THE
USURER'S
DAUGHTER

THE USURER'S DAUGHTER

Male Friendship and Fictions of
Women in Sixteenth-Century
England

Lorna Hutson

London and New York

First published 1994
by Routledge
11 New Fetter Lane, London EC4P 4EE

Simultaneously published in the USA and Canada
by Routledge
29 West 35th Street, New York, NY 10001

First published in paperback 1997

© 1994 Lorna Hutson

Typeset in Palatino by
Ponting–Green Publishing Services,
Chesham, Buckinghamshire
Printed in Great Britain by
T.J. International Ltd, Padstow, Cornwall

British Library Cataloguing in Publication Data
A catalogue record for this book is available from
the British Library

Library of Congress Cataloging in Publication Data
Hutson, Lorna
The usurer's daughter: male friendship and fictions of
women in sixteenth-century England / Lorna Hutson.
p.   cm.
Includes bibliographical references and index.
1. English literature–Early modern, 1500–1700–History and
criticism.   2. Women and literature–Great Britain–History–
16th century.   3. Shakespeare, William, 1564–1616–
Characters–Women.   4. Male friendship–England–History–
16th century   5. English literature–Classical influences.
6. Masculinity (Psychology) in literature.
7. Friendship in literature.   8. Sex role in literature.
9. Humanists–England.   10. Men in literature.
I. Title.
[PR418.W65H87   1997]
820.9'003–dc21   96–44587

ISBN 0–415–16261–0

CONTENTS

CONTENTS

ACKNOWLEDGEMENTS

Friendships and debts are topics of this book; I feel privileged here to acknowledge my own. I owe most to Terence Cave, Lisa Jardine, Stephanie Jed, Victoria Kahn and Lyndal Roper for their encouragement and criticism in the very earliest stages of writing and ever since. Warren Boutcher, Gina Bloom, Laura Gowing, David Norbrook, Bill Sherman, Erica Sheen, Nigel Smith and Alan Stewart all read and responded to drafts of the work, for which, and for their friendship over the past few years, I would like to thank them warmly. To my colleagues at Queen Mary and Westfield College, especially Bryan Chyette, Neil Kenny, Elizabeth Maslen, Suzanne Raitt, Jacqueline Rose and Morag Shiach, and to the members of the Graduate Seminar, thanks for lots of moral support and intellectual stimulus. I would particularly like to remember Jim Reilly, whose wide-ranging intellectual enthusiasm embraced the ideas in this book. Without the initial provocation and continued interest of Routledge's Sue Roe and Talia Rodgers, of course, the book itself would not have been. I would also like to thank my father, John Hutson, for his help with the German. Thanks also, for support and encouragement, to Ros Ballaster, Sara Brown, Rosemary Danielian, Cathy Darcy, Frances Dewhurst, Charlotte Dormandy, Doris and Nora Hutson, Derek Sheil, Vicky Strang, Sandi Toksvig and Margaret Yuill.

I must conclude by claiming sole responsibility for the final text, with all its errors. 'As a wise householder profits', says Erasmus, quoting Xenophon, 'both from friends and enemies, so an intelligent reader may learn from error, as well as from what is well expressed.' And so I hope.

NOTES ON TRANSCRIPTIONS, REFERENCES AND ABBREVIATIONS

The reader will find that in many cases sixteenth-century texts have been cited from a contemporary, rather than modern edition. It is part of the purpose of the book to argue that we are better able to understand the formal properties and fictive concerns of sixteeth-century literature if we do not abstract these properties and concerns from the social exchanges in which the production, circulation, annotation and giving of books played a part. Choosing to cite so much sixteenth-century English, however, has necessitated some pragmatic decision-making in the interests of intelligibility. I have silently expanded all contractions (i.e. commō becomes common) and given the modern equivalents of obsolete letters such as the long 's' (ʃ) and the open-bowled thorn (otherwise indistinguishable from the modern 'y'), so that 'yᵉ' and 'yᵗ' become 'the' and 'that'. I have transliterated 'i' as 'j' where a 'j' would normally appear in modern English (i.e. 'iudgement' becomes 'judgement') and all middle 'u's have become 'v's where a 'v' would appear in modern English, i.e., 'haue' appears as 'have'.

In locating citations from sixteenth-century texts, I have tended to give signature rather than folio references, as the latter are notoriously unreliable (citation from Painter's and Fenton's stories are an exception to this rule-of-thumb; beware, if consulting these, of duplicated folio numbers in the originals). Where possible, the publisher as well as the place of publication has been given in notes and bibliography.

The eclectic (or, flatteringly, 'interdisciplinary') nature of my approach has resulted in a shameless appropriation of arguments from articles across a range of academic journals, so that it has seemed undesirable to abbreviate any of their titles in bibliography.

ix

The only abbreviations to record here are, therefore, the *DNB* (*Dictionary of National Biography* ed. Leslie Stephen, 1885–) and the EETS (Early English Text Society). Shakespeare is quoted from the Arden editions, and translations of classical texts are taken from versions in the Loeb Classical Library.

INTRODUCTION
The signs of friendship

'Why have my sisters husbands,' Cordelia asks King Lear, 'if they say / They love you all?'[1] A simple enough dismantling of the emperor's clothes: the sisters' eloquent protestations of filial love contradict their matrimonial promises. Either one or other utterance (or both) must, under the duress of Cordelia's scepticism, confess itself to be mere rhetoric, a betrayal of faith.

Simple enough. Yet the implied logic is disturbing. In *King Lear*, it seems, the power of eloquence is dramatized as a form of social agency which is demonically oblivious to the material and emotional significance of the bonds of love which it forges and breaks with such facility: 'that glib and oily art / To speak and purpose not', as Cordelia says (I.i.223–4). But why, we might ask, should its exposure in *Lear* be connected with the betrayal of matrimony, anticipating the infidelity of Cordelia's sisters to their husbands? For Goneril and Regan both prove unfaithful as if in capitulation to the inevitable logic of Cordelia's pronouncement. Their initial mobilization of tropes, and subsequent employment of servants whose skills in persuasion match their own seem to render perfectly intelligible to us their dissatisfaction with their husbands' beds.

Repeatedly, in Renaissance drama and prose fiction, the sexual betrayal of men by women is associated with the expression of profound anxiety over the power of vows and pledges to assure the continuity of love or friendship. The pledge or token of faith seems to be in constant danger of being reduced to a material play of signs, without spiritual accountability. So Hamlet accuses Gertrude of

1

> such a deed
> As from the body of contraction plucks
> The very soul, and sweet religion makes •
> A rhapsody of words[2]

while Othello famously finds his handkerchief transformed from a pledge of faithful love into a rhetorically persuasive proof of his wife's infidelity.

The trouble with all this is not that we find it incomprehensible, but that it seems too familiar and intelligible to need explanation. But what are the terms in which we find it so intelligible? The terms of psychoanalysis which readings of Shakespeare have already informed? The complex rhetoric of Shakespearean tragedy seems to go on offering us special insight into the psycho-sexual dynamics of relations between men and women. No one, surely, could be perverse enough to want to understand the crisis Lear confronts in his daughters, Hamlet in his mother or Othello in his wife in terms of a sixteenth-century socio-economic discourse of friendship, rather than in terms of contemporary discourses of sexuality and the psyche.

But what if we were to reverse our usual assumptions, and to think of the troubling sexuality of Shakespeare's heroines as a dramatic effect, rather than motivating cause, of whatever crisis is being represented? In Shakespearean tragedy the (real or supposed) sexual transgression of women becomes significant because it disturbs so profoundly the imaginations of highly articulate men. But what if this were expressive, not of any eternal truth about men's imaginations or women's sexuality, but of a historically specific transition in socio-economic relations in which Shakespeare's dramatic rhetoric were itself implicated? And what if the sense of crisis provoked by this socio-economic transition were concerned not with the love between men and women, but with women as signs of love and friendship extended between men?

My book enlarges upon these hypotheses. It interprets sixteenth-century fictions of women in relation to what men understood was happening, under the combined impact of print and humanism, to the meanings of 'friendship' and 'service' in this period. It will argue, broadly, that in the course of the sixteenth century, the notion of 'friendship' between men was transformed from that of a code of 'faithfulness' assured by acts of hospitality and the circulation of gifts through the family and its allies, to that of an

2

instrumental and affective relationship which might be generated, even between strangers, through emotionally persuasive communication, or the exchange of persuasive texts.

'Friendship' as I define it throughout the book, is evidently an economic dependency as well as an affective bond. Prominent though such an understanding of the word seems to be in sixteenth- and seventeenth-century literature – one thinks of the speaker of Shakespeare's twenty-ninth sonnet wishing himself, 'with friends possest', or Aemilia Lanyer lamenting the loss of her 'great friends' – it is not commonly invoked by late twentieth-century critics in their interpretation of this literature.[3] This is in a sense understandable, since the friendship articulated in literature tends to be, reflexively, *about* literature; that is, it tends to articulate itself as arising from the intimacy of shared reading and writing. What this book seeks to do is not to deny that bonds of under-standing and mutual sympathy are produced by shared reading, but to argue that we should not collude with Renaissance human-ism's account of itself, by believing that such bonds of intimacy represent an altruistic, non-instrumental form of 'friendship'. More precisely, my book seeks to historicize the *topos* of friendship as the bond between 'minds that think alike', insisting on the gendered nature of that *topos* in this period, and locating it in the objectives of the humanist reading programme which, in the course of the sixteenth century, transformed the education of Englishmen.

The code of 'faithful friendship' which pre-dated the advent of humanism in England had, as the historian Mervyn James makes clear, a very precise regulatory function. It was, essentially, a system of credit articulated through the exchange of gifts and services between a lord and his 'fee'd man'. By responding to his servant's needs, overlooking his debts, offering him gifts beyond what he could claim as annuity or by letters patent, a lord ensured that his servant would be faithful to him ('Frendes my good lorde I have none above you') while the servant could trust to the future of the relationship: 'fully resolved you are my good lord . . . I may boldly build upon . . . your continewance of good favors'.[4]

This exchange of gifts and services had a semiotic as well as material import, for 'the gift', as Marcel Mauss has written, 'necessarily entails the notion of credit'.[5] The word 'credit' in-cludes in its range of meanings the idea of trust or belief. Within the system of gift-friendship that Mervyn James describes as practised by the Tudor nobility, the 'credit' entailed by the gift consists first in the obligation to reciprocate and second, in the deferral of that obligation into the future, thereby assuring the 'continewance' of good faith between partners in the relationship. It is one of the main contentions of this book that English humanism, with its stress on the practical efficacy of persuasive rhetoric, undermined the dominance of this system of credit, and replaced it with quite another.

As this is rather a large and enigmatic claim, let me illustrate it with an example. In 1514 Erasmus published an emended edition of his *De Copia* together with the first edition of his *Parabolae*, which carries a prefatory letter to his friend, and the editor of the second edition, Peter Gilles. The *Parabolae* is a collection of witty 'parallels' or analogies deriving from Plutarch, Xenophon and others which Erasmus intended his readers to adapt, in the form of similes or metaphors, to enhance their compositions in Latin. In his letter to Gilles, however, Erasmus explicitly invokes the credit system of gift-friendship in order to elevate, by comparison, the innovative significance of his book as both a gift and a sign of the friendship between himself and Gilles:

> Friends of the commonplace and homespun sort, my open-hearted Pieter, have their idea of relationship, like their whole lives, attached to material things; and if they ever have to face a separation, they favour a frequent exchange of rings, knives, caps and other tokens of the kind (atque alia id genus symbola), for fear that their affection may cool . . . or actually die away through the interposition of long tracts of time and space. But you and I, whose idea of friendship rests wholly in a meeting of minds and the enjoyment of studies in common, might well greet one another from time to time with presents for the mind and keepsakes of a literary description . . . Minds can develop an even closer link, the greater the space that comes between them. Our aim would be that any loss due to separation in the actual enjoyment of our friendship should be made good, not without interest, by pledges of this literary kind (id huiusmodi pignoribus literariis, non sine foenore sarciamus).[6]

At first these sentiments look very familiar to us. Indeed, they seem to require no explanation. Naturally, we think, the bond of sympathetic understanding of which Erasmus speaks is stronger than that of the instrumental loyalty guaranteed by material tokens (*symbola*). But the exchange of rings, knives and caps here deprecated by Erasmus represents a particular institution of the gift as the 'pledge' or 'wager' of the good faith and honour of friends to one another. In the form of pledge or wager, that aspect of the gift which defers into the future the obligation to reciprocate becomes, as it were, the whole of its meaning. The gift becomes a 'surety' or 'assurance', its semiotic value as witness overwhelming that of its material value as favour. Marcel Mauss thus defines the pledge as an exchange in which 'an object, generally of little value ... a glove, a coin (*Treugeld*) or a knife ... binds the honour of the one who hands it over'.[7] There is danger as well as credit in the pledge, for both giver and recipient are bound through it to fulfil an obligation to one another.

The gift as pledge or wager appears frequently in the medieval romances scorned by Erasmus and his fellow humanists. In the thirteenth-century romance of *Amis and Amiloun*, for example, two knights who have sworn to 'hold togider in everi nede / In worde, in werke, in witte, in dede' are forced to part, and so renew their troth with the exchange of gold cups which, as they say, 'tokneth our parting'.[8] The subsequent hazards of fulfilment of the mutual obligation structure the romance, the expansiveness of its narrative representing the temporality of deferral in which the truth of friendship, as the obligation to reciprocate in times of need, may be tried.

It is, I think, important to recognize the way in which Erasmus (quite characteristically and, it would seem, self-consciously) *displaces* both the credit and the danger of the gift-as-surety into the insecure but productive ('interest-bearing') operation of the gift-as-persuasive text. Though his use of the *topos* of epistolary friendship as consisting wholly in the 'meeting of minds' (which, as Natalie Davis points out, was a 'slight exaggeration', since Gilles helped to promote Erasmus[9]), Erasmus can offer his *Parabolae* as a gift which not only cancels time and distance, but *enhances* friendly communication. The literary pledge (*pignus*) thus not only obliges giver and receiver to one another in good faith, it actually yields something extra to both and to others, by way of the 'interest' (*foenus*) it bears.

Thus Erasmus brings about the displacement of credit and danger. For whereas the gift-pledge assured a bond between men by signifying the continuance of their spiritual closeness when physical distance intervened, this book-as-gift *advertises* an existing closeness (the friendship of the dedicatory epistle) and, as a manual of persuasive rhetoric, explicitly facilitates the epistolary generation of bonds of close friendship between men who may be strangers to one another. For what was the 'interest' of which Erasmus spoke, if not the enhancement of his readers' persuasive ability consequent upon their making use of the *Parabolae*? 'Do you intend to persuade?' he wrote to Gilles, enthusing over his gift, 'Nothing gives you greater penetration . . . Nothing else makes your point so convincingly'.[10] If the use of the *parabolae* increases persuasive power to such an extent, then what it offers to readers is greater access to credibility, to being *believed* by strangers who may then become 'friends'. As such, the gift, the literary 'pledge' (*pignus*) itself destabilizes the meaning of the gift as a pledge, for it undermines the power of the gift to assure the giver's good faith. Erasmus indicates his awareness of this by his choice of an example to show off the effectiveness of his *Parabolae*. In demonstration of his parabolic ingenuity, he offers to Gilles a witty analogy between the mixing of wine and hemlock, and the persuasive blending of outspokenness and flattery. As wine, the antidote to hemlock, nevertheless enhances its poisonous efficacy when mingled with it, so frankness, the antithesis of flattery, may be so skilfully mixed with the latter that 'you are flattering your friend most insidiously while you give the impression of perfect frankness'.[11]

This final move in Erasmus' letter belies the sense of security by which he seems at first to distinguish the friendships of men of letters from the 'commonplace' friendships which need to secure their doubts with pledges and tokens. For, as we see, if one effect of the textualization of friendship is the development of closer bonds of sympathy through the exchange of sentiments ('minds can develop an even closer link, the greater the space that comes between them'), another effect is to produce insecurity in a new form, one that was to be far more productive (in the creation of fiction) than the insecurity that moved men to pledge their good faith in the exchange of gifts. For a radical lack of assurance now haunts – as a result of the literary gift – the signs of friendship themselves. Who is going to be able to separate the wine from the hemlock, to distinguish the false frankness from the true, or, as Kent warns of Goneril and Regan, to know whether deeds will 'approve' the passionately persuasive 'words of love' (I.i.183–4)?

At this point in my introduction, the import of its argument for the representation of women remains rather obscure. The part women have to play in any crisis of the semiotics of male friendship seems very minor, hardly enough to account for their very extensive and complex representation in Renaissance drama and prose fiction. Now, the centrality of women to the fiction and drama of the English Renaissance is something no one denies, although opinions have changed about what this centrality means. At one time, it was interpreted as proof of the progressive liberalism of the humanists in their attitudes to women's education and significance generally, especially in view of the Protestant stress upon the sanctity of marriage.[12] Gradually, however, such views have been discredited, and it has even been contended that in many of its aspects, Renaissance humanism represented a restricting rather than enlarging of the freedom of women.[13] Given that this is where the argument currently rests, the extensive representation of 'strong' or transgressive women in almost all genres of literature remains something of a mystery. Why were women articulated, characterized and given voice as never before in sixteenth-century English fiction and drama when their own access to secular literary production and stage performance was either prohibited or severely limited?

As my title, *The Usurer's Daughter* would suggest, I want to argue that one answer lies in the importance of women as signs of credit between men in the traditional anthropological sense of alliance formation, and in a sense peculiar to the literary culture of humanism, in which the claim to be able to 'fashion' women by addressing them through persuasive fictions of themselves lent a special social credibility to the masculine activity of authorship. In an essay that has become a classic, Gayle Rubin pointed out that what structural anthropology added to Marcel Mauss' theory of the semiotics of gift-exchange was 'the idea that marriages are the most basic form of gift-exchange, in which it is women who are the most precious of gifts'.[14] Recently, historians of late medieval and early modern Europe have begun to interpret the structural dynamics of societies based on lineage and alliance in terms of the impact these had upon the way in which women were considered. While we have no such study of households in Tudor England, the society of quattrocento Florence, described by Christiane Klapisch-Zuber, corresponds in its lineage structure to that of the English noble houses described by Mervyn James. Of the women's position in the gift-exchanges of alliance, Klapisch-Zuber writes:

> In Florence, men *were* and *made* the houses. The word *casa* designates, in the fourteenth and fifteenth centuries, the material house ... but it also stands for an entire agnatic kinship group ... In these *case*, in the sense of both physical and symbolic house, women were passing guests ... The marriage that brought a woman out of the paternal house and lineage, the widowhood that led her to return, these incessant comings and goings of wives between *case* introduced a truly indeterminate quality in the ways they were designated: since reference to a male was necessary, a woman was spoken of in relation to her father or her husband even when they were dead ... The determination of a woman's identity thus depended on her movements in relation to the 'houses' of men.[15]

When Shakespeare's Cordelia confirms the good faith of her love for her father in the recognition of its pledged limits ('I love your Majesty / According to my bond; no more nor less' I.i.90–2), she simultaneously makes this assurance explicit in terms of her own stability as a sign of gift-friendship between the houses of men. Unlike Goneril and Regan, she embraces the discontinuity proper to her function in maintaining the troth-plight of marriage:

> Why have my sisters husbands, if they say
> They love you all? Happily, when I shall wed,
> That lord whose hand must take my plight shall carry
> Half my love with him, half my care and duty:
> Sure I shall never marry like my sisters,
> To love my father all.
>
> (I.i.97–104)

As an example of a woman who embraces the inarticulacy and discontinuity proper to the stability and assurance of the gift as pledge of friendship between men, Cordelia indicates how intricately the characterization and voicing of women in Renaissance fiction is tied up with the contribution of persuasive rhetoric to the destabilization of masculine assurance in the signs of friendship. It is the argument of this book, in other words, that there is a very precise correlation between the centrality of women to the fiction and drama of the English Renaissance, and the extent to which that fiction and drama acknowledged its own problematic implication in the highly productive but radically uncertain mediation of friendships resting 'wholly in a meeting of minds'.

Insofar as 'friendship', in the sense understood by this book, means an economic as well as emotional dependency, the book's themes – rhetoric, economics and the representation of women in the sixteenth century – recall those of Patricia Parker's *Literary Fat Ladies*. In that book Parker drew attention to 'the implication of the rhetorical in the economic' in sixteenth-century writing, an implication which she went on to define as an 'ideologically motivated link between the need to control the movements of tropes and figures and the exigencies of social control'.[16] My version of the relations obtaining between humanist rhetoric and sixteenth-century concepts of the economic is slightly different. For it seems to me that Parker's stress on *control* – the handbook codification of tropes – fails to take seriously enough the economic implications of tropes and figures in their practical capacity to transform the conditions of exchange in the contexts of daily life. For sixteenth-century men educated according to humanist methods, rhetoric was less a method of control thematically concerned with 'increase' than a practical technology for the production of persuasive fictions to enable the transmission of knowledge and the facilitation of relationships.

In *The Practice of Everyday Life*, Michel de Certeau describes certain modern French theorists' uses of story-telling as 'an art of making *"coups"* with the fictions of stories'. What de Certeau says about the art of the narrative *'coup'* is helpful for thinking about sixteenth-century rhetoric: both are techniques '"immersed in practice"' and in temporal and spatial contingency; both assume 'many masks and metaphors' and constitute 'an undoing of the proper place (le lieu propre)'.[17] To 'undo the proper place' is to recompose the elements of propriety, to translate them into new places. So it is with English humanism: what 'economic' implications it has are bound up with its rhetorical and dialectical undoing and transforming of the media through which relations of service and exchange had hitherto taken place; this includes, for example, effects upon the flexibility of legal procedure in the area of property transmission and credit relations, and upon the 'invention' and transaction of knowledge in the form of arguments and historical precedents persuasively facilitating projects for practical economic change in the immediate future.

All of this undoing of economic propriety and of the traditional codes of 'faithful friendship' by the rhetoric of humanism was given fictional expression in stories of women who, one way or another, transgressed the proper limits of their function as conveyors of wealth and pledges of friendship between the houses of men. There are dozens of such stories, mostly derived from Italian collections and published in England around the middle of the sixteenth century; constraints of space and considerations of tedium have meant that I have only been able, in the course of the book, to analyse two or three. In one unusually light-hearted story (most of them are violent and retributive) many of the themes of this book – 'good husbandry', rhetoric, friendship, uncertainty about women's chastity and the power of equitable probation to investigate treachery – come together. So a summary of this story may conveniently serve to conclude this introduction by giving an indication of how the book's argument is to be is arranged.

The story concerns Ulrico, a Bohemian knight, who returns from the wars to take up the 'husbandry' of his estate by marrying a wife and living on his rents.[18] Unfortunately these are not enough to support the couple and Ulrico decides to leave his wife, Barbara, at home while he goes off to the court of the King of Hungary, since as she puts it, 'by service shall you credit winne . . . favour with the prince, acquaintance in the court'.[19] The martial skills of the feudal knight are thus transposed into the persuasive skills of the sixteenth-century courtier, and the corresponding loss of ability to assure good faith by the signs that are now employed in persuasive rhetoric is expressed in Ulrico's anxiety about the chastity of Barbara. While the narrator rebukes Ulrico for insufficient 'credite of his loving wife', he also recognizes the predicament, 'for who is able to make assurance of a womans chastitie or tell by signes except he were at the deede doinge, that she hath done amisse?'[20] However, Ulrico's mental husbandry turns this very insecurity to good account, for he acquires a magic image to warn him of danger to his wife's chastity, and proceeds to wager on his 'assurance' of her ability to resist the persuasive skills of two Hungarian knights who propose to try and seduce her. Ulrico's assurance triumphs, as Barbara manages, on pretext of an assignation, to lock up each of her would-be seducers in the dungeon, where she sets them to spin flax. Back at the court of Hungary, Ulrico sues the knights on the strength of the wager, for the forfeit of their lands. The case is taken to the court of Chancery and 'when the Lord Chancellor had framed and digested in order the whole discourse of this history ... after much talke and discourse of the performance of this compact, *pro et contra*' sentence was finally given to the effect that Ulrico and his heirs should possess the lands of the two knights. The narrator comments that 'yt seemed to be pronounced with greate Justice and equitie, for example in time to come'.[21]

This story – untypical only in the narrator's sanguine faith in the chastity of its heroine – contains most of the topics treated chapter by chapter in this book. The whole plot of economic increase is a proof of Ulrico's 'mental husbandry', a concept explained in the book's first section. The significance of a figure like Barbara – a good 'housewife', whose housewifery is less like housework than like the subversive principle of her husband's economic plot – is explored in the first chapter, which deals with the centrality, to English humanism, of the classical text underlying the fiction of the housewife: Xenophon's *Oeconomicus*. This chapter argues not only that Xenophon's *Oeconomicus* was a crucial text in shifting the moral boundaries of economic thought (including those which determined Western attitudes to usury, and hence to capitalism), but that its central paradigm – that of the husband who 'fashions' an unruly woman through his skill in the timely production of fictions – became an emblem of the socially transformative potential of humanist literary culture itself. Shakespeare's dramatic output establishes itself within this paradigm, alleviating the scandal of theatrical imposture by identifying theatre as a site of humanist textual 'husbandry' in which socially transformative (and hence prophetic) fictions of the relations between men and women could be produced.

The second chapter demonstrates how humanist rhetoric undoes the proper place of friendship as the surest form of capital investment in a traditional economy. Conceptually speaking, humanism relocates the instrumentality of male friendship, translating it from alliance and gift-exchange to persuasive communication. Women, symbolically indispensable to the conception of friendship as gift-exchange, become caught up in friendship's new economy of representation in ways that actually narrow the scope for positive representations of their agency.

The middle section, 'Anxieties of textual access', tries to find a critical approach to the new forms of mid-century prose fiction of which the tale of Barbara and Ulrico is one example. The Barbara and Ulrico story is typical of this kind of prose fiction in that it

11

seems to articulate a social world which is feudal, except that men's fortunes depend not on their skill in fighting, but on practices of 'mental husbandry' which involve the ability to plot strategy and make economic use of enemies. Recently, feminist work on 'romantic' prose fiction of this sort has observed that one of its distinguishing features is the new centrality of the woman as subject and addressee. I agree, but argue that the new centrality of women to romance coincides with a broad redefinition of prose romance itself. From being a tale of chivalry concerned with recounting valorous deeds, romance becomes a plot of courtship concerned with displaying the author's dialectical virtuosity, or skill in emplotment. Formally, and as a social transaction, therefore, sixteenth-century prose fiction articulates masculinity in terms of a 'husbandry' of plotting rather than a commemoration of skill at arms. Any assessment of the significance of sixteenth-century romance for women readers needs, I think, to take this into account. Moreover, if the printed text of prose fiction is perceived as an advertisement of gifts intended to intitiate a service relation, it becomes possible to read questions of masculine authorship as involved in a wider redefinition of credit relations between men. Chapter 4 examines some of the issues at stake here, analysing them in relation to contemporary changes in the legal place of trust and credit. Here, once more, the story of Barbara and Ulrico typifies the concerns expressed in other texts of the period, for it attempts to compensate for the lost power of the word as pledge of faith, by means of the deployment of a *pro et contra* rhetoric of uncertainty in the equitable probation of a case of suspected betrayal.

The prose fiction of the 1560s–1580s holds little to detain the non-specialist, but the drama of the latter part of the century – the drama of Shakespeare – is still current today. It seems of crucial importance, therefore, to emphasize the extent to which the formal and thematic concerns of this drama may be identified with those of the mid-century prose fiction which we dismiss as representing a remote and inaccessible social world. My final section on theatre examines in some detail the connections between Shakespearean drama, Terentian comedy and the prose fictions and legal discourses of Reformation humanism. In doing so it challenges the tendency of recent criticism to explain the sixteenth-century perception of the erotic dangers of the public stage exclusively in terms of the 'gaze'. Such a critical approach obscures the extent to which one of Shakespeare's great achievements – the compelling emotional intelligibility, or probability of his drama – depends upon a rhetoric of uncertainty, expressed in metaphors of 'error' or 'blindness'. Recognition of this is important, for Shakespeare's rhetoric of uncertainty acknowledges a culpable 'deceitfulness' in its own working, which it locates, with devastating effectiveness, in its innovative 'characterization' of women. My final two chapters trace the reasons for this, and offer readings of two plays – *The Comedy of Errors* and *The Taming of the Shrew* – in which the characterizations of women bear out the arguments of the book as a whole.

Part I

MENTAL HUSBANDRY

1

THE HOUSEWIFE AND THE HUMANISTS

A painting by Quinten Metsys, now hanging in the Louvre and known as *The Moneylender and his Wife* (*Le Prêteur et sa femme*) presents a couple half-length behind a table. The man is absorbed in the task of weighing coins, while beside him a woman holds open an illuminated book. As her fingers turn the page, an image of the Virgin and Child is revealed to the viewer's gaze; the woman's own eyes are focused away from the book, upon the delicate balancing of the money in the scales.

Quinten Metsys, active in Antwerp at the beginning of the sixteenth century, is perhaps most famous now for his association with the great humanist Erasmus, whose friendship and scholarly correspondence with Peter Gilles he celebrated in a diptych presented as a gift to Thomas More.[1] Metsys' *Moneylender and his Wife*, painted three years before the Erasmus-Gilles diptych, in 1514, has not attracted much art-historical attention. As Panofsky observed, it amounts to not much more than a highly competent 'reconstruction' of elements from paintings by Petrus Christus and Jan Van Eyck. The paraphernalia of the moneylender's occupation – the delicately drawn scales, flanked on the right by a convex mirror and a shiny, open-lidded box for weights, and on the left by a pile of heavy-looking coins, a scatter of nesting weights, a crystal reliquary, a roll of parchment encircled by touchstone rings – may be paralleled, item for item, in Petrus Christus' *The Legend of S. Eloy and S. Godoberta*, painted in 1449 for the Corporation of Goldsmiths in Antwerp. The shelves behind the couple, holding books, papers and household objects, are compared by Panofsky to the book-filled recess above St Jerome's writing table in Van Eyck's *St Jerome in his Study*, now in Detroit. Certain objects on the shelves – the apple, tawny against a pewter dish, and the glass rosary catching the light as it hangs down, have counterparts in Van Eyck's famous 'Arnolfini' marriage portrait, which, of course, also makes significant use of reflection in a convex mirror.[2]

If the objects in Metsys' painting were derivative, its theme – a glimpse into the operations of the world of trade and finance – was much imitated in the course of the sixteenth century. Versions of Metsys' turbaned banker-figure, either counting money with his wife, or taking orders from a client, are to be found hanging in various European galleries, attributable to Marinus Van Reymerswaele. In effect, however, Van Reymerswaele's treatment of the theme is quite different: his images are unequivocal satires on avarice and greed. The woman's gaze, for example, becomes predatory; purses bulge, shelves are crammed, everything twists and warps, from the pages of account books to the winding-sheet that smothers an ancient candle.[3] What Van Reymerswaele has sacrificed is precisely the lack of drama that seems to give meaning to the shiny, reflective or almost-legible surfaces of objects lovingly reproduced by Metsys from the paintings of Christus and Van Eyck. It is a quality which we loosely call 'realism', a verisimilitude which compels and satisfies attention, as if exhausting signification in the accuracy of observation. Svetlana Alpers has suggested that, in relation to seventeenth-century Dutch painting, we should understand this 'attentiveness to descriptive presence' as a particular mode of signifying.[4] According to the logic of this mode, illusionistic virtuosity – such as that achieved by Van Eyck in the Arnolfini portrait, in which he represents himself, the painter, witnessing the marriage as event, reflected tinily in a convex mirror – serves, paradoxically, to efface itself as virtuosity. The tour de force of illusion becomes fidelity to the fact, and the artist becomes, 'one who bears witness to or documents a reality that is prior to him'.[5] That this was precisely the effect Erasmus admired in the painting of Metsys (an effect which he sought, by analogy, to accomplish rhetorically through the composition and publication of his familiar correspondence) has been vividly demonstrated by Lisa Jardine.[6] What, however, might be the significance of Metsys choosing to portray in this illusionistic mode the professional activities of a dealer in finance? Raymond de Roover has explained how, in Bruges and Antwerp at the turn of the fifteenth century, a number of different kinds of merchants, bankers and dealers in valuables served as creditors to those unable to borrow from friends.[7] Among these were the goldsmiths, whose profession

Metsys' figure seems (judging from his resemblance to Petrus Christus' portrait of S. Eloy) to represent. But where Christus' S. Eloy is depicted in the act of weighing a ring (an act of tropical significance in the saint's legendary narrative) Metsys' unnamed dealer in valuables is counting and weighing coins in the presence of his wife. What is meant by the invitation to us, as viewers, to behold this action in this setting? What does it mean to render the accountability of the money dealer's activity in terms of his visibility and, in particular, the visibility of his conjugal status? What, in other words, has the controversial ethical status of the moneylender to do with the inclusion, in the picture, of his wife?

THE ABSENT DOMESTIC WOMAN

In 1541 Miles Coverdale published an English translation of the humanist Heinrich Bullinger's guide to matrimony, *Der Christlich Eestand* (1540). It was to be, in English, an extremely influential text. It went through nine editions by 1575 and was the model for subsequent treatments of the subject.[8] As early as 1543, Thomas Becon had reissued Coverdale's translation under his own name, with the addition of an elaborate preface, imitative of Erasmus' *Encomium Matrimonii*, included 'for the more readie sale'. In 1591, the preacher Henry Smith remarketed it under his name, with a dedication to Lord Burghley. A most popular manual of the seventeenth century, John Dod and Robert Cleaver's *A Godlie Forme of Householde Government* (1610) 'used whole paragraphs at a time' of Coverdale's Bullinger, and the metaphors of the latter 'crop up again and again' in other guides to marriage.[9]

Chapter 19 of Coverdale's Bullinger, entitled, 'Of Covenient Carefulnes and just keping of the house lyke Christen folke' offers what seems to us a predictable enough division of conjugal labour:

> What so ever is to be done without the house, that belongeth to the man & the woman to studye for thinges within to be done, and to se saved or spent conveniently whatsoever he bringeth in. As the bird fleeth to and fro to bring to the nest, so becommeth it the man to apply his outward busines, And as the damme kepeth the nest, hatcheth the egges, & bringeth forth the frute, so let them both lern to do of the unreasonable fowles or bestes created of God naturally to observe theyr sondrye propertyes.[10]

There is, as John Winkler remarked in another context, 'a *lot* of culture packed into this one exemplum from nature'.[11] By the time of Dod and Cleaver's *Godlie Forme of Household Government*, the formula had been enlarged and improved:

> This is also a Dutie (not to bee forgotten) Namely, that Husbands be diligent and Carefull to make provision for their Houses ... The dutie of the Husband is to get goods: and of the Wife to gather them together, and save them. The dutie of the Husband is to travell abroade, to seeke living: and the Wives dutie is to keepe the house. The dutie of the Husband is to get money and provision: and of the Wives, not vainely to spend it. The dutie of the Husband is to deale with many men: and of the Wives to talke with few. The dutie of the Husband is, to be entermedling: and of the wife, to be solitary and withdrawne. The dutie of the man is, to be skilfull in talke: and of the wife, to boast of silence. The dutie of the husband is to be a giver, and of the Wife, to be a saver. The dutie of the Man is, to Apparell himselfe as he may: and of the Woman, as it becommeth her. The dutie of the husband is, to dispatch all things without dore: and of the wife, to oversee and give order for all things within the house.[12]

So striking is the symmetry of the Dod and Cleaver formulation, that, in her influential article surveying sixteenth- and seventeenth-century guides to marriage, the social historian Kathleen Davies reproduced it in the form of a binary scheme:

Husband	*Wife*
Get goods	Gather them together and save them
Travel, seek a living	Keep the house
Get money and provisions	Do not vainly spend it
Deal with many men	Talk with few
Be 'entermedling'	Be solitary and withdrawn
Be skilful in talk	Boast of silence
Be a giver	Be a saver
Apparel yourself as you may	Apparel yourself as it becomes you
Be Lord of all	Give account of all
Dispatch all things outdoor	Oversee and give order within.[13]

Yet there is, for all its predictability, a puzzle about the very symmetry of this formulation of conjugal interdependence. It is, simply, too symmetrical to be anything other than a fiction. Nancy Armstrong, contrasting Davies' schematization of Dod and Cleaver with the discursively amplified role of the 'domestic woman' in eighteenth-century household literature, observes that the seventeenth-century model articulates only one gender: 'the Puritan household consisted of a male and female who were structurally identical, positive and negative versions of the attributes.'[14] Catherine Belsey, likewise, finds a contradiction between Dod and Cleaver's explicit delineation of spheres of responsibility (outdoors for husband, indoors for wife) and the actual allocation of responsibilities that would, in practice, make the household the woman's sphere:

> The husband's responsibilities occupy twenty-nine pages and the wife's, with some repetition, rather less than two. In essence, the wife's responsibilities are to provide a visible model of submission, and not to get in the way, unless her husband is absent . . . the attempt to find a place of authority for the wife results in the renewed insistence on her submission. She is subsumed under the will of her husband . . . a woman is to govern and not to govern, present as example . . . but absent from the place where decisions are made.[15]

The division comes to appear very nearly meaningless: the husband occupies both spheres after all, is both 'indoors' and 'outdoors' all at once, negotiating in the marketplace, and governing the godly household. The woman, as good wife, is merely the example of his ability to govern.

What, then, made this 'natural history' of the conjugal household – the model of husband as hunter-gatherer, and the wife as saver and keeper – so indispensable to humanist moral philosophy? Its provenance is not far to seek: the exemplum as Bullinger uses it derives from a text entitled *Oeconomicus*, written by the Socratian philosopher Xenophon, and from its derivative, a pseudo-Aristotelian text of the same name, but inferior composition.[16] So popular was the Xenophonic formulation with the northern humanists that it inevitably makes an appearance whenever matters pertaining to the household or to women are being discussed in a humanist text of moral philosophy. Thus, in Richard Hyrde's translation of Vives' *Instruccion of a Christen*

Woman, the section on 'shamefastness' requires that women should be sober and sparing in their diet, since the cultivation of habits of thrift,

> 'be in householdyng the womans party as Plato and Aristotle say full well. The man getteth, the woman saveth and kepeth. Therfore he hath stomake gyven him to gether lustily & she hath hit taken from her, that she may warely kepe.[17]

The division of household labour according to the 'natural' properties of the sexes ('stomach' meaning courage or boldness in hunting) in turn dictates their natural properties in other contexts (the man's courageous 'stomach' legitimating his stomach in its other sense as appetite for food and sex).

Versions of Xenophon's natural history of the division of household labour according to the scheme of husband 'outdoors' and wife 'indoors' seem, then, to have been relevant to the humanist project in a variety of ways. What made the model so compelling? Nothing, surely, to do with the the production of a sphere of influence for the 'wife'. For the cultural significance of this natural history concerns men: its function in the sixteenth century was not to legitimate a new version of femininity, but a new version of masculinity. The point of it was not, primarily, to guarantee *in reality* the husband's governance of his wife, but to prove, through a persuasive fiction of the well-governed wife, the legitimate and responsible contribution of a Christian humanist education to the secular and practical spheres of masculine activity. For it was only through the definition of conjugal femininity as the symbolic boundary of 'good husbandry' (the displaced marker of the husband's accountability as head of the household) that good husbandry could come to claim as its sphere nothing less than 'out of bounds-ness' itself – the time/space of opportunity, both for negotiation and for the production of rhetorically persuasive fictions.

XENOPHON'S SUCCESSFUL DISAPPEARING ACT: HOUSEKEEPING LITERATURE AND THE 'BANALITY' OF ECONOMICS

It is actually an effect of the persistence of a hierarchy of values which conforms to that established by Xenophon's gendered division of economic labour that the cultural centrality of an ostensibly gynaecological text (Xenophon's *Oeconomicus*), and its seventeenth-century 'marriage guidance' derivatives has not been taken seriously by critics and historians of change in economic thought. Thus, in a careful and sceptical critique of claims made for the originality of Aristotle's economic thinking, M.I. Finley dismisses in passing the contribution of that second-rate thinker, Xenophon, arguing that although 'the model that survived and was imitated was Xenophon's *Oikonomikos*' yet, 'it was not from *Hausvaterliteratur* that modern economic thinking arose'.[18] For rather different reasons, Kathleen Davies in her article on English *Hausvaterliteratur* or books of 'the art of household', likewise devalues the genre, refusing to allow it any creative cultural force. Davies is, of course, concerned to refute the argument that the Protestant, or, as it is misleadingly called, 'Puritan' doctrine of marriage was liberal in its effects on the position of women in society. In demonstrating the doctrine's far from liberal implications, however, she makes the mistake of underestimating its novelty and prescriptive force, and this is simply because she, like Finley, has been duped by the hierarchizing rhetoric of a gendered division of economic labour which manages, by associating economic prudence with the penny-pinching of good housewives, to make the topic of thrift seem familiar and beneath our notice. The household order prescribed by Dod and Cleaver is, Davies decides 'in fact a picture of a household built on the firm economic base of bourgeois endeavour, whether of the fourteenth, fifteenth or sixteenth centuries'. Marriage guidance literature is, therefore 'a collection of descriptive rather than prescriptive texts, written by authors who were not advocating new ideals for marriage but were describing the best form of bourgeois marriage as they knew it'.[19] Davies can decide that the sixteenth-century humanistic texts derived from Xenophon and pseudo-Aristotle are no different from fifteenth-century antecedents untouched by Xenophonic influence because she has already dismissed the practical economic advice contained in the humanistic household literature as familiar and unnecessary:

> Many of the more peripheral characteristics assumed to be peculiar to Puritan writings on marriage are also to be found in earlier works. Careful prudence and foresight are common features of both; Whytforde's advice to householders to keep a year's rent or income in store 'for chances' is an example of

capitalistic caution, and his remedy for poverty – to spend less – is typical of the rather banal quality of the advice offered by all these conduct book writers . . . Vives, too, was much exercised about the prudent governing of the household . . . the sobriety and prudence described in Roper's *Life* of More are very like the characteristics advised by Bullinger as a means to material prosperity.[20]

And yet, if Vives and Whitford (the latter was, like the former, a humanist and a friend of More and Erasmus) were so concerned about thrift and prudence, would it not be as logical to assume that this is in itself a sign that their texts were not *descriptive* of existing practices, but advocative of practices currently ignored, undervalued or even actively disdained by their readers? It would seem that the humanists valued the moral philosophy of the ancient world for its provision of exemplary authority for the changes in social practice they advocated. Citing the proverb, 'the steppe of the husbande maketh the fatte donghyll', Whitford is drawing on the pseudo-Aristotelian *Economics*, a text which, as Josef Soudek has shown, was widely read between 1420 and 1520 in Leonardo Bruni's humanistic Latin translation.[21] It is a mistake, moreover, to assume that the readership at whom the humanists aimed this literature was confined to the 'bourgeois' householders imagined by Davies. Erasmus recommended the reading of the Aristotelian *Economics* to the duke to whom he dedicated his *Apophthegmata*; Lawrence Humphrey argued in his *Of Nobilitye*, that 'It behoveth also, a Noble man bee skild in house Phylosophie: and be not ignoraunte, in governmente of housholde. Thereof wrate *Xenophon*, and *Aristotle*. Whiche also *Paule* touched, wrytynge to the *Ephesians*.' Leonardo Bruni dedicated his translation of the Aristotelian *Economics* to Cosimo de Medici for, 'to whom else can advice more appropriately be given than to one who owns ample means and desires to preserve them with praise and to increase them with dignity?', while Johannes Herrold, translator of Erasmus, dignified his gift of one such translation to George and Anna Fugger by associating it with the household philosophy of Aristotle and Xenophon.[22]

It is furthermore wrong to assume that 'example[s] of capitalistic caution' typical of householding texts, were already 'banal' to sixteenth-century readers. Indeed, Whitford's advice to have a year's rent in store for chances is *immediately* qualified by reassurance to the reader that such prudence 'is nat contrary unto christianyte, where extreme or very strayte nede is nat perceyved in the neighbour.' Clearly, as Whitford affirms elsewhere, it was more usual to regard surplus in prosperity as bound, both for reasons of charity and in guarantee of future friendship, to be extended to neighbours rather than stored against mischance, for 'thou canst have none so sure castel or garde of thy lyfe: as is love and frendshyppe of thy neyghboure'.[23] One of the great ideological conflicts of Northern Europe in the sixteenth-century – the conflict over credit extension to friends and neighbours, and the legitimacy of exacting interest payments as assurance for the honouring of debts – may be invoked briefly here to demonstrate just how far from 'banal' were the issues raised by the householding texts in terms of the beliefs and practices of their sixteenth-century readers.

It is common knowledge that, as the business operations of northern European merchants expanded during the fifteenth and sixteenth centuries, so they became more reliant on systems of credit which would ensure the honouring of assurances of their wealth at a temporal and geographical distance.[24] In the second half of the fifteenth century, Antwerp overtook Bruges as a business centre. Antwerp's quarterly markets enabled an unprecedented year-round liquidation of debts and credits; previously the end of a fair had marked the ritual closing of exchange, and required the settling of all accounts. As a result of the year-round liquidity of transaction, Antwerp became a centre for the permanent establishment of foreign exchanges, places where 'bills of exchange' might be drawn on reserves held abroad.[25] A practical merchants' guide to account-keeping, translated into English in 1547, makes the Antwerp exchange analagous to what

> we in England ... use in Markettes, [where] there are Goldsmithes which either if we have money will take it to the Market and make a bill to paie it againe at London or where ye will to have it paied, or els will lend you so much in the Market, and take your bill to be paied againe at London or els where, for a reasonable profite'.[26]

There was however, as the same writer notes, a great deal of ideological opposition to this unprecedented increase in the incidence of transferable, profit-making credit relations between men. 'Marchantes who deliver their money by exchange are called usurers and worse then infidels', he wrote, by an 'ignorant and rude sort of people' who 'neyther knowe what exchange is, neither yet how necessary . . . it is for the Marchant, that like as a ship cannot passe the seas without saile and rudder, no more can the marchaunt travaile Countrees without exchange'.[27] If the voice of the non-mercantile population – which this author dismissed as 'ignorant and rude' was one source of opposition, another was the voice of scholastic theology: canon law prohibited as usurious any gain made over the mere principal in any credit transaction. In England in 1487, a statute was passed against so-called 'dry exchange' – considered to be a mere cover for usury – and in 1531 Thomas Cromwell revived a proclamation to forbid exchanges and rechanges; a letter from Richard Gresham (father of Thomas Gresham) to Thomas Cromwell dated July 1538 protests against the measure on the grounds that the prohibition of exchange tends to result in the exporting of specie:

> there is diverse merchants that will shortly prepare th[em-selves] towards Borduus for provision of wines, and f[or lacke of] exchanges I do suppose that there will be some convey[ance] of gold amongst them. I am sure, my Lord, that such exchanges and rechanges do much to the stay of the said gold in England, which would else be conveyed [away].[28]

The issue of credit in commercial relations, of which foreign exchange was one aspect, remained in dispute. Despite the credit crisis and the high incidence of bankruptcy in London in the 1560s, conscience prevailed against the legalization of interest in the Parliament of 1571.[29]

If we want evidence of how both popular and theological opposition hindered capitalistic enterprise outside England, we have only to look at the fortunes of the Fuggers in Germany. Lyndal Roper has explained how, in his declining years, Anton Fugger took to consulting a female sorcerer, a crystal ball gazer. Roper deduces from this that Fugger himself was not immune to the feelings of ambivalence with which people of sixteenth-century Augsburg regarded the pursuit of wealth in general, and the activities of merchant capitalists in particular:

> For sixteenth-century people, wealth was a malignant force. People got rich only by making others poorer. Only by finding treasure . . . could one become harmlessly rich.

Within the city [of Augsburg], wealth was inherently limited, goods were finite and the crucial economic issue was perceived as being the *division* of resources, not the creation of wealth. When Augsburg craftsmen of the 1560s diagnosed the city's ills they laid the blame at the door of newcomers, people who clogged up the crafts ... But popular opinion might also ... identify the wealthy capitalists as the source of the problem, because they had cornered supplies and taken an unfair share ... In the weaving industry, the town's foremost employment ... guild protectionism won the day in a triumph of the belief that wealth was finite and that the common good ought to take precedence over individual gain.[30]

Earlier in the century, the Fugger enterprise had felt the force of opposition in the form of the canon law prohibition on interest-bearing loans. In 1515 the magnate Jacob Fugger paid the expenses of the Ingolstadt professor Johann Eck to go to Bologna to hold a disputation on the practice of collecting interest. At issue, as the historian Heiko Oberman writes,

was the legitimacy of profit-making commerce with capital, a practice long accepted in international banking and financial circles but still encountering organised resistance in Germany, especially among humanists. Thus the practice urgently needed the protective rationale of a new theology of capital. A new interpretation of the church's prohibition of usury was required, an interpretation that would permit smooth financing of investments, especially the rapidly expanding long-distance commerce, without the restrictive overhead of a guilty conscience.[31]

Although Eck and others attempted to shift discussion from a canon law question of permissibility (centring on the prohibition stipulated in Deuteronomy 23:20 and Luke 6:35, and theoretically supported by the Aristotelian conception of money as sterile) towards one of pastoral care (the magisterial discrimination between honest and dishonest exactions of interest), debates in Germany, France and England over the legitimacy of interest were to go on for another fifty years.[32]

Ideological battles are never fought, however, upon a single front, still less upon a single front which is also legislative.

Norman Jones, in his study of the usury debate in England, opens with the observation that, whereas the 1571 Parliamentary discussion of usury was dominated by the idea of God, the Parliamentary debate which legalized interest-bearing loans in 1624 treated the issue as purely economic, a purely secular matter.[33] Evidently, the battle had already been fought elsewhere. The question is, where?

One answer for England might be the conceptual space created, in the circulation of economic projects involving the utilization of interest-bearing loans, by such formulae as 'every man is rather borne to profit his . . . common weale, in revealynge . . . hidden treasure . . . then to seeke after his owne private gaine' or the Ciceronian equivalent, 'nihil est utile, quod non sit honestum' ('nothing is expedient or profitable which is not honest').[34] The latter, taken from Cicero's *De Officiis*, implies the former, for the *De Officiis* is, itself, a sustained philosophical inquiry into the possibility of reconciling, in any situation, the pursuit of what is expedient or profitable (*utilis*) with the pursuit of what is morally right (*honestus*). As the practical value of any moral virtue depends on its being appropriate or fitting (*decorus*) to the contigencies of time and place (*occasio*), the only rule of thumb that Cicero can offer for instant recognition of a clash between the demands of the expedient and the morally honest is the rule of 'common' before 'private weal', the dictum that a man should never pursue his private good at the expense of the whole community.[35] 'The selfe same profyte that is of every private persone is commen profyte', one sixteenth-century translation ran, 'whiche profyte if any man plucke to hym selfe all comforte is dissolved a sondre . . . in lyke manner it is ordayned that it shulde not be lawfull for any man to hurt an other bycause of his private welthe'.[36] As wealth was conceived as finite, and bargaining a struggle for advantage in the disposition of finite resources, we would expect Cicero's representation of *utilitas* or 'profit', even before its philosophical reconciliation with the pursuit of *honestas*, to be ethically circumscribed, dissociated from the pure pragmatics of the marketplace. And, as we expect, the ethical circumscription of the pursuit of material gain takes the form of its translation into an art of household provision, for instruction in which Cicero refers the reader to Xenophon:

But a mannes substance muste bee gotten, by those thinges,

which be farre from dishonestye: and must be saved by diligence, and honest sparinge: and by those same meanes also, it must be encreased. Xenophon the Socratian hathe gone throroughe these thynges very handsomely in that booke which is intituled Economicus: the which we tourned oute of Greeke into latine when we were the same age in a maner, as you are nowe.[37]

Xenophon turns up everywhere. And yet historians of economic and social thought continue to dismiss the efficacy of his text, to deny that it made, through its humanistic revival, a conceptual space for changes in practice. This, as I suggested before, is a measure of the success of the text's complex strategy of simultaneously elevating and deprecating the element of prudential *calculation* which is practically all that the ancient sense of *oikonomia* has in common with the present-day sense in which 'economics' is a science. That Davies and Finley can so easily dismiss the much-imitated Xenophonic model in spite, or perhaps because, of the frequency of its imitation attests to the particular importance of its self-effacement, or self-displacement. For what the humanists perceived to be the value of Xenophon's text was precisely its capacity to offer pragmatic counsel in the prudential and calculating conduct of household affairs in the form of a rhetorical fiction which displaced the ethical stigma of the calculating outlook from the centre to the periphery of the text: from the governing husband to the governed wife. We may cite an article exploring issues in the history of economic thought, published in 1958, for evidence of the enduring power of Xenophon's rhetoric in this respect. The author argues that historians have been mistaken in seeking the origins of economic thought in the utilitarian figment known as 'Economic Man':

Is it not rather in the *mulier economica* in whom we have to recognize the ancestress of those peculiar frames of mind which modern economists have been rashly disposed to regard as the birthright of Economic Man in general or as the offspring of the spirit of capitalism? Commerce and trade have been in ancient Greece too deeply intertwined with warfare . . . to be suspect of fostering a spirit of thriftiness . . . Such propensities are much more likely to arise in the interior of the house and as an object of womanly worries. From the stone age onwards, man's proper attitude towards wealth has been a tendency to spend generously . . . Women, on the other hand, by inborn feelings driven to provide food for hungry mouths of children, were bound early to learn not to rely too confidently on what their male partners may, or may not, bring home from their sylvan hunting excursions. They must have developed a much stronger propensity to think in terms of scarce means; of distribution according to needs; and of provision for an uncertain future by economising and thriftiness. It is significant that even in the fourth century B.C. Xenophon, keeping an elegant and uncertain balance between the aristocratic tradition of *insouciance* and nascent utilitarianism, allows his Isomachus, a model gentle-man (kalokagathos) to leave the spending department of his oikonomia entirely to his wife, after having educated her.[38]

Xenophon may have been a second-rate philosopher but he was, as Philip Sidney pointed out, a first-rate composer of persuasive fictions. In the final section of this chapter, I shall examine some of the ways in which the rhetorical emplotment of the *Oeconomicus* was imitated in humanist texts whose influence in the spheres of economic, social or cultural history cannot be denied. Before I go on to do that, however, I want to look at the form of Xenophon's text itself.

ECONOMICS AS EXEMPLARITY: XENOPHON'S RHETORIC OF HUSBANDRY

Xenophon's *Oeconomicus* was a text that lent itself, as M.I. Finley noted, to imitation. Cicero, recommending it to his son in the *De Officiis*, linked the practical instructiveness of the text with the eloquence that moved him to turn it from Greek into Latin. The cultural significance of Xenophon's art of household, then, is bound up with the exemplarity of its textual ordering. It follows that any exploration of the 'influence' of Xenophon on social thought or practice is also a case study of the extent to which such practical and social knowledge bears the imprint of the rhetorical medium in which it is conveyed.

Sixteenth-century humanism was, in its pedagogical mani-festation, associated with an activity of reading which Victoria Kahn has called 'a practice of examples, or an exemplary practice'.[39] The faculty of interpretation, or skill in understanding the meaning of a text was tied in with the exercise of the reader's judgement and invention in the selection and transformation of elements of the text into *exempla* applicable to future occasions for the production of persuasive discourse. Thus, as Terence Cave writes, this exemplary practice of reading, the principles of which are supremely expressed in Erasmus' *De Copia*, 'constitutes a major episode in the history of imitation theory' by means of which

> the activities of reading and writing become virtually identified. A text is read in view of its transcription as part of another text; conversely, the writer as imitator concedes that he cannot entirely escape the constraints of what he has read. In this respect, imitation is also germane to interpretation, since the interpretative act can only become visible in a second discourse which claims to be a reconstitution of the first.[40]

Some texts, of course, are more 'exemplary', richer in imitative potential than others, because, as Kahn explains, they educate the reader's judgement in the faculty of *decorum*, that is, the art of knowing where and when and how a certain example might be appropriately adapted. Decorum is both a textual and a life skill; a facility in the persuasive structuring of discourse, and a practical capacity for the discovery of resources for action within the contingencies of a particular occasion. So Cicero notes in the *De Officiis* that for poets to observe decorum is to achieve persuasive verisimilitude, while in moral philosophy, decorum, linked to the art of good timing, becomes identical to the strategic virtue of prudence.[41] Texts that enable the reader's sense of decorum, by offering a model of the invention and disposition of examples to greatest persuasive effect within the discourse, might be said to embody an 'economic' or generative principle within an aesthetics which thus values form as potentially transformative, and identifies knowledge with the future uses of imitation. Xenophon's might be said to be one such text, and the science of 'husbandry' that it disclosed to the understanding of a humanist scholar might therefore seem to contribute as much to an identification of masculine power with the economics of using and ordering a discourse, or the contingencies of a particular situation, as with that of using and ordering a wife and household.

We can follow the moves of Xenophon's text as they appeared to a sixteenth-century reader if we use an English translation made in 1534 (and frequently reissued) by the French humanist Gentian Hervet, at the request of Geoffrey Pole, brother to Reginald.[42] Hervet had been one of Thomas Lupset's pupils at Corpus Christi before becoming a tutor in the Pole household, so it may be that the translation published under his name was one to which Thomas Lupset refers, in his *Exhortacion to yonge men* (1531), as being by himself.[43] Whatever the case, it seems certain that there was an interest being taken in this text by a group of humanists connected both with the Pole household and with Erasmus.[44] Indeed, Hervet's translation opens with a note to the reader praising Xenophon 'for his swete eloquence' which caused him to be 'surnamed *Musa Attica*, that is to say, the songe of Athens'; the phrase renders a tribute to Xenophon made by Erasmus in a footnote to his edition of Cicero's *De Senectute*.[45]

Xenophon's text opens with Socrates and Critobolus engaged in an attempt to define the 'art of household' or *oikonomia*. 'I harde', Hervet's translation begins, 'vpon a time the wyse Socrates commone of the ordring of an house.'[46] In the ensuing dialogue, Socrates engages Critobolus in dispute as to whether the art of 'household' (*oikonomia*) is a kind of knowledge (*epistēmēs tinos onoma* – translated by Hervet as 'the name of a science') such as medicine or carpentry. Critobolus affirms that it is, but Socrates problematizes this too facile answer by probing the definition of 'house' and 'household'. Both agree that a man's 'house' means more than the physical enclosure of his possessions within one fixed space; 'a mans house' (*oikos*) they decide must extend to all 'that a man hath' (sig. A2ᵛ). This is already an interesting argumentative move, for it means that the science of ordering one's 'house' will henceforward be taken to include strategies to maximize the advantages, or transform into 'goods and substance' contingencies that contribute to one's well-being but are beyond the sphere of the 'household' in a physical sense. So indeed, Socrates tests Critobolus by asking him if enemies which a man might 'possess' are therefore to be included in his house, as being 'goods and 'substance'? Critobolus demurs, but Socrates proves that whatever is possessed is defined as a 'good' not by any intrinsic quality, but by whether or not its possessor knows how to 'use and order' (*chrēsthai*) it to advantage. So the man who knows how to profit by his enemies may indeed call them 'goods and substance': 'it is a point than of a good husband, and a good order of an house, to haue a waye, to vse his enemies too, that he may get some profit by them' (sigs A4^{r-v}). The art to 'use and order' is thus fundamental to the definition of *oikonomia*, or 'household' as a kind of knowledge, and that kind of knowledge bears a startling resemblance to what we would define as 'economy' in a liberal sense, such as when we speak of the 'economy' of a well-made artefact, or of a text. *Oikonomia* is thus the science which defines itself as the effective use of the possession (*oikos*).

The next phase of the dialogue concerns the exemplarity of the knowledge called *oikonomia*: it is a skill attained by example and practice, not subject to theoretical transmission. So Socrates insists that he cannot teach Critobolus about *oikonomia* because, being a philosopher, he (Socrates) has no household. This is, of course, disingenuous, but the meaning of alerting the reader to the issue of exemplarity will not become clear until a later section in the text. In the meantime, Socrates asks Critobolus to master the art of household by looking at examples of households known to him. Critobolus cannot do this, however, until he has proved his capacity to learn by example: 'Ye must prove your selfe, if ye shalbe able to knowe it, whan ye see them' (sig. B1^v). Critobolus assumes the position of the naive 'reader' of these exemplary households: 'I have seen theim', he says, 'and I know them both, but I have never the more vantage for that' (sig. B2^r). The cause is, says Socrates, that he has looked upon examples of good and bad households

> as ye loke vpon the players of enterludes (*tous tragōdous kai kōmōdous*), not to thintent that ye may be a poete, but for a pastime & a recreation. And peradventure ye do well in that, for ye bee not mynded to be a poete: but where ye be compelled to kepe & fynde horses, will ye not judge your selfe a foole, if ye goe not about to study a remedy, that ye be not ignorant in that behalfe[?]
>
> (sig. B2^r)

The idea of learning by *looking* at a household is transposed through the analogy with looking at a play into a concept of understanding which resembles the humanists' practice of exemplary reading; to consider a play from the point of view of the poet-dramatist is to gain a practical knowledge of its persuasive economy of representation. But Critobolus is 'not minded to be poet', so he never considers the practical architecture of a play. Nor, in fact, is he minded to keep horses. He expresses surprise at the sudden turn of the conversation: 'your mynd is that I shoulde breke horses?', he asks. The horse-breaking example is not, as it turns out, relevant to the discussion of *oikonomia*, except as the analogy which transposes the theme of exemplary learning to the topic which will be all-important: the training of the wife. Socrates declares:

> I canne shewe you some men, the which have so vsed and ordered their wives, that they comfort them and help them toward the increasyng of their house: and some that have suche wives, the which vtterly destroi the hous, and so for the moste part of men have . . . a horse, most commonly, if he be skittishe, and do some displesure, we blame the breker. And a wyfe likewise . . . if he do not teache hir, if she be rude, vnwomanly, and wytles, is not he to be blamed?
>
> (sig. B2ᵛ)

Exemplarity does not, after all, mean learning by example; it means learning by *teaching* by example. The art of household is exemplary because it involves the man practising his own histrionic exemplarity in the training that will transform a 'rude' and 'wytles' partner into a womanly helpmeet. And it is hardly surprising to learn from Kathleen Davies that among 'Puritan' books of domestic conduct, 'the metaphor of horse-breaking was a familiar one – it occurs in Bullinger, Smith, Gouge, and Dod and Cleaver, but Whatley was particularly fond of it, and uses it several times'.[47]

Curious, however, is the turn taken by the text after the concepts of horse-breaking and wife-training have been introduced. For the expected gynaecology is not immediately forthcoming; it is deferred through an extended episode full of double analogies involving military activity and 'husbandry' in the sense of tilling the soil. What seems to be taking place in this section is a deliberate form of mystification. Its final objective is to define the man who has mastered the art of household as the most honourable and necessary of citizens in any state. The occupations of farming and of war, carrying associations of honesty and honour respectively, and traditionally conceded as vital to any state, function as means of legitimizing this new form of 'science' or 'occupation' (more properly, perhaps, an 'art of existence') as something that should be practised by the noblest men of the community.

Xenophon's deferral of the expected amplification and explication of Socrates' introduction of the theme of wife-training also serves to defer any conclusion over the meaning of 'husbandry' itself; by thus opening out a space of suspended definition, Xenophon expands and dignifies husbandry's signifying possibilities until these are quite uncontainable by any one definition of the term. By this process, the prudential practice of husbandry is dissociated from the physical interior of the household; by the time the text relocates 'husbandry' in the supervision of the household and the wife, the term already exceeds supervision of wife and household to the extent that these tasks function like synecdoches, mere parts by which the whole may be recognized.

To motivate the deferral in question, Xenophon has Socrates express a desire to define the noblest and most beneficial occupation in the commonweal (*to koinon* – the community). Craftsmen, Socrates finds, cannot qualify as the noblest citizens since they have 'small leysure to sette theyr mind and diligence to doe theyr friendes any good, nor also the commonwelth', and their labours 'destroy the bodies of them that do occupy those' (sig. B3^v). Xenophon's concern to equate male beauty and leisure as signs of nobility has, *pace* Foucault, a rhetorical purpose here.[48] For the leisure to serve friends and commonwealth that defines the nobleman places him symbolically 'outdoors' in the sense of being unconfined by a narrowing daily routine. It is this sense of patrician freedom that is realized symbolically in the 'outdoors' complexion of men who are not bound to labour as craftsmen. The virtue of symbolism is its transferability; thus other 'outdoor' occupations which do involve routine labour, but are required by Xenophon for the rhetorical purposes of the next phase of his argument (the occupations of farming and warfare) may become impressionistically assimilated to the definition of nobility through their association with health and good looks.

In using farming and warfare as analogies for the art of household, Xenophon's next purpose appears to be to endow his definition of *oikonomia* with the physical dignity and ethical integrity of the one, and the glamour and honour of the other. Thus, when Critobolus has been persuaded of the inferiority of all handicrafts, Socrates proves by the overwhelming authority of the example he offers that 'husbandry' is beyond doubt the fittest occupation for the good citizen:

Let not vs thynke scorne, nor be ashamed to folow [in Greek *mimēsasthai* – imitate] the kyng of the Persis [Persians]. For they saye, that he, supposing the science of warre, and also of housebandry to be most honourable, and also necessary among other faculties, doth regarde and exercise theym wonderfly.

(sig. B4ʳ)

Critobolus expresses our incredulity: 'Do ye thynke', he asks Socrates witheringly, 'that the kyng of Persia careth any thynge for housebandry?' (sig. B4ʳ). Socrates then details the means by which Cyrus retains control of his vast empire; by maintaining garrisons in tributary realms under the surveillance of lieutenants and by rewarding those who cultivate and invest in their lands. As James Tatum has explained, we see in the *Oeconomicus* a thumbnail sketch of the 'economy of empire' by which Cyrus the great rules in the *Cyropaedia*. Tatum argues that 'Cyrus's creation of a court and an empire is essentially an exercise in persuasion . . . however, he does not aim for technical perfection in the ordinary manner of orators. The entire *Cyropaedia*, and not only Cyrus's discourse . . . invites rhetorical study.'[49] Cyrus' imperial economy is plotted as the narrative of a life devoted to the achievement of control over other people by the rhetorical exploitation of their affections. Such exploitation simultaneously displaces itself: by winning the affection of lieutenants, the exemplary ruler diffuses and makes paradigmatic his absolute authority, rendering it the more secure.[50] For readers familiar (as sixteenth-century readers would be) with the *Cyropaedia*, Xenophon's invocation of Cyrus the younger in the context of the *Oeconomicus* detaches the concept of 'husbandry' from the sense of subsistence farming and prepares it for a new and enlarged sense of a rhetorical economy, or a 'use and ordering' of subordinates through persuasion and imitation.

The symbolic husbandry of Cyrus' empire is exquisitely worked by Xenophon in the *Oeconomicus* into a final exemplum which I want to pause over, because it was to become a favourite of sixteenth-century humanists. Lawrence Humphrey's *The Nobles, or Of Nobilitye* (1563), for example, is a polemic arguing for the reformation of the aristocracy through a programme of humanistic learning comparable to that elaborated by Thomas Elyot in *The Boke named the Governour*. In setting out the arguments in favour of a liberal education, however, Humphrey charges the English nobility not with ignorance but with idleness, and launches into a set piece in praise of the 'husbandry' practised by ancient rulers. Pre-eminent among his examples is Xenophon's anecdote of Cyrus in his garden at Sardis:

> That the practise of husbandry was also familyer to kynges, the example of *Cirus* the younger proveth. Who accounted it no stayne, paynefully with hys owne handes to sowe whole fyeldes, to graffe in his Orchardes, cut & border flowers and herbes in hys Garden, and curyously to plant hys trees in seemly order. Nay when *Lisander*, the *Lacedemonian Legate* came to him with presentes, vaunted to hym, that all he saw, him selfe had sowed and set. Whereat he wondring, and viewinge hys purple Roabes, hys bodies beautie, the sumptuous Persian ornaments, embrawderyes of golde and pearle, amazed cryed out, Justly *O Cierus*, men deame thee happy, sith in thee vertue and Fortune meets. For so almoste translated it Cicero out of *Xenophon*. Wherefore learned men, for they see this labour greatly accepted and honoured of the *Consuls* and lords of *Roome*, and the ancient grekes and kinges, thinke it not unmeete or unfitting for oure Nobles.[51]

Through his deployment of Cicero's imitation of the Cyrus exemplum in the context of an education programme for England's governors, Humphrey has produced a reading of Xenophon's *oikonomia* or 'husbandry' as a form of cultural production which enables the government of peoples.

Humphrey's use of Xenophon's example to sum up the potential transformation of the English nobility's 'meane invention and judgement'[52] through a humanist reading programme parallels the persuasiveness with which Socrates' invocation of Cyrus' 'economy of empire' extends and elevates Xenophon's definition of husbandry. As the very strongest form of proof (*tekmērion*) of the effectiveness of Cyrus' rule, Xenophon's Socrates relates how none of the emperor's soldiers ever desert him. Such a proof of persuasive or charismatic virtue testifies implicitly to Cyrus' incessant labour in the art of cultural production – the labour of ensuring the loyalty of a colonized people through the strategic innovation and reordering of customs and codes of living. This cultural work is subsequently stylized as 'husbandry' in the anecdote, made famous by Cicero, of the bejewelled and perfumed

Cyrus in the garden, explaining to an astonished Lysander that he did all the gardening himself:

> Doe ye mervaile of this Lysander? By the feyth that I owe to god when I am well at ease, I never go to diner, vnto the time I have done somewhat, eyther in feates of armes or some poynt of housebandry, tyl I sweate.

(sig. B7^{r-v})

'Sweat' here is the synecdochic detail which, for readers of the *Cyropaedia*, invokes all the Spartan practices of physical endurance – the hunting, the military exercises, the diet of cresses or bread – that mark out the virtuous Persians in contrast to the 'effeminate' Medes who drink wine and banquet, and adorn themselves with jewels and cosmetics. As Tatum points out, it is a sign of the purely rhetorical, rather than ethical value of these differences of *nomoi* or mores for Cyrus that he should, having exploited the chance to expose the 'effeminacy' of the Medes in earlier contexts, finally choose to adapt their practice of using cosmetics to increase his spellbinding power as a ruler.[53] 'Sweat', in other words, is no less rhetorical here, in its setting out and adorning of this textual exemplum of the king with the signs of honest good health, than jewels and kohl would be in the setting out and adorning of his actual presence. The purpose of the Sardis anecdote, as Cicero and Lawrence Humphrey appreciated, is to replace the notion of husbandry as necessary toil with the notion of husbandry as an art of existence which is both the sign and essence of the most fortunate, the rulers of the commonweal. As Cicero puts it, 'in you virtue and fortune meet' ('virtuti tuae fortuna coniuncta est'[54]); it is not exactly that Cyrus is fortunate *because* of his virtuous activity, but that his eminence, which may be considered partly due to fortune, does not exempt him from labour, but rather dignifies the continual prudential labour (which is virtue) of preserving itself. As Xenophon has Socrates explain to Critobolus, the anecdote is told, 'for this cause, that ye may see, that thei that be riche and fortunate, cannot well kepe theim from housebandry' (sig. B7^v).

After a set piece on the praises of rural life, Critobolus agrees that Socrates has sufficiently proved that husbandry is the most honourable occupation in a commonweal. Socrates sums up the argument so far, reminding Critobolus that they have defined the house to be a man's goods, and 'goods' to be all that a man could 'use and order', and that having discovered that most crafts keep men indoors and destroy their bodies, they further decided that husbandry 'semed to be most honourable, and best estemed in cities and common welthes, because it maketh good men, well disposed and well mynded to do good for the common welthe' (sig. C4^v). The shift between defining the art of household as an exemplary knowledge, to be learned by imitation, and the art of 'husbandry' as a dignified 'outdoors' state of being, signifier of patrician good health, substantial leisure and means, and charismatic and surveillant visibility, is marked in the Greek by the movement from *oikonomia* to *georgeon*; in English this distinction is effaced through the homology of 'household' and 'housebandry', emphasizing the conceptual link the text is clearly concerned to make. What finally constructs that link is the use of an exemplary figure – the good husband himself – who is sought under the rubric of the 'good and beautiful man' (*to kalos kagathos aner*) which Hervet translates as 'good and honest man'. In this phase Socrates relates to Critobolus how he has been searching among craftsmen and citizens for the *kalos te kagathos aner*, the true gentleman, in vain, until he heard by reputation of one Ischomachus,

> And for bycause I hard, that Ischomachus was generally, bothe of men, woman [sic], citizines and strangers, called and taken for a good and honest man, methoughte I coulde do no better, than to prove howe I myghte commune with hym. And vppon a tyme, whan I sawe hym sitting in a porche of a churche, for bycause me thought he was at leyser, I came to hym, and sette me downe by hym, and said: What is the cause, good Ischomachus, that ye, which be wont to be ever more occupied, sytte here nowe after this manner, for I have seene you for the most part evermore doing somewhat, and lyghtly never ydell . . . ? Nor ye shulde nowe have seen me, good Socrates, sayde he . . . if I had not apointed with certaine straungers to tary here for them. And if ye were not here, where wolde ye have bene, or howe wolde ye have ben occupied, said I to hym: for I wold knowe of you very fayne, what thynge you do, that maketh ye to be called a good and honest (*kalos te kagathos*) man? The good complection of your body sheweth well ynoughe, that ye byde not alway slouggynge at home.
>
> (sig. C4^v)

Ischomachus, the ideal citizen, is linked with the honourable occupation of husbandry-as-farming (*georgeon*) by the sign of his complexion; his is an 'outdoors' occupation, unlike that of a craftsman. But his being out of doors signifies not physical labour but readiness for negotiation in the public sphere – Socrates finds him at the temple of Zeus in the *agora* or marketplace (Hervet's substitution of a 'chuche porche' would convey to a sixteenth-century reader this sense of a public place for the transacting of business). Xenophon is careful to define Ischomachus' market-place activity as patrician obligation rather than commerce or trading – 'taxes, preastes or subsidies' translates Hervet – but the point is, nevertheless, that the discovery of Ischomachus in the text as 'being outdoors' signifies a state of apparent leisure which is actually preparedness-for-business, a state of being furnished, or possessed, of the means to speak and act to advantage in the public domain. If this quality of 'being outdoors', simultaneously at leisure and 'occupied', is what defines the gentleman, the next question is, how is it achieved? What, in other words, is Ischomachus' gentlemanly 'occupation'? 'I wolde know of you very fayne, what thynge ye do . . .?' asks Socrates. Ischomachus does not answer directly. He does not limit to any profession the perfection of his suspension between leisure and business, the 'beauty' of his timely discovery, awaiting an appointment in the marketplace. Instead he answers, simply: 'in dede, good Socr[ates], I do not alwaye byde at home, for my wyfe can order wel inough suche thynges as I have there' (sig. C5^r).

Thus, by deferral through the intervening definition of 'husbandry' (*georgeon*) as the most noble and necessary occupation in the commonweal, this *topos* of the well-ordering of the wife comes to acquire a special symbolic and political significance. The wife becomes the displaced marker of all that resists definition in the art of 'husbandry' – all that, by definition, would close off husbandry's potent identification with the practical mastery of temporal and spatial contingency and the rhetorical transformation of propriety. 'Husbandry' as Xenophon defines it, is dignified by being identified with the acquisition of a practical, exemplary knowledge resembling the humanist concept of 'decorum' – that is, the capacity of invention and judgement to order speech and action to meet the demands of the occasion. This practical knowledge is, in turn, elevated by association with the imperial economy of persuasion practised by Cyrus the Great, and discovered as the potential of every man who has a wife at home. Xenophonic husbandry is the new masculine ideal of the sixteenth century, the textually acquired but practical art of existence that identifies the man of liberal education, good birth and reasonable means as the most necessary member for the defence and maintenance of a commonweal.

THREE HUMANIST EMPLOTMENTS OF XENOPHON'S HOUSEWIFE: BULLINGER, LUPSET AND ERASMUS

Many years ago, O.B. Hardison's *The Enduring Monument*, in establishing the centrality of rhetorical categories to the evaluation of literary genres in the Renaissance, discovered the period's favourite paradigm of the exemplary heroic poem to be not Virgil's *Aeneid*, as might have been supposed, but Xenophon's *Cyropaedia*.[55] There can be no doubt that, through the *Cyropaedia* and the *Oeconomicus*, Xenophon's impact on the sixteenth century was enormous. At the risk of being reductive, two main reasons may be advanced for this. First, his texts taught, as a practical art, the histrionic and dialectical economy of managing and exploiting the affections and anxieties of one's subordinates. Second, the rhetorical emplotment of each of his texts, or what Sir Thomas Elyot called the 'swetenes' with which he 'invented and ordered his warke'[56], offered a model for the eloquent legitimation of the application of thrifty and prudential principles of resource management to areas of life which had traditionally rejected such principles as being compatible neither with honour nor with Christian charity. The existence of texts such as Dudley Fenner's *The Artes of Logike and Rhetorike*, which contains *The Order of Householde* (1584) suggests that, in the course of the sixteenth century, instruction in the practice of *oikonomia* was inseparably linked to instruction in the capacity to produce its legitimating rhetoric.[57]

Thus, we find that Heinrich Bullinger's imitation of Xenophon in the *Christlich Eestand* owes its formidable impact on English marriage doctrine to Bullinger's ingenious rhetorical emplotment of the Xenophonic housewife as the legitimating trope of arguments otherwise hesitantly advanced to persuade the reader of the compatibility of economic carefulness and the words of Christ. Moreover, this use of Xenophon by Bullinger plays a significant part in the sixteenth-century's ideological struggle over the legitimation of usury. For Bullinger's innovative arguments advocating the sanctity of carefulness in household management were first formulated by way of an attack on the radical communism of the German Anabaptists. The Anabaptists took their cue from Luther's early fulminations against the usurious aspect of the investment practice known as *Zinskauf*. Alleging the authority of Christ's commandment to love one's neighbour as oneself, and his injunction against usury ('Lend, hoping for nothing again', Luke 6:35) the Anabaptists refused to pay *Zins* of any kind, whether rent or fief, and established their own communistic ethos as being nearer to the charitable teaching of Christ.[58] In a treatise entitled *Von dem unverschampten fräfel* ('Of the shameless outrage') Bullinger mobilized an impressive set of arguments against the impeccable scholastic credentials of the Anabaptists' objection to the interest-bearing *Zinskauf*. He argued that interest on loans was not incompatible with Christian charity; in particular, he refuted the scholastic and Aristotelian doctrine of money's essential sterility. Far from being a neutral medium of exchange, money was, he said, 'the nerve, art, diversification and readiness for production (*fertigung*) of all trades'. The investor of capital was entitled to a share in profits made with his money so long as these were taken without disadvantage to his neighbour ('nit ze nachteyl dem nächsten').[59]

Such a ground-breaking shift in ethics (Bullinger's rejection of the scholastic objections to interest-bearing loans anticipated Calvin's) necessitated a reformulation of boundaries around neighbourly and unneighbourly practices. If making profits on productive loans was arguably compatible with Christ's love commandment, then harmful usury (*wücher*) must be redefined as one of those financial practices whereby neighbours defrauded one another, or took what was not their own. A reconceptualization of the very basis of good neighbourhood was necessary. Bullinger used the words of St Paul to the Thessalonians to argue against the Anabaptists that the 'brotherhood and love which is from God is not such that they have all things in common . . . For then the virtue of compassion and sharing is taken away.' Compassion (*barmhersigkeyt*) for one's neighbours was, Bullinger argued, far from being rooted in communism; rather it was the effect of care for the individual household ('die eigenschafft und sorg der husshaltung') as prescribed by St Paul.[60]

42

Bullinger's anti-communistic, pro-usury arguments helped change the climate of opinion on the ethics of capitalism in England, though no one would think so from reading histories of the subject. This is because Bullinger's controversial arguments on marketplace ethics entered English thought via *Hausvater-literatur*.[61] Contemporaries, however, made no mistake about 'householding' literature's relevance to the usury debate: no less an author than Shakespeare alluded to Coverdale's Bullinger to suggest this. For Bullinger's favourite Old Testament example of God's blessing of economic self-sufficiency was the story of Jacob ('an image of all good action', Bullinger called him in the *Fräfel*[62]) who, in Genesis 30, got the better of his master, Laban, by a cunning practice of animal husbandry which he justified by a stout affirmation of his need to provide for his own household as well as Laban's. Shakespeare's Shylock famously alleges Jacob's practice against Laban as his own ethical model: 'This was a way to thrive, and he was blest: / And thrift is blessing if men steal it not.' The editor of the Arden edition remarks that 'The Laban story has not been found in any sixteenth-century book on usury'.[63] But Shylock's words reproduce exactly Bullinger's distinction between Jacob as exemplary householder, and the thief exhorted by St Paul to steal no more: 'War gestolen hat der stale nit mer sonder arbeite . . . mit der handarbeit' (Coverdale translates: 'Who so hath stolen saith Paul, let him now stele no more but labour with his handes'). Here, in Coverdale's translation of Bullinger, Shakespeare and his contemporaries might read how 'the man in his gayning and occupyng' should imitate the thrifty and 'faithful dealing of Jacob' as opposed to the 'cowetuouse desayt of Laban'.[64]

Bullinger transposed the example of Jacob's thrift along with the rest of the *Fräfel*'s arguments justifying the compatibility of Christian charity and economic prudence into his *Christlich Eestand*, but with this difference; in the *Eestand*, he omitted the *Fräfel*'s explicit distinction between productive and harmful usury, plotting the distinction instead as one between 'ordinate' and 'inordinate' uses of *oikonomia*, which, in its ordinate form, he essentialized as a part of God's plan of human and animal nature, manifest in the distinctive labouring properties of the sexes, male and female, husband and wife. Thus, the chapter on household care begins with an injunction to the householder to delegate care to his wife: 'So dann ouch din wyb', or, as Coverdale translates it, 'If thy wife be vertuouse and trustye, let hyr be also carefull in

keping and providyng for thy house. For siche studye and ordinate care gendreth grete love and encreaseth thy substance.'[65] The
crucial question of the possible impiety of 'carefulness' for material
things determines the rhetorical shaping of the arguments; once
the thought of the housewife has been introduced, the chapter
goes on to reassure readers of the sanctity of 'ordinate' care for
household provision:

> For such studye and care is not forboden, for the godly
> patriarch Jacob thought it necessarye for him and his wife to
> be studiouse for their houshold / Paul affirming it: if a man
> provide not for his owne household he denieth the faith and
> is an infidele. Wherefore all that Cryste speketh agaynst
> carefulnes / he speaketh it gaynst all inordinate mystrusting
> & to much couetouse care and sorow.[66]

Followers of Christ's commandment are those who, in Bullinger,
avoid harmfully usurious arts ('*wücherischen vorteiligen künsten'*)
but provide for themselves, and engage in such commercial
transactions as the *Fräfel* proved compatible with loving one's
neighbour as oneself; in Coverdale's version, these become men
who 'walke ordinately & quyetly, labouryng with their awne
handes, avoydinge usurye, but doyng to other as thou woldest be
done to thyn nowne self'.[67] Crucially, the distinction between
faithful and inordinate dealing in the marketplace crystallizes
around the fact that God has established an 'order' (*ordnung*) in all
things economic. 'Die husshaltung hat ouch ir ordnung glych wie
andere ding',[68] writes Bullinger ('The keeping of the house has its
order, just as other things do'), and the order of householding, or
economics, is, of course, the Xenophonic natural history of man's
right to speculate abroad, and woman's obligation to be accountable at home.

Of course, the usurer continued to be *named* throughout the
sixteenth century as the antithesis to all good neighbourhood and
true friendship between men. Nevertheless, Bullinger's writings
had established a conceptual space in which practices of calculation and prudence relating to the provision of the individual
household need not be condemned wholesale as usurious and
unneighbourly. But where the positive valorization of *oikonomia* in
the *Fräfel* was supported by explicit arguments in favour of the
productivity of interest-bearing loans, the injunction to thrift in
the *Christlich Eestand* and its many derivatives was rhetorically

inferred from a 'reading' of God's intention to bless economic prudence by providing two sexes, one of which might conveniently serve as a housewife.

Bullinger's was not the only humanist text to effect this sort of enabling displacement of the circumscriptions traditionally imposed by Christianity on marketplace ethics and practice. Thomas Lupset, a friend of Erasmus, and fellow humanist, published in 1531 a text of moral philosophy dedicated to his erstwhile pupil, Edmund Withypoll, but meant as a guide to all young men of Withypoll's social status and vocation. Edmund was the son of Paul Withypoll, named by G.R. Elton as the 'leading capitalist' of the London of Henry VIII. Naturally, however, Lupset's treatise is no straightforward endorsement of capitalism; modelled, perhaps, on Cicero's reconciliation of *honestas* and *utilitas* in the *De Officiis*, Lupset's is a text *'perswading young men to walke in the pathway of honeste'* by probable argument. It establishes, for practical guidance, a threefold moral hierarchy, of which the highest concern is care of the soul, the second the body and third, the pursuit of worldly goods.[69]

The poor third after care of soul and body, merchandising as Lupset teaches it, would hardly thrive, since the temporal and spatial mastery that is a crucial ingredient of successful negotiation are circumscribed at every turn:

> Labour you muste for your lyvynge in a dewe order, as in the thyrd degree of your thinges. If matens, masse, or a sermon is to be harde, set your marchandise aparte for a season, & prefer the mattens of your soule ... If the tyme require to have you take a mele ... let not your marchandise defer the going therto in a dewe tyme ... If you espie a pore man to be in nede of your helpe, hast to helpe him before any care of making a bargayne ... In making your bargayne, kepe faith and promise: decieve no man with any gyle or false color ... For the gaines that you shuld get ... be conteined vnder your thyrde ... wher the breking of faith and promise ... sore hurteth your soule, in whom resteth your chief thought.[70]

Lupset's humanistic techniques of persuading his reader by probable argument, rather than tenets of faith, would seem by his own criterion to be quite inapplicable to the negotiating practices of his pupil's daily life, where 'color' and 'similitude' are not allowed, lest they deceive judgement in matters of transaction.

Just before he leaves this 'iii care', however, Lupset's argument suddenly becomes expansive and exemplary, declaring positively 'the course of an honest mans lyfe in this worlde to growe in ryches'. The margin announces 'housewife', and the text reveals that 'the best portion of wordly ryches' is 'to procure to have plentie of frendes', and

> to vse accordingly your wife, when the time shall come that you shall have one. For to opteyne substance of goodes, it lieth as moche in the wife, to kepe that you bringe home, as in your travayle to bryng home. And surely, onlesse she be the keper and sparer, the husbande shall littel go forward in his labour of gettynge: And the very trouth is, that there is noo yvelle housewyfe but for her fautes the good man is to be blamed. For I am vtterly of this opinion, that the man may make, shape and forme the woman as he wil. I wolde go farther with you in this thing & shew you somewhat of the wey to order your householde, if I sawe not this matter largelye intreatedde of dyvers philosophers ... Specially I wolde you redde with most diligence, the propre boke, that Xenophon writeth herof: it is called oeconomia, that is to say, the craft to order and kepe an howse, where this auctour geveth such counsell, for all the course of an honest mans lyfe in this worlde to growe in ryches, vnder the meanes of discretion and wisdome, that noo man in my mynde can sey more therin, or better: the whiche judgement of myne I doubt not but you wyll approve, whenne you have redde the sayde worke: it is translated out of greke into latine by one Raphaell, but in his translation, the worke leseth a greatte parte of the grace, that hit hath in the greke tonge, and also his translation in many places is false: and it playnly appereth, that Raphaell vnderstode not wel, what Xenophon wrote in greke. I have therfore, for dyvers of my frendes sake, translated the same worke out of greke tonge into englyshe, and you shall have the same with my good wyl, when your pleasure is to rede it.[71]

Only at this point in the text does Lupset wholeheartedly and confidently embrace the object of economic practice – to accumulate worldly goods – confidently, because he identifies the practice, as he understands it from Xenophon, with the legitimating 'grace' of its articulation in Greek, and therefore with his capacity, as a humanist scholar, to transmit a practical rhetorical appreciation of the text's persuasiveness to his pupil, and to unlatined readers.

Lupset's identification of the practical value of Xenophon's *Oeconomicus* with the potential of humanistic translation and imitation to enrich persuasion and transform cultural practice leads us nicely on to our final example of a rhetorical use of the *Oeconomicus* to shape an encomium of humanism itself. The text in question is Erasmus' epistolary portrait of Thomas More, an important source for much that endures in More's reputation as the man for all seasons: versatile, charismatic, public-spirited yet family-oriented.[72] Erasmus' portrait, published in 1519, claims to be a response to Ulrich von Hutten's request for a description of his friend, and offers itself as a faithful and accurate observation in the manner of Flemish painting; there is, however, no denying that it is also a fiction of good husbandry, an adaptation of Xenophon's emplotment of the housewife to express the practical contribution that humanistic learning might make to the state. Erasmus thus plots an account of More as an exemplary instructor of wives just after he has introduced the topic of More's devotion to Greek literature, the importance of which he intially downplays, characterizing it, indeed, almost as a prodigal straying into *belles lettres* from the paternal path of the law. Marriage is also introduced as if it might be read as an 'unfilial' desertion of the Church Fathers through the rejection of priesthood.[73] Both these apparent extravagances or eccentricities are, however, subsequently recovered through Erasmus' use of Xenophon as a way of 'proving' More's exemplary husbandry, so that they emerge as the investments that finally maximize the ethical and practical effectiveness of More as an agent and speaker in the public sphere.

The phrases in Xenophon which Erasmus particularly recalls are occasioned by Socrates asking whether Ischomachus' bride was already skilled in household matters when he married her; Ischomachus replies

> howe coulde she have ben so, whan she was but fiftene year olde whan I married hir? and afore she hadde ben so negligently brought vp, that she hadde but very littel sene, very littel herde, and very lytel spoken of the world.
>
> (sig. C5^r)

Oddly enough, however, the subsequent proof of Ischomachus'

effectiveness as an exemplary teacher of wives takes the form of an anecdote more remarkable as an allegory of the exemplary practice of reading than as a naturalistic account of a wife's efficiency in peforming housework. Socrates cues Ischomachus by asking how his wife reacted to all his teaching about the division of labour between husbands and wives, and the reply is a history of how distressed she once was at not being able to find a certain object stored in the house when her husband asked for it. Ischomachus relates how he told her sententiously that not to have a thing ready for use is the definition of poverty, and they subsequently re-ordered the household so that their knowledge of where every-thing was would quickly bring it to hand (sigs D2^v-D4^r). This, the figure of woman as agent of rhetorical retrieval, or 'readiness for use' would seem to be the last link in the conceptual chain which identifies *oikonomia* as that 'science' (*epistēmē*) which positions men metaphorically 'outdoors', in a state of 'leisure' or readiness to 'sette their mindes and diligence to do theyr frendes any good, or the commonwealth'. Ischomachus' position on the outside of this ordered household thereby symbolizes his mastery of it as a necessarily hidden investment, so that it emerges, in Socrates finding him 'at leisure' and yet occupied, in the form of a readiness, an easy extemporaneity in the conduct of all his affairs. More's conduct is throughout Erasmus' portrait, of course, char-acterized by just such ease, an ease supremely expressed in Erasmus' climactic praise of his facility in speaking:

> It would be difficult to find a more felicitous extempore speaker, so fertile are both his mind and the tongue that does its bidding. His mind is always ready, ever passing nimbly to the next point; his memory is always at his elbow, and as everything is held, so to say, in ready cash (velut in numer-ato), it puts forward promptly and without hesitation what time and place demand.[74]

In this praise of ease and fluency are echoes of Erasmus' textbook exposition of the hidden labour, the thrifty (*frugifer*) husbandry of texts of which it is the achievement. In the 'ratio colligenda exempla' in the *De Copia*, Erasmus explains how the practice of reading ancient literature for its transformative, exemplary poten-tial, will give the reader access to a facility such as More's, a capacity to order and structure arguments as if they were 'on hand and in ready money, as it were' ('in promptu vel ac in numerato').[75]

Thus it is that in the final image of More, his aforementioned devotion to literature emerges as not eccentric but *central* to his effectiveness in active, political life. And the practice of imitation and exemplarity through which this is achieved is thematized in Erasmus' portrait of More's deliberate espousal of the virtues of a 'chaste husbandry' rather than 'immoral priesthood', since the essence of this husbandry is expressed in an exemplary practice of teaching and ordering the behaviour of those in his household. Indeed, Erasmus' More outdoes his exemplar Ischomachus by actively *choosing* an ignorant and ill-brought up girl for his bride, having learned from the Greek text the positive advantages of the exemplary economy of such learning:

> he chose for his wife an unmarried girl, of good family, and quite inexperienced as yet, having always lived in the country with her parents and sisters, which gave him the more opportunity to mould her character to match his own (quo magis illi licerat illam ad suos mores fingeret).[76]

In its own way, each of these three uses of Xenophon's identification of *oikonomia* as a fiction of wife-training may be read as an undoing of the proper place of the Christian layman. In each the Christian layman is able to transgress the permitted bounds of his worldly activities to the extent that such transgression redefines him as a good husband. Thus Bullinger's reading of Xenophon enabled him to release the Christian occupier into the negotiating time/space of the open market, under the Pauline injunction to provide for wife and household; by the end of the century, all Bullinger's cautious hesitancy of expression on the subject ('sorg-sam syn oder husshaltung ist nit von Gott verbotten' – 'it is *not forbidden* of God to be careful, or keep house') would be quite redundant; by 1592 Thomas Nashe could complain that the text that Bullinger used to justify household provision was too fre-quently in the mouths of the godly.[77] The texts of Thomas Lupset, Lawrence Humphrey and Erasmus likewise demonstrate how the humanists' commitment to exemplary practice (whether in textual production, or in the management of everyday life) enabled them to recognize in Xenophon's discourse of husbandry a series of dignifying metaphors for the contribution which they, as human-ists, might (unlike their cloistered scholastic opponents) make to the prosperity of their worldly patrons, and to the commonweal.

And what, then, of the decidedly non-satiric treatment of the moneylender in the portrait by Quinten Metsys? Is it possible to ascribe the positive qualities in Metsys' portrayal of an occupation so regularly scapegoated to the artist's unusual decision to represent this occupation as an 'art of household'? Inscribed on the original frame of Metsys' picture, according to his seventeenth-century biographer, was a verse of Leviticus, 19:36: 'Just balances, just weights shall ye have.'[78] Marketplace accountability, expressed in the conformity of standards of measure and weight, is rendered by Metsys as visibility. The accurate representation of evaluation (the valuables being weighed) seems to be for our benefit; through Metsys' faithful depiction, we become witnesses, qualified to give an account of the moneylender's good faith and true dealing. Metsys' 'art of describing' thus constructs beholders as both neighbourhood and congregation, the spiritual and secular community to whom pledges of faith and measuring standards in the marketplace are accountable. Thus, while the wife's gaze is drawn, like ours, to the moneylender's weighing activity, her turning of the page makes the finely depicted words and images in her book of hours also the objects of our gaze, creating a further sense (implicit, too, in the tiny reflection of the man reading the scriptures in the view of the church) in which reading is communal, and continuous with other acts of devotion, such as participation in the Mass. Behind the wife, an open door, giving onto an animated conversation between two men, suggests that the worldly consequence of faithless dealing may be identified with the risks it brings to the soul – as Lupset said, the 'breking of faith and promise ... sore hurteth your soul' while 'an vntru tonge, which bringeth a man out of credence' was 'a thing very hurtful for marchantes'.[79] In Metsys' organization of the images, the suggestion of the merchant's simultaneous accountability to God and to his neighbours seems to be made dependent on the presence of his wife, who, placed between the thresholds of the Mass and the marketplace, but directing her eyes at her husband's occupation, personifies our act of witness as its moral boundary.

There is a sense, then, in which Metsys' painting resembles the early humanist texts we have been discussing; like them, it enables a dignified, non-grotesque version of marketplace activity to become visible as part of the division of labour in the conjugal household. Only, of course, as in the humanist texts, the division is not one of labour, but of ethical accountability in an economy of representation. Thus, for all its ethically positive effect, Metsys' construction of the moneylender as good husband reminds us that one of the things Xenophon and his sixteenth-century imitators understood by 'husbandry' was a handy signifying system which enabled the strategic ennobling of practices of uncertain ethical validity, while displacing, through sexual difference, fears about their consequences. In the course of the sixteenth century, as credit relations between men were gradually transformed from spatially fixed and temporally flexible relations of friendship to transferable but temporally specific relations secured by financial interest, Xenophon's concept of 'good husbandry' became indispensible to discursive representations of the changes taking place. The purpose of the ensuing chapters will be to trace and analyse the effects of such representations upon the construction of female sexuality in plays, poems and *novelle* by men, and upon the access of women to cultural production in comparable forms.

2

ECONOMIES OF FRIENDSHIP

The textuality of *amicitia*

In the eighth tale on the tenth day of Boccaccio's *Decameron*, a young Athenian nobleman called Gisippus loses, in the space of a sentence, all his prestige as the head of his household, and consequently all his friends and his goods and substance:

> Gisippo, rimasosi in Atene, quasi da tutti poco a capital tenuto, dopo non molto tempo, per certe brighe cittadine, con tutti quegli di casa sua, povero e meschino fu d'Atene cacciato e dannato ad essilio perpetuo.

> Meanwhile in Athens, Gisippus was held in such low esteem by almost everyone that it was not long before factional strife in the city forced him to be driven with all his household out of Athens, poor and destitute, and condemned to perpetual exile.[1]

The fictional example of Gisippus serves to qualify what has so far been said about the accumulation of 'capital' in the sixteenth century. The 'capital' Gisippus here loses is the readiness of others to assist him in times of need; being 'poco a capital tenuto' (held in low esteem) he becomes vulnerable to enemies, helpless and destitute. Judging by the notes in Ruscelli's edition of Boccaccio, the use of 'capital' in the sense of 'esteem' had already become obscure in Italian by 1552[2]; the word nevertheless provides a striking reminder of how contingent upon *honour* and *the assurance of friendship* was, in that period, the agency of what we would now call 'capital'. Indeed, Boccaccio's 'capital' seems close to what Pierre Bourdieu calls 'symbolic capital' when he defines it as 'the prestige and renown attached to a family and a name' which is 'readily converted back into economic capital'. This prestige,

52

assuring the co-operation and help of friends, kinsfolk and neighbours is, he argues, 'perhaps *the most valuable form of accumulation
in a society in which the severity of the climate . . . and the limited
technical resources . . . demand collective labour'.*[3]

The last chapter touched on the question of sixteenth-century
attitudes to credit and capital insofar as its argument was concerned with the capacity of a Xenophonic literature on the 'art of
household' to break down the sense of there being an ethical
contradiction between the prudential imperative to provide for
one's own, and the Christian obligation to lend freely to others.
But the chapter also placed the humanistic genre of household
literature within the context of a broader sense in which Xenophonic *oikonomia* or 'husbandry' was understood to signify the
transformative potential of the humanist education programme
itself. What needs to be addressed at this point, then, is the
question of the impact of that humanist programme upon the way
in which relations of exchange, reciprocity and affection between
men were henceforward to be imagined. Thus, where the last
chapter considered the new humanist ideal of masculinity in its
individual aspect, this chapter will be concerned with social and
relational aspects of the same ideal: if 'good husbandry' was a
figure for the practical efficacy of a humanistic education in
classical literature, how were the operations of this new form of
symbolic capital to be imagined in relation to the traditional
operations of symbolic capital as prestige, honour, friendship and
alliance? Here, as before, a figurative text, much imitated by
sixteenth-century humanists, provides the clue: this time, our
text is Boccaccio's reworking of a tale about the testing of friendship between two merchants into what sixteenth century readers
understood as an allegory of the transformation of alliance-
friendship by the technology of a humanist education.

We saw in the last chapter how, in the early years of the
sixteenth century, the humanist Richard Whitford had to go out of
his way to assure readers that, although, 'thou canst have none so
sure a castel or guard of thy lyfe: as is love and frendeshyppe of
thy neyghboure', yet, 'it is nat contrary unto christianyte, where
extreme . . . nede is nat perceyved in the neighbour', to store up
wealth against mischance. By the end of the sixteenth century,
however, such qualifying hesitations on the subject of economic
prudence had become redundant. For by this time it was generally
conceded that trust in friendship was no longer the surest form of

capital investment; the newly powerful agency of money had taken its place. In his book on this subject, entitled *Of Golds Kingdome in this unhelping Age* (1604), the lawyer Edward Hake included a poem entitled 'Trust to thyselfe, and not to thy friends nor kinsfolkes', in which a wise little lark, whose nest is in danger of being 'displaced' by the reapers when the farmer begins harvesting, remains secure while the farmer unsuccessfully tries to round up first neighbours and then cousins and kin to help him in the labour of bringing the harvest home. The farmer's frustration is 'the case of all men that do lay / Their hope of help in kinred or in frend' the poem concludes, while other poems in a similar vein lament the failure of men to 'speak or write' to aid the causes of their professed friends, 'if gold come not betweene'.[4]

The pervasiveness of such laments should not fool us into thinking them merely 'conventional', nor prevent us from reading in them the traces of a credit system based on bonds of reciprocal service and gift-exchange, and predating the systems of transferable credit with which we are familiar today. For, as Marcel Mauss, long ago, and Paul Millet, recently, have argued, a system of credit, far from being the the final phase in the development of a monetary economy, is in fact present in the exchange practices of the most archaic societies, in the institution of the gift. As Millet explains, using the model of 'reciprocity and kinship distance' established by Marshal Sahlins, a crucial difference between the credit system secured by interest payments and that instituted in the exchange of gifts and service is that the latter, unlike the former, actively seeks to prevent the equalization of accounts which would terminate the relation between debtor and creditor. Millet cites an author who was quoted in more than one sixteenth-century text on the ethics of credit relations. This is Hesiod, the author of *Works and Days*: 'Take fair measure of your neighbour and pay him back fairly with the same measure, or better, if you can; so that *if you are in need afterwards, you may find him sure*' (my italics). Millet comments,

> The aim, then, is not merely to wipe out the original obligation, but, if at all possible, to create a counter-obligation, thereby converting the former creditor into a debtor . . . This ensures that exchanges between pairs of individuals will continue into the future. Only when a relationship is to be wound up is the debt settled with any precision.[5]

Evidently, what distinguishes such a credit system from the

transferable credit secured by a recognized rate of interest is its local specificity and temporal imprecision; the creditor does not stipulate the time when the favour is to be returned, for the temporal extension of the debt itself creates the bond of 'friendship' that assures the creditor of help in his own future wants. As in the Athenian economy described by Millet, so in sixteenth-century England; the words 'give' and 'lend' were not clearly distinguished, and the practices of both, and of selling goods for 'days of payment' instead of ready money, were considered to create the bonds of 'trust' which were part of good neighbourhood. Thus, in a little poem on friendship in his *Floures of Philosophie* (first published in 1572), Hugh Platt, assuming that friendship involves credit extension, warned debtors against ingratitude:

> If friend in time of scarcitie
> Some golde of him would bid thee fet,
> When he shal come to aske his owne
> Couldst thou in heart deny the debt?[6]

Similarly, in her *Sweet Nosgay* (1573), a versification of the moral sentences of Platt's book, Isabella Whitney took it for granted that a function of affluence was to bind friends to oneself as assurance against the times of 'scarcitie':

> None in adversitie hath help
> except they prospered have
> And by that means have purchast frends
> of whom they ayde may crave.[7]

At the same time, the degree to which 'faith' or 'trust' or 'assurance' was well placed in these friends could only be tried by misfortune:

> Prosperitie wyll get thee friends
> but povertie will trie
> for then, except they faythfull are
> apace from thee they flye.[8]

In the debate over usury, those who opposed the legalization of interest, argued that 'trust' between men was the object of credit-extension: 'no man should sell his wares which he trusteth, any dearer than he doth for ready money', wrote William Harrys in his *The market or fayre of Vsurers* (1550), for 'there must nedes be lendyng and trusting to thyntent that many a pore fellow may have wherewithall to begynne'.[9] When Isabella Whitney made a mock will and testament fondly satirizing the London which poverty forced her to leave, she upbraided the city for refusing to 'lend and trust' to her, and for being such a poor friend:

> And now hath tyme put me in mind
> of thy great cruelnes:
> That never once a help wold finde,
> to ease me in distres.
> Thou never yet, woldst credit geve,
> to boord me for a yeare;
> Nor with Apparell me releve,
> except thou payed weare.[10]

In another poem by Edward Hake, 'The liberall mans Expostulation with Golde', the speaker observes that although he has no wish to put gold to usury, or lock it in a chest, but rather with it to help friends (including 'Booke-men wanting meanes'), yet it flies him, confounding its proper use as an agent of liberality.[11] Here the operative opposition is that between the malign force of gold hoarded, or communicating only with itself, and its benignity as the facilitator of social relations.

Boccaccio's novella, with which we began, is a history of friendship. In it, the strength of the affection between two young men, Titus and Gisippus, enables Titus to incur a debt which costs Gisippus not less than everything; when, in his extremity, Gisippus believes his faith to have been misplaced in his friend, he resolves to die, and only at this point is he recognized by his friend, and his sacrifice liberally repaid. The story concludes with a paean to friendship:

> Santissa cosa adunque e l'amista . . . Quali stati, qua' meriti, quali avanzi, avrebberon fatto Gisippo non curar di perdere i suoi parenti . . . per sodisfare all'amico, se non costei? . . . chi avrebbe Tito senza alcuna dilazione fatto liberalissimo a communicare il suo ampio patrimonio con Gisippo, al quale la fortuna il suo aveva tolto, se non costei?

> (Friendship, then, is a most sacred thing . . . What estates, what rewards, what advancements could have made Gisippus indifferent to the loss of his kin, . . . to satisfy his friend, if not friendship? . . . What would have made Titus so ready to share his extensive patrimony with Gisippus, whose own had been taken by fortune, if not friendship?[12])

Friendship here, for all its idealization, seems firmly rooted within an economics of liberality and timely reciprocity. And yet, if this exhausts the significance of Boccaccio's tale, why should it have been singled out, among the *novelle*, for the lavish attention bestowed upon it by sixteenth-century writers? What did they find in this *topos* of ideal male friendship?[13] In England, the story's exceptional popularity among writers of poetry, drama and prose fiction may be traced to a lively English version of the tale made by Sir Thomas Elyot for his *Boke named the Governour* (1531). Elyot's provulgation of the history occurs as part of a project to educate the nobility along humanistic lines, through a programme of exemplary reading. The exemplary status of the history as a 'figure of perfet amitie' is therefore stressed, and set in a context of related moral virtues, benevolence and liberality. 'Benevolence' is introduced after the manner of Cicero's treatment of the theme in the *De Officiis*, as an economy of generosity that binds men more effectively and assuredly than the tyrant's economy of fear or the miser's of hoarding; Elyot's first example, taken from the *Cyropaedia*, proves Cyrus richer than Croesus of Lydia, the wealthiest man in the world, on the strength of being able to count upon friends to supply him with 'redy' money if, as Cyrus says, 'I have nede of any to occupy'.[14] In its opposition to inert 'treasure' (surplus money otherwise occupied might be usury) the employment of money in 'friendship' is thus thematically linked to liberality, and to the practical tropics of gift-giving, involving the rhetorical arts of timeliness and apparent lack of calculation.[15]

Sir Thomas Elyot's version of 'Titus and Gisippus' deserves our attention, then, because its innovative textual strategies (it is probably the first *novella* in English) are introduced into the language not as part of a literary experiment, but as the appropriate vehicle for exemplary instruction of the nobility in the virtue of *amicitia*, the economy of perfect friendship between men. The story (using both Boccaccio's and Elyot's words where appropriate) may be summarized as follows: in the time of Octavius Caesar, a Roman senator, Publius Quintus Fulvius, sent his son, Titus, to study in Athens with the son of his friend, Chremes, a boy called Gisippus. As the two boys studied and lived together, they grew inseparable, sharing all tastes, opinions and possessions (Elyot says they were also alike in looks). In time Chremes died, and because 'by the goodes of his father', Gisippus 'was known to be man of great substaunce', he had rich marriages offered to him, so that his 'frendes, kynne and alies' (in Boccaccio, *amici* and *parenti*) urged him to take a wife, 'to thintent he mought increase his lygnage and progenie'.[16] Initially Gisippus was reluctant, but he came to delight in the beauty of his chosen bride, Sophronia, to the extent that he invited Titus to look at her and admire her with him. Titus, on seeing Sophronia, was so overcome with desire that he became ill, agonizing with himself on the conflict between his newly conceived love, and the loyalty he owed to his friend. Gisippus, however, learning the cause of his friend's pain, had no hesitation in offering to give up Sophronia to him; the only doubtful point was the means by which this might be effected without provoking hostility between his kin and friends, and those of Sophronia's father. So Gisippus counselled Titus to engage with him in a device, whereby he would take part in the public witnessing of the marriage by kin and friends, while Titus, by a passage which connected their chambers, would enter and take over in the marriage bed. For, as he reasoned, 'natwithstandinge any ceremony done at the tyme of the spousayles, the marriage natwithstandinge is nat confirmed, untyll at night the husband putteth a rynge on the finger of his wyfe, and unloseth her girdell'. To continue in Elyot's words:

The day of maryage was commen. Gysippus accompanied with his alyes and frendes came to the house of the damosel, where they were honorably and joyously fested ... The covenantes were radde and sealed, the dowar appointed, and al other bargaynes concluded, and the frendes of either parte toke their leave and departed, the bride with a fewe women (as was the custome) brought into her chambre. Than (as it was before agreed) Titus conveyed him selfe after Gysippus retourned to his house ... Now is Titus in bedde with the mayden, nat knowen of her, nor of any other, but for Gysippus. And first he swetely demaunded of her, if that she loved hym, and dayned to take hym for her husbande, forsaking all other, which she all blusshing with an eye halfe laughing halfe mourninge (as in poynte to departe from her maydenhede, but supposinge it to be Gysippus that asked her) affirmed. And than he eftsoones asketh her, if she in ratifienge that promise wolde receyve his rynge, whiche he hadde there all redy, wherto she consentynge putteth the rynge on her finger and unloseth her gyrdell.[17]

Titus and Gisippus then make a confession of the situation to
Sophronia, who in distress returns to her father's house. Titus
decides to face the Athenians publicly, with an oration in his own
and Gisippus' defence. His brilliantly structured declamation
representing the marriage as the work of providence on earth,
manifest in the powers of true friendship, succeeds in convincing
the Athenians that Sophronia is indeed truly and justly married to
Titus. Gisippus, argues Titus, perceived by his wisdom:

> (as I dought nat, but that ye do) that it was the very provision
> of god, that she shuld be my wife, and nat his. Wherto he
> gevynge place, and more estemynge true frendship than the
> love of a woman, where unto he was induced by his frendes,
> and nat by violence of Cupide constrained, as I am, hath
> willyngly granted to me the interest that he had in the
> damosell: and it is I, Titus, that have verely wedded her, I
> haue put the rynge on her fynger, I have undone the gyrdell
> of her shamfastnes. What will ye more? I have lyen with her,
> and confirmed the matrimonye, and made her a wife.[18]

However, Gisippus, by consequence, 'they adjudged unable to
enioye any possessions or goodes lefte to him by his parentes'[19]
and not long after despoiled and banished him from their city. He
made his way to Rome, hoping to meet Titus, but so beggarly did
he look that on the occasion of his seeing his old friend in the
street, Titus seemed not to recognize him, and looked the other
way. Gisippus, despairing, came to a place where a murder had
been committed, and did not resist being arrested on suspicion.
On the scaffold he was recognized by Titus, who, unable to bear
hearing his friend pleading guilty, 'denied it, and affirmed,
with reasons and argumentes that he was the murderer and nat
Gysippus'.[20] Thus they contended for guilt and death to the
wonder of the assembled crowd, until from its depths the real
murderer pressed forward, moved to confess and acquit both, for
their friendship and innocence. Such was the comfort of the Senate
and the whole people at this spectacle, that the real murderer was
discharged, and the rare example of Titus and Gisippus' friendship published in the annals of the city.

There are difficulties with this as a figure of ideal friendship
according to the model of reciprocity with which we began. For
the 'assurance' or 'trust' that seems, under such a scheme, to be
the objective of the gift-exchange, is here problematized by the

exchange itself having been successfully effected with the help of deception, and of Titus' declamatory skills – skills which might be perceived, in retrospect, to facilitate the breach of trust between men. The instrumentality of the friendship of Titus and Gisippus, turning as it does on the retrospective justification of deception by persuasive arguments, comes near to contradicting the model I sketched out at the beginning of this chapter. For in that model, the instrumentality of friendship was valued at a higher rate than the instrumentality of monetary exchange precisely because the former created a form of *long-term accountability* which rendered powerless the latter's scope for short-term deception. Thus, in writing of ancient economies, Bourdieu contrasts the 'exchanges of the familiar world of acquaintance based on *trust* and *good faith*' with the unaccountability of the marketplace, and observes that even in the ancient marketplace, men

> aim to minimize the risk . . . by transforming the impersonal relationships of commercial exchange, which have neither past nor future, into lasting relationships of reciprocity: by calling on guarantors, witnesses, and mediators, they are able to establish, or re-establish, the functional equivalent of a traditional network between the contracting parties.[21]

If witnesses and guarantors offer the 'functional equivalent' of friendship by minimizing the risk of deception, then what is story of 'Titus and Gisippus' doing by redefining the agency of friendship itself as a shared project of deception, involving clandestine vows and mystifying rhetoric?

Sixteenth-century readers of Elyot registered the ambivalence of the new definition. For while authors added Titus and Gisippus to the classical list of ideal pairs of male friends (Orestes and Pylades, Damon and Pythias, Theseus and Pirithous, Scipio and Laelius), they tended, when recalling the text formally and structurally, to produce readings which emphasize *the susceptibility of male friendship to betrayal by persuasive arguments*. The most frequently imitated aspect of the story is the *exemplarity* of the discourse in which Titus and Gisippus communicate with one another. An imitation most famous and influential in its own right was John Lyly's *Euphues* (1579), in which the hero is a prodigally eloquent Titus, who seems to be transported by the facility of his own exemplary reasoning into justifying the stealing of his friend's mistress. Lyly's own friend, Thomas Watson, wrote an erudite sonnet collection entitled *Hekatompathia*, which included a sonnet justifying Titus' right to Sophronia by exemplary reasoning: 'and here by examples he proveth unto him (calling him by the name of *Titus*, as if himself were *Gysippus*) that Love not only worketh alteration in the mindes of men, but also in the very Gods themselves' (one of the arguments used by Elyot's Titus to convince the Athenians of his case). And George Pettie invoked the story as an example of the liability of bonds to be broken: 'Yea, the most faithfull bond of frendship betweene *Tytus and Gysippus*, thorow luste was violated.'[22]

In the twentieth century, male commentators have not had difficulty in accounting for the story's exceptional influence. For them it marks (in conjunction with the dissemination of Cicero's *De Amicitia*) a transition from the instrumental and socially unequal ties of friendship fostered by feudal society, to a new 'modern' concept of friendship as pure affection, preceding and exceeding all instrumentality. John J. Major argues that in Elyot the story is 'a striking illustration of the theme that friendship between men is more to be honored than the love of a man for a woman'. According to this reading, what is fundamental about the relationship between Titus and Gisippus is not the narrative proof of its ultimate reciprocity, but its survival of the supreme test: 'the relinquishing of one's beloved for the sake of friendship.'[23] This sounds familiar, but the formulation relies on the misleading transformation of the value Sophronia represents to Gisippus in terms of *alliance* (kin and friends) into an intrinsic emotional quality belonging to their love relationship. In fact, neither Boccaccio nor Elyot ever gives this impression. Elyot's Titus insists that Gisippus decides between the persuasive forces of two forms of friendship: 'more estemynge true frendship than the love of a woman, *where unto he was induced by his frendes*' (my italics), while the subjectivity of Sophronia in Boccaccio is so limited by her function in the narrative, that her ability to make a virtue of necessity and switch her affection from Gisippus to Titus is commended as being *savia*, wise.[24]

If the story of 'Titus and Gisippus' has tended to be read as signalling the emergence of a 'modern' concept of friendship, (recognizable as such by the basis of affection in the bond of intimate mutual understanding rather than instrumentality), then it is worth asking why. Historians who support the theory that the word 'friend' begins, in the early modern period, to designate an emotional rather than instrumental bond, note the increasing application of the word to an exclusive relationship, a pairing of similarly-minded people. So Lawrence Stone differentiates, for example, between singular and plural uses of the word in the eighteenth century. Naomi Tadmor has, however, convincingly argued that, whether singular or plural, the word 'friend' in the eighteenth century most commonly designates a general and heterogenous category of guardians, protectors and supporters, who may or may not be kin, but are always in the position of being instrumental, to the extent that it makes semantic sense to be 'friendless' even when one has friends, if one has no access to their help.[25]

Tadmor's conclusions seem true for the sixteenth-century, too. In this period, the formulae from Cicero's *De Amicitia* that suffuse all genres of literature have been read as the signs of the age's commitment to a belief that friendship between men should ideally conform to the intimate and unbounded nature of the relationship which Laelius claims, at the outset of Cicero's text, to have existed between himself and Scipio Africanus:

> but yet, I take such fruite of the remembraunce of our frendship, that I thinke I lyved happilie, that with Scipio I ledde my lyfe, with whom I hadde a joynct care, for the common wealthe, and for our private causes, with whom bothe in peace and warre I tooke lyke parte: yea, and wee agreed evermore in love, mynde, pourpose and opinion, in whiche thyng the whole pithe of frendship standeth.[26]

Yet Cicero's text, although it has Laelius continually define true friendship against attachments founded in the cynical hope of gain, itself never pretends to sever friendship from instrumentality, and is indeed relegated by Cicero in the *De Officiis* to a mode of instruction in the ethical pursuit of 'profit' (*utilitas*). In fact, *pace* John J. Major's desire to idealize, in the story of 'Titus and Gisippus' both male friendship and sixteenth-century humanism ('this ideal of self-sacrificing devotion which finds its outlet in service to country and friendship between men'), Cicero and the English humanists perceived rather that the commonweal was likely to be threatened by men who cultivated too assiduously the *utilitas* of personal friendships. Knowing when not to privilege friendship over the wider interests of the community is one of the cruxes of the reconciliation between *honestas* and *utilitas* in the *De Officiis*.[27]

At the same time, Cicero undoubtedly upholds friendship in the *De Officiis* as the best form of security. A sixteenth-century translation runs:

> There is nothing more profytable to such as be in authoritie then to be loved of all men, and to be dradde is both a reproche and no surety ... But of amyte and love I have spoken in an other boke which is entitled Lelius.[28]

Ciceronian friendship appears thus also in Thomas Lupset's *Exhortacion to yonge men* in 1535: 'Always your frende shall be more profitable to you than any tresure or goods', he wrote. 'Howe you shall knowe them that be worthy to be your frendes, & by what menes, and what way frendes be both gotten and also kept, ye shall best lerne in Ciceros littell booke, *De Amicitia*.'[28] When John Harington translated the *De Amicitia* in 1550, he dedicated it from prison to Katherine Willoughby, Duchess of Suffolk, 'in whom the freendelesse dayly find their defence', explaining to her that she should see here in 'learnyng auncient' what she herself had 'by nature used'.[29] Indeed, the extensive theorization of friendship in the *De Amicitia* and the *De Officiis* sets out not to refute the instrumentality of friendship, but to set it within an ethical and political context, as Harington says, 'a civile rule to leade my life by'. Cicero's text thus rendered by Harington into a lively exemplar in English ('a glasse to discern my freendes in') is the result of his comparing of a French translation with 'the latine auctor', so that by 'plainely openyng and learnedly amending of the sence, whiche in the freenche translacion was somewhat darkened . . . me thought a new spirite and life was geven it'.[30] The saturation of the literature of sixteenth-century England with *De Amicitia* formulae (affirming, for example, the communality of goods between friends, the sharing of opinions, the similitude of studies, the superiority of friendship over kinship) is a sign of countless such acts of 'translation' having taken place. A literary assimilation of the *De Amicitia* then, may be saying less about the age's commitment to a new theory of non-instrumental male friendship, than it is about a *displacement* of the instrumentality of male friendship into the communicative action represented by the persuasive mobilization of arguments from classical texts.

The story of 'Titus and Gisippus' is also, of course, about communicative action and the persuasive mobilization of texts. Indeed, it seems to define the affection arising from the boys' 'similitude of studies' as a source of dynastic and political power superior to that commanded by the instrumental friendship of kin and fictive kin, the *parenti* and *amici* of Boccaccio's text, and the 'frendes, kynne and alyes' of Elyot's rendering. By persuading one another with exemplary 'counsel' to take socially transgressive action to remedy their situation, and by using similar techniques of reasoning to justify the consequences of that action, the friends mark out a new space in which to control the transference of symbolic capital outside of the economy of agnatic kinship, or of lineal inheritance. In the end of Elyot's story, Titus restores Gisippus to his 'landes and substance' in spite of his kindred, while in Boccaccio, he 'first made him joint owner of all his treasure and possessions, and then gave him to wife a young sister of his, called Fulvia'.[31] To read 'Titus and Gisippus' as a story which introduces into early modern culture a new ideal of masculine friendship as 'affective' rather than 'instrumental' is surely to misrecognize as uncalculated the vastly superior instrumentality proved by Titus and Gisippus' version of 'friendship' over that practised by the 'frendes' that found Gisippus his bride. It would seem that, by this history, the cultural instrumentality of friendship – its power to control the transference of wealth and honour – has not been replaced but *displaced* into a new affective medium. What that medium might be, and how its potential might have been imagined by English humanists intent on bringing about the reformation of the commonweal, is the subject of the next section.

PERSUADING BACHELORS TO MARRY: PRODUCING REASONS

In the last chapter, I suggested that the ideal of 'good husbandry' represented, for the humanists, the potential for social transformation which lay latent in their programme for educating a new elite of 'governors' in the arts of persuasive communication[32]. In this section I mean to explore the implications of this identification of communicative power and conjugal status, probing the terms in which the politicians, propagandists and educationalists of the 1530s predicated their vision of a prosperous commonweal on proposals for the reformation of both the educational and sexual habits of the nobility and gentry.

In societies organized around the economy of the gift, the power of friendship is nowhere more apparent that in the creation of alliances through the exchange of women – 'the supreme rule of the gift' as Lévi-Strauss put it.[33] From the eleventh century onwards, the nobilities of France and of England had consolidated their territories through the practice of what Georges Duby has called 'the lay aristocratic model of marriage'. This involved a strict discipline which, in contrast to the exogamy practised by cognatic kin groups (who tend to wish to widen their affinity) restricted the number of unions to the very minimum required to assure continuance of the family line; a practice, in other words, of exclusive primogeniture. The aristocratic household consequently maintained, in addition to the lord and his lady, a retinue of *juvenes* or bachelors. Of these Duby writes:

> These bachelors were abductors by their very nature, for they were always tempted to take by force from another household the wife that would make them, at last, into elders (seniores). But now this dream of abduction was carried inside the very house that provided for the young men, in the house of the patron who gave them shelter, who 'retained' them, and who every night went to bed with his own wife. The favours of the lady thus became a stake in a competition among the bachelors of the court, a game that was similar in every point to the tournament.[34]

Though Duby is here referring to the French aristocracy of the twelfth century, his version of the instituted sexual frustration and promiscuity of the bachelors corresponds remarkably to Thomas Starkey's derogatory description of the sexual arrangements of noble households in early sixteenth-century England. Starkey, requested by Thomas Cromwell to produce a discourse on 'what thing it is after the sentence of Aristotle and the ancient peripatetics that commonly among them is called policy', responded with the first part of what was to become *A Dialogue between Reginald Pole and Thomas Lupset*. In this text he explored, dialectically, 'the decay of our commonweal', justifying by the authority of Aristotle what might otherwise seem to be an unchristian concern with the questions of how to increase material prosperity. Like his contemporaries, More and Rastell among them, Starkey found that the chief cause of England's extreme poverty was the underpopulation caused by the nobility's enclosure of arable land, and the marriage practices by which they consolidated their inheritances.

Exclusive primogeniture meant that the younger sons who were not living idly in the monasteries were swelling the ranks of bachelors in the retinue of noblemen, a 'great multitude of serving men' which, as Starkey complained,

> in service spend their life, never finding mean to marry conveniently, but live alway as common corrupters of chastity. Wherefore there would be, as I think, an ordinance that no gentlemen nor other of the nobility take to his service greater number of men than he is able to promote and set forward to some honest fashion of living, and lawful matrimony; and so by this mean the multitude of them should be minished greatly. And forebecause that many there be now which cannot find good occasion of marriage because of poverty, and lack of art or craft to live, I would think convenient, forasmuch as we have many wilds and wastes in our country, that the prince and other noble men should build them houses in places convenient . . . and give such tenements to their servants, their heirs and assigns, paying yearly a little portion as chief rent . . . By the which mean, as I think, the great number of them would be glad to set themself to matrimony, and so we should not only have the people increased in number, but also the waste grounds well occupied and tilled.[35]

Here Starkey seems to fuse, in his vision of 'waste grounds well occupied and tilled' a policy for reversing enclosure and encouraging arable farming, with a vision of increased population, brought about by 'enticements to marry'. He was certainly serious about the latter, outlining at great length his proposals for remedying bachelorhood:

> This thing should much entice men to marriage, specially if we gave unto them also certain privileges and prerogative, after the manner of the old and wise Romans, as to all such as by matrimony increased the people with five childer, that they should pay nother task nor tallage . . . and beside that meseemeth it were a convenient pain, that every bachelor . . . should yearly pay a certain sum . . . the which sum should ever be reserved in a common place . . . to the dot [dowry] of poor damosels and virgins.[36]

Starkey's arguments found an echo in those of other texts in circulation among the humanists around Thomas Cromwell at that time. Eric Carlson writes that in 1535, 'Cromwell initiated discussions which resulted in a draft for an entirely new code of canon law . . . which attracted international Protestant attention'. Cromwell was also involved, with John Rastell, in the drafting of a bill to prevent young men from marrying 'till they be of potent age'.[37] In 1532, Richard Taverner, who was to become one of the foremost popularizers of Erasmus' writings in England, published a translation of Erasmus' *Encomium Matrimonii* which appealed to some of the same arguments as those put forward by Starkey, observing that the Romans exempted bachelors from civic posts 'but such as had encreased with chyldren the commune weale, to them they ordeyened a reward'.[38] Taverner made it clear that the publishing of a vernacular version of Erasmus's text was propagandistic; to Cromwell he writes that

> he thought it a thynge full necessarye and expedyent, to translate it into our vulgure tong, and so under your noble protection to communicate it to the people, namely when he considered the blynd superstition of men and women which cease not day by day to professe & vow perpetuall chastyte.[39]

Another author, David Clapam, selected Cornelius Agrippa's *Sacramento Matrimonio Declamatio* as a suitable text to translate in the service of Thomas Cromwell. Clapam offers the text to Cromwell's married son, Geoffrey, as an exemplar of the policies of reform through the encouragement of matrimony and the humanistic education of the nobility with which his father is associated:

> I verily thynke, it shall no less farther, to dedycate the same to you, that are a very true patrone of honest life in wedlock. Whereto shuld I speake of your vertuous education, for the which your right honorable father my good lord hath been very diligent? And surely his care in that behalf hath not ben only for you, but for manie other; yea, the thing that he specially wisheth and desyreth is, that the youthe of this hole realme of England shulde be brought up vertuously, namely the noble mens chyldren, in good litterature . . . to the great advancement of the commonweal.[40]

Clapam's explicit association of the younger Cromwell's exemplarity as one brought up in 'good literature' as well as practising

'honest life in wedlock' illuminates another aspect of the humanists' irritation with the inability of noble households to contribute
productively to the commonweal. Not only were the gently-born
serving men they harboured 'common corrupters to chastity',
their education in service did not prepare them to make any
contribution to civil life:

> look what an idle rout our noblemen keep and nourish in
> their houses, which do nothing else but carry dishes to the
> table and eat them when they have done, and after give
> themself to hunting, hawking . . . and all other idel pastimes
> and vain, as though they were born to nothing else at all.[41]

The hunting and hawking about which the humanists were so
scornful, had been, of course, a part of what traditionally constituted the 'education' that a child received when put out to
service with an aristocratic family. As Mervyn James writes,

> The style of education provided is aptly summarized in the
> fourteenth-century metrical romance *Ipomydon*, where the
> instructions of King Ermones for the upbringing of the
> young hero Ipomedon in household are as follows:

> > Tholomew a clerk he toke
> > And taught the chylde uppon the boke,
> > Both to synge and to rede;
> > And after he taught him other dede
> > Aftirward to serve in hall,
> > Bothe to grete and to smalle;
> > Before the kyng mete to kerve,
> > Hye and lowe feyre to serve;
> > Bothe of houndis and haukis game
> > After he taught hym, all and same,
> > In se, in field, and eke in ryvuere,
> > In wodde to chase the wild dere,
> > And in the feld to ryde a stede,
> > That all men had joy of his dede.[42]

Humanist texts on the education of the nobility, such as Elyot's
Boke named the Governour and Humphrey's *Of Nobilitye*, were
designed to replace such courtesy books as *Stans Puer ad Mensam*,
the precepts of which *Ipomydon* translates into a narrative of social
advancement. Throughout the humanist texts runs a polemic

against the old style of education in the noble household, with its versified literature of courtesy and chivalry, explaining how to carve and wait, and how to fight, hunt and hawk.[43] Indeed, the humanists' disdain for the old occupation of the nobleman and his retinue is signalled by the very mention of hawking. (Hunting seems to be acceptable; it is certainly part of Cyrus' exemplary education in the *Cyropaedia*, where Xenophon explains it as a rhetorical method of knowing territory for strategic military purposes. 'As for haukyng, I can finde no notable remembraunce that it was used of auncient time amonge noble princes; observes Elyot, 'sens whiche tyme vertue and noblesse hath rather decayed than increased.'[44])

The education which the humanists offer instead is one based in 'good literature', a programme of exemplary reading and imitation, beginning with fables and poetry (Aesope, Lucian, Homer, Virgil), going on to military history (Livy, Caesar, Xenophon) and moral philosophy (Aristotle's *Ethics* and Cicero's *De Officiis*) with rhetorical instruction in Quintilian's *Instituitio Oratoria*, Erasmus' *De Copia*, and Rudolph Agricola's *De Inventione*. Parents might worry about their sons not growing up, under this programme, to be 'tall men', wrote Edward Hake in 1574 , 'Nayth'lesse it is not ment to make / tough Champions of the same / but only for the common weale / good governours to frame'.[45] What, however, did the humanists envisage as the material contribution that the nobles' exemplary education in good literature would make to the 'commonweal'? We have already seen how, in Humphrey's *Of Nobilitye*, the productive nobleman is defined negatively, by contrast with the idle nobleman, who 'garded with a rout of servaunts . . . Learns nought but customably & courtlike to entertaine gentlemen' and who fails to practice the exemplary 'husbandry' of the ancient nobility of Greece and Rome.[46] The polemic common to the humanist texts, then, seems to oppose the idle household which maintains a retinue of bachelor younger brothers to a new, but hazily defined concept of nobility and gentry engaging in a kind of 'husbandry' that involves matrimony, the persuasive mobilization of classical texts, and the remedy of the economic ills (underpopulation, the decay of towns, the export of raw materials and import of luxuries and trifles) that beset the realm. So Humphrey defines the husbandry of the reformed nobleman as intellectual: he will increase his patrimony 'with the care and tyllage of the mynde'.[47]

While Starkey's *Dialogue* set the terms for many of the statutory reforms that were undertaken, both immediately, and in the course of Elizabeth's reign, to remedy the state of the economy,[48] a certain conceptual elision operates in his text which suggests that what we would assume to be the desired outcome of economic reform – the creation of wealth – was quite inconceivable to its author. Thus, while Starkey blamed the poverty of the realm on the idleness of a third of the population, he was not in favour of increasing and diversifying craftsmanship in the interests of consumerism; 'craftsmen and makers of trifles are too many', he argued.[49] Like other men of his generation, he perceived wealth to be finite, the crucial remedy for poverty being a redistribution of resources. Hence his interest in the transformation of marriage and inheritance practices; understanding wealth and power to reside in the assurance of friends, rather than the accumulation or usurious use of gold, he conceives of productive civil relations between men as the creation of bonds of trust through the gift-exchange of alliance. It is for this reason that he wishes younger sons to have a part in the patrimony, and contrasts the more prosperous economy of alliance and kin-friendship to be found operating through the smaller household units and patrimonies on the Continent, with the idle bachelorhood of the English: 'A knight or a mean gentleman shall have as many idle men here with us in England as shall in France, Spain or Italy a great lord, signior of many towns and castles' objects 'Lupset'. Since it is inconceivable that wealth be honourably employed outside of the economy of liberality, patronage and alliance, 'Pole' wants to know whether this does not mean avarice, 'what do they with their possessions and riches? Do they heape it togidder in coffers and corners, without applying it to profit and use?' 'Nay, not so sir', replies 'Lupset',

> but they *marry their childer and friends therwith*, and so keep up the honour of their family thereby ... But with us it is contrary: I have known younger brethren go a-begging, whereas the elder hath triumphed and lived in pleasure like a great prince of a country.[50]

It is no wonder, then, that in Starkey's vision, the project for transforming serving men into husbands seems to be the answer to England's problems of unchastity and idleness and underpopulation all at once. No longer rationed to eldest sons, the contracting of matrimony will ensure productive social relations. Starkey's objection to handicrafts and trades springs from the assumption that these do not increase wealth, but are parasitic upon the 'husbandry' of the land. His vague conflation of the arable and matrimonial responsibilities of that 'husbandry' under his proposed scheme (by which people will be 'increased in number' and 'the waste grounds well occupied and tilled') works to suggest that the productivity of alliance and marital negotiation is a kind of 'natural' increase, like the productivity of the earth itself.

Precisely the same effect occurs, interestingly enough, in Taverner's translation of Erasmus' *Encomium Matrimonii*. Here, the duty of replenishing the commonweal with children is continually likened to care of the land; he is 'no dilygent husband' who tends only the 'redy growen' as he is 'an undyligent cytizen in the publike weal' who makes no provision to have an heir. 'Yf he be punyshed whych neglecteth his grounde . . . what punyshment is he worthy whyche refuseth to tylle that ground [women!] which tylled beareth men?' The natural crop of wedlock includes friends, allies and kin: 'There accreseth by the meanes a swete flocke of alysses / ther is dubled the number of parentes / of bretherne / of systerne / of nevewes.'[51] We should compare Lévi-Strauss's notorious citation of the Arapesh informants of Margaret Mead when questioned why they prohibited incest: 'Marry your sister! . . . Don't you want a brother-in-law?'[52]

And yet, if Starkey's *Dialogue* explicitly proposes to achieve an increase in the communication of wealth in the commonweal through the 'traffic' in women, he nevertheless implicitly predicates the achievement of the commonweal upon the circulation of another sort of wealth. This is the *communicative action* of the dialogue itself, which is defined in opposition to a selfish concern with one's private weal:

> You know right well, Master Pole, that to this all men are born and of nature brought forth: to commune such gifts as be to them given, each one to the profit of other, in perfit civility, and not to live to their own pleasure and profit, without regard to the weal of their country . . . little availeth treasure closed in coffers which never is communed to the succour of other.[53]

Evidently, the 'idle rout' in the households of noblemen who merely served and ate and hawked, 'as if they were born to nothing else at all', were born to this: to 'commune . . . each to the profit of other' in textualized dialogue, like 'Pole' and 'Lupset'. For the dialogic 'communing' of knowledge composed and transmitted as a *text* produced a 'traffic' in new modes of persuasive reasoning, or ratiocination. The Cromwellian administration's appreciation of the propagandistic value of the press is well known, but more was at stake in commissioning the composition or translation of texts in the humanistic genres of dialogue, or *declamatio* or *suasoria*, than mere 'propaganda'. For humanistic logic was shifting the study of ratiocination from the analysis of the formal validity of 'fixed patterns of argumentation which guarantee that from any true premisses whatever one can only infer a true conclusion' to an interest in the 'practical certainty' or 'probability' achieved by 'arguments which can be counted on to win in debate'.[54] Accordingly, humanist educational practice caused the analysis of argumentation (logic) to become increasingly identified with the practicalities of text-exegesis or even translation, the 'invention' and 'judgement' with which readers analyse 'the dialectical structure of a text, trace the reasons and arguments to their "places", identify resources of diction and ornament, and then consider the ordering and disposition of the elements thus assembled'.[55] Erasmus' *Encomium Matrimonii* is a *suasoria*, an exercise 'in persuading or dissuading a person or assembly from a given course of action', of a kind which, along with the related forensic exercises of *declamationes* or *controversiae* the humanists were concerned to revive as pedagogic methods for producing minds furnished with argumentative skill, on the model of the ancient advocates.[56] The forms of 'proof' used in the arguing of *controversiae* – the validity of which were debatable, not formal – were comprehensively set out by Quintilian in the *Institiutio Oratoria*, Book V, viii–xii, in a section which closes with the explanation: 'This was a task which required all the more careful handling because the declamations, which we used to employ as foils wherwith to practice for duels in the forum, have long since departed from the true form of pleading.'[57] Nevertheless, the resulting codification of 'a class of proofs that are wholly the work of art and consist of matters specially adapted to produce belief' ('pars . . . probationum, quae est tota in arte constatque rebus ad faciendem fidem appostis'[58]) was to contribute to the development of humanistic logic, or dialectic. Lorenzo Valla, as Lisa Jardine and Anthony Grafton have shown, used this section (Book V) of the *Institutio Oratoria* to provide new ratiocinative techniques for his *Dialecticae Disputationes*, substituting the scholastic treatment of syllogism with methods for arguing *'probabiliter*, or *verisimiliter* – for 'likelihood', or the closest approximation to truth that circumstances will allow'.[59] These techniques were, crucially, both *affective* and *productive of discourse*: Erasmus makes his eleventh and last method for acquiring *copia* in the *De Copia* depend 'upon the copious accumulation of proofs and arguments' ('accumulatione copiosa probationem et argumentorum') for which he gives a compressed version of Quintilian's discussion of artificial proofs in Book V of the *Institutio Oratoria*.[60]

Taverner's interest in Erasmus' *Encomium Matrimonii* was more, then, than 'propagandistic' in our narrow sense; he valued the text both as an affecting argument, and as a mode of instruction to the general reader in the techniques of arguing 'probabiliter'. Throughout his translation, he points up the variety and artifice of Erasmus' proofs. The opening is signalled in the margin as 'the narration' and at various points other strategies are highlighted: 'why than (ye will say) dyd Christ himself abstain from wedlocke?' is marginally noted as a 'confutation' and the story of the Titans' rebellion against Jupiter is 'a fabule and the exposition therof'. There is also a 'similitude' (husbandry) and 'a proverb'.[61] The whole text celebrates generation as the fruit matrimony yields to the commonweal; yet the Erasmian metaphor of generation also recalls the *De Copia*, where, as Terence Cave observes, 'the profusion of the natural world becomes a model for *copia* in discourse'.[62]

By the 1530s in England, the service of the gently-born *puer* in a *familia* or household was already coming to be associated with the skills of inventing probable arguments to enable action. David Starkey has explained how, in the Privy Chamber of the Royal household by 1525, 'diplomatic service was seen as much a part of a Gentleman's job as the monarch's domestic service'.[63] One of the King's Gentlemen of the Privy Chamber at that time, Henry Knyvett, tasked his own servant to translate a humanist text on household service, the *oiketēs, sive de officio famulorum* by Gilbert Cousin, who served both as secretary and domestic in the household of Erasmus. The young Chaloner identifies the act of recognizing his failings as a servant with the text-exegetical skills by which he learns, through translating Cousin's aguments, what constitutes expedient service. Cousin's text itself explicitly criticizes the 'evil custom vsed . . . inespeciall amonges Anglishmen, to heape abowte them for a shew only, a superfluous nombre of waytynge men', and concludes with a polemic on the civilizing value of service in a humanist household, where textual analysis prepares the servant to enter 'those disciplines for which the tounges were furst ordeigned'.[64] Chaloner was later to describe his household service as having 'confirmed his youth and mind in humanistic studies' (studiis humanioribus), while to his erstwhile master he became a 'familiar friend and counsellor'.[65]

As in the Royal household, so among the friends and servants of Cromwell. Cromwell seems to have been exceptionally aware of the potential of the new humanistic mode of reasoning for the achievement of reformation. Thus, when Sir Thomas Elyot, among others, drew attention to the similarity of Inns of Court moots to the declamationes of the Roman orators, arguing that if only English lawyers did not have to read 'fardelles and trusses of the most barberouse autors', they would bring 'the pleadyng and reasonynge of the lawe, to the ancient fourme of noble oratours', it was Cromwell who instigated the reform whereby the Inns of Court became centres of eloquence, with weekly readings from 'some Orator or book of Rhetorick, or else some Author which treateth of the Government of a Commonwealth'.[66] Skill in reasoning probabiliter was what Cromwell also sought in the men who advised him on economic and social policy. So Starkey wrote to Cromwell, hoping that he would find 'powar in my wrytyng & probabyl persuasion',[67] while William Marshall, who was to draw up a forerunner of Elizabethan schemes for poor relief, chose to translate for Cromwell Lorenzo Valla's De falso credita et ementita Constanini donatione declamatio, which, as Hannah Grey wrote, used artificial proofs both as historical reconstruction ('a method of ascertaining what was or is or will most probably be true') and as instruction in rhetorical persuasion ('procedures by which these findings might be rendered persuasive'). Marshall's translation of Valla – undertaken because there was, as he said to Cromwell, 'never better boke made . . . for the defasing of the Pope of Rome' – reveals the extent to which the 'propaganda' of the English Reformation was characterized by its investment in the Quintilianesque techniques of artificial proof.[68] And so it was with texts on the reformation of social mores, such as matrimony. The significant innovations of the Cromwellian texts on matrimony in this respect may be assessed by contrast with pre-Cromwellian texts, such as William Harrington's *In this boke are conteyned the Commendacions of matrymony* (1528). Harrington's text is not a humanistic translation, nor does it take the form of a *controversia*; what it lacks are the 'witty argumentes, quycke reasons' that drew Taverner and Clapam to the texts of Erasmus and Cornelius Agrippa. Harrington relies for his argument only on what can certainly be proved by adducing Scriptural authority; by avoiding all controversial arguments (such as, for example, the celibacy of Christ) he ensures that his text is not ambivalent, but he also deprives it of persuasive potential.[69]

Cromwell's appreciation of the persuasive and intellectually generative effects of *ratio artificialis* in the spheres of social and economic policy seems to have led him to begin the practice, later used in Elizabeth's reign by noblemen, of recruiting scholars from Oxford and Cambridge to 'gather' and read for him.[70] As the work of Lisa Jardine and William Sherman has shown, the activity of gathering and organizing information into a persuasive text, or 'directed reading' of texts, was to become the dominant medium of relations of 'service' between the nobility and the educated gentry of the second half of the sixteenth century.[71]

If we turn again at last to reconsider the location of the future 'productivity' that will uphold and increase the commonweal as envisaged by Starkey's and Taverner's texts, the ostensible promotion of matrimonal 'husbandry' as the imaginary multiplier of households, kin, friends and patrimonies seems, in fact, to be a metaphor for another, perhaps more productive form of 'civility' between men. For by their methods of reasoning, each text suggests that the most significant form of increase, or generation, is the textual effect of persuasive *communication* of which 'friendship' is given as the pretext, or motivating force. Thus Starkey introduces, between Pole and Lupset, a Ciceronian 'true friendship':

> Much time past, Master Pole, I have desired greatly to commune with you, being moved thereto by the great friendship and familiarity which of youth growing betwix us is now so by virtue increased and confirmed that nature hath not so sure and band ... to couple and join any hearts togidder in true love and amity.[72]

Erasmus' *Encomium Matrimonii* likewise takes the form of a

fictive epistle, written by a family friend to a young bachelor. He calls himself the young man's 'frend and lover', but, having invoked the 'streghte alyaunce' and 'olde frendshyp contynued from our chylhode betwixte us' as reasons for the young man's acting upon his advice, he then proceeds to ask the young man to disregard these. Neither 'love of your frends' nor kinship should, he proposes, 'ayde my cause . . . if I shewe nat by *clere reasons*' why 'ye by myne advise shall chaunge thys mynde' and 'levyng bachelorshyppe, a forme of levynge both barren and unnaturall, shall gyve yourself to moste holy wedlocke'.[73] The persuasive power of kin-friendship has here been explicitly displaced by Erasmus into probable reason, cutting its affective power loose from the bonds of a specific relation, into a technology available to all men, a transferable instrument for the creation of credit. And it is characteristic of the reforming texts of the 1530s not only to rely for their persuasiveness on probable reason, but to thematize the affective and generative power of argument thus as a relation of fictive kinship, or friendship between two men.

When the translation of Erasmus' *Encomium Matrimonii* was incorporated by Thomas Wilson in *The Arte of Rhetorique*, its proofs of the 'commonweal' responsibility of bachelors to marry were used by Shakespeare for the first seventeen of his *Sonnets*. So the similitude of husbandry appeared: 'For where is she so fair whose uneared womb / Disdains the tillage of thy husbandry?', and the young bachelor was lovingly rebuked as a 'Profitless usurer', failing to engage in the true 'traffic' of alliance. With the eighteenth sonnet, however, the poet makes a transition from generating arguments for marriage, to celebrating the generative power of the sonnet form itself: 'But thy eternal summer shall not fade . . . When in eternal lines to time thou grow'st.' As I have argued elsewhere, the sequence of sonnets that follows transforms its subject, the young bachelor, into a store of analogical 'proofs' ('Speak of the spring and foison of the year; / The one doth shadow of your beauty show, / The other as your bounty doth appear') and proves the published textual effect of the communicative pretext of 'friendship' between the two men to be a more generative form of 'husbandry' than that which 'in honour might uphold' a patrimony through the power of friends and allies.[74]

ALLIANCE-FRIENDSHIP AND THE 'STOLEN MARRIAGE' MOTIF: HUMANISTIC TRANSFORMATIONS OF A CULTURAL SYMBOL

Returning from our digressive exploration of the associations forged, in the texts of the 1530s, between wealth, matrimony and the persuasive communication of knowledge, it becomes possible to see how Boccaccio's 'Titus and Gisippus' could be read by sixteenth-century humanists as an allegory of the increased access to symbolic capital which would accrue to men who had acquired skills in the technology of artificial proof. Boccaccio's original was a traditional test-of-friendship story; it was he who transformed the tale of eventual compensation for extreme self-sacrifice into a celebration of the potential power of friendship conceived as humanistic *amicitia* – dialectical counsel and persuasive communication in emergency. Boccaccio's innovation was to introduce the presence of a *sensus communis* or body of common opinion (Gisippus' friends and kin) which would displace the original focus on the problem of adequate reciprocity as the barrier to be overcome by the power of friendship.[75] Although he had access only to an incomplete manuscript of Quintilian's *Insitutia Oratoria*, Boccaccio was evidently not ignorant of Book V, with its crucial discussion of the significance of artificial proof. Indeed, scholars have pointed out that he summarizes in his *Genealogia Deorum* precisely that passage in which Quintilian laments the decline of the *declamatio*, and justifies, in so doing, the codification of 'artificial proof' that was to be immeasurably significant to the development of humanistic logic and text-study.[76]

In its position in the *Decameron*, the 'Titus and Gisippus' story's celebration of a communicative power derived from the study of literature bears a certain allegorical relation to Boccaccio's own poetic project as represented in the *Genealogia Deorum*; Titus' winning of Sophronia may be read figuratively, as a *translatio studii*, or transmission of culture through literature.[77] Elyot's version, however, relocating the story within a study programme designed to ensure the contribution of noble houses to the the ideological reform of the English public weal, orients this communicative power more pragmatically. Elyot is quite explicit about identifying true friendship between men as a text-mediated relationship, arising not just from similitude of studies, but from a humanistic, as opposed to scholastic, curriculum:

where the studie is elegant, and the mater illecebrous, that is to say, swete to the redar, the course wherof is rather gentill persuasion and quicke reasoninges than over subtill arguments or litigious controversies, there also it hapneth that the studentes do delite one in an other.[78]

In his and subsequent sixteenth-century versions, the practical efficacy of the friends' technology of 'gentil persuasion and quicke reasoninges' is stressed, as between them, they employ *ratio artificialis* initially across a dialogic space of amity and mutual understanding (*suasoria*, or counsel) to produce their project, and subsequently, across a space of forensic hostility (*declamatio*), to justify that project's cultural transgression. Sixteenth-century readers of Elyot recognized the initial dialogic exchange between Titus and Gisippus as a form of dialectic; indeed, when the martyrologist John Foxe made a Terentian-style comedy of 'Titus et Gesippus' in his schoolteaching days, he dramatized their discovery of the plot of impersonation as if it were the result of an oratorical consultation of places of argument (*loci communes*) 'just as one thing happens to come into the mind from another' the speaker says, 'the place of similitude instantly presents itself'.[79]

We can, then, read Elyot's 'Titus and Gisippus' within the context of the *Boke named the Governour,* as a figurative history of the *textualization* of the medium through which relations of friendship and service between gently born men were subsequently to take place for the good of the commonweal. This textualization of friendship, whereby the instrumental value of what is shared tends to be identified with its confidentiality as a knowledge transaction, is implicit in Cicero's representation of ideal friendship in the *De Amicitia* as the relation subsisting between Scipio Africanus and his second-in-command, Lelius. For, according to Livy's history of the war against Carthage, the fortunes of the Romans turn when they are blessed with a general (Scipio the Younger) whose relations with his second-in-command are constructively confidential. Livy's very first mention of Laelius positions him 'in the know' concerning Scipio's crucial stratagem for the taking of New Carthage, at a point in the narrative when even the reader is still ignorant: 'Of this his purpose no man was privye, but onely C. Lelius', as a sixteenth-century translation runs.[80] English humanists thus seem to have appreciated the Ciceronian ideal of friendship as the instrumentality of a relationship involving the dialectical invention of plots and projects to overcome impediments to action; 'Many thynges be impeched by Nature which by counsayle be shortly achieved' Elyot quotes Livy as saying, and 'counsayle . . . may be named a perfecte Capitayne, a trusty companyon, a playne and unfayned frende'.[81]

Fashioning thus an ideal of textualized friendship for the governors of the commonweal, Elyot nevertheless figured that 'weal' or 'wealth' in traditional symbolic form as the consolidation of a patrimony by alliance. But the alliance is, of course, of initially dubious legality; Titus marries Sophronia by stealth, and only in retrospect justifies his action to her kinsfolk by his skill in the use of artificial reason. Before we leave the subject of the humanist textualization of the symbolic capital of friendship, then, we need to consider the implications of Boccaccio's and Elyot's adjustment of a traditional motif – the motif of the clandestine marriage – to fit their model of humanistic, consultative friendship as the medium through which the prestige capital of traditional friendship might be accumulated.

To explain the nature of service relations in the bachelor households described by Thomas Starkey in the last section, I quoted from George Duby's account of the 'lay aristocratic model of marriage' in twelfth-century France. Bachelors, said Duby, were 'abductors by their very nature'; their literature of courtly love and their pastimes of tournaments were expressions of a 'dream of abduction' involving the desire to 'take by force from another household the woman that would make them into elders (seniores)'.[82] Evidently if, as Bourdieu argued, the 'prestige and renown attached to a family and a name' is, in a traditional society, 'the most valuable form of accumulation', then alliance – the exchange of women – is the dominant mode of such 'accumulation'. By the same token, however, where practices such as exclusive primogeniture limit access to symbolic capital, a mythology or a literature is produced in which the motif of appropriation – the dream of seducing and marrying the heiress to a noble line – becomes prominent.

Such was the literature of chivalric romance – the traditional educative literature of the nobleman – which humanism sought to replace. In a study of the links between sign theory and family structure in the Middle Ages, Howard Bloch interprets the linguistic strategies that characterize certain genres of medieval literature – *chanson de geste*, ancestral romance, troubadour lyric –

in terms of the marital strategies upon which agnatic kinship depends for exclusive control of power, wealth and prestige. Following Duby, he describes how the 'spatial' or cognatic calculation of kinship which dominated in the ninth and tenth centuries gave way, with heritable military tenure and transmissable patrimony, to a 'vertical' or agnatic model of calculating kinship by paternal descent. As an 'aristocratic practice of signs'[83] (most obvious in the differentiating codes of heraldry) agnatic lineage has much in common with the genealogical and etymological biases of early medieval history and grammar. All three share a tendency to accord value by 'strategies of origin', recovering the identity and significance of their subjects from dispersion and obscurity by founding them in a linear relation of descent from an authoritative original. As the medieval grammarian relocated words in relation to their original, 'proper' union of sound and meaning, so the family histories of the great lineages, the *chansons de geste*, claimed to represent events according to a logic of derivation, a 'natural order' of telling. The dominant figure in these histories is metonymy which, as Bloch explains, is the figure of the sacred relic (the sword, for example, of an ancestor), which makes value an effect of its contiguity with the vanished wholeness of the past.

At the same time, the disruption of agnatic linearity through the creation of irregular alliances – adultery or clandestine marriage – was expressed in genres which presented a challenge to its semantics of origin: troubadour lyric and ancestral romance. While troubadour lyric is interpreted by Bloch as a disruption of etymological grammar by the adulteration of metaphor, the 'marital romance' challenges the 'natural' linear order of narrative in the *chanson de geste*, expressing 'uncertainty about the integrity of lineage' in a form that 'both progresses and resists progression'.[84] This erratic form exploited the tension between the aristocratic model of marriage as a treaty between two houses, controlled by its publicity, and the contradiction in canon law, which emphasized the privacy and voluntariness of the marital union, recognizing the validity before God of the secret plighting of troths. Thus, according to one model, the 'trial' of the knight in the wilderness, and in exile in pagan lands, can be read as corresponding to the process by which his secret troth-plighting with an heiress comes to attain a full public validity. As Bloch says, the strategies of origin by which the *chanson de geste* confers validity make it a genre incapable of imagining a future[85]; not so the romance, which may endow nobility in retrospect, through a second generation. We witness the knight exiled and wandering, performing deeds that prove his worth; in a complementary movement, the son born of his illicit infiltration into a noble lineage is being brought up and prepared by the narrative for the ultimate trial in which, confronting his father in combat, each will legitimate the other's part in the clandestine union, enabling the long-awaited entry into the patrimonial lands.

For example, in the late fourteenth-century romance of *Sir Eglamour of Artois*, printed in England in the mid-sixteenth century, Eglamour is a retainer in the household of Sir Prinsamour, earl of Artois ('for that he was a man full bolde / With the erle was he holde / In householde night and daye') He loves Prinsamour's daughter and 'ryght heyre', Chrystabell, but is warned by his chamberlain not to overreach himself; however, he asks the earl for her hand, 'for I have you served many a daye'. The earl plights a troth to give him Chrystabell and Artois on condition of ridding the land of a number of giants and wild beasts, all of which Eglamour performs. The earl then rather unreasonably accuses him: 'Thou art aboute as I understande / for to wynne Artoys and all my lande / And also my doughter clere' and demands his departure forthwith. Eglamour enters Chrystabell's chamber, tells her of his adventures and his prospect of exile and they 'plight trouthes'. Her subsequent pregnancy and exile without her husband takes on the penitential aspect of a trial or proof of the truth of this union. Their son, brought up unknown to either of them in Egypt, fights in a tournament where his mother is the prize, and without either knowing the identity of the other, proves worthy of his own mother's hand; they plight troths, but the union is prevented from being formalized publicly in the instant his mother recognizes in the blazon of an abducted child on his coat of arms, the tale of her own separation from her son. 'Forsothe my sonne', she tells him, 'I am afrayde / That to syb maryage we have made.' The moment in which the banns of one marriage are forbidden thus begins the process by which an earlier, clandestine union will come to light and prove its validity. Degrabell, the son, challenges a stranger to prove worthy to take his mother from him, and that stranger is, of course, Eglamour, who at last enters into possession of Artois.[86]

According to Bloch, aristocratic forms of medieval literature are 'deeply rooted in the evolving legal ethos of their time'.[87] What, we may ask, is the legal ethos which corresponds to the romantic narrative's restrospective legitimation of Eglamour's 'abduction' of Christabell and the land of Artois? The reader's position in such a narrative corresponds to the position of the witness in a trial by ordeal, validating both prowess and penance. Bloch writes that 'the structural model of romance is that of the inquisitory deposition, a transcribed eyewitness account of what has taken place in a realm beyond the law'.[88] Deeds of prowess thus 'prove' the knight's worth by the testimony of an immanent deity (in England, the *iudicium dei*, or the proving uncertain causes by invoking the testament of God through a combat or an ordeal remained an essential part of judicial procedure up to the thirteenth century[89]) but that testimony must, in turn, be witnessed in the commemorative publicity of the courtly text.

What is significant about this from the point of view of the text's status as a fantasy of social advancement is that a similar legal logic of witness obtained, in the canon law that held good throughout Europe before the Reformation, on the question of 'stolen' or secret marriages. In the ninth and tenth centuries the Church had succeeded in creating a legal loophole to combat the aristocratic consolidation of power through strategic alliances by postulating that the validity of marriage rested in the voluntary expression of consent, or plighting of troths, between two individuals, rather than in the public ceremony of alliance.[90] This opened up the potential for subversion of dynastic policy by rebellious lovers, and created an anomaly in the law of matrimonial contract which persisted up until the Reformation. It is spelt out by William Harrington in his *Commendacions of matrymony* in 1528 (italics show underlinings made by a sixteenth-century reader in his copy):

> this consent which doth make matrymony ought to be expressed *and shewed in open and in honest places afore the presence of honest lawful witnesses called specyally therefore* . . . for & it be otherwyse, that is to say yf the man & woman or theyr proctours do *make matrimony secretly by them selfe without any recorde or but with one witnesse that is called matrymony clandestinat whiche for many causes is forboden by the lawe.* And they which done make such matrimony are accused in that dede doynge, notwithstondyng *that matrimony is valeable and*

holdeth afore God into so moche that the one of the same forsake the other and take other, they lyve in a dampnable aduoutry.[91]

These apparently self-contradictory pronouncements on the validity of clandestine marriage, both of which have been underlined by a contemporary reader – *'forboden by the lawe'* while being *'valeable . . . afore God'* – may be understood in terms of archaic legal concepts of proof as witness of the immanence of God, and consequently of the legitimization of marriage through a ritualized process of witnessing a troth to which God has already been witness. So, at various stages the process of witnessing – by close friends, by one's kin or friends and gradually, through drinkings, festivities, banns and solemnity of a ceremony – brings the individually initiated union into the control of the community at large. Thinking about marriage in this way enables us to understand the 'clandestine' promise as the arrested part of a process of valorization, rather than the illegal opposite of the valid contract. The significance of 'witnessing' is manifest in Van Eyck's Arnolfini portrait, in which the artist's imaging of the private scene of the couple's marriage is offered as proof of his presence there ('Johannes Van Eyck fuit hic') which validates the 'faith' or 'trowth' (*fides*) by which the couple are bound to one another.[92]

The romances identified by Bloch as especially concerned with matrimonial issues – *Boeue de Haumtome* and *Gui de Warewic*, *Ipomedon* and *Partenopeu de Blois* were precisely those which retained their relevance and popularity for readers in early sixteenth-century England. So, for example, Richard Hyrde, in his translation of Vives' *Institution of a Christen Woman*, added to the list that Vives gave of pernicious popular romances, 'In Englande Parthenope, Genarides, Hippomadon, William and Melyour, Libius and Arthur, Guye, Beuis and many other'.[93] In certain of these romances, such as *Ipomydon* and *Amis and Amiloun* (which is a tale of clandestine marriage and the ideal friendship of two bachelor knights) the heroes are serving in the household of an heiress in a 'domestic' capacity.[94]

It is likely, then, that readers in early sixteenth-century England whose expectations had been formed by familiarity with the legal ethos expressed in the narrative structure of chivalric romance, would have understood the legitimation of the clandestine marriage to reside in the prolonged act of 'witness' constituted by the hearing of the tale. In Boccaccio's and Elyot's 'Titus and Gisippus', however, the clandestine marriage is validated or made legitimate not through the process of witnessing, but through the persuasive power of a declamation. This was a revolutionary strategy, decisively transforming the moral significance of the clandestine marriage in subsequent fiction. In England, Elyot was the first of Boccaccio's translators to recognize that the private deliberations between Titus and Gisippus, and Titus' subsequent formal declamation in their defence were the cruxes of the story's cultural significance. For although 'Titus and Gisippus' had been englished for the printer Wynken de Worde by a writer called William Walter in 1523, it is evident from a reading of Walter's translation that he missed the significance of *ratio artificialis* to the reciprocal benefits bestowed by Titus and Gisippus upon one another. Judging by the complete indifference displayed by William Walter to the structure of Titus' declamation, the narrative paradigms with which he was most familiar derived not from a rhetorically informed knowledge of classical literature, but from chivalric romance.[95]

Thus it is that when Elyot's Gisippus explains to Titus that 'natwithstandynge any ceremony done at the tyme of the spousayles, the mariage natwithstanding is nat confirmed untyll at night that the husbande putteth a rynge on the fynger of his wyfe, and unloseth her girdell'[96], he is invoking the canon law's privileging of private consent and sexual consummation over public alliance-negotiation, in a manner familiar to readers of romance, and all too often assumed by modern critics to 'affirm the primacy of love' over 'bargains'.[97] As we have seen, however, the economy of deferred reciprocity that is friendship ensures that a 'bargain' of a kind is involved here; Titus' skill in reconstructing alternative but highly probable versions of motives and events at the scene of the crime dictates the form taken by his reciprocal attempt to sacrifice himself for his friend, whom he later finds circumstantially accused of murder: 'Titus denyed it, and affirmed with reasons and argumentes that he was the murderer and nat Gysippus'.[98] Titus, master of the techniques of artificial proof, is in one sense the exemplar of the ideal humanist 'nobleman', exhibiting the mental 'husbandry' of the ancient nobility of Greece and Rome. At the same time, however, he resembles the demonic Other of that same ideal: the 'supposed husband', the histrionic imposter, whose ability to persuade a courtroom by probable argument of his guilt or innocence becomes indistinguishable from his ability to betray husbands and fathers of the chastity of their wives and daughters. The removal, in fiction, of the spiritually expiatory validation of clandestine marriage into a realm of argument conducted *pro et contra* between men, was to produce a literature featuring men who seem obsessed with the problem of 'reading' the probable signs of clandestine sexual activity between their wives or daughters and the male 'friends' to whom they risk having given the persuasive edge by having (in friendship) communicated too much.

Part II

ANXIETIES OF TEXTUAL ACCESS

The first section of this book has been concerned with the humanistic reformation of the ruling class of sixteenth-century England through an education based in the exemplary reading of classical literature. I have tried to show how important were fictions of *women* in giving the socially transformative potential of humanism a vivid and enduring imaginative form. Thus, the practical efficacy of a humanistic education in enabling a man to manage people and situations (*oikonomia*) was pre-eminently expressed in the fiction of the husband who could 'fashion' his wife. At the same time, a humanistic vision of how the benefits of friendship might operate through persuasive communication (*amicitia*) was expressed in the story of how a daughter could, by liberally educated men, be clandestinely given in marriage against the wishes of her powerful but less literate kindred and friends. Both these fictions of *oikonomia* and *amicitia* tested the limits of the feudal conception of 'lordship' and 'service' as a dominant model of masculine social relations, for *oikonomia* theoretically transformed all men into 'good husbands', while *amicitia* displaced the expressive medium of instrumental friendship from the lordly bestowal of gifts to the familiar exchange of texts.

Implicit throughout the first section, then, has been an argument for taking seriously the impact of humanism upon popularly held notions of what constituted the noblest form of masculinity, as well as upon how masculine relations of affection, trust and economic dependency should henceforward be initiated and maintained. To men such as Sir Thomas Elyot and Lawrence Humphrey, noble masculinity was to be located in the practice of persuasion rather than in physical valour. 'By the meane of his dignite', wrote Elyot, the humanist knight, 'shuld more effectually with his learning and witte assayle vice and errour ... havinge ther vnto for his sworde and his speare, his tung and his penne.'[1] At the same time, men in the service of these humanist noblemen were no longer to function as 'tough Champions' or retainers, but as 'good governours' for 'the common weale',[2] that is, men skilled in the dialectical evaluation and transmission of persuasively argued texts. No longer exhaustively signified by the activities of hunting, hawking, fighting and waiting at table, the gentleman's 'service' in a noble household was more likely to consist of some activity connected with the organization of knowledge into texts: intelligence-gathering, secretaryship, scholarly reading, tuition, diplomacy, stewardship, surveying.

Inevitably, such transformations in the expressive medium of masculinity and of masculine social relations found their way into fiction. What follows in the next two chapters is a reading of the English prose fiction of the 1560s and 1570s as the formal and thematic expression of concern about the pervasive textualization of the signs of masculine honour, and of the signs of credit and trust between men. Unfortunately, the fictions central to my discussion – William Painter's *Palace of Pleasure* (1566–7), Geoffrey Fenton's *Certaine Tragicall Discourses* (1567) and George Pettie's *A Petite Palace of Pettie his Pleasure* (1576) – are, because of our alienation from their formal and social preoccupations, very rarely read. As I have no intention of refuting the charges of tedium regularly levelled against the prose fiction of this period, it may be fairly asked how I can justify devoting two entire chapters to their interpretation. There are, I would argue, three good reasons for doing so.

The first reason concerns its popularity. Although we find these stories now all but unreadable, the fact of their contemporary popularity is attested by numerous allusions and exemplary imitations.[3] As for evidence of their cultural survival in forms that we continue to find emotionally intelligible and compelling, we need look no further than Shakespeare. It is true that studies which examine Shakespeare's plays in relation to these sources have never seemed to account for anything very much. However, this is not in itself an argument that the subject is exhausted. For while specific *novelle* have been examined as sources for specific plays, there has never seemed to be any question about what the *novelle* themselves, as a cultural form, were saying to contemporary readers. It may well be that, once the formal and thematic concerns of these *novelle* begin to emerge as central to the culture of sixteenth-century humanism, it will not be hard to see ways in which a number of Shakespeare's plays dramatize concerns which are very similar.[4]

The second reason concerns women. This is a book about fictions of women, and if the English *novelle* of the 1560s and 1570s were 'new' in any way, they were certainly new in the centrality they accorded to women, and to stories about the courtship of women by men wanting marriage. The critic Caroline Lucas has recently seen in this fact a way of linking sixteenth-century prose 'romances' with twentieth-century pulp romance. The analogy enables her to apply to sixteenth-century prose the critical strategies of readerly resistance that have been developed as part of a feminist politics of the reappropriation of those forms of popular culture (soap opera, Harlequin romances) that have been disparagingly associated with women.[5] My own reading of the prose fiction of the 1560s and 1570s as being fundamentally concerned with the definition of *masculinity* rather than femininity does not preclude attention to the position of women as subjects and readers of this fiction. It does, however, aim to revise the impression given by Lucas' (otherwise very helpful) account, that the centrality of women to this form of fiction was motivated by men's desire to anticipate and cater for women's tastes. For if, as I shall argue, this fiction is primarily concerned with the emergence of textual communication as the new medium in which manhood is to be tried, then its preoccupation with lengthy speeches of courtship made to women, rather than lengthy descriptions of combats between men, may have less to do with the anticipated pleasure of women readers than with the displacement of masculine agency from prowess to persuasion.

The third reason turns on its head the modern reader's objection to having to attend to what is tedious and unintelligible about this fiction.[6] For there is no point in trying to smooth away difficulties of interpretation by attempting to make the collections of Painter and Fenton conform to familiar models of story-telling. Histories of prose fiction, probing these texts with modern expectations of narrative coherence, are baffled precisely because these fictions feel even stranger and more remote than forms of story-telling – saints' lives, chivalric romances, pilgrimages – that we think of as more archaic. We find them, in a very real sense, unreadable: the principle according to which material has been selected and organized, whether within individual 'histories' or across a collection of tales, simply eludes us. What is the common denominator for Painter's selection of episodes from Livy, of *novelle* from the second day of Boccaccio's *Decameron*, of apophtegms from Plutarch? How are we meant to make sense of the exasperating redundancy and radical discontinuity of Fenton's *Tragicall Discourses*, in which competing intepretations of the same set of narrative circumstances are offered to the reader without one being privileged or authorized over another? If we find ourselves unable to imagine exactly what reading strategies these narratives are inviting, our difficulty may, in itself, provide a clue as to what these stories are 'about'. For I believe that these stories focus very precisely the implications of English humanism in its attempt to relocate the social agency of masculinity, and of male friendship, in the mastery of strategies for the evaluation and imitation of persuasive texts. It is for this reason that any historicist criticism, especially a feminist criticism, needs to pay attention to them. For any redefinition of masculinity that makes it depend thus upon skill in persuasive writing (an activity which is as near as can be to the centre of all cultural and mythic production in a literate society) is bound to have serious repercussions for women, and for their own access to how 'femininity' is to be defined.

3

FROM ERRANT KNIGHT TO PRUDENT CAPTAIN

Masculinity and 'romantic' fiction

WOMEN AND 'ROMANCE': THE NEED TO DISTINGUISH CHIVALRIC ROMANCE FROM BANDELLIAN *NOVELLE*

Shortly before the close of adventures in the first book of Diego Ortunez's *Espejo de Principes y Cavalleros*, translated by Margaret Tyler as *The Mirrour of Princely deedes and Knighthood* (1578), the Emperor Trebatio of Greece, famous, invincible and no less than eight feet tall, is hastening back to the Princess Briana, whom he left long ago in a cloister by a river between the Hungarian cities of Buda and Belgrado. Having been unfortunately sequestered on an island for twenty years by the enchantress Lindaraza, Trebatio had been unaware of Briana's having borne him two sons, Rosicleer and Donzel del Febo (the Knight of the Sun), who have, in the intervening chapters, performed the 'princely deedes' that have made them 'mirrours' of knighthood, reflecting the virtue of their lineal ancestry, even in its obscurity. Even as the narrative defies credulity, assuring us that Trebatio is, by magic, the same age (35) as he was when he left, bringing Briana (who was 14 then) to 'just one yere under him', it exhibits a somewhat surprising topographical precision, specifying the exact door through which the knight will pass before he is reunited with his beloved. Briana's lodging is, we are reminded, in a separate quarter of the cloister (which is throughout called a 'monastery'):

> wherto she had a posterne gate towardes the wood, by which *Clandestria* had carryed *Donzel del Febo* and *Rosicleer* to nursing, & by this gate no man either entred or went out but by *Clandestrias* leave. Shee was groome porter and kept the key hir selfe. And for to cover this matter which the Emperour

would in wise have known, it was very fit that Clandestria was ther in company.[1]

Briana's 'wise and discrete'[2] gentlewoman, Clandestria, is an apt person to 'cover this matter'; that is, to mediate and temper the emotional shock of Trebatio's making himself known to the woman with whom, under a stolen identity, he consummated a clandestine marriage in the monastery garden twenty years ago, and to whom he now wishes to narrate all that has happened since 'in order up to thys deliveraunce wrought by the knight of the Sunne'.[3] The specification of the 'postern gate', then, serves more than a local reality effect; its purpose is to suggest that Clandestria's rhetorical management of this final stage in the protracted nuptials of Trebatio and Briana will match, in its discretion and wisdom, her earlier meriting of Briana's confidence when she ensured the safe delivery, and secret nursing, of the precious burden carried in her mistress's body.

Clandestria is, then, a positive representation of women's agency in a world governed by the 'bio-politics of lineage'. It would be wrong to dismiss her role, and that of her mistress, Briana, as expressive of sixteenth-century women's 'exclusion from the public sphere'[4], for no 'public sphere' of masculine agency exists in the *Mirrour of Princely deedes* beyond the princely deeds of chivalry that legitimate Trebatio's lineage. Briana's motherhood, 'her "blood" and all that it brought to the family in terms of ancestral force (virtus)'[5] is just as important to the story of this lineage's foundation as Trebatio's paternity, and Trebatio, enchanted as he is for twenty years, is hardly active in public life. What Margaret Tyler seems to have perceived in choosing to translate this Spanish neo-chivalric romance is the way in which such narratives offered scope for representing female agency. For she makes the preservation of the lineage by Briana and Clandestria analagous to her own act of writing, which she sees as contributing to the transmission of ancestral *virtus*. Translating Ortunez's Spanish, she actually adds references to women as custodians and deliverers of the valour of men. Thus, in Chapter 15, in which the first of Briana's noble children issues precipitately from the monastery and into the world by a nursery 'misadventure', Ortunez points to the hand of providence behind the accident; Tyler, however, recalls the personification of such providence in ancient epic as the presiding of female deities of motherhood and wisdom, Venus and Pallas Athene:

and you which reade this history may be brought by good reason to give credite to this my report, sith you your selves are witnesses of the evident presence of the Almightie in so certaine danger. As the learned well know, *Achilles* hath his *Palaice* in *Homere*, and *Aeneas* his *Venus* in *Virgill*, Godesses assistaunt unto men in their daungerous conflictes.[6]

Being 'assistaunt unto men in their daungerous conflictes' is clearly how Tyler, in her dedication, sees herself. For she stresses the danger, to England, of Spanish invasion, and offers her book to Thomas Howard, as a text that will stimulate valour, or 'animate . . . and set on fire the lustie courages of young gentlemen to the advauncement of their line'. And it is 'courage', or greatness of heart, that signifies the young Thomas Howard's own noble lineage, for, as she says, Howard has

> given no small signification in this your noble youth of . . . wisdome and courage . . . it being the only support of your ancestors lyne, so the same likewise will maynteyne your ancestours glorye . . . to the joy of your kinred and frends, whom not a few your parents good deserving hath assured unto you.[7]

Among these beneficent 'frends', though 'last in worthinesse', she counts herself.

One remarkable thing about Tyler's dedication is its innocence of humanistic discourses of *oikonomia* and *amicitia*. Thomas Howard derives his virtues lineally from his parents, and Tyler owes her friendship, expressed in her gift of the book, to him by virtue of his descent from his parents, 'at whose handes I have reaped especiall benefit'.[8] His friends, like his dependants, are thus 'assured' to him by their allegiance to the line to which he belongs; for, as Alan Stewart has pointed out, the conception of friendship expressed by the word 'assurance' had 'its roots in medieval systems of allegiance'.[9] The purpose of Tyler's book – 'to animate and set on fire the lustie *courages* of young gentlemen' is therefore consonant with feudal conceptions of male and female contributions to lineal virtue.

Recently, Tyler's translation – in particular, its robustly argued preface – has received a good deal of critical attention. Helen Hackett locates its fascination: 'it poses exactly the question which occurs to the modern critic, namely: "if women were the main readers of romances, why did they not write them?"' and she quotes Tyler: 'my perswasion hath bene thus, that it is all one for a woman to pen a story, as for a man to addresse his storie to a woman.'[10] Hackett's version of the question is indebted to Caroline Lucas' pointing out of the association that has existed since the sixteenth century between that category of fiction we refer to as 'romance', and the readership of women. Lucas writes:

> Romantic fiction has, for the past 400 years at least, been associated with women. Women have constituted its subject matter, its consumers, and later its producers as well. Romantic fiction has also, perhaps more than any other genre, been ridiculed, criticised and condemned. These two observations may not be unconnected.[11]

My argument with reading the significance of Tyler's act of translation within the context of a perceived association between women and 'romance' is that it confuses the cultural values generically embodied (even nostalgically) in a late *chivalric* romance such as *The Mirrour of Princely deedes* or the *Amadis de Gaule*, with the very different cultural values that belong inextricably to the new, humanistic form of 'romantic' prose fiction which authors such as Fenton, Pettie, Lyly and others were beginning to address to women. For it is clear that although Tyler's *Mirrour* affords scope for positive representations of women, it nevertheless harks back generically to a time in which 'romance' was precisely not a disparaged literary form associated with women, but one in which the values of the lineage culture were articulated, preserved and exemplified.

We can see the contrast between the cultural values associated with chivalric romance and those associated with the earliest humanistic 'romantic' fictions, or 'Novelles', if we compare the dedication of Tyler's *Mirrour* with William Painter's dedication of the second tome of his *Palace of Pleasure*. (Of course, Painter himself does not address his collection to a woman, but his was the collection which had most influence upon the writers of prose fiction in the following decade, all of whom assumed that women would be their readers.)

Painter, who in 1560 had assumed the office of Clerk of the Ordinance, dedicated the second volume of the *Palace of Pleasure* in 1567 to the Master of the Queen's Armory, Sir George Howard. He was later discovered to have amassed a private fortune by falsifying the accounts of the Armory in collusion with Ambrose Dudley, Earl of Warwick, to whom he dedicated the first *Palace of Pleasure*.[12] The stealth and illegality of Painter's private *oikonomia*, however, is less important here than the way in which it relates to his view of the importance of translating prose fictions. First, Painter contrasts with himself the misanthropic Timon of Athens, in that he wishes, in his 'unfolding of sundry Histories, from the coverture of foren language' to benefit humanity. The first volume, he says, was

> adressed to the right honorable the Erle of Warwicke, for respect of his honor, and my calling. This the second, by like band, your Worship may justly claime as a just tribute, nowe this moneth of Novembre, payable. Or if your Curtesie woulde not deale so roughly with your bounden creditour, yet for dutie sake I must acquite and content that which hath so longe ben due. The same I offre now, not with such usurie and gaine as your benevolence and singular bountie, by long forbearing hath deserved, but with suche affected will and desire of recompense, as any man alive can owe to so rare a friend.[13]

Painter goes on to praise Howard less for his ancestry than for the providence he shows in maintaining the Queen's armory in 'Readinesse ... for tyme of service' which 'care of things continually resting in your breast, hath atchieved suche a timely diligence and successe, as when hir majesties adversarie shal be ready to molest, she shall be prest [i.e. ready] to defend'.[14] Finally, he offers as the objective of his translation the desire to stir up, not men's 'courages', or hearts, but their minds. Each history, writes Painter,

> like a lively image representeth before our eyes the beginning, ende and circumstaunce of eche attempte. The same ... by probable examples, stirreth up sluggishe mindes to aspire and terrifieth the desparate ... from enterprising thinges unseemly.[15]

Despite a superficial similarity in the invocation, by both authors, of the nobility of their patrons, the dedications of Tyler and Painter differ in significant and representative ways. First, Painter does not assume that his position as receiver of benefits from Howard is 'assured' as a part of his long-standing allegiance to parents and kin; rather, he sees himself as having had 'credit' or patronage from various benefactors connected with the Armory – first Warwick and now Howard – which he wishes to be seen to recompense with the textual equivalent of 'usurie and gaine'. The implications of that metaphor will be the subject of the following chapter, but here it is sufficient to remark that although Tyler and Painter share the assumption that the 'friendship' between themselves and their patrons involves recompense for benefits received, Painter's version of the bond is a much more mobile one.

Second, where Tyler praises Thomas Howard's 'wisdom and courage' as deriving from his 'ancestors lyne', Painter praises George Howard for his 'readinesse' and his 'timely diligence'. This humanistic version of a militaristic nobility, defending the realm from invasion, is concerned less with valour than with mental preparation, and provision for eventuality.

Finally, where Tyler's translation was conceived as a preservation of the memory of noble deeds, to stimulate valour in modern knights, Painter makes it clear that his histories are designed to contribute to the mind's ability to provide for its own enterprises, judging 'by probable examples', the likely 'beginning, ende and circumstance of eche attempt'.

What does this mean for an understanding of Tyler's achievement in its relation to a burgeoning genre of 'romantic' prose fiction which was to be associated, for centuries to come, with women readers? The implications are these. It is, first, important to appreciate the translucent intelligence of Tyler's writing, which manifests itself both at a stylistic level, and in the formal analogy which she permits to be inferred between the agency of women in the romance of lineage which she translates, and her own service in translating. Consequently, however, a just appreciation of Tyler's artistry forces an awareness of its contingency upon definitions of masculinity that accord with the culture of feudalism, or of agnatic lineage. It is therefore seriously misleading to link Tyler's writing to the 'romantic' fictions which began to be addressed to women, first by Geoffrey Fenton in 1567, and subsequently by those whom Lucas calls the 'Elizabethan romancers', Pettie, Riche, Greene, Lyly and Sidney. For the significance of women as addressees and subjects of the romantic fictions of these authors is intimately linked to the humanistic disparagement of the values embodied in the kind of chivalric romance that Tyler translates. Indeed, the centrality of women to the plots of this newer 'romantic' fiction is a direct consequence of its increasing devotion to the representation of *masculine* social agency as 'civil' rather than martial, and as celebrating victories of mental readiness rather than physical courage. It is, in other words, when fiction ceases to be solely concerned with feats of chivalry, and begins to incorporate the endless reasoning *pro et contra* of which modern readers despair, that the genre begins to be associated specifically with women.

I would not want to be understood, however, to be arguing for the desirability or the possibility of distinguishing between 'romance' and 'novella' on a transhistorical, generic basis.[16] Evidently, even in the moment of the humanists' deprecation of chivalric romance, and in the very midst of the diffusion of the *novelle* of Bandello in France and England, there was a reinfusion of 'romance' elements into the newer, more densely rhetorical and humanistic plot structures. What I would argue, however, is that these post-Bandellian 'romances', however ostensibly concerned with knights, ladies and tournaments, neither uphold the values of a feudal culture, nor maintain the definitions of masculinity and femininity that are a part of that culture's social and economic relationships. Thus, for example, it is indisputable that Philip Sidney's revisions of the *Arcadia* had the effect of enhancing its 'romantic' rather than its *novella*-like qualities. Yet Sidney's knights are not heroes, as Tyler's Trebatio is, because of being fantastically tall and strong, but because, like Painter's dedicatee, George Howard, their minds are prepared for any eventuality by the exemplary reading of histories. Thus, in the revised *Arcadia*, the knight Palladius improves the success of the Helots' rebellion because he 'by some experience, but *specially by reading of histories*, was acquainted with stratagems' (my italics).[17]

What I would suggest, then, is that Tyler was able to justify her position as a translator of romance precisely to the extent that the romance in question was *not* a part of the humanistic culture that was engaged in redefining elite masculinity according to a practice of reading. In what remains of this chapter I shall argue further that even as women's significance within sixteenth-century romantic fiction increased – that is, as fiction increasingly represented 'civil' rather than martial forms of social action between men – the scope for positive representations of the powers of female judgement (such as the discretion and wisdom displayed by Briana and Clandestria's formation and execution of plans to preserve the lineage) actually, in the short term, narrowed. First, however, what needs to be defined is the way in which a masculinity achieved by 'reading of histories' might manifest itself as the heroic subject of the histories concerned.

PLATS OF FORTIFICATION, PLOTS OF COURTSHIP

In her study of Elizabethan prose fiction as a genre written for women, Caroline Lucas cites as innovative the fiction of William Painter and Geoffrey Fenton. Painter, she writes, 'was one of the first Elizabethan fiction writers to realize the great market potential provided by women readers, and to cater for it'. And she observes that Fenton goes even further in the direction of 'feminizing' prose fiction, for he dedicates his *Certaine Tragicall Discourses* to Mary Sidney, and represents himself as 'rejecting the marvels of men's worldly achievements in favour of "the mervellous effects of love"'.[18] In writing thus, Lucas is quoting from Fenton's introduction to the first of his narratives, which concerns the reinstatement of an impoverished heir by the means of the love borne by his arch-enemy towards his sister. But Fenton's declaration is worth quoting in full:

> I meane not here to restore to memory the wonderfull pollicies and artificiall devises of our Ancestours in making plats and firm foundations . . . muche less trouble you with a reaport of their ingenious trauaile . . . with places heretofore impassable to open and make waye to their huge armies [in the margin: Hannyball forced a passage for his armi through the Alpes] but have in present intente to discover unto you the merveillous effects of love.[19]

Lucas reads Fenton's two categories of historical narrative – accounts of successful military stratagems and stories of love – as antithetical, understanding the 'public' world of war as that which is ostentatiously abandoned (to please women readers) for the 'private' world of romance. In fact, however, Fenton's is not an apology, but a boast; the two kinds of history are not antithetical but analogous, and their analogy lies in the marvels they both tell of *efficiency* in strategy and discourse, military and civil. Ancient histories of the Roman republic record military stratagems or 'plats' which enable access to 'places heretofore impassable';

modern histories, however, will discover how emotionally persuasive communication (the 'effects of love') can achieve things
equally 'merveillous' in the conversations, or textual exchanges of
civil life.

The centrality of women to such fiction is not, then, necessarily
a concession to the tastes of women readers, nor even a con-
cessionary move from the 'public' to the 'private' sphere. Rather it
is that fictions of women, focusing men's narratives of persuasive
efficiency, become coextensive with the enterprise of authorship
itself as the medium of masculine social advancement. For, as
humanism relocated the space of trial for masculine *virtus* from
battlefield to text, so anthologies (rhetorical 'gatherings' of poetry
and fictional history), appearing in print before other men's eyes,
became the new place in which men displayed the cerebral
equivalent of chivalric prowess, in virtuoso deployments of their
skill in probable argument.

How do stories in such anthologies characteristically work, and
how do they position women as readers and subjects? Survey-
type accounts of the fiction of the 1560s, having recourse as they
must do to paraphrase, understandably refrain from commenting
on its redundancy, internal inconsistency and exasperating preoccupation with passages of *pro et contra* deliberation between
men, and with densely-argued harangues and epistles delivered
to women. Nevertheless, to omit to notice these aspects is, as it
were, to fail to recognize the hero of this fiction. For heroic
masculinity, in these narratives, finds its image in the reader's
becoming aware of the extent to which all contingency, all
circumstance, has its own strategic potential as emotionally persuasive argument for or against a particular case. Thus, for
example, literary criticism has traditionally been rather hard put
to account for the popularity of the *novelle* of Bandello with French
and English translators who were not exactly complimentary
about his eloquence.[20] Yet it seems that Bandello offered scope for
humanistic translation, or what Belleforest called the 'enrichment'
of the narrative by 'sentences, the adaptation of histories, orations,
epistles according as the case required'. It is this exemplary
quality, this potential of narrative elements to be redeployed as
emotionally persuasive *argument* that constitutes the importance
of Bandello for Belleforest; the Bandellian text becomes a kind of
stronghold, a terrain to be 'plotted' anew, and thus conquered. So
Belleforest writes, 'Cest embellissement donc (je ne l'appelleray

plus traduction) pourra servir d'enseigne vainqueresse sur le fort de mon auteur' ('This embellishment, then – I will no longer call it "translation" – will serve as a flag of conquest over the fort of my author').[21] In his own turn, of course, Belleforest was read in exemplary and strategic fashion by English schoolboys. So the 11- or 12-year-old Philip Sidney and Fulke Greville wrote their names in a copy of Boaistuau's and Belleforest's *Histoires Tragiques*, which their tutor's records suggests was used as a source of 'example[s] ... phrases and sentences in ... frenche'.[22]

We need, then, to pay attention to the heroic role of the text itself as potential for the display of the dialectical equivalent of feats of chivalry. Any of Belleforest's translations of Bandello would illustrate the point I am trying to make; the story I have chosen to consider here has no special merit, other than that it seems to have been rather popular (it finds its way into both Painter's and Fenton's collections, and crops up as an exemplary argument in the first of Pettie's *novelle*). In Bandello's version, this story tells of a knight called Filiberto da Virle who is in love with madonna Zilia Duca, a beautiful young widow who has the management of a large estate in Moncalieri, in custody for her son. Filiberto is so in love that he promises Zilia anything in return for one kiss; her bargain, however, is that he keep silent for three years. Having successfully prevented Filiberto from entering into the *lunghi ragionamenti* (long discourses) of love by which he had hoped to win her, Zilia has thus obliged Filiberto to retire from courtship, and to seek his fortune by combat on the fields of Gascony, where Charles VII is waging a fierce battle against the English. Filiberto is so successful in leading the siege of Rouen, fighting with the English captain, Talbot, and finally performing in a tournament, that the king advances him to greater and greater honour and familiarity, sorrowing only that he cannot *ragionar seco* (converse with him). A proclamation is made of reward offered for Filiberto's cure; Zilia hastens to the knight's bedside, but he knows she comes for money, rather than for love of him, and so he makes love to her without speaking. Finally, her guilt is confessed to the king, and her punishment by death staved off only for Virle's sexual gratification and his pleasure in showing her the estates (larger than hers in Moncalieri) bestowed upon him by the French crown.[23]

What was this story saying to the men who translated and read it? At first sight it seems to conform to a model of masculine *virtus* that is essentially chivalric and feudal. For in chivalric romance, as Howard Bloch has written,'the ordeal of battle is reduced to the proportions of a single hand-to-hand combat . . . a knight's prowess, his place within the chivalric hierarchy, is determined by his succcess in . . . encounters with daemonic dwarfs, outlaws and giants'.[24] According to Bloch, the romance's account of the battle conforms to the act of witness that mediates between the place of warlike encounter outside the law and the courteous place of legitimate social hierarchy; specifically, this act of witness brings the knight to the notice of a lord or prince in whose gift lies the possibility of advancement.

Examples of this 'becoming visible' abound in chivalric romance. In *Sir Eglamour*, a king's squire looks on as we are treated to a blow-by-blow description of the hero's combat with a fierce boar:

> The squer stode and beheld them two
> He went agayne and tolde so
> Forsothe the boar is slayne.[25]

Hearing the squire's description of Eglamour's fight and his 'riche armes', the king himself hastens to the scene, and, finding Eglamour 'ouerthwarte' the dead beast, pronounces, 'manfully thou hast slayne this boar' and later offers Eglamour his daughter, 'with a riche rynge'. Eglamour declines, and goes to Rome, where he slays a dragon in full view of the emperor himself:

> The emperour of Rome, laye in his toure
> And fast beheld Syr Eglamoure
> And to his knights gan saye
> Do crye in Rome, the Dragon is slayne
> A knight him slewe with might and mayne
> Manfully by my faye
> The Emperour had a doughter bright . . .[26]

The relation of the legitimating act of witness to the recognition structure of romance narrative assumes a certain self-consciousness in a late romance like the *Amadis de Gaule*, where Amadis (whose identity no one knows) gains renown at the court of King Languine through the mediatory help of 'Urgonde la Mescognue' ('Urgonde the unrecognized'), a supernatural being who is clearly a personification of the theme.[27] An earlier romance, *Ipomydon*, where the hero wins advancement as much for his courteous education as his physical strength, is no less marked by such mediatory moments of recognition. The lady of the household notes how her new servant is 'feyre and shape wele / Body and armes every deale / But she kowde wete for no cas / Whens he came ne what he was'. So she arranges to watch his hunting from a pavilion in the forest. Ipomydon, nobly educated as he has been, shoots with facility 'both bucke and doe' before the eyes of his lady, who concludes that 'of hunting . . . he cowde jnoughe', and determines to marry him.[28]

The fantasy of thus becoming visible through one's merits to a powerful patron would seem to account, in part, for the popularity of the the the story of the knight of Virle. Before Rouen, in combat with Talbot, and at jousting, he proves his valour in the eyes of the King of France who, as Painter writes,

> was very sory that a gentleman so valiant was not able to express his minde, which if it might be had, in councel would serve the state of the common wealth, so well as the force and valour of his body had til then served for defence and recovery of his places.[29]

There is, however, a crucial difference here. For where the valour of Eglamour, Ipomydon and Amadis constitutes *in itself* the merit which earns them notice, Virle's valour is 'read' by the king as the sign of his mind's ability to 'serve the state of the common wealth'. The medium in which Virly's potential would be fully realized, in the king's opinion, is not combat but discourse, the medium where he might 'express his minde'.

That the problem of becoming visible to a patron should thus be expressed as a problem of access to a public discourse (in which to prove one's ability to serve the common wealth) would have made perfect sense to young men seeking advancement in mid to late sixteenth-century England. When George Gascoigne was invited by Lord Grey to go hunting in the 1570s, he was rather less skilful than Ipomydon had been, apparently managing to shoot nothing but carrion deer. What should have been (and no doubt was) a humiliating failure in chivalric self-display, was transformed by Gascoigne's translation of the incident into another medium. The medium was that of emotionally persuasive argument – poetry – in print. In a poem dedicated to Lord Grey and entitled 'Woodmanship' Gascoigne proceeded to allegorize his failure in shooting as the failure of his skills in dialectic and rhetoric to gain him patronage or office in a corrupt society, where those

Who can not speake, nor write in pleasant wise,
Nor lead their life by *Aristotles* rule
Nor argue well on questions that arise
Nor plead a case more than my Lord Mairs mule

are nevertheless taken up by patrons, the men who 'hit the markes that I do misse / And winne the meane which may the man mainteyne'.[30] Inviting Lord Grey to become the interpreter of his allegory, Gascoigne indicated that a gracious exposition would prove the author's apparent incompetence to be, after all, an example of his ability to exploit the occasion for a display of gifts of the mind. Moreover, once published in Gascoigne's collection, *A Hundreth Sundrie Flowres*, the poem became visible to eyes other than Grey's, defining any gracious exposition as a potential act of recognition and patronage. Indeed, Gascoigne made this function of his printed collection quite explicit in the apologetic epistle appended to the second edition, in which he excused his coming into print by appealing to the very difficulty symbolized by the silence of the knight of Virle – the difficulty of getting noticed not for proportion and physical valour, but for brilliance of mind. 'As I seeke', he wrote, 'advauncement by vertue'

> so was I desirous that there might remaine in publike recorde, some pledge or token of those giftes where with it hath pleased the Almightie to endue me: To the ende that thereby the vertuous might bee incouraged to imploye my penne in some exercise which might tende both to my preferment, and to the profite of my Countrey. For many a man which may like mine outwarde presence, might yet have doubted whether the qualityes of my minde had bene correspondent to the proportion of my bodie.[31]

Gascoigne, like the fictional Filiberto da Virle, had sought advancement as a soldier, but he wanted to show that he could 'as well persuade with Penne, as pearce with launce or weapon'.[32] The printed collection of fiction was explained by Gascoigne as his attempt to ensure for himself the space that Virle, in Bandello's story, had been denied: the space in which to express the qualities of the mind.

It becomes possible to understand, then, the attraction of the Virle story; to see how it reflected the enterprise of humanistic translation and publication embarked upon by Belleforest, Painter and Fenton and others as authors and seekers after patronage. A puzzle nevertheless remains. For why should these authors produce, from the hint of Bandello's original narrative, a version of the story which makes explicit the idea that Virle's military exploits are indisputable signs of 'wisdom, for the direction of a common wealthe or countrey'?[33] Of course, the King has seen evidence not just of Virle's strength in combat, but of his skill in strategy, for he 'mayde hym Capteyne of diverse holdes, with charge of fyftie men at armes'.[34] Yet why should there be a perceived connection between the captain of military forces, and the gifts of an author's mind published in hope that they might be employed in Gascoigne's words, 'to my preferment, and to the profit of my Countrey'? And what has either to do with the peculiarly violent vengeance taken by this plot and other Bandellian plots upon the bodies of women?

Perhaps the first question to ask concerns the kind of service for which printed collections of poetry and fiction might have been expected, in the mid to late sixteenth century, to serve as qualification. In an unpublished paper on the participation of scholars in intelligence work in Elizabethan England, William Sherman qualifies the historian Wallace MacCaffery's authoritative view that policy was formed almost entirely within the charmed circle of the Privy Council. In the state papers, argued Sherman, 'there are hundreds, if not thousands, of papers offering information bearing on policy which were prepared by individuals outside – and sometimes well outside – that charmed circle'.[35] How did these papers reach the Council? Walsingham's personal secretary, Nicholas Faunt, describes among his responsibilities the compilation of books of information useful to the state, including

> discripcions most exactly taken of other Countries . . . as by discoveringe the present state of their goverment[,] their alliances[,] dependencies etc. with many other discourses[,] devices[,] plottes, and projects of sundry natures etc. all which sometimes may serve to verie good purpose, which wilbee dayly delivered to the Secr.: especially if hee bee known to make accompt of vertuous imployment and of men that are liberally brought up, and have their mindes elevated through . . . arts and faculties.[36]

'Vertuous imployment' is practically Gascoigne's phrase. The assumption appears to be that the secretary, in his own mediatory and influential position, can expect to receive 'plots' and 'projects' for the commonweal, composed by men educated in the liberal arts who hope for preferment. (One might consider here as exemplary the career of the aptly-named Hugh Platt, whose collection, *The floures of philosophie with the pleasures of poetrie*, came out the year before Gascoigne's *Hundreth Sundrie Flowres*, in 1572. Platt wrote no more poetic collections, but was subsequently knighted for his service to the Privy Council in the form of his delivery to them of discourses, 'inventions' and projects delivered to them on agricultural improvement, fishing, mnemonics and remedies against famine.[37]) While we might find it hard to perceive the connection between the political 'plot' or 'plat', and the anthology of rhetorical flowers in prose and verse, Elizabethan policy-makers evidently recognized in the latter skills appropriate to the composition of the former. For, as I have argued elsewhere, an essential connection was perceived between these two kinds of text at the level of probable argument; these 'plots' or 'plats' were not only conceptual schemes for the better organization of means and resources, but *discourses ordering or 'emplotting' arguments of their own probable success*.[38]

Clearly, then, a liberal or humanistic education was envisaged as a preparation for such textualized intelligence service. The Secretary of State, Francis Walsingham, set out in a letter to his nephews instructions for the exemplary reading of histories which leaves us in no doubt as to his assumptions on this issue. He advises the young men to 'Read also Titus Livius and all the Roman histories which you shall find in Latin, as also all books of state both old and new, as Plato, de Rep., Aristo. polit., Xenophon . . . orations'. Reading these histories, he says,

> you have principally to mark how matters have passed in government in those days, so have you to apply them to these our times and states and see how they be made serviceable to our age, or why to be rejected, *the reason thereof well considered shall cause you in time to come to frame better courses both of action and counsel as well in your private life as in public government*.[39] (my italics)

This last phrase of Walsingham's – 'better courses of action and counsel' – describes a mind adept in the classical virtue of prudence; that is, the ability to discern the latent good in any situation and to find the means to pursue it.[40] The idea of 'prudence' is really our clue to understanding the connection, in sixteenth-century humanist pedagogy, between the exemplary reading of histories, and the mind habitually concerned with the strategic 'emplotment' both of practical policy (courses of action) and of persuasive arguments to justify that policy (counsel). According to humanist education theory, readers of classical history would attain prudence both by attending to its thematic examples and by noting the rhetorical ordering of the examples as arguments within the discourse as a whole. For the reading skills that enable prudence resemble those that prepare for rhetorical composition. Both oratory and prudence deal with what is contingent and uncertain to human knowledge. Victoria Kahn writes: 'Just as the orator is guided by decorum in adapting his speech to the exigencies of the moment, so the prudent man enacts decorum in the moral sphere by responding to the particular and contingent in human affairs.'[41] Both are concerned with the discovery of means to act or speak in relation to knowledge that is merely 'probable', that is uncertain. Both, therefore, are concerned with the provision of means to make the unforeseen 'visible' in relation to what is already known and to the requirements of the situation. Metaphors of vision and provision dominate Sir Thomas Elyot's very lengthy account of 'prudence' in *The Boke named the Governour*. Prudence involves circumspection, providence, opportunity and the ability to 'beholde and foresee the successe of our enterpryse'.[42] Rhetorical composition resembles prudence in its concern with foresight, with discursive provision of the means for victory.[43]

Interestingly, humanist prescriptions for reading history become clearest about the connection between prudence and oratory when their subject is *military history*; specifically, the campaigns related in Livy's third decade, in Caesar's Gallic wars, in Xenophon's *Cyropaedia*, and analysed in such books of stratagems as Frontinus, and Machiavelli's *Arte della guerra*. In the sixteenth century little time was lost in translating these books into English: Frontinus by Richard Morison in 1539, Livy by Sir Anthony Cope in 1544, Xenophon by William Barker in 1552, Caesar by Arthur Golding in 1565, and Machiavelli by Peter Whithorne in 1566.[44] This, then, is the point at which to return to the opening of Fenton's *Tragicall Discourses*, to reconsider the meaning of his invocation of military history – the history of 'the wonderfull pollecies . . . our Auncestours in making platts and firm foundations' as a model for his own discourses of current affairs, demonstrating 'the merveillous effects of love'. Fenton makes explicit the central argument of this chapter, namely, that it was classical military history which offered the primary conceptual model for fictions of civil courtship, in which men's victories over women, over fortune and over one another were imagined as successful projects of *access* by means of emotionally persuasive texts which conveyed the 'effects of love'.

How could this be? In the first place, classical military history, especially Livy, afforded a fund of metaphors for the unfamiliar cerebral processes involved in the definition of prudence and the experience of enterprise. For example: when, in *The Boke named the Governour*, Sir Thomas Elyot defines that aspect of prudence called 'circumspection' he illustrates it with reference to Quintus Fabius Maximus, who, by keeping his soldiers moving along high ground, frustrated Hannibal's desire for a decisive engagement. These are, of course, the tactics of delay for which Fabius Maximus is famous, but Elyot translates them into a graphic metaphor for the mental ability to assume a position of pragmatic vantage with regard to any situation, to 'beholde on every syde farre of' and to judge 'what lackethe, howe and from whens it may be provided'.[45] The complexities of political contingency are reduced, in military history, to the conceptually vivid contours of physical emergency.

Second, it is military history in which the crucial connection between the prudential and the oratorical – the conceptual organization of resources for action and their probable justification in discourse – emerges most strongly. So Livy and Caesar are valued because the graphic intelligibility or 'plat' of any campaign is matched by the persuasive immediacy of the discourses designed to make it effective. It will seem to the reader that he 'seeth the ordre of hostes' wrote Elyot, and that he 'hereth the Counsayles & exhortations of captaines.' He went on to single out Xenophon's *Cyropaedia* as a text in which instruction in the 'well ordring of hostes' was inseparable from the 'swetenes' with which the author 'invented and ordred his warke'.[46] And if it was military history which properly succeeded the chivalric romance, this was so less because of its subject matter than because of its rhetorical emplotment. In the *Defence of Poetry* Sidney praises Xenophon's *Cyropaedia* above other fictional discourses – certainly above the *Amadis de Gaule* – because attention paid to the emplotment of its examples will enable the reader to reproduce their instructive potential, for 'so far substantially it worketh' he writes, 'as not only to make a

Cyrus ... but to bestow a Cyrus upon the world to make many Cyruses, if they will but learn aright why and how that maker made him'.[47]

Interestingly, when Sidney talks about the plot of the *Cyropaedia*, he identifies the military captain – Cyrus – with the provident emplotment ('substantial working') of the fiction itself. This recalls, once more, the example of Filiberto da Virle, whom the King of France assumed would, on the evidence of his captainship of the French soldiers, be skilful in oratory. Clearly, the figure of the 'prudent captain' – Cyrus, Filiberto da Virle, Quintus Fabius Maximus, Scipio Africanus, Hannibal – is somehow analagous to a humanistic conception of the significance, for men, of reading historical narratives as argumentative resources for use 'as well in ... private life as in public government'[48]

Unlike the knight errant, who simply fights and follows the chivalric code, the captain responsible for soldiers on a military campaign embodies the very imperative that makes prudential acivity – that is, the constant and unceasing emplotment of present circumstances to prevent future disaster and ensure good fortune – a habit of the mind. The *Cyropaedia* redefines the art of warfare in terms of this habit of creating ongoing means for provision against emergency. Cyrus asks his father to reward a man who has taught the art of warfare – *taktikōn* in Greek, translated by Barker as 'feates of chivalrye' – and his father scornfully replies, 'did this man ... emong his matters of warre, make any mention of household governance (*oikonomia*)?' and he goes on to explain that enmity lies not so much in the power of the foe as in the extremity of circumstances, 'thinges themselves', and that the skill of war lies, 'in care of provision and prest courage of travell' to transform this circumstantial enemy into a source of 'goods and substance'. 'I allow him for a travellous captain', says Cyrus's father, 'which (god not hindering) can provide, both that his armie have thinges nedeful abundantly, and also prepare that their bodies be strong and lustie.'[49]

In the English Xenophon, then, we find very explicitly delineated the figure of the military captain as a model of foresight and circumspection, of 'plotting' in the sense of anticipating and providing for the physical agents of good fortune. However, the physical agents of any campaign – the soldiers – obviously have to be emotionally committed to the hazard of their lives in the conviction of success. Material providence has therefore to be supplemented by discursive providence, or a virtuoso ability to emplot the circumstances of the present and of the immediate and the remote past within a providential narrative, promising imminent good fortune. Whithorne's translation of Machiavelli focuses on the difficulty of executing any plan once the soldiers have succumbed to fears about its ill-fatedness. The great difficulty is 'to remove from a multitude an evill opinion . . . where cannot be used but woordes', he writes, 'wherefore it was requisite that the excellent Capitaines were oratours, for that without knowing how to speak to all the army with difficultie may be wrought any good thing'.[50] Accordingly, the fourth book of the *Arte of Warre* moves from 'plats' and directions for the ordering of soldiers on the ground, to the ordering of motivating forces in contingency. Morison's translation of Frontinus has chapters on 'how to dissemble adversities' and 'how to put away feares that soldiers conceave in unlucky chances,' full of examples of the success of captains in rapidly re-emplotting or reinterpreting misfortunes as part of a narrative that might give the soldiers 'good hope and comfort that some profit shuld followe thereof'.[51]

Obviously military history of this kind offered a very different position to the male reader from that afforded him by chivalric romance. For military history positions the reader as 'travellous captain' rather than as *chevalier errans*, that is, it offers him a vantage point from which to survey the entire narrative as a terrain to be advantageously ordered as *potential for emplotment*. Surely herein lies the difference Sidney pointed to when he acknowledged that the *Amadis de Gaule* moved men's hearts to the exercise of courtsey, liberality and courage, but for all that it wanted 'much of a perfect poesy'. The *Amadis de Gaule*, unlike the *Cyropaedia*, does not enable the masculine reader to become, through reading, the prudent captain who masters the plot in an exemplary way, as if it were a treasurehouse of arguments to be used in persuading men and women to act in accordance with a plot of his own.[52]

What is new about romantic prose fiction after Bandello, then, is that heroic masculinity no longer figures as 'courtsey, liberality and courage', but as the capacity to read strategically, in Sidney's words to 'use the narration as an imaginative ground plot of a profitable invention'.[53] This capacity for the exemplary reading and re-emplotment of histories is repeatedly personified as the activity of a 'prudent captain'; so a poetic allegory of prudence written in the 1570s runs: 'Like as the Capitayne hath respect, to trayne his souldiers in aray / So learning doth mans mind direct.'[54] And the space in which this allegorical captain was supposed to achieve his victories was not an archaic 'man's world' of physical combat, but a modern world of textual exchange, representing the real significance of letters and discourses in the late sixteenth century as crucially mediatory both in providing intelligence for the augmentation and defence of the realm, and in obtaining men's preferment, or what Gascoigne called, 'the meane, which may the man meyntaine'.

For a real-life example of the double function of letters and probably-argued discourses in both serving the commonwealth (maintaining its defence) and mediating the preferment of authors, we should (briefly) consider the career of Geoffrey Fenton himself, once his days of translating and publishing romantic fiction were over. After much assiduous translation and dedication, Fenton obtained, in 1581, the post of Secretary of State for Ireland. In October 1586, we find him writing to Burghley from Cork with a detailed description of his survey of the coastal towns of the region. Throughout his description, he balances the the need for financial provision to fortify a 'doubtful' or vulnerable bit of coastline, with the need to provide information and arguments to 'assure . . . the people inhabiting the maritime parts, being for many respects to be doubted most'. Fenton reports how he has been making financial provision for fortifications against invasion, and offering textual provision (intelligence) to counter the inhabitants' doubts about England's 'care of their safety'. Finally, he refrains from describing the state of certain harbours west of Cape Clear (which location Burghley notes in the margin) 'for that they are less doubtful than others, both by their situation and the fidelity of the people'.[55]

We could hardly have a more vivid example of the identification of military strategy and probable persuasion, of the complimentarity of 'plats of fortification' and well-plotted arguments. But Fenton's second letter in connection with this enterprise adds another dimension to our understanding of the significance of textual exchange as the medium of his public service. For not only do letters conveying intelligence constitute Fenton's service, they also *enable its recognition as service*, structuring relations of dependency. Thus, in his October letter to Burghley, Fenton mentions a local alderman, whose letter to himself he encloses in a further communication with Burghley dated 7 November. The alderman's letter is a careful matching of reports concerning the rumoured departure of a Spanish fleet from Biscay, headed for Ireland. Fenton refers its contents 'to be weighed by your lordship according to the probabilities' and he explains that in its author

> I found very faithful assistance, both to discover the unsoundness of some gentlemen, as also to stay and assure them; if it would please your lordship to take knowledge thereof, and bestow a letter of thanks on him, it would not a little encourage him . . . besides, he is very anxious to depend on your lordship.[56]

Burghley is to judge from the enclosed letter not only the 'probabilities' of its arguments concerning imminent invasion, but also the quality of the alderman's service, in the expression of his mind. The state of the Irish coastline, space of military engagement, is mediated to Burghley as an object of provisional knowledge, or probability; thus it is that letters, manipulating uncertain and probable intelligence, have taken over from the battlefield or the tournament as the medium in which the virtues of men are to be tried and known, and in which these virtues are to be recognized by the encouraging promise of further relationship.

In Fenton's own prose fiction, and in that of his imitators, notably Pettie, it is women who serve as the symbolic analogues of the textual/spatial medium of uncertainty over which the prudent man must assure his hold, and as the mediatory interlocutors through which his 'Nobleness of minde' is proved when persuasion succeeds in getting one of them to promise marriage to him, in spite of her kinsmen or rival suitors. Thus, Filiberto's 'love' for madonna Zilia is expressed as a strategic attempt to gain entry to a stronghold, echoing precisely his subsequent, successful siege of Rouen. She is first described as intractable territory, 'so hagardlyke and enclyned to crueltie that she semed rather to take her begining, among the desertes and craggie places of *Scavoye*' than to be native of the 'fertil feldes' nourishing the 'curtoyse ladyes' in the place of her son's patrimony, Montcalieri.[57] Her care of the estate, and refusal to entertain suitors is both offered to women readers as an example of good housewifery (notes in the margin observe that 'gentlewomen ought to be skilful in housekeping' and gloss Zilia's activities as 'the charge of a mistres or governour of household') and subsequently avenged by the narrative as the symbol of all that prevents men gaining public recognition for their humanistic qualities of foresight, resolution and discursive virtuosity. Virle makes it clear, wooing Zilia, that these are the job qualifications he is showing off. 'My case alas', he observes,

> differeth not much from the condition of the pollitike capteine, who, . . . beyng careful to kepe his soldiours from slaughter, . . . planteth his ordinance & battery in the face of the forte, . . . that . . . the soldiours maye more saffelie give charge upon the walls, and performe the expectation of their capteyne.[58]

The soldiers he means not to waste here are his prudential linguistic resources; later, at Rouen, he confirms the 'inward dexteritie' thwarted by Zilia's treachery when he becomes 'the first that was seene upon the walles makinge waye to the souldiers to enter the breache'. Finally, when the King rewards Filiberto with possessions, Fenton describes these as 'townes and holdes'; strategic sites, requiring prudence to maintain, and therefore symbolic of the valuable masculine asset that was nearly wasted by Zilia's 'vaine glorie and conceite of a chastitie invincible'.[59]

The most significant effect of the displacement of heroic masculinity in the prose fiction of the 1560s and 1570s, then, is the way in which it transforms the violence explicitly wreaked (in genres such as *chanson de geste* and chivalric romance) by men upon men, into a vengeance visited by the narratives themselves upon their heroines. Women stand in, as victims, for the indirection or inadmissability of rivalry between men within the medium of persuasive argument that wins its victories by eliciting affection, and simulating 'the effects of love'. Of course women always represented the struggle for power between men in the symbolic form of alliance-gifts, or adulterous wives, but in these forms they were not necessarily implicated as interlocutors in a version of that struggle being enacted at the level of textual exchange. Yet this is how women are implicated, time after time, in the stories of courtship told by Fenton, Painter and Pettie. An example, again of a popular and much imitated story, might be that of 'the constancy of Dom Diego'. In this story the 'presumtuouse arrogancie' of Diego's beloved Genivera in entertaining doubts about his faithfulness and not even responding to the letter in which he explained 'th'equitie of my cause', is avenged when Diego's friend, Roderigo, has her new lover killed before her eyes by one of his servants who then offers 'the point of hys naked dagger to her white and delicate necke, threateninge, that if she contynued in these tearmes hys handes sholde performe the sacrafize of her life, to the shadow of the villain she lamented so much'.[60]

Of course, it cannot be denied that the new focus upon textual exchange meant that women were more central than ever before to the plots of romantic fiction, and this arguably had some positive side effects. Thus, as Caroline Lucas writes, George Pettie 'does expand women's roles, giving them depth of character, allowing them to be highly articulate', but, as she also observes, his conclusions inevitably re-emplot the active implication of the women in the textual exchanges of courtship as reasons to condemn them, whether for excessive forwardness or excessive chastity.[61]

We may, I think, understand the inherent contradiction in the positioning of women readers by Pettie's text as another effect of what I have, throughout this chapter, been referring to as the displacement of heroic masculinity from combat to textual exchange. Almost all of Pettie's stories concern courtship, conducted through letters or orations delivered to the woman alone, in an attempt to persuade her against the necessity of her obedience to friends and kin in the matter of her matrimony.[62] In chivalric romance, the motif of the 'stolen marriage' is indeed one through which rivalry between men may be enacted; a young bachelor may, through a clandestine contract, defeat the opposition of a powerful seigneur. But the text of chivalric romance is not expected to function, as Pettie's *Pallace* does, as the medium in which is displayed (before men) the author's heroic capacity to husband and fashion the minds of his female readers. That this was indeed the function of the *Petite Pallace* becomes evident in Pettie's prefatory letter to his second publication, a translation of Guazzo's *Civile Conversation*, in which he refers to his *Pallace* as the first proof that men have had of his valour, 'havynge already past the Pikes in a daungerous conflict without wounde of honour'.[63] *Pace* Juliet Fleming's brilliant account of Pettie as a 'ladies' man', it could be argued that it is not so much the presence of the woman reader that makes Pettie's text 'manly enough', as the visible interpellation of the woman reader before a readership of men.[64] For although Pettie's *Pallace* ostensibly addresses itself, by means of the first prefatory epistle, to 'gentlewomen', a second prefatory epistle from 'G.P.' to 'R.B.' creates the fiction of the whole book as the record of an intimate textual exchange between men, proof of their *amicitia*, which has accidentally escaped into public view.[65] This epistle contains asides in Latin which make light of the main text's preoccupation with courtship and marriage, indicating that what Pettie exhibits in his writing is no effeminate yielding to the desires of women readers, but a truly humanistic proof of manhood as a masterful rhetorical 'husbandry' of the desires of a female interlocutor or reader, fashioning the woman as subject by offering her a compelling fiction of herself.

4

USURERS' DAUGHTERS AND PRODIGAL SONS

The gendered plot of authorship in the 1570s

The last chapter re-examined the issue of the relation between women and romantic prose fiction in the second half of the sixteenth century. It put the question, 'if romances were addressed to, and concerned with women, why did women not write them?' The increasing devotion of sixteenth-century romantic prose fiction to the representation of civil, rather than martial, forms of masculine social agency (that is, to plots of courtship, rather than deeds of knight errantry) was not found to enhance the scope for positive representations of female social agency. The new form of romantic prose fiction, derived from the *domestici ragionomenti*[1] of Bandello, produced, through its very privileging of exemplary reading as a basis of masculine social agency, a gendered split in its educative orientation towards readers. Women were offered examples of conduct to imitate, or take warning by, while men were asked to identify with male protagonists who used such examples flexibly and pragmatically, as resources for the emplotment of prudent undertakings and persuasive discourses. The reason for this was nothing less than the connection between the textual display of skill in emplotment and in probable reasoning exhibited by the translators and authors of romantic prose fiction, and the function of the printed and dedicated text in bringing those skills to the notice of a noble benefactor who might wish to employ the author in some form of intelligence service.

This chapter will once more be concerned with the Judith Shakespeare that never was, that is, with the question of why the decades leading up to the flowering of the English Renaissance in the 1590s were so uncongenial to the emergence of women's writing, given, as Virginia Woolf put it, that 'every other man . . . was capable of song or sonnet'.[2] If being capable of song or sonnet was also proof of eligibility for political service, then our question about gender turns on larger issues we have been investigating about the *function* of the printed text as the advertisement of those skills now redefining relations of service and friendship between men. Those skills were, as we have seen, founded in the humanist dialectician's interest in 'probability': 'arguments which can be counted on to win in debate'.[3] The relationships which such text-exegetical and textually productive skills were to initiate and make operational were conceived, however, as long-term exchanges of services and benefits secured not by wages, but by a form of credit extension known as 'fidelity' or 'trust' or 'good faith'. It was in the course of the 1570s that a discrepancy became apparent in the conceptual basis of the technology of probable reason as a facilitator of relations of civil service and friendship, and the dependence of traditional conceptions of service and friendship on the extension of credit as proof of trust. The problem of authorship in the 1570s, and the gendered mode of its solution will be best understood, then, as part of a wider debate about the need to redefine credit relations, and to combat what was being perceived as a crisis in the power of pledges of faith to bind men to one another in relations of reciprocal obligation.

CONTEXTUALIZING WOMEN'S WRITING IN THE 1570s: ISABELLA WHITNEY AND THE 'ELIZABETHAN PRODIGALS'

I have been arguing all along that fictions of women in the sixteenth century map out the visions and anxieties of men in response to the perceived textualization of their social agency as a result of humanism. In this section I want to show how, in the decade after the diffusion of Bandellian fiction in English, legal and moral anxieties began to get the upper hand, and to express themselves in the censorship and condemnation of fictional and dramatic writing. The result may be seen in the mode of self-presentation adopted by a generation of writers whom Richard Helgerson has called 'the Elizabethan Prodigals'.[4] These writers found themselves obliged to contain, by various strategies, the moral objections being raised to the enterprise of authorship as a means of gaining employment. The strategies of containment they adopted tend to draw a parallel between two apparently unrelated areas of experience: first, condemnation of the falsehood inherent in 'prodigal' and 'usurious' contracts between men, and second, the problems of assuring the chastity of wives, sisters and daughters. Parallels tend to be drawn through the adaptation, in their texts, of Bandellian fictions. This in itself serves as an index of the extent to which these fictions had become available to men's imaginations as ways of thinking through the problems attending the increasingly textualized bases of friendship and service. As the 'prodigal' writers use them, these fictions are being used to legitimate the enterprise of authorship itself. The first question to be asked, then, concerns the rhetoric of authorship in the the 1570s and 1580s; in what ways was it different from that of earlier decades?

The successful career of Geoffrey Fenton as Secretary of State for Ireland suggests that there was, in 1567, no clash of interests perceived between the use of print to advertise humanistic text skills for public service, and the choice of Italian histories of romantic courtship as a vehicle for the display of such skills. By the 1570s, however, attitudes no longer seem to have been so liberal. In 1570 Roger Ascham's *The Schoolmaster* was published, with its famous pronouncement against the prudential histories that had overtaken in popularity the older forms of chivalric romance. The *Morte Darthur*, he wrote 'is good stuff to . . . laugh at', but

> ten *Morte Darthurs* do not the tenth part so much harm as one of these books made in Italy and translated in England. They open, not fond and common ways to vice, but such subtle, cunning, new and diverse shifts to carry young wills to vanity and young wits to mischief, to teach old heads new school points, as the simple head of an English man is not able to invent.[5]

In 1582, Stephen Gosson, refuting Thomas Lodge's contention that drama might be 'an image of truth' chose, like Ascham, to scorn the improbable dramas of chivalric romance for their silliness ('nothing but the adventures of an amorous knight . . . encountring many a terrible monster made of broune paper') while at the same time condemning the comedies plotted according to the probable arguments of Italian fiction and drama as positively vicious. The *'Palace of pleasure*, . . . baudie *Comedies* in *Latine, French, Italian,* and *Spanish,* have been thoroughly ransackt to furnish the Playe houses in London', he wrote; 'Howe is it possible that our Playmakers headdes, running through *Genus* and *Species* & every difference of lyes, cosenages, baudries, whooredoms, should present us any *schoolmistres of life* . . . or *image of trueth?*[6]

I propose to treat the question of the emergence of a verisimilar drama on the London stage in the following chapter, but Gosson's objections are nevertheless relevant here, because they demonstrate the extent to which the opposition to the theatre shared ground with moral opposition to Italian prose fiction. The moral objection to both was tied up with a formal appreciation of their redefinition of heroic masculinity as skill in strategic re-emplotment; this, as I have been arguing, took the form of making the reader or auditor aware of the extent to which all contingency, all narrative circumstance might be available for use as emotionally persuasive argument. In this way, both humanistic *novelle* and neo-classical drama were considered to be formally instructive in the forging of ambiguous contractual relations which, based in merely local acts of persuasion, might gain a man credit with his interlocutor, without rendering himself legally obliged or accountable. As 'schoolmasters' of such subversive ethics, these fictions were perceived by men like Gosson and Ascham to be threatening to the traditional forms of alliance-friendship, which depended on unambiguously signalled 'assurances' (sworn promises, gifts, acts of hospitality) of allegiance and fidelity between houses.

It was in response to the moral reformation on behalf of which Ascham and Gosson wrote, that 'the Elizabethan Prodigals' – who included George Gascoigne, George Whetstone, John Lyly and Thomas Lodge – all at one time or another adopted the figure of the repentant prodigal as an enabling authorial persona. This phenomenon has been explained to some extent, but aspects of it remain puzzling. Why, exactly, was the clumsy fiction of 'prodigality' necessary to these writers? What was it apologizing for, and enabling, in their writing?

In a gift economy, prodigality may be understood as the abuse, by anticipation, of the reciprocal flow of gifts and credit from benefactor to recipient and back. For within a gift economy, the act of giving, or the extension of credit, is a sign of trust in the other's ability and worthiness. The recipient knows this, and understands his honour to be at stake in the obligation to reciprocate, thus 'ending up on the right side in the process of gift giving'.[7] Marcel Mauss has spoken of the way in which honour is linked to 'the meticulous repayment with interest of gifts that have been accepted, so as to transform into persons having an obligation those that have placed you yourself under a similar obligation.'[8] An example of the signifying power of timely reciprocity, in which the recipient acknowledges trust and returns benefits, is clearly articulated, as we saw in the previous chapter, in William Painter's dedication of the second volume of his *Palace of Pleasure* to George Howard:

> This the second [volume] by like band, your Worship may justly claime as a just tribute nowe this moneth of Novembre payable. Or if your Curtesie woulde not deale so roughly with your bounden creditour, yet for duties sake I must aquite and content that which hath so long ben due. The same I offer now, not with such usurie and gaine as your benevolence and singular bountie, by long forebearing, hath deserved, but with such affected will and desire of recompense, as any man alive can owe to so rare a friend.[9]

Painter's text fits decorously into the model of gift-friendship, and becomes a rich sign of recompense for benefits received. This is precisely, however, what the texts of the self-styled 'prodigals' of the 1570s and 1580s did not, or could not, become. Indeed, their rhetoric of prodigality may be interpreted as acknowledging themselves guilty of the anticipation, or imposture, of a relation of trust and indebtedness to a powerful friend. It is as if the prodigal author, by projecting among indifferent readers a potential benefactor, had implicitly perverted the 'true' nature of the book as a gift to a benefactor in gratitude for benefits received, and had attempted to transform it instead into an instantaneous source of credit. For the prodigal is, by definition, one whose self-love (*philautia*) anticipates the benefactor's trust in him, and aims 'to hazard that goodwill and credite . . . to gain more'.[10]

The difficulty faced by the authors who styled themselves as 'prodigal' in this way was quite real. For humanism's transformation of service relations among the elite from retainership to knowledge-transaction posed a considerable problem in the question of initiating the relationship of patron and client, or lord and scholarly servant. In his work on the importance of published translations as a means of gaining patronage, Warren Boutcher notes that the 'relative visibility' of the sixteenth-century translator contributes to our understanding of his choice of text and approach: 'A socially marginal translator may be offering an advertisement of his humanistic qualifications in specific areas, such as secretarial, political or diplomatic work, and even his usefulness to specific causes.'[11] We speak easily of the printed text's advertising function, but only with difficulty could such a model for the mobilization of relations of mutual obligation between strangers be reconciled with the assumption that such relations were and should be grounded in the proximity of kinship and/or neighbourhood, making the dedicator of a text a man who was already reciprocating benefits received from his 'friend'.

It seems, then, that the texts that took refuge in the rhetoric of prodigality during the 1570s and 1580s were engaged in producing a solution to the impropriety of their own use of print, and their advertisement of skills in probable argument, as means of initiating the kind of relationship traditionally founded in long-term familiarity and mutual good faith. Thus, in republishing the text of his *A Hundreth Sundrie Flowres* after it was banned by the Court of High Commission, George Gascoigne was forced to acknowledge that the tactics he had adopted to make the book look like a private gift were nothing but a fiction to conceal the text's function as advertiser of his talents to a benefactor as yet unknown. He further admitted that the subject matter of the book – including, as it did, fictions which frankly advertised the usefulness of rhetorical methods of proof in promoting adulterous liaisons and clandestine marriages – was not the most appropriate advertisement of his fitness for employment. 'But', as he wrote,

> since the oversight of my youth had broughte me farre behind hande and indebted unto the world, I thought good in the meane time to pay as much as I had, untill it might please God better to inable me. For commonly the greediest creditor is appeased, if he see his debitor willing to pay any thing. And therefore being busied in martiall affairs (whereby I also sought some advauncement) I thought good to notifie unto the world before my returne, that I could as well persuade with Penne, as pierce with launce or weapon; so that yet some noble mind might be incouraged to exercise me in time of peace.'[12]

The rhetoric of prodigality is enabling for Gascoigne here in two ways. First, it excuses the impropriety of 'claiming credit' or coming into print without already having a benefactor to whom to give ('dedicate') the text. Second, it pretends to disown the inherently 'prodigal' or credit-abusing potential of arguments which work by ambiguity, arousing anxious conjecture (what Gascoigne calls a 'jealous suppose'[13]) by characterizing the heroes of conjectural argument (Master F.J. and Erostrato in *The Supposes*) as admonitory examples, moral allegories of his own mis-spent youth. Gascoigne's avowedly 'prodigal' text, therefore, both disowns and advertises the efficiency of a mode of writing which works by witholding interpretative assurance, and which refuses to become obliged by what it may seem to have promised.[14] Clearly, it was this mode of writing which Gascoigne wanted his readers to be impressed by, even as he tried to contain (by moral signposting) its apparently disturbing implications. An attitude of repentant prodigality was adopted so as to have it both ways: 'For although I have been heretofore contented to suffer the publication hereof, only to the ende men might see my Methode and maner of writing', he wrote, 'yet I am nowe thus desirous to set it forth eftsoone, to the ende all men might see the reformation of my minde.'[15]

Gascoigne set the example for the strategies of self-presentation used by other authors. Thomas Lodge, defending the value of Terentian-style comedy and Euripidean tragedy as bases for an English drama in his reply to Stephen Gosson's *The School of Abuse*, was then subject to a personal attack in print by Stephen Gosson in *Playes confuted in five Actions*. Lodge responded in a way which perhaps seems curious to us, with a text entitled *An Alarum against Usurers*, exposing the practices by which usurious creditors exploited needy and prodigal debtors in contemporary London.[16] Other prodigals, such as John Lyly and George Whetstone went straight into repentance, combining in a single text models of persuasive reasoning, and admonition against the abuses of credit and friendship with which it was associated. Thus Lyly's *Euphues* is both a 'Titus and Gisippus'-style betrayal of Philautus by Euphues, *and* the story of Euphues as the prodigal son (for *philautia*, or self-love, is the attribute of the prodigal).[17] George Whetstone's *Rocke of Regarde* addresses itself to 'young gentlemen' who tend to be 'tired out right with prodigalitie'. After sections devoted to sonnets, and to the retelling of Bandellian narratives addressed to women, it ends with an account of the 'adventures of P. Plasmos', recognizably identified as a young prodigal:

And nowe to the condition of P. Plasmos in the prime of his unthriftines it appeareth by his fonde triumph that hee was infected with [self-love] the overthrow of many younge Gentlemen, who seeing sufficiencie in themselves to be advaunced, to winne credite and acquaintaunce, so farre passe the boundes of their abilitie, that long before countenaunce taketh note of their desertes . . . they are gladde of meane maintenaunce at home with their friendes.[18]

Now, the story of the prodigal son is irreversibly gendered, but it is not clear at this point why the configuration of author–reader relations which it seeks to articulate should likewise be so, nor what the implications of their emplotment in the fiction of prodigality would be for women writers.

We are lucky enough, however, to have an example of a woman writer of the 1570s who, like the prodigals, wished to use print to initiate a credit relation, that is, to find herself employment. Isabella Whitney's *A Sweet Nosgay, or pleasant Posye*, published in 1573 (the same year as Gascoigne's *Hundreth Sundrie Flowres*) is both self-conscious and ironic about about the impropriety of claiming gift-status for the nosegay/text that is, in fact, shamelessly constructed as an artefact intended to initiate a service relation, through its rhetorical demands upon the reader's credit. Whitney goes beyond her male counterparts in admitting to the lack of ability to reciprocate that prevents others from giving her credit, and obliges her to improvise a fiction of ability in print, being 'so weake in Purse' that 'none me credit dare'.[19] But even as her assessment of the problem seems more sharply perceptive than the cumbrous fictions of prodigality, it is also, for that very reason, less productive as a legitimating rhetoric.

Whitney opens her *Swete Nosgay, or pleasant Posye: contayning a hundred and ten Phylosophicall Flowers*, by materializing the metaphorical *florilegium* in an intimate gesture of giving: 'When I (good M. MAINWARING) had made this simple Nosgay: I was in minde to bestow the same on som dere frind, of which number I have good occasion to accompt you chiefe (sig. A4r). Reflections on the inadequacy of the gift and the extent of her indebtedness, however, catch the gesture up in hesitant deliberation:

> But waying with my selfe, that although the Flowers bound
> in the same were good, yet so little of my labour was in them
> that they were not . . . to bee esteemed as recompence for the

least of a great number of benefits, which I have from time
to time (even from our Childhood hetherto) receaved of
you: Yet least by me, you might be occasioned to say, as
ANTIPATER said by DEMADES of Athens, that he should
never [fi]ll him with geveing, I woulde to shewe my self
satisfied, gratifye your Guifts; . . . But ceasing to seeke by
benefits . . . to accquit your curtesies, I come to present you
like the pore man which having no goods, came with his
handes full of water to meett the Persian Prince withall, who
respecting the good wyll of the man, did not disdayne his
simple Guift: even so, I being willinge to bestow some
Present on you, by the same thinking to make parte of
amendes for the much you have merited, to performe the
dutie of a friend, to expresse the good wyll that should rest
in Countrie folke & not having of mine owne to discharg
that I go about (like to that pore Fellow, which went into an
others ground for his water) did step into anothers garden
for these Flowers.

(sig. A4^r)

For all the clumsiness of the repeated conjunctions 'but' and
'yet', the reasoning here is tautly controlled, and its objectives clear.
Like Margaret Tyler recalling the 'manifolde benefits receyved' of
Thomas Howard's parents, or Barnabe Googe 'accounting [him]-
selfe as bounde' for the 'nombred heapes of sundry frendshypps'
extended to him by William Lovelace, dedicatee of his *Eglogs,
Epitaphes and Sonettes*,[20] Whitney articulates her book as the token
acquittal of a debt which belongs to that category of credit relations
characterized by Marshall Sahlins as a 'generalised reciprocity',
that is, the 'overwhelming but unspecified obligation to reciprocate'
obtaining in the exchanges of benefits within families, or between
dependents or friends who are 'close'. I use the last word advisedly,
for Sahlins' model makes relations of credit in pre-capitalist society
intelligible in terms of a scheme of reciprocities traversable along
an axis of 'kinship distance'. Thus, the 'closer' the relationship
(whether in kinship, or in affection, or in such physical proximity as
neighbours or household members) the more its credit relations
conform to the extreme of 'generalised reciprocity'. At the other
end of the spectrum, the 'distance' between participants in an
exchange (foreigners, strangers, even enemies) requires that their
relations of exchange and credit involve the mistrustful anticipation

of each other's double-dealing in cunning bargaining and pitiless usury.[21] Whitney's invocation of a shared childhood and 'the good wyl that should rest in Countrie folke' (by which she means inhabitants of the same county) thus serves to narrow the 'kinship distance' between herself and Mainwaring in the eyes of readers, even as the genre in which she expresses their relation – the printed epistle – inevitably exploits a fiction of physical distance or absence between friends as a pretext for creating a public and enduring illusion of closeness.[22]

None of this was new when Whitney wrote, of course; Natalie Davis, in a lecture drawing on the theories of Mauss and Sahlins, has drawn our attention to a medieval tradition in which the transmission of learning in manuscript was considered to be a part of the responsible stewardship of God's gifts. This tradition persisted into the age of print, so that the sixteenth-century printed anthology was offered, similarly, as a gift or acquittal of debts. Commenting on the difference made to the nature of gift-exchange by the advent of the printed book, Davis notes that the 'printed epistle now carried the patron's praise far and wide, both adding to the value of the gift for the recipient and taxing the donor's ingenuity in finding ways to multiply dedications for the same work'.[23] In fact, of course, the latter aspect tends to negate the former, or at least, it disturbs the conceptual *direction* of the flow of benefits from donor to dedicatee, since the obligation extending into the future created by the act of giving is anticipated, even pre-empted by the credit claimed in the advertisement of the text's gift-relation to the recipient. The gesture of giving or accrediting *in print* is thus constantly in danger of cancelling out, by anticipation, the temporality of reciprocity, and reversing itself to become an improvisation or fiction of credit instantaneously accruing to the author as the professed 'friend' of the dedicatee.

Whitney seems to have to have been aware of this effect of print; indeed, it would not be too much to say that is one of the themes of her book, taken as a whole. The book is explicitly divided, by changes of typeface, into three discrete sections, the first of which, thus 'presented' to Mainwaring, is the collection of Hugh Platt's *Floures of philosophie* (originally published in 1572) turned into verse (sigs B2r-C5r). Following this, a section of 'Certain familiar Epistles and frendly letters by the Author: with replies' (sigs C6r-E2r) dramatizes Whitney's friendly relations with a range of correspondents. These seem to form an extended kin group: brothers, sisters, a cousin and two friends to whom she signs herself, variously, 'your lovyng (though lucklesse) sister', 'your loving sister', 'your poorer kinswoman', 'your welwiler', 'your welwiling Countriwoman' and 'your most lovyng Cosyn'. Reading through the letters, one is struck by the way in which they exploit the condition of being physically separate from friends as a pretext for the articulation of exchanges of counsel, appeals for help, enquiries after health that are public proof of 'friendship'. Thus Whitney begins with an appeal to her 'brother G.W.' to let her know of his vacation whereabouts so that she may 'hearken' of his 'health' and inform him of the ill luck that obliges her to rely on friends:

> But styll to friendes I must appeale
> (and next our parentes dere)
> You are, and must be chiefest staffe
> that I shall stay on heare.
>
> (sig. C6^r)

The letters are far, however, from being reducible to appeals for help on the author's behalf; they constitute a varied exchange, one of the effects of which is to build up an image of the reliability and soundness of Whitney's own judgement as a counsellor to relatives and friends. To one 'Master T.L.' she writes, remarking that his good nature is abused by professed friends who 'fleece' him of his goods. Her analysis of the situation resembles the arguments of the humanists against bachelorhood: 'He that hath not a wife, . . . is alwaies left alone and forsaken. His servauntes steele from hym, his felowes bribe from him, his neighboures dispise him, his frendes regard him not.'[24] So, too, T.L.'s plight is in Whitney's view the consequence of his 'single state' and she advises him to marry (sig. D7^v). A verse prefatory to the whole book 'in commendation of the author' suggests that these letters be read as proof of the practical operation of the moral philosophy expressed in the 'Flowers': 'And that it is no fable, you shall see, / For here at large the sequel will declare / To Cuntrey warde, her love and friendly care' (sig. B1^v).

In this new context, as part of the drama of affective and instrumental friendships played out in her verse letters, the gift-aspect of the moral theory of friendship, the 'nosegay', suddenly makes its appearance again, this time as if intended for another recipient. Having written to her brother in request of news and of help Isabella begs, in return, that he should

> Receave of me, and eke accept
> a simple token heare:
> A smell of such a Nosegay as
> I do for present beare
> unto a vertuous ladye, which
> tyl death I honour wyll.
> The losse I had of service hers,
> I languish for it styll.
>
> (sig. C6ᵛ)

Of course, it might be said that the 'nosegay', being a collection of rhetorical material, is a gift in which all readers have a share, but Whitney's ingenious use of the metaphor of scent (which might be taken to express the inability of a 'nosegay' to be depleted or devalued by being shared) actually has the effect of making us more aware than before of the extent to which giving in print corresponds to the creation of a *fiction* of a relation constituted through the reciprocal exchange of benefits which elicits from readers the benefits of 'credit' as an author. Offering a scent of the printed nosegay in the first of her printed familiar epistles, Whitney draws attention to the function of both (i.e., the book itself) as ambassadors of her merits to the 'vertuous ladye' for whom, lacking a referent, the reader is irresistibly compelled to construct a hypothetical existence which in turn reflects back on, or 'advertises' Whitney's readiness to serve in some virtuous employment.

Whitney's familiar epistles come to a comically abrupt end when the author suddenly declares herself 'wery of writing', and expresses her leave-taking of the rhetorically purposive genre of the epistle by means of a mock will and testament. The mock will and testament was, as I have argued elsewhere, recognized in the sixteenth century as having links with the popular festive pastime, and the menippean 'true confession from the underworld', in which unreliable travellers or dying festival fools expose the madness and hypocrisy of 'things as they are' in the real world.[25] In literary terms the mock testament tends to lay bare the material bases of a genre's intelligibility to readers. Thus it is that Whitney's testament abruptly reverses and abandons the improvisation of credit through the epistolary invocation of friends and admits, with an endearing irony, the exigency and over-extension of resources that motivates coming into print in London:

> The Aucthour (though loth to leave the Citie) upon her friendes procurement, is constrained to departe: wherfore (she fayneth as she would die) and maketh her WYLL and Testament, as foloweth: With large Legacies of such Goods and riches which she most aboundantly hath left behind her: and ther of maketh LONDON sole executor to se her Legacies performed.
>
> (sig. E2^r)

London, both executor and bequest, is fondly characterized as the heartless friend, whose economy belies the rules of reciprocity and kinship distance, since all here, even neighbours, live amidst an abundance of goods and services that must be openly and immediately transacted for ('Thou never yet, woldst credit geve / To boord me . . . Nor with Apparel me releve, / Except thou payed weare' (sig. E2^v)). Consequently, while enumerating the riches that are also uncompromisingly financial regulators of conduct and position, Whitney dramatizes herself as entirely without place:

> What makes you standers by to smile,
>   and laugh so in your sleeve[?]
> I thinke it is, because that I
>   to Ludgate nothing geve.
> I am not now in case to lye
>   here is no place of jest:
> I dyd reserve, that for my selfe,
>   yf I my health possest
> And ever came in credit so
>   a debtor for to bee.
> When dayes of paiment did approch
>   I thither ment to flee
> To shroude my selfe amongst the rest,
>   that chuse to dye in debt;
> Rather then any Creditor
>   should money from them get.
> Yet cause I feele my selfe so weake
>   that none mee credit dare:
> I heere revoke: and doo it leave
>   some *Bankrupts* to his share.
>
> (sig. E6^r)

Whereas we think of poverty as insolvency, and assume indebtedness to define a potentially insecure state of accountability, Whitney expresses even the temporally specific entrustment of being someone's debtor in London as being very desirable, if only she could bring it about. 'Whole in body and in minde / But very weake in Purse' (sig. E3^r), the testament ironically belies the preceding fiction of a generalized indebtedness to friends and kin, revealing indebtedness itself as a prosperity comically beyond the author's reach. Translating herself as a speaking subject into the marketplace in which her fiction is due to appear, Whitney confesses, with astonishing candour, the rhetorical trick of mobilizing credit in print; for all the circulation of epistolatory credit in her fiction, London offers no sanctuary to the author who cannot incur a friendly debt, being 'so weake / that none mee credit dare' unless, of course, as she goes on to say, 'these Bookes' that she is presently in process of writing come to be bought by actual and potential 'friends' (sig. E6^r).

Read in the context of the prodigal anthologies of poetry and fiction composed by men in the 1570s, Whitney's text is striking for its awareness that one of the newly emerging social uses of the printed book – the initiation of a credit relation through indication of readiness for service – could perfectly well be adapted to women's needs. Women too have friends, need to borrow money and to live somewhere, and are capable of producing fiction and poetry in the interests and on the topics of these relations and wants. What Whitney's text makes us aware of, in other words, is the strict irrelevance to a real woman writer of the figure of female sexual betrayal which always lurks somewhere about the plot of author–reader relations as articulated by the Elizabethan prodigals.

The rhetoric of prodigality, I would argue, contributed to the legitimation of masculine authorship at the expense of sexualizing the terms of women's relation to rhetoric and to publication.[26] Prohibiting women thus from access to the production and transmission of texts was fundamental to the process by which such textual exchanges became, for men, the dominant medium of credit extension and friendly relationship. In the next two sections of this chapter, I shall explore aspects of this process, by examining the ways in which stories of actual or potential female prostitution were employed by men to give imaginative form to the displacement of credit from a bond of trust based in kinship or neighbourhood, to a more fickle and easily transferable benefit to be bestowed and acquired through the exercise of probable argument.

THE RHETORICAL GIFT OF ANGELICA: HOW THE TEXT CANCELS 'KINSHIP DISTANCE'

When Whitney hesitates over the presumption of giving so inadequate a gift to Mainwaring, she eases her embarrassment by invoking the example of the Persian Prince Artaxerxes, who famously recompensed with gold the handful of water offered him by a dutiful subject, 'as occasion of the place, and myne abilitie at this instant serveth'.[27] The example appeared so often in printed dedications that it became a joke; presenting his translation of Virgil to his brother in 1582, Richard Stanyhurst laughed at the 'swarme' of unlatined *'wooden rhythmours'* whose books invariably boast *'Artaxerxes*, al be yt hee bee spurgalde, beeing so much gallopt . . . in thee dedicatorye epistle'.[28] And according to Nashe in 1593, there was no author that Harvey could cite 'which hee hath not stalefied worse then . . . the presenting of *Artaxerxes* with a cup of water, usde in every Epistle Dedicatorie'.[29] As early as 1563, Lawrence Humphrey calls Artaxerxes an 'olde forsworne president', deploring his own deployment of the example as an argument to persuade the gentlemen of the Inner Temple to receive the gift of his *Of Nobilitye* 'Probablie', he writes,

> it is my constraint of proffering, emplieth your necessitie of taking . . . But with more force to move ye . . . somewhat meane I to saye, whye ye ought to take it. With open mouth loe curtesy, the refuge, roade & succour of al afflicted, the patronesse of hartye though meanest presentes: fearing stayne in ye in this, crieth ye may not spurne so humble, so iust, so hearty proffer. Now hyeth she to vouch her old forsworne presidentes, of . . . *Artaxerxes*, who so much prised, the heaved up handes of his well wishing subject, though but filled with water: as he bought the liccour with golde.[30]

Humphrey here admits the contradiction involved in the concept of the dedication as both a gesture of giving and an argued case for its own gracious reception. After all, if the dedicatee is under 'necessity of taking' by the author's public 'constraint in proffering', the affective proof is redundant, for the transaction may be said to have already happened. And this explains why socially marginal authors could not, as Stanyhurst noted, dispense with Artaxerxes, whose example articulates a sense in which the gift is not, in fact, an acquittal of debts, but a demand for credit. The gift is merely the signal, from the donor in straitened circumstances, of an 'ability' which will be much more valuable to his friend when his cupped hands have been symbolically transformed into a vessel of gold.

Geoffrey Fenton's *Tragicall Discourses* opens with a story about this very difficulty, in which the barrier of kinship distance and of the embarrassed 'inability' of the poor but nobly educated man who has received credit from his erstwhile foe, are overcome by the passive 'becoming visible' of a potential gift in his possession which needs only to be rhetorically offered to elicit more credit, and thus become the basis of a lasting and productive exchange. The story was imitated by Thomas Heywood as the sub-plot of his Xenophonic play of good husbandry, *A Woman Killed with Kindness*. As Heywood's adaptation shows, the question of propriety in 'kindness' – that is, the extension of credit to those who are or are not 'kin' – is assumed to be one with the question of *oikonomia*, or wife-taming. An examination of how Fenton's story might have been read and understood by men like Heywood, then, should prove revealing.

In Fenton's story, the city of Siena harbours two noble families, the Salimbeni and the Montanini, who, in spite of their parents having been 'mirrours . . . of perfect frendship',[31] had become such irreconcilable enemies that eventually the sole survivors of the feud on the Montanini side were Charles and his sister Angelica. Angelica was endowed with such beauty that even those that hated the Montanini 'could not close their mouthes from her due commendation'. 'Suche', Fenton reasons of Angelica,

> is the operacion and force of true vertue . . . exposinge in lyke sorte suche frutes as seame wondrous in the eye of the worlde, and excede the common imaginacion of men, by reducinge the confusion of kindreds into an entier of ever-lastyng amytie, and of a mortall enemy to make a most assured frende.
>
> (fol. 6ʳ)

The friend eventually assured by the 'operacion and force' of Angelica is an heir of the Salimbeni, Anselmo, who becomes 'most subject to the viewe and contemplation of her beautie' (fol. 6ᵛ). As Angelica becomes visible to the family enemy, the 'glisteringe shewe' of the Montanini property, 'in the open gaze and eye of the whole worlde passing by in the streetes' (fol. 10ʳ) is desired by a 'peltynge marchaunt never nourished in anye skole of cyvill or curteous education' (fol. 10^r) who, 'thinkinge it no offence or grudge of his conscience to enlarge his livynge with the porcion of his neyghboure'(fol. 8^r), tries to force Montanino into selling his patrimony. In refusing, Montanino falls foul of a law according to which noblemen living in Siena must pay a tax of 5000 ducats or lose their lives. Being 'not hable to levye by any credit or assistaunce of his frendes' (fol. 11^r) the required sum, Montanino offers his house as security for 5000 ducats to the merchant, but the latter, now sure of profiting by his death, argues that the value of 'so small a plat of inheritaunce' is not worth the 'use and interest of so greate a summe of money' (fol. 11^r). None of the Sienese citizens are able to help, 'seing their maister usurer made dif-ficultie to advaunce the value'(fol. 11^r), and it falls to Anslemo Salimbeno to consider the redemption of the enemy of his kin. At first he thinks of Charles' death as his opportunity to enjoy Angelica, but pages of deliberation on the virtue of liberality make him decide, nobly, to pay all the Montanini debts with interest. As Bandello, in the original of Fenton's history, exclaims:

> Che un amico per suo amico, un parente per l'altro, o chi si sia, con sicurezza o pegno in mano, paghi per altri danari, non e percio cosa che tutto il di tra uomini non si costumi. Ma un nemico voluntarimente paghi buona somma de moneta per te, ne motto te ne faccia, o riccerchi esser de la restituzione cauta, questa e ben cosa insolita, mirabile, lodevole, e cortesissima liberalita, che di rado, anzi forse che non mai fu usata.

> That one friend or kinsman should pay money for another, or that anyone should do so with security or a pledge in hand, happens every day. But that an enemy should volun-tarily pay a great sum of money without requiring a word, or being at all cautious about repayment, is surely a most unusual, wonderful, praiseworthy and most courteous liber-ality which has rarely, perhaps never before, occurred.[32]

Such liberality naturally obliges Charles to his old enemy, but he finds himself with nothing worthy 'to present the frendshipp of SALIMBENO' except himself and his lovely sister, who protests violently against the proposed 'prostitution of her chastity' only agreeing on the condition that, having presented 'this pore carkasse' to Salimbeno, her brother will not prevent her immediate suicide (fol. 26ᵛ). Montanino's position, then, is recognizably that of the prodigal author whose potential for service must somehow become known through being presented in such a way as to anticipate and elicit the credit that will enable him to be in a position to bestow real benefits. So Salimbeno, moved by the hyperbole of trust implied by Montanino's dedication of his unendowed, unallied and penurious sister, responds by turning her from a rhetorical into a real gift: presenting her with a rich dowry so that she will be a worthy match for him, and dividing his land with her brother, so that he will be an able ally and brother-in-law.

Anselmo's recognition of the 'vertue' of Charles Montanin in the beauty of Angelica may be understood as a metaphor for a noble stranger's recognition of the virtue of an educated mind in a well-made text. Thus Gascoigne, as we saw, published to reveal 'the qualityes of minde' as 'correspondent to the proportion of my bodie'.[33] What needs to be emphasized in this reading, however, is that the woman, as metaphor for publication, does not function as a token of alliance according to 'the supreme rule of the gift', but rather expresses the way in which the 'gift' itself has become problematically identified with the social agency of persuasive communication between men.

The story thus legitimates a textualized *amicitia*, or an 'entier of everlasting amytie' above the principle of kinship or 'kindred' as the basis for masculine friendship and credit relations. In doing so, however, it makes Angelica's sexuality bear the symbolic burden of uncertainty as to whether or not Charles Montanin was making a 'prodigal offer', hazarding the chance of Anselmo's refusal, or offering a real gift of value to the house of Montanin. Either Angelica meant to die, or Charles is a fake, a prodigal and hypocrite; who knows?

In Heywood's well-known adaptation, *A Woman Killed with Kindness*, this uncertainty about Charles' intention is identified with the emotionally persuasive power of Heywood's dramatic fiction itself. At the same time, the moral ambiguity implied by this identification is contained in the main plot's redefinition of such dramatic communication as the 'kindness' which deals so effectively with the threat of adultery (i.e., it persuades an adulterous wife to die).

Thus it is that in Heywood's play, the plots of *amicitia* (the reconciliation of enemies through the rhetorical gift of a sister) and of *oikonomia* (taming of a wife by rhetorical and histrionic skill) are dialectically related. Both dramatize the problems of extending credit to men who are not kinsmen without either forcing them into positions of servitude, or suffering their encroachment upon one's own estate and kinswomen. The heroes of both plots – Charles Mountford and John Frankford – face antithetical versions of the same dilemma. Frankford's gentlemanly independence in liberality is the mirror image of Mountford's gentlemanly independence in extreme want, and as Mountford's depends on a sister's uncertain chastity, so Frankford's depends on the uncertain possession of a wife:

> I am a gentleman, and by my birth
> Companion with a king; a king's no more
> I am possessed of many fair revenues
> Sufficient to maintain a gentleman.
> Touching my mind, I am studied in all arts,
> The riches of my thoughts, and of my time
> Have been a good proficient. But the chief
> Of all the sweet felicities on earth,
> I have a fair, a chaste and loving wife.[34]

By the early seventeenth century it had become a commonplace to observe that kings, while they might create noblemen, could not create gentlemen. But while such formulations enhanced the pride and independence of the gentry, they simultaneously drew attention to the difficulty of imagining, in response to their implicit rejection of relations of feudal dependence, a new basis for the contracting of credit relations between gentlemanly equals. Thus, Mountford, reduced to utter poverty, betrayed by the usury of a so-called friend and unfriended by his own kin, cancels out the inconceivable obligation of servitude to the enemy who has paid his debts by offering him his sister, Susan. But the gesture, in Heywood, is explicitly theatrical, calculated to move his old enemy, to 'amaze his senses, and surprise / With admiration all his faculties', so that he will respond, as he does, by endowing the sister and proclaiming, 'All's mine is yours: we are alike in state'.[35] The complementary plot concerning John Frankford is linked through Frankford's receiving of the intelligence of Mountford's affairs from a man to whom he then extends liberal credit and friendship: 'Had the news been better / Your will was to have brought it, Master Wendoll', he says, 'I know you sir, to be a gentleman / In all things, your possibilities but mean; / Please you to use my table and my purse.'[36] Wendoll, however, repays this kindness with sexual betrayal, as if compelled by Frankford's over-precipitate cancellation of kinship distance.'This kindness grows of no alliance between us', is his puzzled comment,

> I never bound him to me by desert.
> Of a mere stranger, a poor gentleman,
> A man by whom in no kind could he gain,
> He hath placed me in the height of all his thoughts . . .
> And shall I wrong this man? . . .
> And yet I must. Then, Wendoll, be content;
> Thus villains when they would cannot repent.[37]

As the dearth of 'kin' or 'kindness' which threatens Mountford's gentlemanly estate is overcome by an effective rhetorical show of 'kindness' (pretending to offer his sister) so the too-great familiarity or 'kindness' shown by Wendoll to Frankford's wife is neutralized as a threat to Frankford's gentlemanly estate by the Xenophonic 'kindness' with which the good husband punishes his wife. Heywood, who was clearly interested in the Xenophonic emphasis on the importance of theatrical role-play in the practice of husbandry, draws continual analogies between the real economy of Frankford's estate, and the rhetorical economy of discursive ability by which he maintains it. Thus, for example, Frankford's decision to isolate his adulterous wife in another mansion from his own is articulated both as proof of his substantial wealth, and of the prudence and sense of decorum which defines him as a gentleman: 'A man cannot say by my old Master Frankford . . . that he wants manners, for he hath three or four', quips the servant, leading Frankford's wife away kindly to her death.[38]

EQUITABLE REMEDIES FOR A LOSS OF TRUST: COMMUNICATING THE DISORDERED LIFE OF THE COUNTESS

Fenton's story of Angelica Montanini, and Heywood's adaptation of the story in *A Woman Killed with Kindness*, both demonstrate the indispensability of fictions of women to the humanist reconceptualization of men's economic and social dependencies, or friendships. In the final section of this chapter I want to explore the way in which women were fictively implicated in what might be argued was the most serious and consequential aspect of the reconceptualization of friendship in sixteenth-century England: the crisis of usury. Economic and social historians have tended to portray the sixteenth-century debate for and against the legalization of interest as a struggle between the forces of religion and capitalism, or between material and spiritual cultural values.[39] In the context of the present book, which is throughout concerned with the effects of humanism's textualization of masculine social agency, the representation of usury is of interest because it focuses the issues in a broader struggle over the signifying power of material exchanges in the formation of relationships. Thus, where other discussions of usury in this period deal with the direction of the theological debate, or ways of charging interest, or with technical definitions of kinds of usury, I shall concentrate on the meaning of usury as a symptom of the displacement of friendship from its position as the primary objective of (non-mercantile) credit extension. Seen from this perspective, the crisis of usury becomes moral and semantic as well as material, involving questions about how to signify good faith, and how to assure the fulfilment of promises without evacuating the practical and emotional bonds of mutual trust. These questions, I shall argue, found their solution not in parliamentary debates for or against the legality of interest, but in the humanistic changes of legal procedure which were formally expressed both in the drama of the period, and in stories such as the following about a usurer's daughter.

Much of the prodigal fiction of the 1570s and 1580s redeems its own impostures of credit through fictions addressed to, and about, women. Thus, although Whetstone's *Rocke of Regarde* is, as a whole, addressed to 'young gentlemen' in danger of being 'tired out ryght with prodigalitie', the first of its stories is an admonition to women, a warning against the 'wanton toyes' which are 'read in thousand bookes'[40] of the depraved life of the Countess of Celant. The Countess' sensational story was famous in its time; John Marston wrote a play (*The Insatiate Countess*) about it. For us it is conveniently summarized by Paul Salzman:

> Bianca Maria, the title character, is married at 16 to Viscount Hermes, who recognizes her 'wanton spirit' and keeps her, accordingly, in check. After his death she marries the Count of Celant, who promises her liberty within marriage; she

soon leaves him to live a promiscuous life in Pavia. She is courted by Valperga, Count Massimo, soon tires of being his mistress, and turns to his friend, Roberto Sanseverino, Count Gaiazzo. When Valperga, after this ill-treatment, makes her character known, she tries to persuade Sanseverino to challenge him, his refusal to attack leads to his rejection by the Countess, who returns her favours to Valperga, and tries to persuade him to murder Sanseverino. The two friends put their heads together and realize the wickedness of the Countess, whose true character they proceed to reveal at every opportunity, driving her out of Pavia to Milan. There she captures the heart of Pietro de Cardone, an inexperienced young Sicilian, who is easily persuaded to take revenge on the Countess's two former lovers . . . He kills Valperga, and reveals the Countess's part in the murder after he is imprisoned, saving his own life and beheading her. The Countess confesses her faults on the scaffold before being beheaded.[41]

No wonder Whetstone addressed the story to women readers. It is obviously an admonitory tale about the consequences of not obeying husbands. But why tell it in an anthology otherwise devoted to the composition of songs and sonnets by men, and the exposure of the 'new kinde of usuries' practised by merchants on young gentlemen?

Although Salzman does not mention this detail, Bianca Maria is supposed by Bandello to be of *legnaggio non molto stimato* (a lineage of low esteem)[42], being the daughter of a usurer of Casale in Montferrato, and his Greek wife, erstwhile servant of the house of Mantua.[43] Usury, however, seems to play no great part in the action, until, at a climactic point in the story, when Valperga and Sanseverino exclaim: 'Is it possible that the earth can breede a more pernicious monster than this most pestilent beast? This is truely the gift of her father's usury.'[44] Painter here follows Belleforest closely: 'Est-il possible que la terr nourisse un Monstre plus pernicieux que ceste malheureuse? C'este vrayment la lie des usures de son pere.' 'La lie' though related to the verb 'lier', to bind, actually means the thickened binding agent, the dregs, and so figuratively refers to the baseness of Bianca Maria's usurious descent.[45] Painter's translation, however, points in another direction. Lineage is an effect of alliance, which in turn binds by 'the supreme rule of the gift'. The symbolic power of the alliance/gift to bind men in long-term relations of mutual, friendly assurance becomes, in the person of Bianca Maria, a binding power to betray trust and divide and destroy men.

Shortly after their conference, the two noblemen resolve that, as it is 'the true marke and badge of nobility' (P.fol. 211^v) to communicate knowledge for the commonweal, they should publish their experience,

> and in all the companies where they came, the greatest parte of their talke and communication was of the disordered life of the Countess of *Celant*: the whole citie rang of the sleights and meanes she used to trappe the noble men, and of her pollicies to be rid of them.

> (P.fol. 211^v)

The reflexivity of this is obvious: in Belleforest's, Painter's and Fenton's versions, the novel is entitled *The Disordered Life of the Countess of Celant*; it is this publication which redounds to the credit of the author for the good of the commonweal. But the nature of the communication is not expressed in the idiom of sexual defamation: 'sleights and meanes' used to 'trappe the noble men' had a very specific resonance in the London of the second half of the sixteenth century in relation, not to women, but to the practice of usury, as exposed for gentleman readers by prodigal authors.[46]

It is not at all clear, however, why the 'sleights' and 'pollicies' of the sexually voracious Countess should thus take up the symbolic position of a discourse proving the humanistic 'nobility' of authors in uncovering the contractual abuses of the marketplace on behalf of the commonweal. Evidently, we need to examine more closely the ways in which Bandello's original novella has been adapted or re-emplotted by the French and English translators.

In Bandello's story the first husband of Bianca Maria, Ermes Vesconte, dies in the second paragraph, and Bianca Maria is being courted by two principal contenders, Gismondo Gonzago and the Count of Celant, Baron of Savoy. Bandello makes it clear that Gonzago is the favourite of the house of Mantua, and the Marquise of Montferrato is urging his suit, when, to her annoyance, the Count of Celant intervenes, and wins Bianca Maria by the sheer eloquence of his courtship.[47] Bandello's sentence to this effect becomes, in the French and English versions, a model 'Oration of the Count of Celant to his Ladie', running to several pages. Each version stresses, in military terms, the 'fine force' of the Count in intercepting the 'fynal consommacion' of Bianca Maria's marriage to Gonzago, and his prudence in using 'the nexte offer of conveniente tyme' to find his lady 'all alone & (as he thought) somewhat disposed to heare his discourse' (F.fol. 142^r). Although he could, he argues to her, allege 'a thousande other reasons' (F.fol. 143^r) to plead his cause, the oration is in fact built around two, both of which are immediately recognizable as opportunistic re-emplotments, in the prudential battle for victory over Gonzago's rights, of the narrative's own exemplary arguments addressed to readers. First Celant pleads a wife's right to liberty: 'Have you now forgot the sondrye miseries you endured under the gouvernement of your late husband, *Seigneur Hermes*?' (F.fol. 142^v). Next, he throws into doubt the reality of Bianca Maria's sense of obligation to the house of Mantua. As the narrative has stressed the physical emplotment of Casale as 'a percell of thinheritaunce of the *Marques montferrat*' (F.fol. 136^r), Celant's argument is clearly a tactical re-emplotment – backed, confusingly for women readers, by the authoritative marginal note: 'A contracte forced, is a vyolacion of mariage' (F.fol. 144^v). As the Count pauses in his speech, Bianca Maria replies evasively that 'the sondrie benefits of the Ladie marquesse had bounde her to a thankefull consideracion to her power' (F.fol. 143^v), an appeal to dependence on 'consent of friends' such as was used, as Church court records show, by women trying to avoid being drawn into binding themselves by a contractual promise to a man in conversation alone.[48] In the military and prudential terms in which the Count's courtship is expressed, however, this conditional response becomes a contingent time/space which it would be folly to waste: 'Therle, seynge so faire an enterey, . . . judged yt no point of good husbandry to loose his . . . corne for wante of getting' (F.fol. 144^r). He therefore 'recharged' Bianca Maria and urged her to 'assure me by the breath of your owne mouth of the faith and loyalty of maryage'(F.fol. 144^r). She is thus persuaded on the sudden, and they exchange promises in words of the present tense such as perform a binding contract, and leap into bed together, 'pour mieux asseurer le fait' as Belleforest drily comments.[49]

What has happened here? The narrators of each of these versions appear to have no doubt that, in intercepting Bianca Maria's impending marriage thus, the Count of Celant 'shewed forth his Nobleness of minde, when he understoode . . . that an other was ready to beare away the price' (P.fol. 199^r). At the same time, the narratives *foreground the merely probable nature of Celant's arguments* by virtue of having already used them to prove the opposite case: that firm husbands like Vesconte are good, and that real obligations bind young widows to the goodwill of their noble friends when making contracts of marriage. Celant's triumph therefore represents both an oratorical/prudential victory over fortune, and, at the same time, an ambivalent credit facility, a displacement of the binding force of the very 'faith and loyalty' he seeks to assure, from its basis in simple trust to a customary form of words, or code of behaviour, to its flexible mobility as a probable reason to be taken into consideration for or against the following of custom, or the trusting to forms of words.

The consequences of Celant's victory for the nobility in the world of the fiction is at first represented as a credit facility. After having been so easily persuaded by probable arguments to make a binding contract of marriage, Bianca Maria seems to become a catalyst for the making of false assurances. All her lovers promise largely, without thinking of words as pledges of faith to be redeemed. As Valperga and Sanseverino become rivals for the Countess's favours, these inflationary exchanges of credit multiply. The crisis is provoked by the Countess's exaction of deeds in accordance with the prodigal promises made to her by both her lovers; she wants them to destroy one another. Her apparent liberality of credit acquires its own sinister binding force in the form of 'using the advauntage of [their] promise[s]' (F.fol. 154^v) to destroy their 'mutual conversacion' (F.fol. 155^v). To understand how the story resolves this crisis of trust between men at the expense of women, we must digress to investigate historical links between humanism, usury and the development of contractual actions at common law.

THE DISPLACEMENT OF CONSCIENCE: FROM SPIRITUAL *FIDEI LAESIO* TO EQUITY AT COMMON LAW

In his chapter on 'faith or fidelitie, called in latyne FIDES' Sir Thomas Elyot defines the Latin term across a variety of kinds of relationship, to denote a bond of allegiance: 'belevynge the pre- ceptes and promyse of god it is called faythe. In contractes betwene man and man it is communely called credence. Betwene persons of equall astate or condition it is named truste.'[50] Moving on to consider promises, however, Elyot voices a lament to be heard more than once in the course of the century. The binding force of good faith, he writes,

> is now come into suche a generall contempt that all the lerned men in the lawes of this realme . . . can nat with all their study devise so sufficient an instrument, to bynde a man to his promise or covenaunte, but that there shall be some thinge therein espied to brynge it in argument if it be denyed. . . . Which is one of the principall decayes of the publike weale.[51]

In the late fifteenth and early sixteenth century, the ecclesiastical courts oversaw the enforcement of sworn promises through an action known as *fidei laesio*. The bulk of cases were commercial: the promise was usually a debt for goods purchased, but the issue was the danger to the defendant's soul in having violated his sworn promise. The action therefore pertained to the realm of conscience, of spiritual health, and it was brought *on the promise*, not the debt. There were signs, as R.H. Helmholz writes, of 'a quasi-religious seriousness with which many of the promises were made' and he cites examples: '"By my faith, I shall faithfully pay the said sum before the feast of Michaelmas next."' Often the promise was made with a pledge of faith *in manum dextram*.[52] At common law, however, verbal promises of this kind were not enforceable. No action of debt could lie on a mere promise to pay money, for this was a 'naked pact' or 'nude parol' and *ex nudo pacto non oritur actio*. The existing common law action of debt as failure to pay for material goods received, however, was practically useless; its method of proof was the archaic 'wager of law', for which a debtor had merely to swear his innocence of the charge, along with the help of eleven other compurgators, usually hired oath-helpers, known as 'knights of the post'.[53]

What took place in the course of the sixteenth century was this: the spiritual courts' hold over the action of promises disappeared completely between 1500 and 1550.[54] At the same time, the common law action of debt was clearly inadequate as a remedy for the growing numbers who found themselves in difficulty over the recovery of sums or goods owing to them. With the abolition of auricular confession, the ultimate court of conscience, and with the demise of the spiritual courts' extension of conscience into the realm of public expiation for promise-breakers, a legal and moral vacuum opened up around the practices of extending credit and assuring that promises would be fulfilled.

This is the moral and legal vacuum with which the humanistic literature of the 1560s and 1570s is intimately bound up. Gascoigne's *Supposes* (1573) turns on the impossibility of proving, in law, an imposture of identity, or a credit fraud. In the course of the play, there occurs an exchange in which the comedy's hero, Erostrato (who is a stranger in the town of Ferrara, where the comedy takes place), is masquerading as a servant called Dulippo, when he decides to confound the designs of his rival in love, the lawyer Cleander, by offering him some unhelpful information regarding his suit. Cleander begs to hear what the false Dulippo has to say, but Dulippo professes to want to be assured that Cleander will keep it confidential. 'What assurance shall I have?', he asks, and Cleander replies, 'I lay thee my faith and honesty in paune'. 'A pretie paune', comments the false Dulippo, 'the fulkers [Fuggers] will not lend you a farthing on it.' We should contrast this comment on the worthlessness of verbal assurances with the crisis in Fox's *Titus et Gesippus* in which a verbal agreement between Simo and Chremes is pledged *in manum dextram* and threatens to become actionable at law. Evidently Gascoigne's false Dulippo knows all about worthless assurances, since his very identity is one; and to the extent that he is the hero of the comedy, its hero is also the credit facility of his impostures, the 'supposes' that generate action without any accountability, or any basis in truth.[55]

Gascoigne's reference to the usurious securities of the Fuggers in this passage is also worth remarking, for this is his own addition to Ariosto's original, and it brings the English *Supposes*, published in the 1570s, into dialogue with contemporary debates on the meaning of trust and credit. In the debate on usury in the Parliament of 1571, Thomas Wilson 'by examples proved' the 'ruines of the commonwealth when such practices for gaine should be' and 'Hee heere shewed in the practise of the Lowe Countreys of Germany, and namely the doinge of the Fulkers to the verie beggaringe of greate and mighty Princes'.[56]

The 1560s and 1570s saw a huge rise in the volume of litigation connected with credit extension, debts and payments, bills and obligations; the incidence of bankruptcy also soared.[57] Everywhere one looks in the fiction and poetry of this period, one finds references to the difficulty of assuring the performance of verbal promises. We have already noted how the 'methode and maner of writing' of which Gascoigne was justly proud in his *Adventures of Master F.J.* characteristically secured the reader's credit precisely to the extent that it created uncertainty and lack of assurance about what was being promised by the text, and to whom. Anthologies of prose and poetry in these decades all register, with greater or lesser degrees of rhetorical sophistication, the implications of what Gascoigne first explored. So, for example, the most influential anthology of the period, the *Paradise of Dainty Devises* (1578) turns out to be far more concerned with the perplexing problems of assuring promises between men than with the vagaries of heterosexual love. Here is a typical selection of the sentiments expressed across a range of poems by different contributors: 'Beleeve not him that once hath broke his troth / Nor yet of gift without desert be free'; 'In my accompt the promise that is vowed / Among the good is holden such a debt'; 'By deedes in dout, as though no wordes can binde / O faithlesse freend, what can assure your mind'; 'Let not in word thy promise be more large: / Then thou in deede art willing to discharge'; *'Like well thy frende*, but trye him ere thou love'. Addressing the reader himself as a 'friend', certain of these poems appear to belie their own counsel, expecting to create credit through rhetorical proof, rather than a trial of trust.[58]

The figure of the usurer emerges in these years as the demonic personification of the rigidity of the common law over the question of 'nude parol' or verbal evidence for contracts. For the effect of the legal objection to 'nude parol' was twofold: as well as precluding the recovery of goods merely promised, it rendered void the use of verbal evidence as proof of a debt's discharge. In response to the first problem, creditors increasingly used sealed bonds to ensure that their debtors' promises were good in law; but a creditor was then in the position to sue twice on the same bond, if the debtor had not taken the precaution of getting written proof of having paid. The usurer, then, became by definition any creditor who, 'will have the parties that borrowes money of them wrapt in Statutes, and Bonds'[59], that is, any creditor who, justly fearful or mistrustful of extending credit on verbal promises, requested his debtor to be 'bound' in a sealed obligation to return the credit by a specific date. An unconscionable creditor might withold the bond, persuading the debtor with 'fained wordes' that 'bare wordes were good discharge / For matters of recorde'.[60]

An anonymous interlude of the 1560s, *Impatient Poverty*, demonstrates how the taking of bonds, though universally deplored, was practically necessitated by the way in which credit extension, in a gift economy, operates primarily as a sign of friendship and trust. Impatient Poverty, furious because 'A knave wolde have rested me, I owe him but xl pens', is advised by Peace to bear the insult to his good faith patiently and pay 'with fewe wordes dyscretelye / Another tyme ye shal be the better truste'. Impatient Poverty, however, vows to wage his law, or to 'let it be tryet by manhode'. Like Isabella Whitney, the fictive Impatient Poverty clearly regards his own indebtedness as a 'credit' to his trustworthiness, so that the precipitate calling in of the debt becomes a violation of that sign. In the circumstances, however, his impatience justifies the figure of 'Haboundance' in taking bonds for every petty sum owed to him when he 'sells for longe dayes', and in suing for the bond twice, even when his debtor has discharged payment.[61]

Thus it was that, as well as representing the procedural rigidity of the common law in relation to verbal promises, the usurer personified the crisis of 'friendship' in Marshall Sahlins' sense of a relation of 'balanced reciprocity' about half-way along the axis of 'kinship distance'. As antithetical to the 'true friend', however, the usurer is not detachable from the prodigal, for both collude in violating the rules of reciprocity and kinship distance. During the 1570s and 1580s, more and more young gentlemen from outlying counties were converging upon London, and demanding credit from strangers not as a sign of friendship, but rather as the prerequisite for acquiring powerful 'friends'. These are the types with whom Gascoigne identifies himself in *Woodmanship*, when he, deciding to try to win friends at court, 'shot the wronger way / Thinking the purse of prodigalitie / Had been best meane to purchase such a prey'. Such are also the young men to whom Whetstone addresses his *Rocke of Regarde*, prodigals who, 'seeing sufficiencie in themselves to be advaunced, to winne credite and acquaintaunce, so farre passe the boundes of their abilitie, that longe before countenaunce taketh note of their desertes, they are gladde of meane maintenaunce at home with friendes'.[62]

The 'prodigal young gentleman' and the prodigal text, therefore, are alike conceived as efficient causes of the usurer's violation of 'friendship' in that they demand financial credit not as a sign of trust in their ability to reciprocate, but as a hazard to gain that ability. Both therefore debase credit-extension as a sign of friendship. Thus, in Heywood's *A Woman Killed with Kindness*, the penurious Charles Mountford confuses Shafton's offer of money as a sign of friendship: 'Sir, I accept it, and remain indebted / Even to the best of my unable power', he says. When he finds himself sued for payment of the bond, Charles denounces not only Shafton, but his own unfriendly kin as 'Usurers'. In the texts of the 1570s and 1580s, usury is characteristically thought of as histrionic or hypocritical in this way, a practice of extending credit to strangers under pretence of friendship. Whetstone calls this 'a cusnage under the couler of freindship' in which 'freindship new, by greting oft' produces a 'kindred coynde in cousners stampe'. The practice of credit extension begins in a friendly manner: 'Some pettie summe on small assurance lend, / if youth be slowe, at leasure bid him pay / Sometimes bestowe good counsell as his friend . . . lend him his turn to serve, yet binde him sure.'[63]

Dialogic texts which debated the question of usury, such as Thomas Wilson's *Discourse uppon vsurye* (1572), William Harrys' *The market or fayre of Vsurers* (1550) and Thomas Lupton's *Sivqila* (1580) advocated the return of credit extension to its traditional status as a sign of friendship, an emplacement of trust in the debtor. If lending for gain were utterly abolished, the meaning of trust, they argued, would be restored: 'although they [merchants] would not truste so many a one whom they truste now, yet woulde they truste some of them rather then they woulde kepe their wares.'[64] These dialogues conjure up an idealistic or nostalgic vision in which promissory discourse is binding at the level of conscience; so the inhabitants of Lupton's imagined world of Sivqila are

> the faithfullest meaners, and truest dealers that are in all the world . . . but when it is once spoken or promised it is as sure to be kept and performed as though the partie that promised it were bound in a thousand pounde.[65]

So what was happening in the years between the abolition of the spiritual court of conscience at which promises could be called to account, and the establishment of a common law of contract? The development in law exactly parallels that of humanistic literature. For even as humanism, with its stress on the efficiency of probable argument, problematized the signifying power of the word as pledge of faith, so it introduced into the English common law a secular 'conscience' in the concept of *equitable interpretation*, which enabled the judge to interpret the sentence of the positive law according to the exigencies of a particular case.[66]

According to the jurist Christopher St German, equity was 'a ryghtwysenes that consyderyth all the partyculer cyrcumstaunce . . . observyd in every lawe of man'.[67] Urged by the imperative of conscience, or *synderisis*, to investigate the particularity of the debtor's and creditor's circumstances, which had heretofore been hidden by the generality of the positive law, the equitable judge would no longer preside like an umpire over a contest or wager of law, but would actively weigh the arguments on either side of the case. And St German's first example illustrating the need for an equity at common law was that of the debtor who, having paid his debt, had taken no written acquittance of his bond, and so, by the refusal of 'nude parol' as evidence, was bound to pay more than once. This became a stock example among writers on equity, as did its complement, the example of the creditor of a promise who, without making a sealed bond, had no redress if it were not performed.[68]

If the positive law on the invalidity of unwritten evidence could not change, judgements of cases would have to start being more flexible, invoking, according to particular circumstance, 'the excepcion . . . secretly understand in every general rewle of every posytyve lawe'.[69] The theory of equitable interpretation, based in Aristotle's assertion in the *Ethics* that 'when the lawgiver owing to the generality of his language left a loophole for error to creep in' the judge may 'fill the gap by . . . such an enactment as he would have made, *if he had known the circumstances*' (my italics), was closely related to the practice of *interpretatio extensiva* in humanist translation,

> a technique whereby the orator borrows a basic knowledge of the *ambiguorum genera* from the logician and 'invents' an ambiguity or 'interprets' a disadvantageous word in the relevant text in such a way as to support his interpretation of that text according to *aequitas*.[70]

Interest in jurisprudential equity cut across divisions between common and Chancery law, as well as across spiritual differences. At the same time as Christopher St German was setting out for the English reader the new learning about equity to be found in Aristotle and Jean Gerson, Thomas More was trying to persuade judges of the common law courts to mitigate the rigour of their procedure by following his example in Chancery. By the time Edmund Hake wrote his *Epieika* at the end of the century, equitable practice was no longer confined to Chancery, but had become a part of the common law, through the development of actions on the case.[71]

According to J.H. Baker, the most significant effect of the equitable development of the common law through the sixteenth century was 'the development of actions on the case for not performing promises, and failing to pay debts'. 'Why', he goes on to ask, 'was the law so long in providing a remedy for the breach of simple contract?'[72] In the context of our discussion of the cultural significance of trust as the assurance of a friendship, it becomes clear that the conceptual problems were many. That the positive law could not be altered to make mere words actionable was obviously essential; less obvious (to us) as a conceptual barrier was the refusal to compromise the flexible temporality of friendly reciprocity. In law, this meant that *nonfeasance* or 'not doing' was no trespass; the inability to conceive of delay in fulfilment as damage to the creditor was essential if friendship was to remain the objective of credit extension. This position is made very clear by David Ibbetson's analysis of a well-known case of 1532, in which the Coventry cloth dealer, William Marler, attempted to sue '*in assumpsit*' (i.e., for non-performance of a promise) rather than bring an action of debt.[73] Clearly, friendship had been involved here, for the debt of £4 13s. 8d. was originally owing by one Thomas Wilmer to William Marler's father, but his son let the matter drop, even though Wilmer promised it to him on his father's death. The terrible inflation of these years, and the decline in the Coventry cloth trade obliged Marler to seek recovery of the money, rather than maintenance of the friendship. His legal difficulties arose from the need to present a *nonfeasance* or non-performance of the promise as a trespass, and so avoid the useless action of debt.

Finally, we come to the hub of the legal transition from archaic conceptions of debt as a trial of trust, to the humanist relocation of the trial in the ability of an individual to assess or reconstruct probable *motives* on which to argue the existence of a real debt between the parties involved. For one of the objections made to Marler's suit was that he had given no good 'cause' or 'consideration' for Wilmer's promise. The so-called 'doctrine of consideration' was actually a displacement of the pledge of faith into arguable motive. To overcome the problem of mere breath not being actionable at common law, there developed the equitable procedure of arguing that a certain circumstance offered good 'consideration' for the existence of a promise in this case, making the promise actionable in law.[74]

From our point of view, then, the move from *fidei laesio* to *assumpsit* is equivalent to the displacement of the binding force of trust from the purgatory jurisdiction of the ecclesiastical courts as courts of conscience, to the equitable, motive-reconstructing jurisdiction of secular courts presided over by men whose sense of likelihood or probability was constructed from the exemplary oratorical storehouse of their shared education on the classics. Edmund Plowden, whose humanistic uses of equitable interpretation seem to have been extremely influential in the development both of the law and English drama,[75] argued and won a case in 1566 which will serve to demonstrate the displacement I describe. An action of trespass had been brought against one Edmund Baynton, brother to the deceased Andrew Baynton, for cutting down a wood which he claimed belonged to him by his brother's conveyance. For the plaintiffs, William Fleetwood argued that without evidence of a contract or conveyance, Baynton was indeed a trespasser. Plowden, however, maintained that there were three good considerations for the likelihood of a conveyance of the land having been made to Edmund Baynton. The first was the affection of Andrew Baynton for heirs male of his body, the second the continuance of the land in the name of Baynton and the third, the goodwill and friendship owed to Edmund Baynton as a brother. On the subject of the first, Plowden's argument is an Erasmian one of the importance of good husbandry; the object of marriage is procreation, but the father is to provide for the issue. On the second, he argues continuance of the land in the name is a good consideration, because its import is to exclude women,

> And divers good reasons might move him so to do. For God has divided the rational creatures into two Sexes, Male and Female, the Male is the Superior, the Female the Inferior, . . . Also, Men are for the greatest part more reasonable than Women, and have more Discretion to guide and manage Things than Women have, for to govern and direct is more suitable to the capacity of the Male than of the Female . . . And as a Woman is not fit to govern in Things of a higher

Nature as Man is, so is she not as fit to govern in things of a lower Nature, which perhaps *Andrew Baynton* considering apprehended that the profits of his land would not be so well expended and employed by Females as by Males nor the Lands so well ordered, nor Hospitality so well kept up . . . and that there would not be so great Comfort and support to his Race, or Kindred, or Allies, or Friends and Acquaintances, as well as to the Country in general where he and his Parents dwelt, if his Inheritance should come to Females . . . Also if his Inheritance should come to a Female, in all Probability she would take a Husband . . . and consequently she and the whole Inheritance would be subject to the will of a Stranger, and be governed by him . . . and no Man would willingly suffer a Stranger to reap the Fruits of his Labour, and therefore such of his blood to whom he desires to leave his substance is an Heir Male, and the want of an Heir Male is a great Grief. For which reason God says by his prophet *Elias* to *King Achab*, whom he intends to plague, *I will kill of* Achab *him that pisseth against the Wall*, which is but a Circumlocution of Males only.[76]

From here it was but a short step to Plowden's third consideration, that brotherly love bound Andrew to Edmund Baynton, and was therefore good consideration for having conveyed the land to him in default of the male heirs whose absence was such a great grief. Plowden's successful argument, winning against Fleetwood's objection *ex nudo pacto non oritur actio*, obviously binds men together through the relegation of women to a position of difference. But it does so not through the absolute and unvarying validity of the arguments (which obviously would not work in most cases, since their cumulative implication would be to disallow that affection can bind men through relations of alliance where husbands are always strangers) but through the plausibility of those arguments in this particular case. What binds men, in other words, is the sharing of the right and the educational ability to mobilize arguments drawn from the exemplary reading of classical texts as evidential consideration for the existence of contracts, while women sustain this evidential economy as it were from the inside, forming the commonplace material of its argumentative negotiations, and figuring the sense of duplicity at its heart.

CONCLUSION: THE MISOGYNY OF EQUITY

Equity, then, is humanist dialectic in its hermeneutic aspect, a method of assessing, through the reconstruction of probable motives, the validity of another person's story, or the likelihood of their intention and ability to fulfil a promise. If we turn now to the resolution of the crisis of faith brought about in the story of the Countess of Celant, we can see that it is this binding power that compensates men for the loss, through the sharpened negotiating edge that probable reason gives to their conversation, of a sense of security in each other's good faith. Belleforest and Fenton signal early on to readers that Bianca Maria's facile persuasion by the Count represents an inability to hear and try the justice of his reasons with equity. Belleforest's Count delivers his reasons 'à la bonte de vostre esprit & équite de vostre jugement' ('to your good will and the equity of your judgement'). But of course Bianca Maria is not educated to hear causes as Sidney's Euarchus does, 'letting pass the flowers of rhetoric and marking only whither their reasons tended'.[77] When Fenton has Bianca Maria reply that 'the sondrie benefits of the Ladie marquesse had bounde her to a thankfull *consideracion* to her power' (F.fol. 143ᵛ), it is a signal that something has gone awry. Benefits received from the Marquise should bind the young widow to grateful reciprocity on this occasion, not to the mere *pro et contra* consideration of whether they provide motivating evidence of the existence of a contractual bond. As a woman, she lacks the privilege of an invention and judgement copiously developed to assess what is and is not 'good consideration', and so her appropriation of the motif of the prudent man's skill in reasoning *in utramaque partem* subsequently defines her as irrationally mobile as Fortune herself, the demonic antithesis of the prudential orator.[78]

The impending crisis of trust between men is signalled by the invocation of a discourse of *amicitia* to describe the cohabitation and interdependence of the rival lovers, Valperga and Sanseverino. Valperga, 'enjoyed a mutuall conversacion with therle *Sanseverino*, wyth suche indifferent familiaritie, that for the moste parte they used but one bedd, and one borde, wyth one purse common betwene them both' (F.fol. 155ᵛ). First Sanseverino's fidelity to his friend is tested, when the Countess asks him to take vengeance against Valperga. Sanseverino takes refuge in plausible discourse:

The Lord *Sanseverino*, hearing this discourse, promised hir to doe his best, and to teache Valperga to talke more soberly of hir, whome he was not worthy for to serve, but in thought. Nothwithstanding he sayde more, than he ment to do, for he knew . . . that *Ardizzino* had a juster quarrell against him, by taking that from him which he loved . . . Thus he concluded in mind stil to remain the frend of *Ardizzino*.

(P.fol. 208ʳ)

Sanseverino 'promised hir', but his promise is expressed in a free indirect discourse which presents it to the reader as a stylized parody of amorous extravagance: he would 'teache Valperga to talke more soberly of hir, *whome he was not worthy to serve, but in thought*'. These flowers of rhetoric come to be gathered as evident tokens against him when the Countess takes back Ardizzino Valperga as her lover, and undermines the latter's trust in his friend's fidelity:

Syr, said she, is the Counte of Gaiazzo one of your very frends? I think (answered Valperga) that he is one the surest friends I have, and in respect of whose friendship, I will hazarde my selfe for him no less than for my brother, being certaine that if I have nede of him, he will not faile to do the like for me.

(P.fol. 209ᵛ–210ʳ)

The Countess goes on:

And that you do not thinke this to be some forged tale, or light invention, or that I hard the report therof of some not worthy of credit, I wil say nothing else but that which himself did tell me' . . . when in your absence he used my company. He sware unto me without declaration of the cause, that he could never be mery . . . before he saw you cut in pieces.

(P.fol. 210ᵛ)

Ardizzino Valperga, shaken by report of this oath, is almost persuaded that his trust in Gaiazzo has been misplaced. What prevents him at the last minute from believing the Countess, however, is her final urging that he take action against Gaiazzo. Seeing her 'concluding upon hir own quarrel, his conscience throbbed' says Painter (fol. 210ᵛ), while Fenton's Ardizzino 'entred into a pawse, measuring in the secret of his mynde, the tearmes of her present malice, with thexperience and diverse proffes of the fydelitie of his frende, whom he knewe to be more assured in vertue' (fol. 159^r). Both conclude to the effect that he 'wold give no credit to false report without good and apparent proofe', in order to examine which he 'tooke his leave of hir to goe to *Milan*, . . . to reveale the matter to his companion, and direct the same as it deserved'. Once in Milan, 'he imparted to *Gaiazzo* from point to point the discourse of the Countess' (P.fols 210^v-211^r).

The Countess alleges the *exact words* of Sanseverino's swearing of his bad faith to Ardizzino. What she says is no more than the truth and its near persuasion of Ardizzino figures a quasi-allegorical choice: does the assurance of friends depend, as the tradition would have it, upon the performative truth of the promissor's word? Or can bonds between men accommodate each other's rhetorical and strategic uses of promissory discourse, through mutual identification, across the space of the text, the lawcourt or the theatre, as judicous evaluators of the evidence according to probability and equity? The story proves the latter, with Ardizzino employing his 'conscience' in an equitable weighing of the Countess' words against proofs of his friend's fidelity. This move in the narrative redeems the men's erstwhile prodigality as clients of the Countess, and transforms them into the paradigm of the prodigal author whose experience qualifies him to benefit the commonweal with the exposure of the abuses that secretly threaten its good order. And, of course, that same setting out of abuses of faith in apt and convenient discourse serves to regain the prodigal author's access to the credit and friendship that he nearly lost in trusting to the heady facility of his own rhetorical credit.

The story of the 'Countess of Celant' is not, after all, anything to do with female sexuality. Its concern is, rather, to counter the charge of 'prodigality' inherent in texts which instruct men in probable argument, and to neutralize the anxiety voiced by Sir Thomas Elyot, when he observed that nothing nowadays 'can bynde a man to his promise' without there being 'something therein espied to brynge it into argument'. If skill in probable argument could problematize trust between men, it could also restore it, by urging men to practice 'equity' in their judgement of one another's discourse. The effects of this masculine hermeneutic of 'equity' on the representation of women endures most obviously and influentially in the drama of Shakespeare, which will be the subject of the last two chapters of this book.

Part III

THE THEATRE OF CLANDESTINE MARRIAGE

FANTASIES OF FREEDOM FOR WOMEN? THE 'LOVE MATCH' IN SHAKESPEARE

One of my justifications for devoting the last two chapters to the consideration of obscure prose fiction was the conviction of its relevance to our understanding of Shakespeare. The convoluted and mean-spirited tale of the Countess of Celant might seem far removed from the dazzling scope of Shakespeare's imaginative concerns. Yet to the extent that it defines heroic masculinity as an act of persuasion which both achieves a clandestine marriage, and proves threatening (through female sexual infidelity) to male friendship, the story has much in common with Shakespearean themes.

We do not, however, immediately recognize the thematic resemblance between Shakespearean drama and humanistic prose fiction, largely because of our common-sense presumption that Shakespearean dramatizations of secret marriages represent romantic fantasies of defiance against parental coercion rather than allegories of masculinity as persuasive power. We assume an opposition between the romantic love match and the economically motivated 'arranged marriage' (though in fact, of course, creditless strangers and younger brothers usually stand to benefit, in Shakespeare's fictions, from the winning of a Bianca, an Olivia, a Rosalind and so forth). Furthermore, critics interpret the popularity of the 'love match' theme in commercial drama to be a concession to the tastes of women. Thus Andrew Gurr gives his section on plays of clandestine marriage the title of 'Juliet's rebellion' and goes on to observe: 'Shakespeare's presentation of marriage was relatively "new", in that his plays uphold the power of love over parental authority.'[1] But why should we assume that the clandestine marriage, a dominant theme of the Bandellian prose fiction from which *Romeo and Juliet* derives, represents the interests of women in marriage, rather than those of men in authorship? Recently, historians examining Church court records have argued that the polarization of 'individual freedom' and 'parental coercion' that continues to inform the social history of marriage in this period is misleading. For it seems that women were less likely to think of kin and friends as constraints upon their freedom of choice than as supporters of their matrimonial interests: 'I must be ruled by my freendes as well as by myself' as one woman is recorded as saying.[2] Because men controlled the occasions of contractual negotiation, clandestinity in the act of betrothal was far more likely to be in their strategic economic interests. Men who were in debt might, for example, try their luck in forging a sudden and casual contract, as Lancelot Grimshawe did in 1610, when he persuaded Anne Foote to plight her troth to him as she was delivering laundry.[3] And it was because women knew that they were vulnerable in such situations that they made use of the appeal to friends. Laura Gowing writes that

> The roles that men and women play in the rituals of courtship mean that men propose and women answer, and faced with proposals that they do not intend to accept, women use the idea of kin in a way that is peculiar to them. Alice Dawson, testifying to the court in 1580, said that two men held her captive and tried to make her agree to marry John Bothewyd ... she responded with tactics she knew would keep her from legally binding herself to him: 'she not having any entent to conract matrimony at the presente did without any deliberacon answer I yf her frends good will might first be therunto obtained and otherwise not.[4]

Why, then, do we assume that the love match represented in drama is 'Juliet's rebellion'? Simply, because we have become collusive with the Shakespearean mode of representing the themes that dominated the prose fiction of the 1560s and 1570s. For, underlying Shakespearean drama, we find stories of the productivity of equitable probation – or of probable reason – which, as we have seen, is the subject of so many Bandellian prose fictions of male bonding and clandestine courtship. Thus, for example, in *Othello* we have a play in which a man's social agency is expressed as a victory in the persuasion of a woman into a clandestine marriage, the stability of which is subsequently undermined by persuasions of her sexual infidelity. The equitable model of probation is, then, twice overproductive: first in securing the legal validity of Othello's clandestine marriage through equitable process, and second, in transforming the (admirable?) vocality and assertiveness of Desdemona into ambiguous proofs of her sexual infidelity.

At first it appears that no equity exists in Venice, for Iago warns the clandestinely married Othello of the magisterial license that Brabantio enjoys with respect to the law:

> Are you fast married? For be sure of this,
> That the magnifico is much belov'd
> And hath in his effect a voice potential
> As double as the duke's; he will divorce you,
> Or put upon you what restraint and grievance
> That law (with all his might to enforce it on)
> Will give him cable.[5]

In the law court, the Duke appears to justify Iago's words, granting Brabantio the right to read 'the bloody book of law . . . in the bitter letter / after its own sense'. The inexorable letter of the positive law, however, finds its equitable loophole in the hearing of Othello's moving narration of the circumstances that led up to the marriage. Brabantio's case for prosecution, based on the argument that Othello must have used magic ('For nature so preposterously to err . . . / Sans witchcraft could not', he reasons) is dismissed by the court as 'poor likelihoods'. The result, however, is that in proving his own marriage valid, Othello has rendered persuasive the hypothesis that Brabantio denied, namely, that a tendency to 'err' might be in Desdemona's own nature. Having thus won his case against another man by merely probable arguments, Othello is himself haunted by their own sinister emotional compulsion, treacherously deployed in the name of honesty and friendship by Iago: 'make me to see't, or at least so prove it / That the probation bear no hinge, nor loop to hang doubt on', Othello begs, unable to bear the imaginative productivity of doubt.[6] But Othello's doubts about Desdemona are replicated in the doubtfulness of the signs by which her 'character' is made known to an audience or reader; scholarly commentators are put into the position, interpretatively speaking, of a sixteenth-century jurist consulting his commonplace book for ways in which to gloss her speeches and actions, to make them 'probable', one way or another.[7] Masculine practice in the equitable probation of uncertain arguments thus becomes, in Shakespeare, the basis of dramatically persuasive characterization, especially of women.

The example of *Othello* suggests that the formal and thematic concerns of the drama relate broadly, as well as specifically, to those of the humanistic *novelle* of the 1560s and 1570s. Like the *novelle*, we may find that Shakespeare's plays dramatize the conceptual difficulties of translating masculine social agency into a capacity to persuade both friends and enemies, without endangering the means by which one distinguishes friends from enemies. In the *novelle*, acts of persuasion, or of the transmission of probable intelligence, are ambivalent proofs of male friendship, for their efficiency is inseparable from a kind of treachery; we saw this in the example of the Count of Celant's triumphant and secret act of persuasion which, winning Bianca Maria, betrayed the House of Mantua. In another such story, the tale of 'Dom Diego', a young gentleman first wins a blonde and glittery mistress called Genivera through his skill in sonneteering; her doubts about his faith and desertion of him send him into despair and exile, but she is won back by the agency of Diego's 'friend', Roderigo, who works as an intelligencer, determined 'to sound by some secrett circumstance afarr of, the doinges and determination of the girle'. He discovers, by entering her household and pretending friendship to her servants, that she has secretly married her steward. Roderigo kills the steward, an act which is moralized as a 'notable example . . . proving the ordynarie sucesse of secret contractes and mariages made by stelthe', the blame for which must lie with 'indiscret mothers . . . who . . . suffer their doughters to comunicate matters of love with their howshode servantes'.[8] Both of these stories of Celant and Diego enable us to see how ambivalent are the victories of masculine persuasion; Celant's conference with Bianca Maria in the house of the Marquise of Montferrat, Roderigo's infiltration of Genivera's household; each is an image of masculine social agency as potentially threatening to the honour and wealth of the household. But the threat is not acknowledged to reside in the masculine agency of persuasive communication; rather it is misogynistically displaced in fictions of women's inclination towards facile persuasion into clandestine marriage contracts.

In a general way it may be said, then, that humanism brought with it a perception of how much more productive and efficient the textualized services of *amicitia* would be in promoting a household's interests than traditional friendship (with its cumberous hospitality, gift-exchanges and openly negotiated alliances) could ever be. But at the same time, the operation of such *amicitia* was always going to be perceived as stealthy and treacherous. The sense of treachery was expressed, in prose and drama, in fictions of easily persuaded women, who represented the other side of the productivity of *amicitia*; that is, the new vulnerability of households to stealthy depletion and loss. So Brabantio's house becomes, thanks to Othello's clandestinity, as open and friendless as a remote country 'grange'.[9]

What follows will be an attempt to develop these themes into an understanding of the concerns of dramatists and moralists in the years just before Shakespeare began to write for the stage. In this section of the book I face the exact opposite of the problem I encountered in the last; where my discussion of the prose fiction of the 1560s and 1570s was encumbered by the obscurity of its subject, Shakespeare is too much argued over, too well known. It seems necessary, therefore, to place the arguments of the next two chapters in the context of current literary critical and socio-historical debates about Shakespeare and the subversions of 'patriarchy'.

Recently, the idea of 'Juliet's rebellion' – that is, the idea that Shakespearean drama appealed to female fantasies of romantic freedom of choice – has (somewhat unexpectedly) received support from an otherwise convincing argument that Shakespeare's family romances are internally subverted by the transvestism of their original staging. In an article that looks set to become a classic, Stephen Orgel has ingeniously argued that the liberating energies of the English transvestite theatre were responsible both for arousing a certain form of sexually focused anxiety (anxiety about the potential effeminization of men) and for enabling the allaying of a different form of anxiety, also sexually focused (anxiety about the sexual fidelity of women). Commenting on objections to the theatre by John Rainoldes (1599), Philip Stubbes (1585) and William Prynne (1633), Orgel observes that these writers conflate the assumption that the response to theatre is erotic, with the assumption that male sexual excitement is 'effeminizing' and therefore homoerotic.[10]

Orgel goes on to argue that a transvestite theatre served to allay, as well as arouse, sexual anxiety, because anxiety for the chastity of women, on which assurance of paternity and of the honour of a male household depends, was greater than anxiety over sodomy. He suggests that two levels of tranvestism – on the stage and in dramatic fiction – chiastically served to neutralize one another.[11] This formulation is the crux of his argument that a peculiar tension of subversive and yet tolerated sexual energies generated by a transvestite theatre enabled a drama in which 'fantasies of freedom' for both men and women could be played out. The supporting part of his thesis – that Shakespearean drama may be characterized as a fantasy of freedom for women as well as men, depends on three related assumptions, which I shall here adumbrate. The first is that the existence of a commercial drama argues for parity in the intelligibility of its fictions for both men and women:

> The fact of a large female audience must have had implications for the development of an English popular drama. It meant that the success of the play was significantly dependent on the receptiveness of women ... theatres are only viable insofar as they satisfy their audiences.[12]

The exclusively male stage, apparently, enables and contains the representation of fantasies of sexual liberation in which both men and women are implicated, because it always maintains a hypothetical distance from the oppressive patriarchal structure of marriage; there is much virtue in the 'if' which prevents Rosalind and Viola from being women and wives. For the patriarchal family structure, argues Orgel, oppressed men and women in equal fashion:

> Women are commodities in this culture, certainly, whose marriages are arranged for the advantage or convenience of men ... the distinction here is between fathers and children, not between the sexes; this is a patriarchal society. Fantasies of freedom in Shakespeare tend to take the form of escapes from the tyranny of elders to a world where children can make their own marriages ... it works for women as well as men: the crucial element is the restrictive father, not the sex of the child.[13]

The third point ties up the other two, by arguing that if the instrument of the oppressive patriarchal family structure is the enforced marriage, then dramatic fictions of escape from the miseries of enforced marriage, through love matches or adulteries, were practically made for the pleasure of the female audience.[14] At this point, Orgel returns to his insistence that the sexual danger identified by anti-theatrical polemic was exclusively homoerotic, thereby proving its insulating capacity to enable an experience of 'liberating theatrical freedom' for women.

I have dwelt upon the stages of Orgel's argument, because it conveniently spells out a number of popularly held assumptions about Shakespearean drama with which it will be the purpose of this chapter to contend. The first is the assumption that the popularity of Shakespearean drama is an index that its construction of cultural fantasies must have implicated its audience equally in the 'reception' or construing of the significance of the fantasies concerned. Orgel's argument – that 'theatres are only viable insofar as they satisfy their audiences' – reduces the variable conditions and effects of 'reception' to the measurement of 'consumption', which is, of course, commercial success. But does the yardstick of commercial success pre-empt other kinds of discrimination from operating within an audience to differentiate modes of 'reception'?

For all its popularity Shakespeare's drama had a rigorous intellectual basis in the deliberative or hypothetical structure of Terentian comedy as it was rhetorically analysed in every grammar school.[15] Far from being a rigid intellectual straitjacket, the rhetorical analysis of Terentian comedy enabled the achievement of a drama that carried emotional conviction as an unfolding narrative of events – 'a kind of history'[16], as Shakespeare himself defined it – by investing the representation of those events with the impression of an intelligible combination of causality and fortuitousness. Shakespearean drama could not have been further, in this respect, from the morality plays' presentation of events as syllogistic arguments, nor from the loosely sequential narratives of 'romance' plays such as *Sir Clyomon and Sir Clamydes*, with their arbitrary miracles and *deii ex machina*.[17] Even Shakespeare's most ostentatiously improbable drama, *The Winter's Tale*, explicitly alludes (for those who could catch the reference) to the theories of Donatus and Evanthius, the grammarians whose analysis of Terence set the model for humanist grammar-school practice.[18]

'Reception' of such a drama might be significantly divided,

then, between auditors with and without grounding in the rhetorical analysis of a credible plot. Citing the examples of the lawyer John Manningham, and the Caroline play-goer, Lucius Cary, Andrew Gurr observes, that 'both of these educated playgoers, whatever their strength of memory or hearing, thought of the essential medium as words'.[19] Manningham, of course, was also alert to the *order* of discourse in the sense of plot. He recorded having seen, in *Twelfth Night*, a play 'like the commedy of errores or *Menaechmi* in Plautus, but most like and neere to that in Italian called *Inganni*'.[20] The French translator of the Sienese play, *Inganni*, Charles Estienne, urged French dramatists to follow 'the custom of the ancients in their so-called new comedy', precisely because the rhetorical disposition of the argument of new comedy facilitated its pleasurable and persuasive reception among auditors: 'la façon de disposer & pursuyure leur sens & argument . . . pour donner recreation aux auditeurs' ('the disposition and pursuit of sense and argument . . . to give an audience pleasure').[21]

An understanding of persuasive verbal technologies for the production of fantasy might seem of scant relevance to the emotional complicity of an audience in that fantasy's reception. The apparent irrelevance would hold, were it not for the fact that the sexual disquiet to which theatre gave rise in the 1580s and 1590s was not, as Orgel suggests, exclusively or even predominantly focused on the homoerotics of its staging. In fact, as much anxiety centred on the association of the persuasive technology of the dramatic fiction with a form of plot involving the *problematization of good faith between men*, and the disruption of alliance-friendships by secret love affairs. As Estienne said, the probable arguments of Roman new comedy concerned nothing but 'marriages, love affairs and such things' ('ne parlans d'autre cas de mariages, amours & semblables choses').[22] While one strand of anti-theatrical polemic stressed the Deuteronomic prohibition on cross-dressing, another and equally significant strand identified a structural connection between the probably argued plots of Latin, Italian and French dramatic models and a perceived increase in the betrayals of household honour by ingenious schemes for clandestine courtships and illicit adulteries.

In Orgel's argument, this last point would seem to be pre-empted by his opposition of the patriarch as oppressive father-figure to 'children' of either sex, whose rebellious libidinal energy enables them to resist becoming components in his dynastic projects of marriage. The problem with this version of the opposition is that women can never become patriarchs – a banal enough observation, until we consider its implications for 'husbandry' in the extended sense. A young man scheming a love match with the object of his desires necessarily anticipates his own imminent translation into the husband/patriarch liable to be betrayed by the same methods of clandestine courtship which have won his beloved for him. Thus, even in the thick of the fantasy of freedom, the fictive daughter indulging in clandestine courtship becomes the focus of audience suspicion regarding her fidelity as a wife. *As You Like It* offers an image of marriage as unavoidable cuckoldry precisely because it assumes that a woman's agency in clandestine courtship irretrievably undermines the probability of her subsequent sexual fidelity. When Orlando tells Ganymede that his Rosalind is wise enough to be moderate in passion, Ganymede replies,

> else she could not have the wit to do this. The wiser, the waywarder. Make the doors upon a woman's wit, and it will out at the casement; shut that, and 'twill out at the keyhole, stop that, 'twill fly with the smoke out at the chimney.

'A man that had a wife with such a wit', replies Orlando, 'he might say, "Wit, whither wilt?"' to which Ganymede's response is 'Nay, you might keep that check for it, till you met your wife's wit going to your neighbour's bed'.[23] Here the penurious younger brother Orlando, clandestinely (albeit ignorantly) courting the daughter of his woodland patron, is suddenly translated in the imagination of the audience into the householder whose honourable estate is threatened with dissipation by the faithless sexual energy of the woman on whose promise it was founded. This is comic because the exchange foregrounds its own fond homosociality, just as the play foregrounds the purely hypothetical nature of any marital denouement: Orlando takes his Ganymede finally for his Rosalind, 'if there be truth in sight'.[24] In *Othello*, as we have seen, however, the same mental reflex acquires the force of a tragic prediction.

The relative positions of women and men in the 'fantasy of freedom' represented by the Shakespearean love match are not, then, symmetrical, because men are doubly positioned in relation to the audience as successful suitors for social advancement through clandestine marriage, and as anxious policemen, apprehending the implications of their exploitation of clandestinity in fantasies of jealousy that displace their share of culpability onto women. For, *pace* Orgel, it was not the enforced marriage that exercised the imaginations of playwrights, lawyers and governors of London, but the practice of quite another abuse of the contract: the clandestine marriage.

The following chapter will be concerned with substantiating the propositions outlined above in three related sections. First, it will attempt to shift the current critical emphasis in the discussion of Shakespearean drama from the 'gaze' and the 'spectacle' by arguing for the significance of dialectical *uncertainty*, the meta-phorical 'blind spot' or 'place for error' that operates to make a theatre of fantasy emotionally persuasive. Then it will go on to consider the problematic implication of Terentian comedy in the legitimation of clandestine contracts, especially in England, where the ambiguity of canon law remained unreformed. Finally, it will offer an interpretation of prodigal son or 'Christian Terence' tragicomedy as the ideological displacement of legislative refor-mation in matters of prostitution, debt and clandestine marriage in the 1570s and 1580s.

5

HOUSEHOLD STUFF
Terence in the Reformation

CREATING CREDIBILITY: THE DELIBERATIVE USES OF ERROR

In the second act of Terence's *Heauton Timorumenos* (*The Self Tormentor*) a young man called Clinia anxiously scans the distance for the approaching figure of Antiphila, a poor maiden for whose love, we understand, he has quarrelled with his father, as a result of which he has just spent three months in Asia on military service. Already he is worried that while he has been away, Antiphila may have been 'corrupted'; 'Many things concur to confirm this impression in my mind', he reflects, 'the opportunity, the place, her age, the wickedness of the mother under whose control she is, and who has no taste for any thing but cash' ('occasio, locus, aetas, mater quoius sub imperiost mala, quoi nil iam praeter pretium dulcest'). As Antiphila comes into view trailing luggage and maidservants, Clinia breaks down in anguish: 'O Juppiter, ubinam est fides?' ('O God, where is fidelity to be found?') She has evidently, during his absence, turned courtesan.[1]

This movement of mind is typical of the action of Terentian comedy in more ways than one. In a formal sense, it is an example of what, to Renaissance humanists, was a profoundly influential innovation in the structuring of a dramatic representation: that is, the artful and naturalistic joining of the scenes by the anticipation of an actor's entrance. Early writers of Terentian-style comedy, such as John Foxe in his comedy of *Titus et Gesippus*, foreground the device in a way that reveals another aspect of its importance; so Foxe's Terentian slave, Phormio, soliloquizes:

> So while I can, while things are still quiet here, I think it prudent to anticipate with cleverness the troubles that are

163

coming so that later, when they come – that is, when the expected happens – they'll be less painful. But who's that foreigner I see rushing this way . . . ?[2]

Foxe's pedantic insistence (he wrote the play to demonstrate his competence as a schoolmaster) here alerts us to the extent to which this Terentian attitude of 'looking ahead', of 'seeing' the foreigner approach, is also a prudential attitude, a *habitus* of mental preparation, readiness for contingency. It has recently been fashionable to read into Renaissance metaphors of vision the preoccupations of our own intensely scopic culture, emphasizing, for example, the 'spectacular' rather than interpretative or rhetorical aspect of theatre. It is worth recalling, however, that the significance of the 'gaze' and of the longing for 'ocular proof' in Renaissance drama is the product of a *textual* rather than cinematic technology. That is to say, it is a kind of intellectual voyeurism, a readiness to discover potential *signs* of proof, to 'anticipate with cleverness the troubles that are coming'. Thus, in our first example, Clinia's forensic discovery through the places of occasion, place, age, person and motive of the probability of Antiphila's falsehood, render her eventual appearance less a sight to be gazed on than a sign to be read.[3] In its Renaissance development, this produces such figures of obsessive jealousy as the paranoid Thorello of the 1601 quarto of *Every Man in his Humour*, whose figuring forth of the scene of his cuckoldry may also be analysed, like Clinia's deliberations, as an adumbration of dialectical proofs from place, person, motive and occasion:

> Why't cannot be, where there is such resort
> Of wanton gallants, and young reuellers,
> That any woman should be honest long.
> Is't like that factious beauty will preserue
> The soueraigne state of chastitie vnscard,
> When such strong motiues muster . . . ? . . .
> Well (to be plaine) if I but thought the time
> Had answered their affections: all the world
> Should not perswade me, but I were a cuckold.[4]

Later, of course, he does think the time will answer too ('Two houres? ha? things neuer drempt of yet / May be contriued, I and effected too, / In two houres absense'); his only remedy is constant vigilance, to 'checke occasion' with 'euery looke or glance mine eye obiects'.[5] Such Renaissance depictions of desperate fantasies of scopic control encourage, in late twentieth-century criticism, the articulation of ingenious analogies between jealousy and 'spectatorship' in English drama; so Katherine Maus proposes that 'the dynamics of sexual jealousy provides a complex analogy to theatrical performance and response in a culture that tends to conceive of theatrical experience in erotic terms'.[6] If we want to talk in a meaningful way about the representation of women in Renaissance theatre, however, such analogies may be misleading. For however troublingly 'effeminizing' some men may have felt the actual homoerotic gaze of the theatre to be, there is no doubt that the dynamics of sexual jealousy played out in theatrical fictions were deeply implicated in a forensically based dramatic structure which was itself figured as a form of 'error' or 'blindness'. Such metaphors denote the temporary departure from, or loss of, an ability to read signs with assurance, and indicate that space of strategically induced *uncertainty* which fiction itself requires in order to operate effectively. So, again in Foxe's *Titus et Gesippus*, when Titus first begs Phormio to think of a scheme whereby he may occupy Sempronia's marriage bed in Gesippus' place, Phormio says 'Everyone's eyes must be blinded'. He speaks metaphorically, referring to the way in which his dialectically invented plan will deceive the friends and kinsfolk; when things get more problematic, however, and the achieved plan is threatened with exposure, Phormio's metaphor becomes more violent. 'We'll pluck out their eyes', he tells Titus, speaking now of the uses of dialectic as an artificial means of representing what has taken place.[7]

This is not, however, to deny the brilliance of Maus's final analogy between the condition of jealousy and the diagnostic or interpretative relation of the English audience to the drama of their Renaissance; in this drama, she notes, 'we are presented less with a story than with the synecdoche of a story'. Denied full access to or 'control' over 'that which they seem to own', the audience is thus in the position of the jealous husband: 'interpretation' she concludes 'is the attempt to escape the horns of this dilemma'.[8] The observation that English Renaissance drama actually structures or produces a condition of jealous suspicion, a desire to search out and interpret signs of infidelity, has also recently been made by Terence Cave, who locates in Shakespeare's romances and tragedies the emergence of a 'plot of the psyche' which, he notes, 'is very different from anything in the classical canon of recognition plots'. He goes on:

> Its paradigm is the plot of mistaken jealousy. Jealousy also motivates the plot of the *Medea*, but it is a well-founded jealousy, and not associated with a drama of concealment and suspicion. Suspicion and anxiety characterise the modern epistemological plot, and the power of suspicion in Shakespeare's variants derives from the audience's knowledge that it is an aberration, an error.[9]

Cave's concern is with the Renaissance rediscovery of the Aristotelian poetics of recognition. Although a familiarity with the *Poetics* was not common to Englishmen before the end of the sixteenth century (Philip Sidney was an exception) anyone who had attended a grammar school would have assimilated the principles of Aristotelian plot structure through humanist uses of the commentaries on Terence made by the fourth-century grammarians Donatus and Evanthius. It may be possible, then, to derive what Cave identifies in Shakespeare as 'a plot of the the psyche' from a comic, rather than tragic paradigm; specifically, from Terentian comedy as adapted for the education of Renaissance schoolboys using the *scholia* of Donatus. If my argument is correct, the plot of mistaken jealousy, either as a fully-fledged drama, or in motif-form denoting a type of character, emerges through the writing of Shakespeare and Jonson as the gender-specific solution to a historically specific problem. It represents, I will argue, the victorious conclusion of a struggle to appropriate the enormous cultural power implicit in the Terentian formula as an instrument for the production of credible dramatic fantasies, without endorsing the ethical threat entailed by an outright acknowledgement that the credibility created out of speculation and uncertainty is a more productive instrument of social relations than the assurance of good faith or integrity.

The conditions for such a drama were structurally present within the deliberative mode of Terentian comedy, to which the attention of sixteenth-century schoolboys was drawn by the *scholia* of Melanchthon, which built upon the analytical method of the fourth-century grammarian Donatus. Some sense of how a sixteenth-century schoolboy might have been encouraged to understand the formal principles of the example with which I began – Clinia's anxiety about Antiphila in *The Self Tormentor* –

may be gained from considering the marginal notes appended by Melanchthon to this scene. Thus, in a typical edition of 1574 we find that at the point at which Syrus, a slave, intervenes to correct Clinia's impression of Antiphila, Melanchthon had noted: 'Error Cliniae praebet occasionem sequenti narrationi' ('Clinia's error supplies the occasion for the following narration').[10] In a set piece of narrative rhetoric, Syrus then describes the scene of his own encounter with Antiphila earlier on, at her house:

> Well then, to start with: when we came to the house, Dromio he knocks at the door. Out comes an old woman. The moment she opened the door, in went Dromio full tilt and I after him. The old woman shoots the bolt and goes back to her spinning. That's where one could find out, if there's any spot at all where one could find out, what way she's been spending her time in your absence, I mean by breaking in upon her unawares. Why, this way we had the means of reckoning her everyday life (nam ea res dedit tum existumandi copiam / cottidianae vitae consuetudinem), and its that that best tells what a person's character (ingenium) is. When we came on her she was busying herself at the loom; she was poorly dressed and in mourning, I suppose, for the old woman who was dead, and not a trinket on her. What's more, she was dressed like women who dress for themselves, none of that stuff on her cheeks which women use for varnish, her hair not done up, but long and loose over her shoulders, thrown anyhow ... The old woman was spinning wool; there was only one little maidservant beside, and she was helping her to weave, all in rags, dowdy, horribly dirty.[11]

At the close of this iconic description of Antiphila's private life, Clinia's companion, Clitipho, urges him to read the signs it offers:

> Do you take it in about the girl he describes as unkempt in dress and person? That is another sure proof (magnum hoc quoque signum est) that the lady's life is blameless, when the go-betweens are so little cared for.[12]

We might wonder why Syrus did not simply explain the immediate source of Clinia's error: that is, that the costly accoutrements which he mistook for Antiphila's ill-gotten gains were in fact spoils of trade belonging to her courtesan companion, Bacchis, the lover of Clitipho. In a humanist reading of the scene, however, the silly mistake produced by Clinia's earlier forensic reasoning subsequently highlights and enhances the effectiveness of the no more than probable reasoning exemplified by Syrus' narration. So Melanchthon approves Clinia's uncertainty or 'error' in reasoning about Antiphila as the occasion for what he goes on to commend as a 'narratio ornatissima, de moribus Antiphilae, a signis ex ordiens' ('a most ornate narration of the moral character of Antiphila, drawn in an orderly fashion from proofs'), noting against Syrus' explanation of his intrusion into the household: 'ratio est argumenti: quotidiana consuetudo indicat ingenium' ('the premiss of the argument is that the daily habits make known the character').[13]

In fact, this little episode epitomizes the structural principle of Terentian comedy as a whole, which, as Joel Altman notes, was characterized by Donatus as 'a three part fable based on error'.[14] Altman's excellent study demonstrates how Tudor drama developed from the 'profoundly reassuring' syllogistic structure of the morality play towards a deliberative structure based on a radical lack of assurance: the Terentian comedy of bourgeois disputes over marriage in which characters engage in tireless hypothesizing about one another's motives with the inadequate instruments of probable reason.

Latent in Altman's analysis is a suggestion that this deliberative mode of drama depends on the (ethically troubling) recognition that error is culturally productive; that the establishment of probability or credibility is more useful than the establishment of certainty or belief, and that credibility is enhanced by the strategic promotion of error. 'How does one find a basis for action immersed in a world of shadowy probabilities?' he asks. 'Traditionally, through the arts of rational argument – and commentators were quick to observe that these dramas of citizens resembled contentions over a central issue.'[15] At one level, Altman suggests that comedies are deliberative because they are images of the uncertainty of life itself, in which people are willy-nilly forced to find a hypothetical basis for action. But his analysis also enables us to draw the conclusion that the plays are *reflexive* images of the effectiveness of deliberative oratory in that they manage to convince an audience of the credibility of their own working towards resolution, despite the uncertain, indeed highly improbable and ridiculous basis for belief which their resolutions finally offer. It is in this reflexive sense, I suggest, that Melanchthon appreciated the productive potential, the 'occasion' for probable conviction, represented by Clinia's unecessary inquietude over the fidelity of Antiphila. The analytical divisions which Melanchthon recommended that teachers follow in their exposition of Terence were those given by Donatus in a summary appended to every edition:

> Now comedy is divided into four parts: prologue, protasis, epitasis, catastrophe. The prologue is the first speech called by the Greeks πρωτος λογος or the discourse preceding the true composition of the fable . . . the protasis is the first act of the fable, in which part of the argument is unfolded, part withheld in order to maintain the curiosity of the audience (ad populi exspectationem tenedam); the epitasis is the complication of the plot, exquisitely fitted together; the catastrophe is the unfolding of the fable (explicatio fabulae) through which its outcome is proved acceptable (per quem eventus eius approbatur).[16]

'The use of the verb approbo', comments Altman, 'reinforces the sense that the happy ending is the product of a successful application of proofs'.[17] But if proof is established through the unfolding or interpretation of the catastrophe, then the blockage of interpretation, the 'part witheld' of the protasis, exacerbated in the epitasis, may be understood in terms of a calculated strategy of error, a way of engaging the audience in hypothesis, thereby creating, we might say, a dilatory space equivalent in dramatic experience to the 'suspense, partial unveiling, temporary blockage, eventual resolution' of questions posed in Barthes' 'hermeneutic code' of narrative.[18] A 'strategy of error' sounds like deceit, and indeed, the structure is not without reflection on the ethical status of the characters whose dilemma it pretends to resolve, but this ethical reflection has different effects according to gender. What these are, and how they were perceived by humanist commentators, we can best see by examining Melanchthon's adaptation of Donatus' comments on Terence's *Andria*, the most widely-read and best known of the comedies.

The argument of the *Andria* involves what in the sixteenth century would have been considered a disputed case of pre-contract, a 'clandestine marriage'. Pamphilius, son of Simo, has already pledged faith to Glycerium, a woman from Andros, who lives in Athens in the disreputable house of Chrysis, and who, as the play begins, is about to give birth to Pamphilius' child. Pamphilius' father suspects that his son is disobeying him, a hypothesis which he then tests by exacting from Pamphilius a promise to wed the daughter of his neighbour, Chremes. Persuaded by probable signs (no wedding preparations) that it is a hoax, Pamphilius agrees to his father's request. Meanwhile, Chremes is persuaded that Pamphilius' liaison with Glycerium was mere conjecture, and agrees after all to the wedding with his daughter. (Part of the comedy here is that the adults are all so involved with calculating probabilities that they cannot read the meaning of inartificial and undeniable proofs, such as the arrival of Glycerium's baby.) In terms of the reflexiveness of the plot's structure, however, what is most interesting is Donatus' comment on the way the play draws attention to the improbability of its own denouement, and turns that attention into yet another strategy of credibility through the promotion of 'error'. For the solution to Pamphilius' dilemma is a highly improbable romantic contrivance; Glycerium will turn out to be Chremes' long-lost daughter. Far from deflecting attention from the shabbiness of this device, Terence exposes it to scorn through the soliloquy of Davus, Pamphilius' slave, who confides early on to the audience that the *pretium* or assurance on which Pamphilius and Glycerium are building hopes to legitimize their union, is a hackneyed romance in which the foreign orphan turns out to be a respectable Athenian, severed by the tempests of fortune from her true origins:

> Any child she bears they've decided to acknowledge as legitimate. And now between them they've hatched a wild story (fallaciam) that the girl is an Athenian born: 'Once upon a time there was an old gentleman (fuit olim hinc quidam senex) an Athenian, a merchant. He was wrecked on the isle of Andros; he lost his life in the wreck, the girl was cast ashore, and Chrysis's father took in the poor little orphan.' Moonshine! (fabulae!) Seems to me a damned improbable story (me quidam hercle non fit veri simile).[19]

Of course, the 'damned improbable story' will be related again at the end of the comedy as the resolution of all the deliberations. It is the *pars argumenti* that has been withheld in order to hold the expectation of the audience. What Davus' untimely exposure highlights is the extent to which the very withholding of the resolution – the temporal suspension of the audience in 'error' or uncertainty – creates the conditions under which such a silly story can come to have its own kind of contextual intelligibility, can come to be valid as the *explicatio fabulae*. Donatus comments that Davus 'narrates part of the argument (et argumentam partem narrat) and does not believe that it happened as he says, that there might remain a place for error (ut supersit errorem locus)'. At the words 'fuit olim senex mercator' Donatus stresses the point: 'now the whole sum of the argument is narrated to the people, but in order that there might remain something toward error, belief is taken away' ('sed ut restet aliquid ad errorem, abrogatur fides').[20]

In his exhaustive study of sixteenth-century commentators on Terence, T.W. Baldwin observed that the significance of Melanchthon's alteration to Donatus lay in his making not the 'error' but the 'peril' of the characters the focal point of his analysis.[21] Thus, in Melanchthon's marginal notes, every important male character has his own 'epitasis' or 'catastrophe', marking his embroilment in and emergence from the 'peril' of conjecture and uncertainty into which he is cast. But this inflection of Donatus has the effect of drawing attention to an analogy between the ways in which what 'imperils' individual characters may correspond to the 'error' through which the play gains credibility. Thus, in his preface to the *Andria*, Melanchthon sees the play as turning on the issue of Pamphilius' faith, which is drawn into 'peril' by being promised in two directions. First, as he explains, every comedy is divided into protasis, epitasis and catastrophe, and then he goes on

> Moreover comedies usually contain a certain danger, for where is the place for counsel if not in doubtful affairs? And indeed comedy is none other than certain picture of human consultation and its outcome. In the *Andria*, Pamphilius is imperilled in that he must keep faith with Glycerium (vt Glycerio fidem promissam praestet), after having promised his father in error that he will be under his control and marry the girl his father wishes him to. And this is, as it were, the *status* of the play. All counsels, all complaints, all arguments, must be brought back to this place.[22]

Thus, for the duration of the *Andria*, it is Pamphilius' faith or credit (*fides*) that is suspended in doubt and ambiguity, in a way which (as Melanchthon analyses it) has potentially damaging consequences; the resolution of the issue is proof, after all, of the integrity or intactness of Pamphilius' faith as a son and a husband. But just as the comedy works by creating scope, through the strategic removal of certain belief ('abrogatur fides', as Donatus says, 'belief is taken away'), so the conceptual space of uncertainty that comes into being around Pamphilius' imperilled fidelity becomes analogous to the rhetorical negotiation of credibility which the comedy achieves for its own outrageous proofs through the temporal extension of error and confusion. In a sense, then, comedy is inclined to prove that the mobilization of doubts and hypotheses about one's motives and intentions is finally more effective, more emphatically productive of social credibility, than is an unwavering certainty of 'good faith'. At least if one is a man. For it is evident that no such analogy can be made between the deliberative structure of comedy and the woman whose fidelity succumbs to the touch of hypothesis, the withering hand of conjecture. Probable reasoning about her actions and motives brings no correspondent liberation into the space of error, the temporarily exploitable inconsequentiality of other people's confusion and bewilderment. As we saw in the case of Clinia's conjectures about Antiphila, such errors may supply the occasion for 'happy' deliberative resolution through probable reason, but the function of these is to arrest speculation, not to open out its character-creating possibilities through the promotion, in a safe inconsequential space, of further hypothetically-based action and response. The female subject is presented merely as a challenge to surveillance: the only way to 'know' her character is to break in unawares on her household.

'AN HOUSHOLD SOMEWHAT DEFAMYD': REFORMATION ATTITUDES TO TERENCE

In 1520, Thomas More's friend, the lawyer John Rastell, published a translation of the *Andria* under the title *Terens in englysh*, in which the place where Pamphilius met Glycerium is described as 'an houshold somewhat defamyd / To which much wanton company resorted'.[23] If the household was defamed by wanton resort, then how would that affect the status of Pamphilius' and Glycerium's own union? Surely its disreputable place of origin dishonoured both them and it? Yet, as we have seen, the sixteenth century approved the play for its legitimizing of that contract. Specifically, it was admired for a rhetorical skill which could give the most blatantly counterfeit of assurances – the romance of origin – the effect of a proof which retrospectively wiped out all dishonour from the marginal place and the covert manner of courtship.

The discovery of Donatus' commentary on Terence was made in 1433, and its impact on the composition of Renaissance comedy began to be felt in the first half of the sixteenth century.[24] This, however, was also a period in which definitions of the sexual honour of a household were changing, the changes themselves (as we saw, for example, in Starkey's *Dialogue*, with its desire to reform the chastity-corrupting, bachelor households of England) focusing a variety of different investments in a comprehensive project of religious, economic and social reform. Lyndal Roper, writing of Augsburg in this period, has termed this, in a memorable phrase, 'the domestication of the Reformation'.[25] It is not surprising, then, that in this period all over northern Europe, reformers should have tempered their admiration for the rhetorical power represented by the Terentian order of discourse, with a distaste for its identification with fictions which countenanced the prostitution of orphans, and proved the legitimacy of betrothals made in bawdy houses, with the connivance of old nurses and wily slaves. From the 1530s on, there developed an entire subgenre known to literary history as 'Christian Terence', in which the protasis-epitasis-catastrophe structure was adapted by German and Dutch humanists to produce godly dramas for the education of youth. An especially popular model reproduced the Terentian *mise-en-scène* as the parable of the prodigal son, not always with the original parable's benign ending. Perhaps the most famous and influential of these prodigal son plays was the *Acolastus* of Fullonius, which was given a copious English gloss and rhetorical commentary by John Palsgrave in his pedagogical translation of the play in 1530.[26] In the prodigal version of the Terentian plot, the young man's excursus into the world of pimps, bawdy houses and courtesans is made to do moral service as an admonitory example of the consequences of filial disobedience. The son and the error-based plot are thereby redeemed, but the courtesan remains a courtesan, and no *explicatio fabulae* can prove her a marriageable citizen's daughter. In one exceptional case, the *Studentes* of Christopherus Stummelius, a daughter of respectable parents, Deleasthia (enticement) becomes involved with Acolastus, one of the prodigals. In this play, then, a parental permission for a wedding is allowed to clear the sin of pre-marital sex, but the sin is nevertheless foregrounded, and moralized as such. The act in which Acolastus vows faith to Deleasthia begins with an invocation of the metamorphoses of Jove in the rapes of Europa and Calisto (notoriously reminiscent of Chaerea's soliloquy before his rape of Pamphilia in Terence's *Eunuchus*) and ends with an ode to adultery. Jodicus Willichus, whose student Stummelius was, wrote a preface to the 1550 edition of the play in which he explained its protasis-epitasis-catastrophe structure, and commended its improvement upon Terence in the heightened manner of its demonstration that extra-marital fornication was to be condemned, and marriage without consent of parents shown to be unlawful.[27]

In England, as in Germany, the first imitators of Terentian comedy were schoolmasters or university men who were interested in communicating the capacity of the protasis-epitasis-catastrophe structure to persuade the audience into accepting the probability of the solution to the perils mobilized in the plot. This might mean an epitasis capable of promoting sympathy enough in the audience to make the forgiveness of the prodigal's misdeeds imminent in the catastrophe seem affectively 'right', and not arbitrarily contrived. So John Palsgrave, in his commentary on Fullonius' *Acolastus*, made a special note of the 'great artifice used by Fullonius' in the epitasis, where the scene

> draweth shortly on to his *catastrophen*. And of this cause doth Fullonius in the settyng forth of Acolastus his complaynt, use all such rhetoricall preceptes, as shulde serve to make his pronunciation more figurated . . . to move the audience to comiseration.

The conclusion is thus more credible and natural than that which Palsgrave notes is 'used to be shewed now a days in stage playes, whan God or some saint is made to appear forth a cloud, and succoureth the parties which seemed to be towards some great danger, through the Soudan's cruelty'.[28]

Palsgrave's specific approval of the Terentian comic structure's use as a model of eloquent persuasion seems to have been shared even by men who otherwise deplored the socially disruptive effects of dramatic performances open to the general public. Thus Geoffrey Fenton exempted, from his chapter on the the viciousness of theatre in *A forme of Christian pollicie* (1574), 'the Plaies of scollers in actions of comedies or tragedies . . . by the which they are prepared to a boldness of speech . . . enabling their tongues to readye and wel disposed eloquence'.[29]

Even a comedy approving duplicity in contracts of marriage,

such as Foxe's *Titus et Gesippus*, might be accepted, then, in the classroom, where its purpose was to enable the structuring of eloquent discourse. But what was to happen when such probable comedies of stealthy loves made their way onto the common stages of the city? For the first part of the century, performances of deliberative drama seem to have been confined to scholarly institutions and to the households of such men as were associated with the common law and Chancery; thus, as well as publishing the *Andria*, the lawyer John Rastell wrote his own deliberative interlude, *Gentleness and Noblity*.[30] In 1566, Ariosto's *I Suppositi* (which adapts the plots of Terence's *Eunuchus* and Plautus' *Captivi*), was humanistically translated by George Gascoigne and performed to the lawyers at Gray's Inn. Already the sexually licentious implications of the Terentian *fabula* were moving into wider circulation: the play celebrates the powers of mistaken conjectures (supposes) to facilitate and subsequently legitimize a young man's defloration of a citizen's daughter. It is, of course, not known to what extent the drama of the Inns of Court affected other dramatic activity (though Marie Axton has shown that a continuum existed between the lawyers' drama and the drama at Court), but Isabella Whitney's *Testament* in 1573 linked the lawyers' handling of cases to the frequenting of plays by students at the Inns:

> For such as cannot quiet bee,
>> but strive for House or land
> At Th'innes of Court I Lawyers leave
>> to take their cause in hand
> And also leave I at ech Inne
>> of Court, or Chauncerye
> Of Gentylmen, a youthfull roote,
>> full of Activytie: . . .
> And every Sonday at the least,
>> I leave to make them sport
> In divers places Players, that
>> Of wonders shall report.[31]

In the course of the 1570s, there are signs that Italian imitations of Terentian comedy of which Ariosto's *I Suppositi* is a type, were making their way onto the stages of inns and other publicly accessible households, with apparently diastrous social effects. The playwrights or erstwhile playwrights writing in response to recent government initiatives for policing of sexual mores as part of a 'general reformation of manners' make it clear that an offending aspect of this new Italian *commedia erudita* was its investment of sexually licentious fictions with the authority of rhetorical probability. Thus, when Gascoigne's published version of the *Supposes* was seized by the High Commission in 1573, he reissued it with marginal annotations pointing out each deceitful 'suppose' as it occurred, thereby 'policing' the drama's deliberative exploitation of error as if in admonition to the reader.[32] Moreover, he followed the play with another, an exceptionally harsh prodigal son drama called *The Glasse of Government*, in which an 'error' becomes the basis for the magisterial detection and equitable punishment of courtesans and pimps under the law. Although its probability is based on a Terentian *fabula* of error, the play thus eschews any 'Terence phrase', claiming 'Reformed speech doth now become us best'.[33] In 1578, George Whetstone dedicated a new dramatic form to the Recorder of London, William Fleetwood, a key figure in the new initiatives for the policing of illicit financial and sexual activity in the capital. Whetstone's play, *Promos and Cassandra*, is familiar to readers of Shakespeare as sharing a common source (Cinthio) with *Measure for Measure*: it is a play about transforming theatre from a spectacular veiling of magisterial abuses into an equitable instrument for their detection and punishment. In his preface to Fleetwood, Whetstone sees the dramatist's problem as one of adapting the credibility, while condemning the sexual mores of the Terentian plot structure. Native English drama falls short of credibility: 'The *Englishman*, in this quallitie', he writes,

> is most vaine, indiscreete, and out of order: he fyrst groundes his work on impossibilities: then in three howers ronnes he throwe the worlde: marryes, gets Children, makes Children men, men to conquer kingdomes, murder Monsters, and bringeth Gods from Heaven'.

Neither German prodigal son drama, nor Italian *commedia erudita* offer a viable alternative, however, for 'at this daye, the *Italian* is so lascivious in his commedies that the worst hearers are greeved at his actions', while 'the *German* is too holye: for he presentes on everye common Stage, what Preachers should pronounce in Pulpets'.[34]

Gascoigne's and Whetstone's sense of the difficulty of dis-sociating the technology of dramatic probability from the apparent endorsement of lies and sexual infidelity is shared by Stephen Gosson. In a curious passage in his *Playes confuted*, Gosson moves from mocking the improbability of native English drama, to warning of the 'mischief that may privately breake into every mans house' if the error-based structure of Italian comedy is allowed to instruct men in the exploitation of probable arguments and counterfeit assurances in their own projects of courtship.

Sometime you shall see nothing but the adventures of an amorous knight, passing from countrie to countrie for the love of his ladie, encountring many a terrible monster made of broune paper, & at his retorne, is so wonderfully changed, that he cannot be knowne but by some posie in his tablet, or by a broken ring . . . what learne you by that? When the soule of your playes is eyther meere tryfles, or Italian baudery, or the wooing of gentlewomen, what are we taught? paradeventure you will saye, that by these kinde of playes, the authours instruct us how to love with constancie, to sue with modestie, and to loath whatsoever is contrarie unto this. In my opinion, the discipline we gette by playes is like to the justice that a certaine Schoolemaster taught in *Persia*, which taught his schollers to lye, and not to lye, to deceive, and not to deceive, *with a distinction how they might doe it to their friends, & how to their enemies;* to their friends, for excercise; to their foes, in earnest. Wherein many of his schollers became so skillful by practise, by custome so bolde, that their dearest friendes payde more for their learning then their enemies. I would wish the Players to beware of this kind of schooling, least that whilst they teach youthfull gentlemen how to love, and not to love, how to woo, and not to woo, their schollers grow as cunning as the *Persians*. / As the mischiefe that followed that discipline of *Persia* enforced them to make a lawe, that young men should ever after, as housholders use to instruct their families: so I trust, that when the Londoners are sufficiently beaten with the hurte of such lessons as are learned at Plaies, if not for conscience sake, yet for shunning the mischief that may privately breake into every mans house, this method of teaching will beecome so hatefull, that even worldly pollicy without any gramercy shalbe driven to banish it.[35] (my italics)

Gosson's example of the Persian schoolmaster comes from Xeno-phon's *Cyropaedia*, from the crucial sixth book, in which Cyrus' father, Cambyses, instructs him in the *oikonomia* of warfare. One of the things in which Cambyses instructs Cyrus is the necessity of lying and fraud, but he rationalizes this by comparison, as Machiavelli noted, with the strategic use of topography in hunting and warfare.[36] It seems, therefore, that Cambyses' admonitory history of the Persian schoolmaster is Xenophon's way of dis-sociating necessary instruction in the rhetorical arts of fraud from the charge of having endorsed deception as a mode of civil negotiation. In applying Xenophon's example to the effects of contemporary theatre, Gosson points not to the erotics of the drama's staging, but to the way in which such drama reflexively celebrates *probable persuasion* as the means by which young men achieve friends and deceive enemies. Indeed, it makes probable persuasion responsible for a potential subversion of sexual mores in the city. In his proposal for reformation – that young men should become 'householders' to instruct and oversee their own families – Gosson speaks prophetically. For, as we shall see, the problem of policing the sexual mores of households was eventu-ally resolved by the development of an emotionally persuasive drama of surveillant good husbandry.

PROSTITUTION AND CLANDESTINE MARRIAGE: THE POLICING OF SEX IN 1570s' LONDON

Let us consider how sixteenth-century English readers might have perceived cultural difference in the conceptual problems of legitimacy and honour as demarcated through Terentian fictions of access to women. Typically, in Terentian comedy, the woman desired by the young man in contravention of his father's will is sexually accessible because of her poverty, or the infamy of the household in which she finds herself. Discovery of her citizen birth serves to transform the sexually accessible object of desire into a legitimate participant within the socially binding exchanges of matrimony. Yet if the sexual access that initially defined her was tolerated because of her position within a marginal, woman-governed household, her subsequently acquired household of male, citizen relatives does not seem to be affected by the initial endangering, or violation, of her chastity. This seems to articulate a sense that the space of prostitution is prophylactic; it both sanctions the initial violation, and ensures that, once attached to a citizen household, the woman will be protected by the very institution that once made her vulnerable. So, in Roman law, prostitution was an officially tolerated means of dissuading young men from intriguing with married women; its professional practitioners, though wholeheartly accepted within that context, were nevertheless marginal, the *locus* of tainted relations.[37] An extreme example of the position is illustrated in Terence's infamous play, *Eunuchus*, in which Chaerea dresses up as a eunuch in order to rape Pamphilia, whom he has seen entering the household of the courtesan Thais, apparently as a slave. When it turns out that Pamphilia is a free-born citizen, someone tries to scare Chaerea's slave, Parmeno, with the threat that his master will be punished as an adulterer. Parmeno proves the unlikelihood of this with an enthymeme: 'Who ever heard of a man being seized as an adulterer in a house like that?'[38]

Leah Otis' study of prostitution in urban centres in medieval Languedoc suggests that it occupied, in the High Middle Ages, an institutional position similar to that articulated in the *Eunuchus*. A commentary of the customs of Toulouse observes that men visiting houses where women are commonly found for money cannot be charged with adultery 'since the place excuses the same'.[39] Lyndal Roper explains how in pre-Reformation Augsburg, the brothel was a municipal service, through which 'the city was able to celebrate and encourage youthful male virility' while helping 'to keep the town's "respectable" women sexually inaccessible'.[40] Such municipally regulated brothels were rarer in medieval England; the exception, however, was London, with its Southwark stews.[41]

The establishment of chronology in the history of attitudes to prostitution is fraught with difficulty; records of exceptional disciplinary procedures may distort the picture. Leah Otis thus warns against anachronistically backdating to the medieval period the harsh repressive attitudes of the sixteenth century.[42] Lyndal Roper makes the closure of the municipal brothels in Reformation Augsburg vividly intelligible in terms of a displacement of sexual discipline into the household itself. Despite the conceptual radicalism of the early reformers' criticisms of the Catholic tolerance of prostitution, the effect of reform as enshrined in the Disciplinary Ordinance of 1537 was to efface distinctions between commercial and non-commercial sex:

> The sexual discipline which the whole citizenry was to adopt
> was both more all-embracing and less well-defined than it
> had been before the Reformation. Now any sexual relation-
> ship outside marriage, and any occasion on which the sexes
> mingled . . . might lead to sin.

The marginal status once overtly allocated to prostitutes became a
covertly acknowledged category of suspicion embracing all
women:

> Prostitution had previously been regarded as the cure for the
> dangers of male lust, protecting (as all who favoured its
> existence insisted) the honour of the women within the
> household. The wives, daughters and maids for whom they
> feared were their own; and the sexual threat derived from
> the young men of the house. Once the brothel was abolished,
> and prostitutes were considered either as fornicators or
> adulteresses like other women, it is not surprising that such
> care should have been taken to redrawing the boundaries
> within the household.[43]

Historians of early modern England have been reluctant to con-
cede that the Henrican Reformation could have brought about any
comparable change in attitudes towards sexuality, any 'reformation of manners'. There has been a tendency to stress a kind of
continuity in English habits of thought which, as discussion often
turns on evidence from the early part of the seventeenth century,
is just as likely to represent the interiorization through popular
texts, sermons, ballads and other media, of radical changes in
attitude which made their impact at the beginning of the previous
century.[44] As in other areas of English history, so in the history
of the disciplining of sexuality, change may be masked as continuity by the indirection of reform (indeed, it will be my purpose
to argue that the English stage itself helped helped ideological
change look like a timeless structure of the mind). Where Augsburg
and other German city-states made a clean break with the canon
law through disciplinary ordinances and the establishment of
courts for their enforcement, the English equivalent, the bill for the
Reformation of Ecclesiastical Laws, never made it through Parliament. Initiated by Cromwell in the 1530s and later involving the
work of Latimer, Martyr, Cheke, Johannes a Lasco, Cecil, Thomas
Smith, John Foxe and Thomas Norton, it attracted the attention

of Melanchthon, Bullinger and other eminent reformers on the Continent, but was destined to be defeated in the House of Lords in 1559 'by an odd alliance of bishops opposed to any reform and reform minded peers'; its reintroduction in the Parliament of 1571 fared no better.[45] Nevertheless, the position articulated by the bill on the questions of sexual mores testifies to the commitment of these influential men to the early Cromwellian policy which aimed to found the commonweal on the good order of the household.[46] The extent to which men like William Cecil were later willing to co-operate with the initiatives of the city governors in their policing of illicit sex in the city of London suggests that the failure of the bill might actually have generated alternative alliances and means through which to achieve some of its aims.[47] Ian Archer has made a persuasive case for linking an abrupt transition in disciplinary attitudes towards illicit sex in London in the 1540s to the polemics of the Cromwellian phase of the English Reformation. Noting the difficulties of assessing the evidence for change, he nevertheless concludes that the closure of the Southwark stews in 1546, 'marked a decisive break with the past'.[48] Old penalties against harlotry were revived, and required to be enforced by the Lord Mayor. The failure of the *Reformation of Ecclesiastical Laws* meant that sexual offences were still spiritual offences, punishable by the ecclesiatical courts with their penalties of carting and penance, but with the foundation of Bridewell in the 1550s began 'the widening involvement of the secular arm in the punishment of illicit sexuality'.[49] There continued to be large numbers of illicit brothels throughout London (not only in the liberties) which enjoyed the patronage of eminent figures of city and court; nevertheless, a change in attitude is marked by the refusal of Bridewell's governors to regard these clients as exempt from sexual discipline, despite the power struggles that might ensue. Warrants were used for arrest, men were punished as well as women, and the penalties meted out by the Bridewell court included incarceration and whipping. As Archer writes: 'The scope of secular action widened to include the routine investigation and punishment of fornication. Whereas the fifteenth century wardmote presentments were predominately concerned with the professionals, now non-commercial sexual relations were disciplined.'[50]

The extension of official responsibility to the control of extra-marital fornication in general links changing attitudes to prostitution with those expressed in the humanist polemic against the canon law toleration of clandestine marriage. This is a topic which evidently needs to be addressed in order to appreciate the sexual politics of the accommodation of Terence to the English stage, given that the Terentian celebration of its own persuasiveness as fiction is identified as a plot which legitimizes a contract made without consent of parents. The topic engaged the attention of the best minds of the Northern Renaissance, and Erasmus, Brenz, Bucer, Bullinger, Calvin, Zwingli and Rabelais were unequivocally condemnatory of a law so open to abuse as that which founded a matrimonial alliance on the mere consent, or token of consent, between a man and a woman. In this respect the canon law was an assault on the humanist concept of wedlock as a stable union which, responsibly entered into, would guarantee the security of inheritance and the civility of alliance on which a commonweal might be built.[51] Erasmus, commenting on Paul's words to the Corinthians on the subject of divorce, took occasion to sustain a book-length attack on the contradiction of claiming the status of a sacrament for a union so casually entered into. His characterization of the abuses of the contractual power of the mutual promise unmistakably recall the Terentian plot of clandestine betrothal:

> matrimony is contracted secretely in corners, after a stealyng fashyon, betwene boyes and yonge wenches, by the helpe and counsell of baudes and whoares; it is contracted betwene fooles and dronkards, and yet . . . they doo make of this fylthy and ungodly contracte an holy sacrament . . . I do graunt, that there is no matrimonye, without the mutual consent of the partes, but I woulde have a sober & a godly consent, not such a consent as is wonne by craft and giel, and by dronkennes. I would have suche a consent as shulde be made by the counsel, and advyse of both theyr frendes, as is mete and convenient to be, in such a thynge as can never be undone agayne.[52]

A marginal note alerts the reader to 'the preuye contractes of matrimonye betwene partes in corners without consent of the parents', and in page after page Erasmus returns to the topic, employing a rhetoric that may be paralleled in the writings of many of his contemporaries, Catholic and Protestant.[53] But the gravity of the problem called for more than rhetoric: in Geneva and Zurich the ordinances of Calvin and Zwingli rescinded clandestine contracts. In Augsburg, the Civic Marriage Courts established in 1537 successfully abolished the legal claim which sexual consummation of a verbal promise made on marriage. France sent Gentian Hervet to the Council of Trent with an oration arguing the case for the necessity of parental consent to the validity of marriage in canon law. Trent's eventual decree of 1563, the Tametsi, compromised by making the presence of a priest and two witnesses necessary to marriage, but France did not stay for the deliberations of the Catholic Church, and produced its own *Edit Contre Les Mariages Clandestins* in 1556, disinheriting children who contracted marriages against their parents' wills.[54]

In England, however, the reform of clandestine marriage was another casualty of the failure of the *Reformation of Ecclesiastical Laws* to become law; for the whole of the sixteenth century a paradoxical situation prevailed in which 'the English Church clung to a part of the medieval Roman canon law which the Roman Catholic Church itself had discarded'.[55] Yet it is evident that the failure to legislate against unwitnessed and irregular marriage contracts continued to give rise to concern throughout the century. Petitions were received by Henry VIII, requesting that due ordinances and penalties be devised against those contracting secret and unlawful marriages in St John's and Bethlehem in London.[56] When Nicholas Lesse made his translation of Erasmus on divorce about 1550, he insisted on the contemporary application of Erasmus' polemic against clandestine marriage, noting in the margin 'There be some suche contractes in London, the moore is the shame that they are suffred' and concluding his treatise with the impassioned exclamation: 'What yf Erasmus wer now alyve and in englonde, what wold he saye, knowyng we have received the word of god and this wickednes ten fould more[?]'[57]

It was in the 1570s, moreover, that the concern over clandestine marriage came to be associated with the staging of plays in publicly accessible households. Increasing rigour in the investigation and punishment of fornication coincided with an attempt on the part of the city governors to 'convert their power of regulating plays into a power of suppressing plays'.[58] In 1574 the aldermen issued an Act of Common Council establishing their exclusive right to license and regulate dramatic activity in public households. Clandestine contracts were among the first mentioned of their grievances against the practice of staging plays in public inns. The Act begins thus:

Whereas heretofore sondry greate disorders and incoveny-
ences have bene found to ensewe to this Cittie by the
inordinate hauntynge of great multitudes of people, speciallye
youthe, to playes, enterludes, and shewes, namely occasions
of ffrayes and quarrelles, eavell practizes of incontinency in
grate Innes, having chambers and secrete places adjoininge
to their open stages and galleries, *inveglynge and alleuringe
of maides, speciallye Orphans and good Citizens Children under
Age, to privie and unmete Contractes*, the publishinge of unchaste, uncomelye and unshamefast speaches and doinges.[59]
(my italics)

PRIVY CONTRACTS AND EQUITABLE REMEDIES: SEX AND DEBT IN THE PRODIGAL SON PLAYS OF THE 1570s

We may interpret the failure of the *Reformation of Ecclesiastical
Laws* as a sign of the disinclination of some Englishmen to
adopt an all-embracing, Genevan-style ecclesiastical discipline, but we should certainly not take it as evidence of
indifference to the reformation of sexual morality. Nor should
we isolate men's concern over the sexual honour of their
households from the more strictly economic concerns of
Hausvaterliteratur. Richard Whitford, in his *Werke for householders*, warned men to be on guard against 'pryvate and
secret contractes' of love among servants and *familia*, just as
he explained how to spend less, and make thrifty provision
against mischance.[60] To contemporaries, the literature of
prudence and good husbandry was in itself a means of
combating what was perceived (however erroneously) as the
spiritual and legal vacuum left by the failure to establish an
ecclesiastical discipline. Thus, Edward Hake's *Touchstone for
this time present* begins with a lament about the 'state of
Ecclesiastical government', expressing grief that 'the infallible
doome of our conscience (which of the learned is called
Synteresis) holdeth no place of terror amongst us'.[61] The
demise of the Church courts' jursidiction over pledges of faith
in matters of debt and credit was, of course, gradually giving
rise to a secular 'conscience' or 'Synderis' in the form of
equitable process, as outlined by Christopher St German in
his *Doctor and Student*; Hake himself was to write an import-

ant treaty on equity at common law. The *Touchstone* is the document in which Hake begins to set out his views on the remedying of the failure of the reformation of ecclesiastical laws in the form of recommending a humanist-style education in probable reasoning to every son and heir of a family. What is most remarkable about his proposition, however, is that the glaring social problems he assumes it will remedy are first, those arising from the inadequacy of the wager of law in assuring contractual good faith, and second, those arising from the failure of parents to ensure against daughters being persuaded into clandestine marriages.[62]

Of course, not all men were as preoccupied as Hake seems to have been with the locking up of daughters. A satirical reply (probably by another lawyer) to one of Hake's lost pamphlets on the subject of women's freedoms refers scornfully, in female voice, to Hake's strictures against venturing out of the house: 'For what causes wherfore he wold have us restrained of our liberties? "Forsooth bycause of privie contracts, he wold not have us resort to Playes."'[63] But it is important to see that while these legally-minded men express both moralistic and liberal attitudes towards clandestine marriage, liberality tends no less than moralism towards an understanding of the contract as the rhetorical victory of a man over a sensually yielding woman. A poem by the lawyer Francis Kinwelmarsh forms a dialogue in which one man mocks another for being so foolish as to tarry in his matrimonial suit for the 'proofe of / Of freendes, whose wils withold her vow aloof'. The foolish suitor is advised not to be so scrupulous in matching 'words with deedes' since, after all, 'her freendes wote how thy wil is bent'; he is urged to make his lady 'wholly thine', in spite of what he has promised to her kin. The poem is prudential in spirit; it sees clandestinity as an opportunity to argue the case in retrospect, and so win the contract in spite of the family's opposition. There is no mention of the woman's aims and intentions.[64]

Even as committed a reformer as Recorder William Fleetwood expressed a tolerance for this masculine, prudential aspect of the clandestine contracts he encountered in his tireless criminal investigations. Once he found a wedding taking place in a 'secret corner' of the Temple Church between a serving man and an ageing heiress. He told Burghley that he pitied 'the state of the poor young man' and while condemning the marriage as 'lawles', also christened it more indulgently a 'littel comedie'.[65] Belleforest similarly referred to 'ceste Comedie' when he spoke of the Count of Celant's success in matrimonial contract with Bianca Maria.[66]

Invoking the figure of Recorder William Fleetwood suitably brings into convergence the topics of Terentian comedy, clandestine sex and moral reformation with which this chapter has been concerned. For Fleetwood was a lawyer committed to the achievement of the moral reformation through the equity of the common law; his correspondence with Burghley during the years of his Recordership is full of complaints about corrupt evasions of equitable trial involving defendants claiming 'credit' with influential figures at court.[67] This theme of his office became prominent in the reformed Terentian drama of the 1570s. In such drama, the Terentian plot celebrating impostures of credit and clandestine courtships was turned inside out, and its movement towards 'catastrophe' or disclosure was made to mimic the magistrate's task in discovering imposture and bringing it to trial. Sexual and financial impostures were punished. Thus, in Whetstone's *Promos and Cassandra* (dedicated to Fleetwood) the good magistrate Ulrico hears complaints against the usuries of the corrupt Phallax: 'As thou complaynst, agaynst all equity / Houldes Phallax thy house, by this extremity?' The citizen replies: 'and he hath bound me so subtylly / As lesse you helpe, lawe yeeldes me no remedy.'[68] As Phallax holds forfeit the bonds of his debtors, so his master, Promos, deprives Cassandra of her 'credit' by seducing her on the strength of a clandestine vow to marry her and save her brother, which he then refuses to honour:

> The spoyle was sweete, and wonne even as I woulde,
> And yet ungainde, tyll I had given my trothe
> To marie hir, and that hir brother shoulde
> Be free from death, all which I bounde with oathe.
> . . . But no man else is privie to the same.[69]

The 'Christian Terence' plays of the Reformation have a certain formal ingenuity. However, they are not dramatic. In them the emotional compulsion of arguments based in error and uncertainty (the basis of dramatic verisimilitude) cannot survive the inexorable predictability of the punitive denouement. The existence of these plays, however, marks the perception among dramatists of a need for some kind of drama in which arguments based on error could work formally, creating verisimilitude in the Terentian manner, without endorsing a masculine ethos of contract-breaking. Shakespeare, I shall go on to argue, achieved just such a drama in *The Comedy of Errors* and *The Taming of the Shrew*, by transforming the Terentian 'place of error' from a set of arguments about credit impostures and sexual betrayals committed by men, into another set, preoccupied with potential infidelity on the part of women.

6

WHY DO SHAKESPEARE'S WOMEN HAVE 'CHARACTERS'?

Error, credit and sex in *The Comedy of Errors* and *The Taming of the Shrew*

THE INTEREST IN REPRESENTING WOMEN

In sixteenth-century editions of Plautus' *Amphitryon* there occurs a scene (omitted from modern editions) which provides a curious gloss on the play. Amphitryon, having been away from home fighting the Telobians, returns to an errant husband's worst nightmare: he is spurned by his wife, Alcmena, for an imposter. The imposter is, of course, Jupiter, but Amphitryon does not know this yet. The audience, however, is assumed to be familiar with this myth of the birth of Hercules, a knowledge which Mercury (who, as the deity of commerce, presides over the play) exploits in a comment on Amphitryon's noisy self-pity. 'Lucrist', he says, 'quod miserum deputat, nam uxorem usuriam' ('What he counts loss is sheer gain, for his wife is lent out at interest').[1]

We have seen how plots analysed according to Donatus' model of Terentian error (also used in sixteenth-century editions of Plautus, such as that produced by Lambinus in 1576) enhanced the 'credit' of male protagonists to the extent that they problematized the certainty of men's good faith long enough to prove a happy resolution to the whole error-based dilemma. Such plots implicitly identified men's broken vows and credit frauds with the play's happy capacity to persuade us of the possibility of events both fantastic and improbable. But women's credit (and, by association, that of their kinsmen and household) could scarcely thrive in the gossipy air of error and conjecture; as we saw, Clinia's 'error' about Antiphila in Terence's *Self Tormentor* elicited a narrative which was productive only in arresting speculation about her *ingenium* or moral character.

Yet when Plautus writes that Amphitryon's wife has become a source of productive gain or 'usury' to her husband, he is suggesting an identification between the fabulous productivity of the myth (productive of *fabulae* – probable arguments as well as dramatic plots) in being able to reconcile an improbable story about wives being faithful and households increasing in honour while husbands are absent, with a down-to-earth comic scandal of cuckoldry and loss. In *Amphitryon*, sixteenth-century humanists might find a myth of their own ambivalence towards the productivity of credible argument based in error rather than in the assurance of good faith: on the one hand, a threat to traditional conceptions of household honour; on the other, the fantastic possibility of increasing that honour in the happiness of a Jovial imposture and its Herculean effects. So John Foxe has Titus use the *Amphitryon* as an allegory of invincible plotting in his comedy of *Titus et Gesippus*. Titus describes the counterfeit wedding: 'By Hercules, you would have said that Gesippus had Mercury with him for a Sosia, and Jove himself to applaud his plot (*fabula*).'[2]

In this chapter I shall argue that Shakespeare faced and resolved the problem of representing women within the doubtful, gossipy mode of the Terentian plot by picking up the hint in Plautus' *Amphitryon*, that is, by identifying the representation of *women*, rather than men, with the dramatic productivity of 'error'.

Prior to Shakespeare, the representation of women in a Terentian-style drama seems to have been rendered extremely problematic, if not unthinkable, by virtue of the impossibility of reversing the effects of scandal created by conjectural arguments or 'errors' concerning women's credit. A unique solution to the problem exists in Nicholas Udall's brilliant Terentian comedy of *Ralph Roister Doister*, but it involves the eschewing of a deliberative resolution.[3] The credit or sexual reputation of the widow Custance (which is, *pace* Altman, the deliberative issue of the play[4]) is resolved by witness, not equitable probation. Though her contractual good faith to Gavin Goodluck has been cast into doubt by a series of probable arguments (including an ambiguously construed letter, which found its way into Thomas Wilson's textbook of dialectic, *The Rule of Reason*[5]), Custance's honesty is finally assured through the agreement of Tristam Trusty to depose for her against the probation of Sim Suresby. We know (although the trial takes place off-stage) that Trusty's evidence will clear her name, for we have seen with our own eyes that Doister has never had access to Custance's house, so that Suresby's doubts about her good faith to the absent Goodlucke have arisen, as we can testify, from evident misconstructions of her conduct by her suitor, the foolish Doister, egged on by the mischievous Merrygreek. By calling on the audience as witnesses, Udall closes off the Terentian space of hypothesis and deliberation as a 'gappe'[6] that may defame the respectable women of citizen households. This in turn precludes the possibility of drama; as a solution to the problem of representing chaste women in Terentian-style comedy *Ralph Roister Doister* is both a *tour de force* and a dead end.

Udall's example helps to confirm my hypothesis about the problems of representing female chastity in a deliberative mode. The women in Plautus and Terence tend to be already unchaste (they are often courtesans); otherwise they are dramatically insignificant. Their importance to the story consists in their having slept with the young men whose ambition it is to marry against paternal opposition. Shakespeare's women are, of course, unlike these in being dramatically significant, articulate and histrionic. Yet Shakespeare's women are also unlike the equally active and vocal women in the Terentian-style comedy written and imitated by sixteenth-century humanists (Cinthio's *Epitia* and Whetstone's *Promos and Cassandra*; Ariosto's *I Suppositi* and Gascoigne's *Supposes*) in that they are, apparently, *chaste*. Where Whetstone's Cassandra loses her virginity and her 'credit' thanks to Promos' broken vow, Shakespeare's Isabella remains virginal. And where Gascoigne's Polynesta becomes the scandal of Ferrara for having slept with the false Dulippo, no one in Shakespeare's Padua seems to think that Bianca has slept with Lucentio. Where Plautus' Alcmena gives birth to Jupiter's son, Shakespeare's Adriana gives birth to a new kind of drama in which women become productive (that is, dramatically intriguing) not at the level of outward sexual scandal (which would be an explicit loss of their credit within the fiction, implicating male kin in dishonour) but at the level of the audience's uncertainty about their sexual intentions and desires. Why does Shakespeare's Isabella profess virginity and talk about whips and lovers' beds? Is Bianca's modesty and aptness to learn really sexual knowingness? Why does Desdemona show a sudden interest in Lodovico's good looks? Why is it Luciana and not Antipholus who speaks up for men's duty to be discreet in their conjugal infidelities?

It is not fashionable to observe that Shakespeare is more accomplished than his contemporaries in endowing his *dramatis personae* – especially women – with 'character' in the sense of an illusion of interiority and developmental continuity. Yet in spite, or because, of the current critical preference for models of subjectivity which de-emphasize psychological interiority and prefer to focus upon social, semiotic and historical contingency in our experiencing of ourselves as subjects, there remains a need to account for the cultural endurance of fictions of women which seem (unlike the their counterparts in sixteenth-century drama, poetry and prose) to transcend these very contingencies, or to be *too productive*, from age to age, of convincing interpretations.

'AMPHITRYON' AND THE LAWYERS, OR ADRIANA'S BABY

In her wonderfully rich explication of Jean de Coras' record of the trial of the imposter of Martin Guerre, Natalie Davis imagines a situation in which there need never have been a text of the trial. 'Could the woes of the Guerres have come about', she imagines Jean de Coras asking, 'in the Reformed City of Geneva, where an assiduous consistory would never have permitted so youthful a marriage, would have divorced Bertrande betimes, and would quickly have uncovered adultery?'[7] She sees the text, in other words, as having been composed by the Hugenot Coras in *compensation* for the lack of a Genevan-style ecclesiastical discipline to oversee clandestine contracts and credit impostures among Protestants who no longer bared their souls to priests in the confessional. There are resemblances, then, between Coras' text and the writings of English lawyers and dramatists – Fleetwood, Hake, Whetstone, Gascoigne – who likewise record or represent a desire to bring about reformation in the absence of ecclesiastical discipline, through the enabling of men to conduct trials of equity.

Thus it seems at first sight as if Coras' text of the trial, in which the arrival of the real Martin Guerre exposes the deceits and errors of Arnauld du Tilh, resembles the Christian Terence plays of Whetstone and Gascoigne and others in formally suggesting a consonance between Protestant equity and the judgements of God. Indeed, the printer of the second edition advertised it as 'presque vne Tragi comedie' with a 'pleasant and diverting' protasis, followed by an 'uncertain and doubtful' epitasis and a catastrophe, characterized as 'sad, pitiful and miserable in its discovery of hypocrisy and dissimulation'.[8] This description of the case makes it conform precisely to the Christian 'prodigal son' type of tragicomedy, in which the errors mobilized to produce the dramatic and dilatory place of uncertainty and conjecture in the epitasis are discovered in the catastrophe so as to close off dramatic uncertainty completely, to unmask it as 'hypocrisy'.

And yet the effect of Coras' text is more ambivalent and has been (therefore) more productive of interpretation. Acknowledging this, Davis resists the printer's designation of the trial as a tragicomedy, preferring to distinguish it with the name of 'comitragedy'.[9] The difference is that Coras' text preserves, through its encouragement of an emotional identification with du Tilh, a sense of lingering uncertainty about the unmasking of the errors: was du Tilh guilty after all? This sense of uncertainty was to be an important aspect – perhaps the important aspect – of the cultural legacy of the text. Montaigne wrote that it seemed to him that Coras had rendered the imposture of him whom he judged guilty so marvellous and exceeding human knowledge, that he should not have hanged him.[10] The uncertainty in the text is partly the effect of repeated suggestions, in Coras' examination of du Tilh's imposture, of an admiration for his capacity to elicit and retain vast tracts of information about village life and about the personal history and household secrets of Martin Guerre, through the persuasive power of *amicitia*, and, with Xenophonic prudence, to memorize and mobilize this information with such probability that, wrote Coras, it was most equitable to believe the witnesses who testified for the prisoner, for these 'tesmoignent des choses plus approchantes la versimilitude' (testified matters that seemed to have more likelihood) than did those testifying against him.[11] This, surely, was a victory equivalent to that of Cyrus, or Scipio Africanus, both of whom were notable for enhancing the likely success of their histrionic actions by careful research and preparation: indeed, Coras compares the prodigy of du Tilh's feat of memory to that of Cyrus 'who knew the names of all his soldiers' and Scipio Africanus.[12] There seems to be a latent sense of identification between the humanist lawyer, whose memory was so copiously stored with examples as to enable him to produce plausible arguments on either side, and the imposter whose plausibility had convinced an entire village.

It is worth remarking, for the sake of my argument, that Coras' text first came to my notice by way of a 1572 edition of his *Paraphrase sur l'Edict des Marriages clandestinement contractez* which

I wanted to read because of the prominence of clandestine marriage as a theme in the *Histoires Tragiques* which were begun by one of Coras' law students, Pierre Boiastuau. It was in this edition that I found Coras' trial of Martin Guerre. Natalie Davis explains why: Coras's book was 'bought first and foremost by lawyers and judges who . . . wrote notes in the margins, had it bound together with Coras' *Paraphrase sur l'Edict des Marriages clandestinement contractez*, or with other books on marriage law'.[13] And yet, as I read the texts side by side, it seemed to me that the implications of Davis' observation had been missed by literary critics. For Coras' *Paraphrase sur l'Edict* is, like the text of the trial of Martin Guerre, an argumentative supplement to the recent legislation against clandestine marriage. It is written in consciousness of the fact that canon law had not changed (the French were not waiting for the Council of Trent on this issue) so it was desirous to persuade men of the necessity of taking moral discipline into their own hands. But a text, of course, does not so much discipline readers as engage them in argument. So Coras' *Paraphrase* celebrates men's power, as readers, to judge his own arguments, and to apply them in causes of their own. It offers 'arguments and reasons . . . strong enough to render our adversaries harassed, and breathless', as well as 'authorities and examples to refresh them, and . . . win them over, if they are not quite inexorable and deaf to all persuasion'.[14] Reasons are drawn from Terence (*Phormio*) and examples from Terence's *Andria* and Xenophon's *Cyropaedia* to urge the benefits of obtaining parental consent before marriage, but the text is flexible on the issue of sexually consummated betrothal, having 'more regard for the conservation of public tranquillity than for the upholding of the authority of fathers'.[15] Thus, through its idiom of reasonable persuasion, drawing on masculine knowledge of classical examples to 'win over' its readers, the text stresses not the authority of parents over children, *but the shared interests of men as readers in husbanding their wives and patrimonies.*

The very mode of reasoning probably from classical exempla which characterizes the *Paraphrase* also dominates Coras' text of the trial of Martin Guerre. It is, in fact, this mode of probable reasoning which gives the trial the effect of a 'comitragedy' rather than a 'tragicomedy'. For it is through his pleasure in reasoning thus through annotations that Coras conveys the admiration for Arnauld du Tilh remarked on by Davis. We may then conclude that unlike a tragicomedy of the 'Christian Terence' type, which finally unmasks and condemns the productivity of probable reasoning, Coras' text almost celebrates such reasoning as its hero – if not the heroic imposture of du Tilh, then the heroic productivity of his own text among the lawyers. Moreover, if that productivity worked, as Montaigne suggests, to maintain uncertainty about the final verdict, the identity of Martin Guerre, then this in turn was the effect of a conceptual 'usury' in the text – that is, an unresolved doubling of the function of Bertrande de Rols in Coras' judgement. Thus, although Coras admits that it was not probable (*vray semblable*) that Bertrande should not have recognized du Tilh for a stranger, he nevertheless argues that she is *not guilty of having deceived her own husband with intent,* for 'où y a erreur, nous disons qu'il n'y a point de consentement, ni de volonté' ('where there is error, we say there is not voluntary consent').[16] This judgement of Coras' does not square, as Davis says, with the reader's sense of likelihood if she or he discounts sixteenth-century generalizations about the easily deceived intellects and senses of women.[17] Nevertheless, the very ambiguity or error 'works' in the interests of the text, in the sense that it preserves the positive sense of uncertainty about du Tilh's status which prevents the story from degenerating into a *fabliau*, and which even elevates it into a story of 'identity crisis'. The cultural endurance of the story is thus contingent upon the location of error in the unknowability of Bertrande de Rols. As Terence Cave writes:

> Betrande de Rols here becomes, by implication, the figure of female difference: she is the unknown quantity, the one who knows what the men don't know, the faithful wife who may also have abetted the imposter. Any reading of Martin Guerre's story is bound to make Bertrande central to the uncertainty of the recognition (whom did she recognise behind the scenes, in bed?). Central, yet always, in a male dominated society, peripheral: which is exactly why she is a blind spot.[18]

Cave's formulation is very suggestive: in the first place, the idea that someone might 'recognize' differently in front of the scenes and behind them effaces the intention we assume is involved in acts of dissimulation, and suggests an *inherent* and *involuntary* theatrical duplicity. It also, of course, links theatrical duplicity (being different in front of and behind the scenes) with sexuality: 'behind the scenes' = 'in bed'. Where does the oxymoronic figure of the faithful/faithless wife come from? In Coras' text, from the resemblance he detects between his activity of equitable probation, and that which fails to discover the identity of the imposter in Plautus' *Amphitryon*.

Coras evidently liked the *Amphitryon*, for his annotation on its resemblance to the case in hand is very substantial. The episode which he finds the 'finest' (*le plus beau*)[19] of the whole drama is a scene in the epitasis (nowadays omitted) in which Amphitryon, having been refused entry into his own house by his wife, Alcmena, who is indoors with his double, fetches a neighbour called Blepharo to arbitrate between the true and false Amphitryons. 'At last', Coras writes,

> Blepharo is elected arbitrator, to judge which of the two is the real Amphitryon, who, because of the utter likeness between them, doesn't know how to distinguish one from the other . . . Seeing which, Jupiter, in order to demonstrate Alcmena's innocence, discovers in full the whole case to Amphitryon, to set him in peace and love once more with his wife.[20]

Blepharo agrees to try the cause by probable reason ('Faciam id si queo signis palam' – 'I'll do it if I can by open proofs', he says[21]) and his attempts to assess authenticity by testing the memories of the two Amphitryons by means of questions about the recent battle against the Taphians obviously parallels Coras' own procedures in examining du Tilh. But more than that, Jupiter's disclosure of himself in the catastrophe, unlike the unmasking of imposture by the providence of the Christian God, enables the reconciliation of conjugal fidelity ('paix et amitie avec sa femme'), with the appreciation of the productivity of the place of error at the heart of deliberation.

What makes the celebratory acknowledgement of the productivity of such probable impostures possible in Plautus' play, of course, is the location of the error in the involuntary consent of the body of Alcmena to the embrace of the marvellous stranger. The honour of the household is preserved by the suspension of Alcmena between the involuntary error of allowing herself to be violated by the imposter, and its fruits in the disclosure which not only proves her innocence, but, in her parturition and birth-giving, amply compensates for the temporary anxieties of infidelity and defamation in the birth of the hero. Alcmena becomes the paradigmatic 'faithful wife who may also have abetted the imposter', revealing how productive such an oxymoronic location of uncertainty might be in enabling the space of error and confusion to dilate, rhetorically speaking, without an over-hasty termination in the interests of exposing sin and discovering the truth.

If we turn now from mid-sixteenth-century France to the 1590s in England, and from the problems of preventing, without a Genevan ecclesiastical discipline, cases such as that of the Guerres, to the problems of enabling, again without such discipline, a drama of deliberative fiction, we shall find Plautus' *Amphitryon* once again at work, with a wife once again rhetorically 'lent at interest'. Our setting is now London, at the Inns of Court, where we know that 'a Comedy of Errors' was performed for the Christmas revels of 1594.[22]

The theme of error and theatrical illusion seems to have run through the revels at Gray's Inn that year. But Shakespeare's comedy opens inauspiciously for a play that might be expected to generate a place for error through the rehearsal of some urgent dilemma requiring conjecture and hypothesis. For although there is the basis of a legal dilemma – the criminality of Egeon's mere presence in Ephesus – *pro et contra* argument on the subject has already been terminated by the first line: 'Merchant of Syracusa, plead no more. / I am not partial to infringe our laws.'[23] To open a play thus is to take up the dramatic dead end of the prodigal son plays, in which errors having been exposed as debts and impostures of credit, nothing remains but impartial punishment before the law. Thus, for example, in Gascoigne's reformed Terentian tragicomedy, the *Glasse of Government*, one of the issues is the frustration of the magistrate's desire, having arrested the pimp, courtesan and the prodigals, to 'finde any proofe against them, whereby they ought to be punished'[24]. When one of their eye-deceiving devices (an imposture of credit – a claim to kinship with the magistrate himself) is then revealed to him, he is able to try and punish them equitably, and the play ends with the observation that it is 'a happy common wealth where Justice may be ministered with severitie, and no where no mediations or suits may wrest the sentence of the law'.[25]

Shakespeare's comedy, then, begins with an image of the prodigal son plays' death sentence upon the deliberative, dilatory time/space of the Terentian plot. This, of course, is a death sentence to masculine cultural production in humanist terms. For, as a model of counsel taken in emergency or 'reasoning in doubtful affairs',[26] Terentian comedy offered an image, through its own audacity as a fantastic yet plausible fiction, of the effectiveness of deliberation in practical contingency. This is why so often in Plautus or Terence or the *commediae eruditiae* which imitate them, the very unlikelihood of the poet's successful imposition on our belief finds a correspondent materialization in the capacity of desperation – the emergency of the epitasis – to enable the slave's or the lover's last-minute improvisation of the cash, credit or plausibility required to relieve temporarily the moment of crisis. Thus, for example, in Terence's *Phormio*, in Ariosto's *La Cassaria*, or even in the cave episode of Sidney's Terentian *Old Arcadia*, where the extreme constriction of a 'promise . . . tied to so small compasse of time' materialized in the spatially tight spot of the cave, forces Cleophilia to deliberate and produce 'a ground plot' with astonishing facility.[27] In Plautus' *Pseudolus*, the identification between the poet's fantasy and the protagonist's imposture of credit is made explicit when Pseudolus, having not one 'drop of certain counsel' (*gutta certi consili*) insists that he will 'find' (*inveniam*) the cash or credit he needs to get the courtesan for his master, 'like the poet who, once his tablets are in hand, hunts for what is nowhere on this earth, yet finds it, and makes a lie look like the truth' ('facit illud veri simile, quod mendacium est'.)[28]

The effect of the prodigal son plot was to exhaust confidence in the productive power of deliberation, figured in the comedies by the cornucopia of invention elicited from terror- struck slaves in the stormy moment of the epitasis, when time is fast running out, and the severe father returning home to find his sons married to courtesans, or worse. By refusing to countenance the improvisatory credit that allows a dilemma time to resolve itself through some such device as the romance of origin, the prodigal son plot produced the time/space of urban comedy as purely attritive. The young man's impostures of credit are thus conceived purely in terms of taxes on his own substantiality, debts growing to the point where, in Lord Burghley's words, young men 'consume themselves' and 'run into such debts and shifts as they cannot live without danger of the laws without attempting of unlawful acts'.[29] Such are the inhabitants of of the eroding time/space of Ephesus – inadvertently self-consuming prodigals who cannot stop divesting themselves of the 'marks' of their credit, or suffering arrest for debt by excessively thick-skinned officers of the law.

The audience for whom *The Comedy of Errors* was composed and performed, the gentlemen of Gray's Inn, were precisely those targeted by this discourse of prodigality. Thus, Whetstone's *Mirrour for Magestrates* (dedicated to the Aldermen and Fleetwood), begins by noting that there are 'divers worthie Houses called, the *Innes of Court*' which nourish 'the marrow and strength of this happy realm, I mean, the Abilitie of the gentlemen', but laments that this 'ability' is 'much weakned and almost wasted' by the young men's haunting of brothels, dicing houses and ordinaries. Whetstone imagines a London in which this waste would be arrested by the prohibition of 'error' or wandering on the parts of gentlemen and citizens, so that young men might be kept from the seductions of prodigality, and citizens from the 'great inconvenience' that might follow 'when a man leaveth his owne house, and the companie of his wife and familie, and dineth at a dicing house'.[30]

Assuming that the real waste of ability is the prohibition of cultural production of the part of gentlemen, Shakespeare turns the debt-time of the prodigal plays inside out in *The Comedy of Errors*, transforming it into 'season'; the fortunate *locus* of rhetorical improvisation and the affirmation of drama. He does this by displacing from the focus of deliberative trial the sexual and financial misconduct of errant young men, placing there in its stead cause for suspicion of the sexual misconduct of *women* in the conjugal household. Thus prodigal sons both in the fiction and in the audience may identify newly as 'good husbands' for whom the city street and the marketplace ceases to be the predatory places of their victimization by pimps, courtesans and magistrates, and become the symbolic 'outdoors' of readiness for negotiation, the place of Ischomachus in the agora, who produces himself by having already produced the surveillance-space of his wife in the home.

At first comic time and urban space are aggressively, ludicrously attritive, wearing and wasting the substance of the male body. The explicit emergency of time and and strangeness of place – Ephesus, until five o'clock – insteading of freeing the male protagonist of Terentian comedy (no one knowing him by sight, because of his being a stranger, or in disguise) into the fortunate improvisation of wild deceits and impostures, seems rather to exhaust all his rhetorical ingenuity and resistance to the law. One male protagonist from Syracuse (Egeon) has no sooner wandered off the scene into terminal debt at the rate of a thousand marks, but another (Antipholus) wanders on, and proceeds to divest himself

of exactly that amount of his own substance. The want of 'marks' –
signs of credit and kinship – which usually offers opportunity
(*occasio, fortuna*) for the productive counterfeiting of a temporary,
rhetorical assurance, appears in this play to be constrictive to the
point of threatening life. And, at the farcical level of the play's
language, this dangerous loss of sign and substance in the confused
exchange of 'marks' materializes in the blows that disfigure and
make insubstantial a household servant, so that while Antipholus
of Syracuse, handing over a thousand marks to his Dromio, can
identify this movement into the opportunity-space of error with
radical self-loss ('I will go lose myself, / And wander up and
down to view the city', I.ii.30–1), Dromio of Ephesus, finding him,
exhibits as erosions of his body the very signs of kinship and credit
that the Syracusan wants: 'I have some marks of yours upon my
pate/Some of my mistress' marks upon my shoulders' (I.ii.82–3).
The chiastic confusion that intensifies and multiplies the blows
upon Dromio appears, in this early phase of the drama, merely to
wear him away. Dromio hasn't enough skin to stay intact in the
exchange: 'You spurn me hence, and he will spurn me hither: / If I
last in this service you must case me in leather' (II.i.84–5).

It is not only, of course, Dromio of Ephesus who suffers from
this cross-over of intention and effect. In the linear and predatory
time/space of prodigal Ephesus, inexorably drawing on the hour
of five o'clock, nothing grows but debts. A merchant, in conversation with Angelo, the goldsmith, urges:

> You know since Pentecost the sum is due
> And since I have not much importun'd you,
> Nor now I had not, but that I am bound
> To Persia, and want guilders for my voyage;
> Therefore make present satisfaction
> Or I'll attach you by this officer.

Angelo: Even just the sum which I do owe to you
> Is growing to me by Antipholus
> And in this instant that I met with you
> He had of me a chain, at five o'clock
> I shall receive the money

> (IV.i.1–11)

Another purpose has, of course, been crossed here: Antipholus of
Syracuse having received the chain, Antipholus of Ephesus is not
forthcoming with the money. A prodigal son type of *epitasis* has

been condensed and double-crossed; while the insubstantially prodigal Antipholus of Syracuse appears to wander free of the Ephesian law that requires him to pay his debt, the Ephesian citizen Antipholus, though 'Of credit infinite, highly belov'd' (V.i.4) in his own town, suffers the ignominious fate of an Acolastus, being arrested for debt by an officer who appears to be wearing the fleeced prodigal's substance, for he 'goes in the calf's skin that was killed for the prodigal' (IV.iii.16–18). But, at the moment of the arrest, a curious thing happens to the linear temporality of the play, enabling it, after all, to dilate. For, in the moment of Antipholus' arrest, time suddenly doubles back on itself. Dromio of Syracuse, having just rushed to Adriana for the redemption money, notices the hour:

Dromio: 'tis time that I were gone
          It was two ere I left him, and now the clock strikes
          one.
Adriana: The hours come back: that did I never hear.
Dromio: O yes, if any hour meet a sergeant, 'a turns back
          for very fear.
Adriana: As if time were in debt; how fondly dost thou
          reason.
Dromio: Time is a very bankrupt, and owes more than he's
          worth to season.

(IV.ii.54–7)

It is odd that critics single out *The Comedy of Errors* for the formal regularity of its time-scheme, for nowhere except in *The Winter's Tale* is the illusionistic verisimilitude of dramatic time more ruthlessly and comically sabotaged. Here the play ceases to image time as the inexorable sentence of the law, and transforms it into the happy or fortunate 'season', the time/space in which persuasive discourse, introducing error as scope for argument *pro et contra*, may reverse the law's sentence. The difference between 'time' and 'season', as the words were used by sixteenth-century humanists, corresponds to the difference Cicero identifies between *tempus* and *occasio*, or between the Greek *kronos* and *kairos* or *eukairia*. Thus, for example, Gascoigne's poem, 'Woodmanship', which transforms a social gaffe into opportunity to make an argued case for his social advancement, speaks of its own effectiveness as being dependent on being received 'in season' by Lord Grey. The decorum of Gascoigne's invention as a poet becomes analogous to his prudence as an exploiter of the unfortunate social occasion; and, indeed, Cicero's *De Officiis* made poetic decorum analogous to what one sixteenth-century translator of Cicero called, 'this syence of opportunitie of tyme to do any thynge' which 'same selfe defynycion may be the defynycion of prudence'. [31]

In *The Comedy of Errors*, then, Shakespeare is concerned with the inability of 'Christian Terence', or the prodigal son type of plot, to imagine a time/space of 'occasion' or 'season' in which the deliberate introduction of error or ambiguity or uncertainty into discursive exchange is read, not as irresponsible credit fraud with intention to deceive, but as the masculine exercise of prudence. The problem, in dramatic terms, becomes one of breaking down the Terentian identification of men's deliberative energies – their capacity to exploit the temporal and spatial 'occasion' – with their capacity to threaten the sexual honour of other men, by infiltrating their houses and seducing their kinswomen.

Shakespeare solves this problem by identifying female sexuality as the time/space of opportunity itself, thereby ensuring the implication of men's freedom to 'err', while the moral accountability of error is displaced on the conduct of women. The secret of moderation and discipline thus ceases to lie in the magisterial punishment of men, becoming, instead, a question of the *oikonomia* of representation: the husbandry of images of women.

Thus it is that only after the first scene in which women are represented in dialogic consultation with one another – a scene evidently indebted to Xenophon, and to Erasmus' *Coniugium* – is there perceived to be any breach in the play's representation of time as predatory and punitive of young men. This breach opens in Act II, scene ii, in which Antipholus and Dromio of Syracuse indulge in an extended joke over the baldness and masculinity of 'Father Time'. The point of the joke becomes clear: in Renaissance iconography, *tempus* is indeed masculine, but in defining *tempus* as bald, the young men call attention to their inability to conceive of time not as *tempus* but as *occasio*, which, in contemporary iconography, was portrayed as being not masculine, but feminine, and only bald at the back, having in her forehead a lock of hair to signify her ability to be seized and possessed by the prudent man.[32] In making jokes about syphilis and the baldness of 'Father Time', the young master and his servant lay bare the contradictions of the prodigal son discourse. For the sexual/economic anxiety betrayed by these jokes (fear of self-loss, fear of syphilis) may also be construed as a self-defeating refusal to acknowledge the femininity of time as *occasio* or *fortuna*. This in turn signifies a failure in prudence, for prudence is emblematically defined as a man seizing the female Occasio by the forelock, realizing in this gesture the good fortune latent in the error and uncertainty of circumstance.

It is in the moment of the Syracusan Dromio's pronouncement of Time's eternal debt to 'season' that the play explicitly transforms dramatic error from masculine sexual sin into masculine prudential opportunity. Adriana glosses this metaphorical transformation of the play's temporality with an enigmatic request for help from her sister: 'Come, sister, I am press'd down with conceit; / Conceit, my comfort and my injury' (IV.ii.65–6).

With these words, Adriana has taken up, in metaphor, the position of Alcmena in *Amphitryon*. The dramatist's exploitation of the inventive occasion which enables 'conceit' is figured as a sexual pressure on Adriana, and a conception in her womb. According to the paradigm of the reforming discourses of the 1570s and 1580s, of course, the social situation represented so far in the comedy is over-determinedly leading to clandestine sexual transgression: a husband has gone to dine with a courtesan, and while he is absent from his own household, a stranger has entered it, at the invitation of his wife and kinswoman. But in the chiasmus of sexual adventure, nothing seems to have happened. What, then, have the female parts of the play to do with its transformation from a retributive economy of debt and arrest to an expansive 'season' of fortuitous comic discoveries?

It is, in fact, the women whose voices transform the chiastic error (wandering) of the men from an unproductive stasis in subjection to the discipline of the law to a mobile and fortunate mastery of the negotiating potential of urban time/space. In II.i, a scene whose antecedents are the Xenophonic discourses of household, such as Erasmus' *Coniugium*, or Walter Lynne's *Vertuous Scholehous of ungracious women* (n.d.), Adriana and Luciana between them begin to perform the play's function of displacing male sexual and financial conduct from the ideological constraints of discipline. The first words we hear Antipholus of Ephesus speak – 'My wife is shrewish when I keep not hours' (III.i.2) – define her unruliness in terms of the temporal and spatial constriction of *his* negotiating potential. Adriana complains to Luciana, like Xantippe to Eulalia: 'Why should their liberty than ours be more?' and Luciana replies, 'Because their business still lies out o'door' (II.i.10–11). Walter Lynne's Xenophonic dialogue makes the point clear: here, the curst wife, Serapina, is likewise impatient about her husband's absence from the house, but the good wife, Justina, urges her to consider the productivity of her husband's freedom to negotiate, using time and place as he sees fit. 'I knowe', concedes Serapina, 'that he dyd more wyth one worde, then I can do in a hole day.'[33] The work of women indoors cannot compete with the expansiveness of the propitious oratorical occasion for which the prudent man in the marketplace is ready. By acknowledging this, Shakespeare's use of the Xenophonic dialogue of wives makes over to men the right to exercise what Michel de Certeau has described as the art of the narrative *coup* – 'a balancing act in which the circumstances (place and time) and the speaker himself participate'. De Certeau goes on, using the work of Marcel Detienne, to elaborate this use of narrative as 'a form of intelligence that is always "immersed in practice" ... which ... counts and plays on the right point in time (*kairos*): it is a temporal practice ... it takes on many different masks and metaphors: it is an undoing of the proper place (le lieu propre)'.[34] The 'proper' place of men thus becomes an effect of skill in the temporal practice of negotiating such *coups*, of which the *Comedy*'s denouement – the same story as Egeon told at the beginning, only discovered with more timeliness – is itself an example. Thus the whole play works to insist on the contradiction that at least one editor has found in the words of Luciana at II.i.7–8: 'A man is master of his liberty / Time is their master, and when they see time, / They'll go or come.' As Stanley Wells pointed out, if a man is master of his liberty, time is not his master, but his easy-going *mistress*, and he amended the line accordingly in the original spelling edition of the *Complete Works*.[35] Whether or not the emendation can be supported, the tension in the nonsense of Luciana's lines as they stand (and 'Luciana', after all, suggests 'Lucian', the author most associated with the productive un-certainty of nonsense) points towards a resolution consonant with Wells' reading: in the course of the play, male 'husbandry', or freedom to negotiate, begins to justify 'error' (both wandering, and using the spaces of conjecture and uncertainty) as the proper place in which men are henceforward to be culturally productive.

But how is this translation of the sexually and financially irresponsible prodigal into the good husband of his own occasions to be achieved without opening the doors of the citizen household to the wandering threat of male lust? Shakespeare solves the problem by dividing the oxymoronic duplicity of Alcmena – the faithful wife/receiver of the imposter – between three female figures in the play, Adriana, Luciana and Luce. Luciana's is the involuntary error of authorizing male sexual transgression in an exchange in which the response of Antipholus is formally precise about the significance of her words in transforming his relation to the comic *fabula*. Luciana, thinking that she is speaking to Adriana's husband, urges him to do his philandering discreetly:

> . . . if you like elsewhere, do it by stealth,
> Muffle your false love with some show of blindness.
> . . . Look sweet, speak fair, become disloyalty;
> Apparel vice like virtue's harbinger . . .
> Be secret false; what need she be acquainted?
>
> (III.ii.8–15)

Antipholus' endlessly puzzled yet seduced reply leaves him on the brink of explicitly becoming the sexual predator, the violator of household honour. It sustains him in the error of implication, the enfolding of *her* words' deceit. His response refers explicitly to the privileging, in Donatus' analysis and commentary on Terence, of the 'place for error' as the strategically deferred 'unfolding' or explication of the *fabula*, which sustains the audience in expectation, giving negotiating power to an improbable fiction. But where Terence and his followers identify this error-based rhetorical power with the male protagonists' deliberate improvisations of credit, Shakespeare merely implies such a power as the possibility Antipholus gropes towards understanding in Luciana's words. It is thus her words' error that insulates him, as it were, from error's blame. She authorizes his release from ethical constraint upon his sexual conduct and his rhetorical mobility, while she herself becomes a focus of suspicion through the involuntarily seductive implication of her speech. 'Teach me', he pleads to her,

> how to think and speak;
> Lay open to my earthy gross conceit,
> Smother'd in errors, feeble, shallow, weak,
> The folded meaning of your words' deceit.
> Against my soul's pure truth, why labour you
> To make it wander in an unknown field?
> Are you a god? Would you create me new?
> Transform me then, and to your power I'll yield.

O, train me not, sweet mermaid, with thy note
To drown me in thy sister's flood of tears;
Sing, siren, for thyself and I will dote;
Spread o'er the silver waves thy golden hairs,
And as a bed I'll take thee and there lie.

(III.ii.51–2)

In this fantastic double displacement, Luciana's misconstrued speech to Antipholus of Syracuse dissociates the figure of the rhetorically mobile imposter, the supposed husband, from the threat of sexual betrayal, and relocates that threat in the indiscreet or involuntarily ambiguous implication of a woman's words. The displacement is double, for Luciana's words are addressed to the absent Antipholus of Ephesus who, like the husband in the *Menaechmi*, has gone off to lunch with the equivalent of Plautus' Erotium. The absent husband and the bachelor 'smothered in error' are both inaccessible, and therefore morally unaccountable as interpreters of Luciana's words; at the same time, the erroneous address of her speech releases it from exclusive application, and gives it the force of a general authorization and a general image of enticement. The result is to exempt deliberative theatre from the obligation to inquire magisterially into men's sexual conduct (figured as prodigality). The magistrate and the prodigal are henceforward to be united in a new brotherhood: a deliberative theatre that acknowledges men's shared responsibility for policing a sexuality in women which resists all rational control, being itself quite involuntarily seductive, a meaning without an intention.

If the 'folded deceit' of Luciana's *words* frees masculine conceit into a regeneration of error as the inconsequentially conjectural time/space of comic fictions, so, symbolically, do the folds of fat Luce's *body*. In the scene before the intimate exchange between Luciana and Antipholus of Syracuse, the Ephesian Antipholus arrives with his merchant friend at the door, only to find himself reviled and denied entrance. The scene closely resembles the (now considered corrupt) threshold scene in the fourth act of *Amphitryon*, in which Mercury, having borrowed the 'marks' (*signis*) of Amphitryon's servant, Sosia, denies and insults his master, and laughs at the usury of his wife. The escalating verbal battery which follows suggests, in *Amphitryon*, a kind of hymeneal magic: as Mercury deals blows at Amphitryon's credit and self-esteem, his wife indoors has conceived of Jupiter a burden that will not dishonour him. In *The Comedy of Errors*, it is at this point that blows cease to have purely attritive qualities (effacing the 'marks' of masculine credit and kinship), and become associated with sex, and with the female body's capacity to conceive. In *Amphitryon*, the epitasis in which Jupiter appears as Amphitryon, to engage Blepharo in distinguishing the false from the true husband, is justified by Jupiter himself as a deliberative game to prolong the errors until it is time for Alcmena's parturition: 'so as not to terminate this inchoate comedy before time.'[36] In Shakespeare, Jupiter's error-prolonging game of conjecture and probable reason is *materialized*, as Patricia Parker has brilliantly observed, by the female body of Nell, or Luce, the kitchen wench who becomes the porter. 'In the play's own middle', Parker writes,

> we encounter a wall of partition, which keeps the sets of twins from precipitating too early that final recognition scene . . . the figure that guards this wall . . . is a wondrous fat lady . . . she is so fat that she is spherical, like the globe itself: 'I could find out countries in her', says Dromio.[37]

Yet, while Luce's verbal 'Have at you' keeps the husband outdoors in error, the crucial metaphoric significance of that fact that she is, lewdly, all made of 'countries' can only be understood in relation to the scene just discussed, in which Luciana implicitly grants sexual license to the Antipholi. Immediately afterwards, Dromio enters, apparently frightened by the enveloping abyss of flesh which beckons to him in the form of Luce's emollient advances. His reckoning up of 'countries' in all parts of her body both punningly materializes the implication of masculine freedom to 'err' in the irrational wantoness of women, and suggests that the dissolving, procreative magic of sex between men and women is taking over from the forensic deliberations of the law, as a metaphor for the conceptually expansive temporality of the comic, or tragicomic plot.

This metaphor is fully realized in the moment of the epitasis, in Antipholus of Ephesus' arrest for debt. Here, Dromio's terror of being enveloped in the vaginal abyss of Luce is metaphorically transposed into the horror of utter powerlessness, of 'arrest' by the sentence of the law. Dromio of Syracuse condenses this horror – of imprisonment, of inability to 'plead' one's cause, of arbitrary, magical paralysis – in his obsession with the buff leather jerkin of the sergeant who has laid his hand on the shoulder of Antipholus. Adriana asks 'Where is thy master, Dromio, is he well?' and Dromio replies:

> No, he's in Tartar limbo worse than hell.
> A devil in an everlasting garment hath him,
> One whose hard heart is button'd up with steel;
> A fiend, a fury, pitiless and rough,
> A wolf, nay worse, *a fellow all in buff.*
> (IV.ii.32–6, my italics)

Adriana goes on: 'What, is he arrested? Tell me at whose suit?', but Dromio's ignorance of the crossed purposes of the goldsmith and the chain means that (being in error) he is incapable of analysing the arrest as the equitable outcome of a violation of social obligation. Consequently, his answer merely materializes the 'suit' as the arbitrary violence of the law upon the wandering freedom of men: 'I know not at whose suit he is arrested well; / But *is in a suit of buff which 'rested him,* that I can tell' (IV.ii.42–5; my italics). After his departing exchange with Adriana, however, in which time was transformed into 'season', and the mistress of the house 'pressed down with conceit', Dromio's references to the sergeant's leather jacket undergo a subtle transformation. He meets his true master, Antipholus of Syracuse, whom he believes to have escaped the officer: 'What', he asks him, looking about for the sergeant, 'have you got the picture of old Adam new apparelled?'(IV.iii.13–14). Here, the leather jacket has become a second skin: the sexual connotations of this become more explicit as Dromio goes on to define the sergeant as 'he . . . that takes pity on decayed men and gives them suits of durance', one that 'thinks a man always going to bed, and says, "God give you good rest"'(IV.iii.21–6). The build-up of innuendo would not be lost on the Inns of Court audience, for the sergeant's buff jerkin was lewdly associated with the vagina, as John Harrington's epigram on the subject makes clear:

> Kate, being pleas'd, wished that her pleasure could
> Indure as long as a buff jerkin would
> Content thee, Kate; although thy pleasure wasteth,
> Thy pleasure's place like a buff jerkin lasteth.[38]

Or, as Falstaff quips in *Henry IV,* part 1, 'And is not a buff jerkin a most sweet robe of durance?'[39] The inexorable law of Christian Terence, the tragicomic *fabula* which fixed the male audience and dramatist in the relative subject positions of arresting magistrate and arrested prodigal son, has been transformed. The scene of man's arrest by the law has become man's ability to undo this incarceratingly 'proper' place by a timely emplotment of metaphor. Emplotment, being temporal, works by 'unfolding', but this metaphor never quite unfolds, it remains as a 'folded meaning', an implication. The implication is, of course, of sex-behind-the-scenes, no longer in the 'liberties of sin', but in the household. The import of this is left open, a space of meaning which (in the form of innuendo) unites men across the presumption of women's involuntary participation in its construction, and leaves men to husband that participation as they will.

Alcmena's parturition, which ushers in the catastrophe of Hercules' birth, a prodigy of astonishing promise, is rewritten in the catastrophe of *The Comedy of Errors* as the gossiping of the birth of Egeon's family to the Abbess. This is final proof of comedy's power to invest an improbable fiction with negotiating power by mere dilation and deferral. The play as a whole allegorizes the regeneration of men as producers of powerful cultural fanatasies, using the technologies of rhetorical and dramatic probability. The 'schoolmaster' who presided over the conception of prodigal son drama (schoolmasters wrote the plays; in Gascoigne's *Glasse* it is a schoolmaster who discovers the young men's 'errors' to the magistrate) is personified, in all his etiolated malignity, as the 'mere anatomy', Pinch, who is then thrashed and burnt by the vengeful Antipholus. The new place of masculine cultural production, however, requiring that masculine sexual transgression remain an implied possibility, reinvents procreative sex as 'female sexuality' – the truth about women, the 'folded meaning' that gives them dramatic interiority, and a significant dramatic voice. Thus it is a woman, in the act of assuming her motherhood, who concludes this comedy by saying of a man 'Whoever bound him, I will loose his bonds, / And gain a husband by his liberty' (V.i.339–40). For it is the procreative implication of men's (uncertainly) legitimate sexual encounters with women that symbolically releases men from the culturally unproductive bonds of subjection to the discourse of sexual discipline. Unfortunately the solution leaves women as more or less vocal versions of the kitchen wench, Luce, the 'mountain of mad flesh that claims marriage' (IV.iv.152), thereby guaranteeing good husbandry its own productive place of error.

'HUSBANDED WITH MODESTY': SHAKESPEARE'S TAMING OF THE 'SUPPOSES'

The Taming of the Shrew seems to endure in spite of itself. Evidently, producers still find it dramatically compelling and (whether in good faith or in a concession to feminism) believe that the dramatic power which they sense in the text is, if not identical to, at least compatible with the ironizing of the plot by the foregrounding of its own theatrical artifice. Thus, as Leah Marcus observes, recent productions attempt to make strange the taming plot by keeping Christopher Sly in evidence throughout, and having him fall asleep in Act V, so that, 'the reality of the taming plot ... is severely undercut: it has remained "only" a play – or even a dream'.[40] The quarto version of the play, known as *The Taming of a Shrew*, supplies one authority for extending the Sly frame in this way. However, the quarto version is of decidedly inferior composition, though it is not fashionable to say so: for just as the play can only continue to be performed if steps are taken to ironize the audience's relation to the taming plot, so criticism, having rejected attempts to read evidence of Shakespeare's 'humanity' in the standard text of the play, requires that the play's significance now be located in the process of critical interrogation 'of the editorial assumptions by which we have come to "know"' Shakespeare.[41] Such interrogation, calling into question the decisions upon which the relative merits of the two texts are based, endows with a dream-like unreality the question of the standard text's significance as an intended discourse, with historically identifiable concerns. Thus, as this critical approach reveals the authenticating presence of 'Shakespeare' to be a fiction, it simultaneously absolves both the brilliant mind of the man, and the humanist education it represents, of responsibility for a text which has long been an embarrassment. *The Taming of the Shrew* has been made to seem almost entirely the effect of editorial and performative decisions of the eighteenth and nineteenth centuries. The result – 'a fresh sense of the provisionality, even the fragility of our standard text'[42] – preserves the play for critical discourse, as recent productions do for performance, by making us feel superior to those who dreamed there could be such a play – Christopher Sly, Shakespeare's editors.

But *The Taming of the Shrew* is a triumph, not of facile devices foregrounding the artificiality of theatre, but of theatre's power to achieve an intelligibility at the level of emotional response which makes concession to its argument practically irresistible. Specifically, the play triumphs in the efficiency of its fictions of women, which resolve the scandal of sex and imposture that was originally the problem posed by their representation. In the induction, the theatrical representation of women is itself a sexual scandal; by the end of the play, it is a persuasive agent of women's own sexual discipline. *The Taming of the Shrew* was in its own time, moreover, the ultimate legitimation of the drama of clandestine marriage, for it rewrote the drama of household infiltration by clandestine courtships as the drama of a husband's achievement of absolute conjugal discretion; its denouement ushers in, as if prophetically, the profoundly disturbing game of 'supposes' that constitutes what historians have called the 'companionable marriage', in which a wife's conduct is accountable only to her husband, and his accountable to nobody.

The marvel of the play is not so much the fiction of a woman tamed as the transformation of a mere fiction of taming into something so emotionally complex and credible. The response of students of the play in seminar discussion testifies to this, for while they tend to dismiss as unacceptable and even uninteresting the scenes of Petruchio's cruelty, they remain thoroughly compelled by the characterizations of Kate and Bianca as convincing and contrasting individuals. Yet it is in these women's characterizations, and in their counterpointing, that the real innovation of the whole play lies. For, if Andrew Gurr could appeal to our 'common sense' in designating the clandestine marriage theme as 'Juliet's rebellion', a fantasy to please women, then it becomes possible to see how *The Taming of the Shrew* can seem to make a kind of sense to men as a subversion of silly female fantasy. So Gurr writes:

> *The Taming of the Shrew*'s complex reshuffling of the traditional love story, contemplating life after marriage and setting Bianca's conventional posturing in contrast to Kate was in its own way a sensational contribution to the debate between 'young love' and parental authority.[43]

What Gurr makes explicit here may seem easy to disagree with, but it is worth contemplating as the exposition of the otherwise inarticulate 'common sense' of any audience's response to the characterization of Bianca, which in its turn contributes to whatever emotional complicity the taming plot is able, in the theatre, to achieve. Gurr's comment suggests that the character of Bianca helps us to take for granted the idea that the desire for a clandestine courtship and marriage is at once typically female and typical of a certain kind of woman's inherent duplicity ('conventional posturing') once the shallow vanity that motivated her fantasies has been gratified. That these conclusions can be drawn from Shakespeare's version of the Lucentio–Bianca marriage, though sought in vain from a reading of either Ariosto's *I Suppositi* or Gascoigne's *Supposes*, is in itself remarkable. I shall argue that whatever it is that has made *The Taming of the Shrew* so much longer lived, so much more able to transcend its historical moment than earlier taming plots must have something to do with the way in which Shakespeare rewrites the Terentian comedy of *Supposes* as the answer to Bianca's romantic fantasies. For Shakespeare's 'taming of the shrew' is also a beshrewing of his Terentian originals.

In Shakespeare's play, the idea of dramatic verisimilitude which was invariably associated with the rhetorical power and moral scandal of the Terentian *fabula*, is repeatedly caricatured, first in the Induction and then in the staging of Lucentio's plot to 'achieve' Bianca. In the Induction, the nobleman's instruction to his page to 'usurp the grace, / Voice, gait, and action of a gentlewoman'[44] so as to arouse a member of what the anti-theatre proclamations called 'the base and refuse sort' of theatre-goers suggests a provocative confrontation of those who oppose the theatre on the basis that its 'unchast fables, lascivious devises' were 'so sett forth as they moved wholy to imitacion, & not to avoyding of those vyces which they represent'.[45] The sly suggestion that compelling dramatic verisimilitude is indistinguishable in its effects from pornography is taken up in a series of linked references to Ovid and Terence. Arousing descriptions of the nobleman's 'wanton pictures' depicting Ovidian rapes and metamorphoses, 'as lively painted as the deed was done' (Ind.ii.50–7) condense the associations of Ovid, pornography and the libidinal impulse at the heart of the Terentian plot. This is not surprising, for Ovid's centrality to sixteenth-century debates about erotic representation in the visual arts turned on the example of Chaerea's rape of Pamphilia in Terence's *The Eunuch*, in which Chaerea claimed to have been aroused by seeing a lively depiction of Jove raping Danae. 'Was

I, a mere mannikin not to imitate him?' ('ego homuncio hoc non facerem?') asked Chaerea.[46] The conflation of references to *The Eunuch* and to Ovid as evocations of the sexual scandal represented by theatre and by the deliberative plot would have been easily understood; Stummelius, for example, has Acolastus invoke Jove's rapes of Calisto and Europa just as he vows faith to Deleasthia.[47]

Even after the transvestite page has fended off Sly's advances with the offer of another theatrical illusion, this time a 'a kind of history' (Ind.ii.137–40), the dramatic discourse continues to flow replete with the same condensed references to sexually-motivated betrayals achieved by disguise and deception. The scene of deliberation, in which Tranio and Lucentio invent a plot, is stylized as Lucentio's Jove-like desire responding to the sight of Bianca:

Tranio: Perhaps you marked not what's the pith of all.
Lucentio: Oh yes, I saw sweet beauty in her face
  Such as the daughter of Agenor had
  That made great Jove to humble him to her hand
  When with his knees he kissed the Cretan strand.
  (I.i.166–70)

A plot 't'achieve that maid / Whose sudden sight hath thrall'd my wounded eye' (I.i.219–20) is schoolboy-Terence stuff, as Tranio's quotation from *The Eunuch* ('Redime te captum quam queas minimo' 'ransom yourself as cheaply as you can') suggests. These references accumulate to imply an identification of dramatic verisimilitude itself with the plot of imposture in which fictions of women represent the objective of sexual gratification. One such plot was, of course, Ariosto's imitation of *The Eunuch*[48] translated by Gascoigne as the *Supposes*.

The plot of the *Supposes* is recognizable from Shakespeare's version in *The Taming of the Shrew*. In it, the Lucentio-figure (Erostrato) changes clothes with the Tranio figure (Dulippo) and infiltrates the household of Damone, the original of Signore Baptista, to have sex with his daughter, who is called Polynesta. Realizing that he wants, after all, to marry Polynesta, the disguised Erostrato is in great perplexity as to how he will be able to regain sufficient credit as the son of the wealthy Philogano to assure a jointure that will persuade Damone to allow Polynesta to marry him and not his rival Cleander. Like Lucentio and Tranio in *The Taming of the Shrew*, Erostrato and Dulippo solve the problem by a daring credit fraud – what Shakespeare, in his version, called a 'counterfeit assurance' (IV.iv.88) or a 'counterfeit suppose' (V.i.107). The pair borrow the services of a travelling merchant to impersonate Erostrato's father and negotiate the jointure with Damone. Meanwhile, the (mistaken) scandal of Polynesta's having a liaison with one of Damone's servants begins to spread, co-inciding with the arrival of the real Philogano, who despairs of being able to prove in law his claim to the identity and the credit stolen from him by an imposter. The sorrows of the two fathers, Philogano and Damone, are resolved in a romance-of-origin denouement in which the real Dulippo turns out to be the long-lost son of Cleander the lawyer. This has the effect of mitigating the scandals both of the outrageous credit imposture involving the faking of Philogano's assurance, and of Polynesta's having (arguably) slept with a man called Dulippo, since the name 'Dulippo' is now a creditable equal to that of 'Erostrato'. At the same time, of course, the fact of Polynesta's having slept with Erostrato becomes the clandestine marriage whose solemnization is at hand in the catastrophe.

So Ariosto's denouement, with its fiction of Dulippo's gentle birth ('the most fortunate adventure you ever heard ... a man might make a Comedie of it'[49]) is necessary to mitigate the perceived association of deliberative theatre with scandal and dishonour to households. Yet this is the one element of the plot that Shakespeare does not make his own. In his *explicatio fabulae* nothing relieves the anger of the deceived fathers, nor the scandal of how Lucentio and Tranio have blinded these men's eyes with their 'counterfeit supposes' of marriages and jointures.

Baptista: Where is Lucentio?
Lucentio: Here's Lucentio
           Right son to the right Vincentio
           That have by marriage made thy daughter mine
           While counterfeit supposes blear'd thine eyne.
Gremio: Here's packing, with a witness, to deceive us all.
Vincentio: Where is that damned villain Tranio
           That fac'd and brav'd me in this matter so?
                                    (V.i.103–6)

What we need to ask, then, is why, if Shakespeare makes no effort to excuse the legal and moral outrage of Lucentio's and Tranio's frauds, do we feel quite unmoved and undismayed by the whole episode? Ariosto achieves a masterful emotional climax in the epitasis of his play by conveying Philogano's despair at ever being able to prove his true identity and find his son. The grief of Shakespeare's Vincentio, by comparison, is summarily signalled: 'O my son, my son! Tell me, thou villain, where is my son Lucentio?' (V.i.80). There seems to be no reason to become emotionally involved with either Baptista or Vincentio; our attitude to the the deceivers remains benign and tolerant.

The reason for this lies in Shakespeare's careful displacing of the confidence trick at the heart of Terentian theatre. Instead of arising from confusion by the young men's deceptions, the audience's sense of uncertainty and disorientation – the dilatory 'place of error' in which drama achieves credibility – becomes part of the way in which they experience knowledge of Bianca. This is, in effect, a displacement comparable to that which we saw achieved by Coras' *Paraphrase sur l'Edict des Marriages clandestinement contractez*, or Shakespeare's *Comedy of Errors*, where men ceased to be asked to identify either as disciplinary fathers or disobedient sons, and were instead united as practitioners of prudential husbandry.

Brian Morris, editor of the Arden edition, puts the difference between Polynesta and Bianca thus: 'Bianca is unlike Polynesta in that she is a virgin, an obedient, submissive and not unsubtle foil to her shrewish sister.' Bianca's apparent chastity is paralleled with her modesty, in contrast to Polynesta, whose Terentian plot function is, after all, to have engaged in a clandestine sexual liaison with an imposter. But Morris, some pages later, argues that chastity and modesty are not, after all, proper to Bianca. He speaks here of the theme of disguise and metamorphosis:

> the dazzling changes of identity in the manifold disguisings take place, for the most part, in the first two Acts, while the later part of the play is concerned with the longer rhythms of the change of personality which overcomes Katherina. It is upon her transformation that we focus, though we may note the foil which Shakespeare provides for her in her sister. Bianca is the only major character who assumes no disguise and achieves no development. She begins, in I.i., with her own form of covert and clever shrewishness to her sister, securing herself the sympathy of her father and all his household, and she ends the play bidding fair to take up where her sister left off.[50]

Here Morris appears (having revised his interpretation of the first Act as signifying Bianca's modesty) to condemn the character of Bianca for tricking him into believing her 'obedient' and 'submissive' by comparison with the unchaste Polynesta and the shrewish Katherina. His contradictory response accurately conveys how the play works to create uncertainty around Bianca's speech and action, so that readers, actors and audience are obliged to interpret her in retrospect, revising an initial 'mistaken' impression of her modesty in the conviction that the error in judgement that produced it must mean that she is to be read as deceitful. In displacing 'error' or uncertainty thus from our dramatic experience of the 'counterfeit supposes' of the young men into an experience of the gradual revelation of how false have been our suppositions about Bianca, Shakespeare appears to preserve the fact of her chastity, while sinisterly casting into doubt her future fidelity to her husband. Polynesta's frank sexual transgression with Erostrato (for which, in the ethical scheme of the *Supposes*, the young couple appear to be mutually held responsible) has been transformed into Bianca's 'covert and clever shrewishness', her potential to deceive her husband.

This is a devastating rewriting of Ariosto's own solution to the problem of employing a Terentian plot of conjecture and error as the vehicle, not of an academic stylization of Roman drama, but of a drama of sixteenth-century society. For Ariosto's play is fully conscious of the scandal inherent in probable representations of women in sixteenth-century theatre; indeed in his play, conjectural drama is equivalent to the defamatory spread of rumour. His romantic denouement, with its narration of the gentility of Dulippo, is the attempt to resolve what has been foregrounded throughout the play as the problem of a theatre of supposition: its likeness to a theatre of scandal. Thus Ariosto's play opens by forcing the audience's awareness of theatre as the spreading (in the words of Geoffrey Fenton) of 'publike sclanders on scaffold . . . where every eare is open . . . Babling vaine newes.'[51] Polynesta and her nurse appear on stage to whisper confidentially about Polynesta's secret affair; it is better to get out of the house to discuss these things, says the nurse, because, 'in the house the beds, the cupboards, even the doors have ears'.[52] The indiscretion of theatre, its affinity with the mockery of the open marketplace where ballads are sung libelling neighbours as usurers, cuckolds and whores, is furthermore personified in Ariosto's character of

Pasafilo, a parasite who owes allegiance to no particular household, but delights in fuelling the desire of each for scandal about the other. It is Pasafilo who discovers what he supposes to be the great scandal about Polynesta; that she has been sleeping with Damone's servant: 'Who'd have thought it of her? Just ask the neighbours: they'll tell you that she . . . associates only with nuns.' Polynesta's own father says, 'I'm less upset about the event itself, than that Pasafilo should get to know of it . . . whoever wants to keep something secret should tell Pasafilo: only all the people, and those who have ears, nobody else will ever hear'.[53]

In Pasafilo, Ariosto identifies the threat constituted by the Terentian drama of supposition as the threat of discourse escaping the bounds of household solidarity, of the loyalty of members of the household to one another.[54] Neither Pasafilo nor Damone blame Polynesta especially; both recognize the damage done by her transgression as the inevitable and ruinous potential of such things to become food for scandal among the neighbours. With the loss of Pasafilo and his explicit function of foregrounding the meaning of theatre as household scandal, Shakespeare is able to mystify the gossipy conjectures and errors that surround the liaison of Polynesta's likeness, Bianca, so that we understand their operation not as a sign of the peculiar susceptibility of women's sexual reputations to endanger the fame of the whole household, but as the revelation of an unpleasant female character.

Thus, Shakespeare transforms Pasafilo's gleeful broadcasting of the supposed affair of Polynesta and Dulippo into an extraordinary scene of voyeurism in which we and Hortensio look furtively and mistrustfully on from behind the scenes while Bianca flirts with her tutor. Our position of complicity with the spies focuses attention away from the scene's purpose as part of Lucentio's plan to dissuade Hortensio from loving Bianca, and makes us rather aware of a disturbing gap in our knowledge about Bianca herself, as she appears to respond with ambiguous facility to the instructions of her private tutor. Our sense of Bianca's 'character' thereby partakes, in spite of our knowledge that this scene has been staged for his benefit, of Hortensio's own error in supposing this to be proof of her promiscuity, entertaining honest suitors while she flirts with a household servant. Our not knowing whether or not Bianca was party to the duping of Hortensio becomes another strand of the accumulating uncertainties that, as Katherine Maus observed, render the the audience's interpretative position similar to that of a jealous husband.[55] 'Fie on her, see how beastly she doth court him!' and 'See how they kiss and court!' (IV.ii.27, 34) are lines which oblige dramatic productions of the play to stage Bianca as ever more flirtatious, ever more sexually forward, resulting in the apprehension (expressed by Morris) of her as 'covert' and untrustworthy. It becomes difficult, during the play, to retain conviction that the real frauds and sexual predators are, in fact, Lucentio, Tranio and Hortensio himself, the last having stolen into Baptista's house in disguise so that he might 'have leave and leisure to make love to her / And unsuspected court her by herself'. Yet Shakespeare makes Baptista, in contrast to Ariosto's Damone, complicit in the compromising of his daughters' honour through his own use of sexual innuendo. When Kate 'shrewishly' breaks the lute over the lustful Hortensio's head, Baptista cheers him up with the invitation to 'proceed in practice' with his younger daughter: 'She's apt to learn and thankful for good turns' (II.i.165). Such phrases are themselves part of the game of supposes that make women the locus of sexual uncertainty in the play.

The *explicatio fabulae* of the sub-plot, so laboriously signalled by technical references to 'counterfeit supposes' and the 'blear'd' eyes of the *senes*, the Terentian fathers, brings no dramatic shock of relief, then, because we experience it not as the clearing of the parents' sight, but as the progressive blinding of Lucentio's own eyes by the merely apparent candour of his 'Bianca'. Petruchio hints at the unchastity of the clandestinely married couple: 'Come Kate, we'll to bed. / We three are married, but you two are sped. / 'Twas I won the wager, though you hit the white' (V.ii.185–7). Lucentio's whole objective was, in rivalling the other suitors, to gain the universally desired object, to 'hit the white', but in being so easily 'sped' in the sense of being sexually gratified, Petruchio suggests that the union is also 'sped', done for.

The Terentian plot of clandestine marriage is thus tamed by being 'beshrewed'. Its power to make men like Gosson fear that 'such lessons as are learned at Plaies' would bring sexual scandals 'privately [to] breake into every mans house' simply vanishes.[56] By exaggerating such anxious views of theatre both in the induction and throughout the sub-plot through Terentian/ Ovidian motifs of metamorphosis for sex ('Love wrought these miracles. Bianca's love / Made me exchange my state with Tranio' V.i.114–15), Shakespeare both renders the representation of clandestine courtship harmlessly undramatic and relocates the sense of anxiety once associated with it in the duplicity of 'Bianca's love'.

The *Supposes* plot, thus beshrewed in the person of its objective, the soiled white of Bianca, calls for its own husbanding and taming by Petruchio's revolutionary version of the clandestine marriage. For the clandestine marriage between Bianca and Lucentio – so well signposted by the text as a 'Titus and Gisippus'-style attempt to blind the kinsfolk's eyes with a false wedding, while a secret one occurs elsewhere ('Baptista is safe, talking with the deceiving father of a deceitful son . . . his daughter is to be brought to you to the supper . . . The old priest at Saint Luke's church is at your command at all hours . . . they are busied about a counterfeit assurance. Take you assurance of her *cum privilegio ad imprimendum solum*', IV.iv.80–90) was arguably not in itself very subversive of social norms. After all, English communities had, for hundreds of years, found that the ambiguous position in law of the secret contract enabled both the control and accommodation of matches made against the wishes of kin. The function of the community, as Diana O'Hara writes, is best understood as one of witness and participation:

> The participation of particular persons at various stages of the marriage process . . . has to be understood not merely as a means to publication, but interpreted as an expression of kin and community control . . . It has to be asked how . . . participation at the symbolic level of ritual demonstrates the importance of marriage as a personal, family and social event.[57]

Though Lucentio's marriage was negotiated behind the backs of the families involved, it moves frankly and rapidly into the eyes of the fathers and the community, culminating in a wedding feast. Such a progression, with its attendant disputes, was allowed for by the ambiguity of canon law; O'Hara cites a case from the 1550s in which neighbours had apparently sought to prevent the deponent, Alice Cheeseman, from contracting herself to her husband. One neighbour deposed that

> the parishioners bear her that goodwill and affection that when yt was reported she shuld be married to Cheeseman they wer sore agynst yt, and stayed the asking of the banns

and marriage...because the parishioners misliked of Cheeseman ... though she did offend in carnallye knowing Cheeseman before marriage notwithstanding she made as he thinketh recompence in that she being persuaded to forsake him by her freends, she ever said she should have him and in respecte allso that she hath reconciled herself to god and the world by marrying of her husband.[58]

According to this testimony, the operation of clandestine marriage as a way of resisting community opposition appears to have been able to be accommodated by the community involved. The offender reconciles herself to God and her neighbours through the process of witness, absolving herself of the sins of secrecy and unchastity. Not only does her persistence within the context of the dispute appear to be interpreted by this parishioner as a sign of her good faith, but his motivation for intervention in her matrimonial choice is given as being 'goodwill and affection'.

If Lucentio's marriage moves in the traditional direction from clandestinity into community control, Petruchio's, far more subversively, goes the opposite way. Openness is his disguise. He comes as himself to woo, makes solid assurances, calls the banns, gathers the witnesses and is seen before the priest, but only in order to make good in law his right to vanish from the sight of the community, just when their traditional right to oversee the maintenance of good relations between himself and his wife might become compromising to his designs. As his marriage becomes clandestine to the community, of course, it opens up to the audience; it is as if the play were mimicking a humanist book of good husbandry, enacting the historical drama of a print culture's displacement of instruction in marital affairs from neighbourhood into readership, and identifying the exemplary text with the prudence of Petruchio's plot. Where Tranio and Lucentio were modelled upon the quick-witted slave and lover of Roman comedy, Petruchio's histrionic model is the humanist one of successful improvisation grounded in exemplary reading: 'he'll rail in his rope-tricks [i.e., his rhetoric]', as Grumio says (I.ii.110). Many analogues of such histrionic good husbandry might be found. In Erasmus' colloquy known as *Coniugium*, a troublesome young wife is tamed by a man who uses his dramatic skill to frighten her into anticipating a beating so as to enhance the emotional impact of his kindness in relenting, thus shaming her into gratitude. Erasmus describes the man as, 'capable of playing any comedy without a mask'.[59]

Playing comedy without a mask is just Petruchio's forte. Like Livy's Scipio Africanus, he allows competing interpretations to accumulate about his words and actions, clothing himself in the conjectures of others. At first this looks like an abdication of authority and power; the first command he gives, 'knock me here soundly' is clownishly double voiced, rendering him a buffoon (I.ii.7). But the disorienting effects of such self-subversions are far more productive than the new comedy roguery of Lucentio and Tranio.

Petruchio's triumph of open clandestinity, comedy without a mask, is his wedding. Though in obvious contrast to Lucentio's stealthy removal of Bianca to St Luke's, under cover of the 'counterfeit assurance', Petruchio's public ceremony is orchestrated entirely to the end of excluding the very community whose presence is its legitimation. The concept of witness itself becomes rhetorical, a 'reason' or consideration in law to support Petruchio's denial of Kate's presence at her own feast. It is this that requires so much preparation in the way of carnivalesque subversions of ceremony, for such a daring challenge to the community's authority cannot risk its purpose being anticipated. The calculated dialogism of Petruchio's words and actions, their tolerance of competing interpretation, here pays off. Thus, although the waiting community experience some discomfiture at his tardiness, Baptista vehemently condemning it as a 'mockery' of 'the ceremonial rites of marriage', Petruchio's credit remains good through the readiness of others to offer interpretations of his present conduct, based on their previous experience of him as habitually but harmlessly distracted in his words and actions. 'Upon my life', as Tranio says to reconcile Baptista, 'Petruchio means but well,/ Whatever fortune stays him from his word./ Though he be blunt, I know him passing wise; / Though he be merry, yet withal he's honest' (III.ii.21–5).

Petruchio's achievement is breathtaking. Having appropriated all the signs of holiday foolery to distract witnesses from his purpose, he proceeds to allege his absolute right in law to remove his bride from all further witness. Baptista and Tranio, for all their enthusiasm about Petruchio's agreeing to wed Kate are nevertheless shocked and dismayed at this unprecedented abortion of the ceremony.

Petruchio: I know you think to dine with me today,
And have prepar'd great store of wedding cheer,
But so it is, my haste doth call me hence,
And therefore here I mean to take my leave.
Baptista: Is't possible you will away tonight?
Petruchio: I must away today before night come.
Make it no wonder. If you knew my business
You would entreat me rather go than stay . . .
Tranio: Let us entreat you stay till after dinner.
Gremio: Let me entreat you.

(III.ii.183–90)

His speech of defiance which begins 'She is my goods, my chattels, she is my house' and concludes 'I'll bring mine action on the proudest he / That stops my way in Padua' (III.ii.228–33) is shocking less for its explicit statement of the legal position of women in marriage than for its assertion of the action of common law over the traditional authority of the community conceived, by canon law, as legitimating witnesses and participants in the local control of matrimony.

The innovative clandestinity of Petruchio's wedding is the clandestinity advocated by humanist readings of Xenophon, such as Vive's *De Officio Mariti* (translated by Paynell as *The Office and duetie of an husband*) or Erasmus' colloquy, *Coniugium* or 'Marriage'. Texts such as these attempted to compensate for the way in which print culture and humanism, textualizing the signs of friendship between men, had themselves raised levels of anxiety about the security of household honour, by advocating the husband's insistence on strictest discretion about household affairs between himself and his wife.[60] Shakespeare plots the new importance of discretion as the alternative *explicatio fabulae* of his rewritten play of *Supposes*. For before Lucentio's and Tranio's tired confession to having 'blear'd the eyne' of the old folks, there occurs in the play a moment which all critics agree has a peculiar emotional compulsion, although its implications are extremely disturbing. This is the moment in which Petruchio and Kate encounter Vincentio, on his way to being duped by his son. Kate is obliged by Petruchio to greet Vincentio absurdly as a 'Young budding virgin, fair, and fresh, and sweet' (IV.v.36). The scene, as Ruth Nevo comments, 'is structured by New Comedy paradigms . . . the senex is made fun of, in effect, by a pair of tricksters in some subtle alliance with each

221

other not clear to the audience'.[61] Sure enough, the same *senex* will find himself the butt of a tedious (old) new comedy plot. But where the objective of that plot is the revelation of eye-blinding 'supposes', the objective of this is their inadmissibility. To Vincentio, or in the eyes of Kate's kin and neighbours (for Vincentio, as the couple discover, is kin to them through Bianca's wedding), the counterfeit supposes that motivate her actions will remain forever obscure. For Petruchio's pragmatically motivated comedy of supposes has become her reality:

> Then, God be blest, it is the blessed sun.
> But sun it is not, when you say it is not,
> And the moon changes even as your mind.
> What you have nam'd, even that it is,
> And so it shall be so for Katherine.
>
> (IV.v.18–22)

While 'the moon changes even with your mind' might be taken as ironic, and Katherine's whole response strategic, it is useless to conjecture the degree of her scepticism. For if strategic compliance involves its own misrepresentation to others as wholehearted allegiance, scepticism loses its capacity as a site of communicable resistance: 'Pardon', Katherina says to Vincentio, 'my mistaking eyes, / That have been so bedazzled with the sun / That everything I look on seemeth green' (IV.v.44–5). That the sun can be invoked here as a cause is contingent on Petruchio's having denied, after all, that the orb they contemplated together was the moon. Thus, as Bianca has already come to focus one new *locus* of Terentian error – the blind spot of anxiety over knowledge withheld – so Katherina comes to embody another – the wonder of not knowing how it is all done, here expressed in the the permanent enigma of the new-style conjugal household to bewildered neighbours, kin and friends.

Petruchio has created for himself a mobile and histrionic *oikonomia*, a conceptual household over which he rules, and in which he may innovate at will, unimpeded by old customs perpetuated by neighbourhood. As two sets of husbands and wives – Hortensio and his widow, Lucentio and Bianca, settle comfortably into the same-sex alliances that are the traditional repositories of survival techniques in the conjugal struggle, a third set – Katherina and Petruchio – express an entirely new alignment of the resources of cultural production in the sustaining of the marriage contract. For Katherina is directed by Petruchio to instruct other women in the duties they owe their husbands. Like Erasmus' Eulalia in the *Coniugium*, she is both a persuasive fiction, and a fiction of woman as persuasive, diffusing the absolute authority of her author/husband by the volition we can hardly help inferring from her eloquence and coherence as a speaker. For women, then, this dramatic image of a woman tamed anticipates Shakespeare's transformation of the theatre itself into a place in which complex fictions of women become crucial to the representation of heroic masculinity as authorship.

CONCLUSION
Shylock: Why this usurer has
a daughter

When I was writing this book, a number of people asked me whether it was about Jessica, the daughter of Shylock in Shakespeare's *The Merchant of Venice*. At one level, of course, the answer was 'no', since my 'usurer's daughter' had no specific referent in literature, but was meant (as the argument of the book progressed) to indicate how women had, in their transition from being one man's daughter to being another's wife, symbolized the assurance of alliance-friendships between men, and the orderly channelling of wealth from one 'house' or lineage to another. As humanism textualized the friendships between men, or made their value turn upon persuasive skill, men's uncertainty about the place of 'assurance' in the conveyance of benefits through friendship was expressed in a range of discourses in narratives of credit-fraud – of false claims to kinship, disguises, stolen marriages – in which the agents were prodigal unthrifts, pitiless usurers and daughters or wives. As the (dowried) daughter symbolized readiness-to-be-given, or the ability of her male kinsman to be a powerful friend, so the credit-fraud of the prodigal might take the form of 'stealing' that ability by marrying her secretly; alternatively, if the male kinsman were a usurer, then he would be the fraudulent friend. The 'usurer's daughter', then, may be understood as the ultimate fantasy of the creditless adventurer, the hero of fiction, the younger brother, the man-on-the-make. For the persuasion of a usurer's daughter to contract herself secretly, against her father's will, is a victory for rhetoric which undermines no male friendship; there would be no assurance in having her father's friendship rather than his gold.

No literary character fits this description better, after all, than Shakespeare's Jessica, who 'with an unthrift love' did, as Lorenzo says, 'steal from the wealthy Jew'.[1] Why have I not, then, mentioned Jessica, since she appears to be the perfect exemplar of the imaginative crux that I have been trying to describe?

The reason is this. I have been trying to think of both 'prodigality' and 'usury' as the names by which late sixteenth-century Englishmen expressed their apprehension that the traditional regulator of credit – friendship – was now itself being regulated by various rhetorically-mediated projects of economic, social and political advancement. I have, therefore, largely ignored the definition of usury explicit in Deuteronomy 23:20, which equates it with the 'negative reciprocity' of racial difference, sanctioning the taking of interest between Christians and Muslims or between Christians and Jews.[2] In my argument, the financial practice of usury has been invoked as way of understanding specific narratives of historical change in the social relations between men, under the impact of humanism and the technology of print.

Yet the fact undeniably remains that it is Shylock who popularly symbolizes the very crisis in the power to 'assure' male friendship which I have been identifying as my subject throughout this book. And if that crisis stems, as I have argued, from a humanistic transformation of the signs of contractual good faith from the status of witnesses – oaths, pledges, tokens – to the status of probable arguments *pro et contra*, open to equitable interpretation, then the figure of Shylock may be one of its dramatic personifications. For it is Shylock who stands at the unthinkable boundary at which the humanists' fantasy of a pure *amicitia* between likeminded men, apparently unconcerned with material reciprocity yet able to emplot the means of access to hitherto inconceivable sources of honourable wealth, suddenly becomes its own opposite: a paranoid fantasy of anxiety about the stealth, betrayal, depletion, emasculation and bleeding to death of one man by another. In spite, then, of my own hesitation before the complexity of representations of Jews and Judaism in sixteenth-century Europe, I would like to conclude this book with some observation about the implications of its findings for readings of *The Merchant of Venice*. Such observations, however partial and inadequate, will at least prevent what Bryan Chyette has identified as the tendency of critics to disregard the representations of Jews in English literature out of what amounts to a teleological and pre-emptive assumption of knowledge as to what 'the antisemitic strain in English literature' is already going to mean.[3]

And yet it is also important that these are concluding observations, a fact which testifies to the necessity of not identifying Shylock and Jessica as central referents in a book about the humanistic legitimation of rhetoric as a medium in which to forge significant contractual relations between men. For if the argument of this book has substance, then one may say that the anti-Semitism of *The Merchant of Venice* lies in the success with which the play dissociates the qualities of prudent calculation, combined with the strategic problematization of good faith, from the successful self-legitimation of Christian humanist rhetoric onto a figure who functions merely as agent of this rhetorical success: that is, the Jewish moneylender in Christian Europe.

In his study of the case of Bondavid, a Jewish moneylender who sued successfully against an accusation of fraudulent debt collection in Marseilles in 1317, Joseph Shatzmiller has shown that credit relations between Jews and Christians in medieval communities had their own ethical codes. Like their Christian counterparts, the Lombards and the Cahorsins, Jewish moneylenders took pledges and rendered writs in witness and assurance first of the debt and then of its acquittal.[4] In England, during the period of the crown's heaviest reliance on the revenues of the Jewry it eventually ruined and then expelled (1218–72), records of these quitclaims, known as 'starrs' were kept on the Plea Rolls of the Jews Exchequer.[5] However, relations of debt and credit also existed without the assurance of pledge or written acquittance, on good faith alone. The noteboook of a Jewish moneylender in Constanz in 1372 records a loan issued 'without security' (*ohne pfand*), evidently to a debtor with whom the moneylender had a long-term relationship of trust.[6] The medieval Hebrew expression for such a special relation of trust with a client was *ma'arufia*, a word which also signified the long-term monopoly of the relationship, its protection from the competitive intervention of others.[7]

The fact that Jewish moneylenders were not and could not have been at the real centre of sixteenth-century Englishmen's reconceptualization of credit relations through the successive crises of inflation, the fall of the Antwerp exchange, the inadequacy of common law procedure with regard to debts and bonds, the cash-flow problems of gentlemen at court and the complication of promissory discourse by the increasing deployment of *pro et contra* rhetoric,[8] did not prevent the Jew from becoming symbolically central, in a manner analogous to the prostitute, to fictions of the financial/physiological 'cutting off' or 'draining' away of the resources of masculine identity. The centrality of the Jew to this fantasy was promoted, as R. Po-Chia Hsia has clearly shown, by the circulation of Protestant accounts of the ritual murders purportedly practised by Jews on young male Christians.[9] James Shapiro has convincingly argued that such fantasies of emasculation and depletion underlie Shakespeare's fable of the flesh-bond between Christian and Jew in *The Merchant of Venice*. In such fantasies, especially when courtesans are also invoked, the senses of the physiological and economic threat to manhood are intimately linked; Shapiro cites a verse prefacing Thomas Coryat's *Crudities* which refers to Coryat's adventures in Venice: 'Thy Cortizan clipt thee, ware Tom, I advise thee / And flie from the Jews, lest they circumsize thee.'[10] One might add to this the example of Nashe's *The Unfortunate Traveller*, in which the young hero, having lost all credit, falls through a hole 'into the hands of ... a cursed generation', a Jewish household, in which he is threatened with being 'cut up like a French summer doublet', only to be saved by a courtesan by whom he is nearly 'consumed and worn to the bones'.[11]

To this historicized reading of *The Merchant of Venice* in the context of the anti-Semitism expressed in Protestant discourses of ritual murder, I would like to add another dimension, one which refers specifically to the *dramatic economy* of the representation of 'economic' relations between Christian and Jew. For while it is true that Shylock's representation draws upon the myth of ritual murder, that is not the whole story; if it were, there would be less difference than there is between Shakespeare's play and its main source, Ser Giovanni Fiorentino's *Il Pecorone*, in which the 'Lady of Belmont' fulfils the role of the sexually demanding courtesan, while the Jewish usurer prepares the Christian merchant for his knife by stripping him naked. In Shakespeare's play, however, the resolution of a crisis in credit relations between Christian and Jew is not resolved through the symbolic equivalence of the seductress and the usurer. Rather, it is through the dramatic complication of 'the usurer's daughter' – the theft of Jessica from the house sealed tight as a legal bond – that Shakespeare makes his play of Shylock into a playing out of the contradictions inherent within Christian humanist discourses of *oikonomia* and *amicitia*. As the figure of the wife in Xenophon's *Oeconomicus* allows the good husband a monopoly of economic prudence while absolving him of the stigma of thrifty calculation, so does the Jewish householder in relation to the Christian husbands of the *The Merchant of Venice*. But whereas the discourse which the Xenophonic wife enables is that of 'good husbandry', what the Jewish usurer enables is a husbandry complicated by a Christian humanist discourse of *amicitia* – that is, the textualized friendship between men that forms the medium in which a successful plot is conceived and carried out. For it is the Jew, with his murderous insistence that he may 'be assured' of Antonio's bond (I.iii.26), who personifies the anxiety that is always latent in the idea of *amicitia* – the anxiety that the 'love' between like-minded men will not be able to sustain the pressure of the uncertainty, the strategic lack of assurance, that contributes vitally to the rhetorical, and therefore the economic success of their collective enterprise.

In the course of this book, I have been using the word 'uncertainty' as a quasi-technical term for the rhetorical foundation of probable reasoning. In Terentian-style drama, such uncertainty may be identified as the place of 'error' in which the plot gains credibility, and which, deployed by such *dramatis personae* as Shakespeare's Petruchio or Prince Hal, signifies a heroic masculine prudence, an ability to emplot and exploit the conjectures of others to one's own advantage. Of course, not all of Shakespeare's young gentlemen are exemplary figures of such histrionic prudence, but in many cases it is possible to read the drama of their fortunes as one in which skill in probable reason (rather than in the fighting they apparently profess) plays a part. Thus Othello wins his case of disputed marriage through persuasive narration; thus Orlando gains in the forest the education in civil conversation that his elder brother denied him, learning to effect his will by persuasive 'reason' and 'civil sayings' rather than by wrestling or the sword.[12] In Chapter 4 of this book I showed how the self-styled 'prodigals' – the writers of prose fiction in the 1570s and 1580s – were preoccupied with the difficulty of 'becoming visible' to potential friends and benefactors through displays of rhetorical rather than martial skill; the problem they faced was one of initiating the beneficient exchange of texts, or the patronage relationship by means of which they they could signify their abilities of mind. This problem was expressed as the contradiction of being forced into an attitude of 'prodigality', a fraudulent improvisation of the signs of such a relationship of trust and credit, as the means to secure one in reality.

In Ser Giovanni Fiorentino's collection, *Il Pecorone*, Shake-speare found a story expressive of masculine friendship as just such a risky anticipation of the signs of reciprocal ability. Gianetto's father leaves him nothing to inherit but the friendship of his old business partner in Venice, Ansaldo. Ansaldo gives Gianetto the keys of to his coffers so that he will have means and to display his rhetorical ability. 'Spend this' he says, 'and clothe and shoe yourself to your liking, and keep open house for the citizens and make yourself known, for I leave you this thought, that I will love you better, the more you make yourself beloved' ('tanto meglio ti vorro, quanto piu ben ti farai volere'). [13] Gianetto, by this means, becomes 'expert, practised, magnificent and courteous in all things, knowing well how to give honour and courtesy where it was fitting to do so' ('esperto & practico & magnanimo e cortese in ogni cosa; e ben sapeva fare honore & cortesia dove si conveniva'). One of the people to whom he 'renders' this honour is Ansaldo, more than if he were a hundred times his father ('sempre rendeva a messere Ansaldo piu che fosse stato cento volte suo padre').[14] But, of course, Ansaldo is not Gianetto's father, and the credit he gives the young man seems to anticipate some eventual ability to reciprocate. This is indeed the subject of the story. The narrative negotiates the hazards of the Lady of Belmont and the Jew of Venice in its resolution of a central uncertainty: the question of whether Gianetto's talent for being 'beloved' will be able to repay the love Ansaldo has given him. Gianetto's hopes are repeatedly wrecked in the harbour of the Lady of Belmont, who has issued a proclamation that anyone who enters there must sleep with her on penalty of forfeiting their ships if they fail. She thus condenses, as both treacherous harbour and sexually demanding virago, the twin Renaissance icon-ographies of 'Fortune': tempestuous, shipwrecking sea and woman requiring to be mastered.[15] As such, too, she expresses Gianetto's hazard as the performative risk of eloquence, which was commonly associated with difficult sexual encounter (thus Erasmus opens the *De Copia* with an allusion to Demosthenes' words about not risking a visit to Corinth, home of the fabulously expensive courtesan Lais[16]). In symbolizing the contingency of Gianetto's fortunes thus, the story of *Il Pecorone* forces the reader's awareness of a direct correlation between the risk of failure run by Gianetto's courteous rhetoric, and that run by Ansaldo's financial trust in his love. For as Gianetto is nearly wrecked by the demands of sexual conquest, Ansaldo faces ruin, castration and death at the hands of the Jewish usurer. However, Gianetto is helped upon his third voyage by a young lady-in-waiting, who warns him not to drink a drugged potion, thereby assuring his sexual success. It is she with whom Gianetto, as lord of Belmont, rewards Ansaldo in the last line of the story, thus neatly reciprocating the latter's initial credit in him, and transforming his old benefactor into an indebted friend.[17]

The aspect of Gianetto that Shakespeare foregrounds in his combination of Bassanio and Gratiano is, precisely, the uncertainty without which Gianetto's courtesy could not do its rhetorical work. In flirtation and courtship uncertainty is the necessary basis of pleasure, the growing place of love. Words and glances ('fair speechless messages' I.i.164) are not, of course, assurances; Salerio observes that lovers are quick to reap the benefits of their sudden contracts, to 'seal love's bonds new-made', but not to assure them, to 'keep obliged faith unforfeited' (II.v.5–7). But in courtship these uncertain bonds have their own dramatic value; they are the techniques of making oneself beloved. The task Ansaldo explicitly sets Gianetto in *Il Pecorone* comes to be represented in *The Merchant of Venice* in the person of 'Gratiano' (suggesting *grazia* – grace) and in his accompaniment of Bassanio to Belmont on condition of tempering himself to the occasion, 'lest' as Bassanio says, 'I be misconst'red in the place I go to, / And lose my hopes' (II.ii.179–80). The game of the caskets is an allegory of Bassanio's merit in recognizing the extent to which his 'love' for Portia is defined by the uncertainty that surrounds being 'misconst'red' – the hazard of successful self-mediation. Elsewhere in the play, this hazard of fortune finds itself parodied in the graceless Lancelot Gobbo ('gobbo' means 'hunchback'), who seeks a service in Bassanio's household. Believing himself to have achieved this through his eloquence, Lancelot crows with delighted irony: 'I cannot get a service, no! I have ne'er a tongue in my head.' The future looks bright for a man who has proved his virility thus eloquently: 'well, if Fortune be a woman, she's a good wench for this gear' (II.ii.149–59).

The propitiousness of timely speech and a decorous manner, parodied in Lancelot's suit, is seriously expressed in the allegory of successful self-mediation (the mediation of the self through clothes, manners, facial expression and forms of speech) that is the drama of Bassanio's and Gratiano's relationship, and of their expedition to Belmont (hence it is, too, that the rivals of Bassanio are all characterized by Portia and Nerissa in terms of ill-fitting garments and repulsive demeanours). So Bassanio's 'credit' on arrival in Belmont is enhanced by his prudent skill in the use of a mediator, Gratiano, whose signifying makes seem probable or 'likely' the ability of his master in friendship and love:

> Madam, there is alighted at your gate
> A young Venetian, one that comes before
> To signify the approaching of his lord,
> From whom he bringeth sensible regreets;
> To wit (besides commends and courteous breath)
> Gifts of rich value; yet I have not seen
> So likely an ambassador of love,
> A day in April never came so sweet,
> To show how costly summer was at hand,
> As this fore-spurrer comes before his lord.
> (II.ix.86–95)

The sign of friendship or love as the ability and desire to *give* here becomes radically indeterminate. Gratiano's gracious signifying lends credit to Bassanio's approach, but his 'gifts of rich value' are, as we know, not signs of the latter's ability to give, but costly hazards, anticipating Portia's cancelling of all his debts with the rich gift of herself. The collapse of ability into prodigality is expressed in repeated metaphors of Bassanio's courteous enterprise as the venture of a ship, magnificent yet vulnerable upon the seas. So he has, as he confides in Antonio, 'disabled' his estate by showing 'a swelling port' (I.i.124); the suggestion of his ostentatious courtesy as as a proudly swelling sail is picked up in Gratiano's later comment on the tardiness of Lorenzo in love:

> all things that are,
> Are with more spirit chased than enjoy'd
> How like a younger or a prodigal
> The scarfed bark puts from her native bay –
> Hugged and embraced by the strumpet wind!
> How like the prodigal doth she return
> With over-weathered ribs and ragged sails –
> Lean, rent and beggar'd by the strumpet wind!
> (II.vi.12–19)

This speech, which itself anticipates a rapid transition from the enterprise of stealing Jessica to that of hazarding for Portia (Gratiano moves from the pleasure of one to the other: 'I desire no more delight / Than to be under sail, and gone tonight', II.vi.67–8) is expressive not simply of the pleasures of the chase, nor of the risks of venture, but of the play's own proof that the promise of enjoyment is a kind of economy, having a material value (the value of dramatic credibility) contingent upon the withholding of assurance, or the keeping of its 'means', like the ships of Antonio, 'in supposition' (I.iii.15).

In Il Fiorentino's story, the hazards of Gianetto's good fortune are rehearsed and resolved through the perceived equivalence of the Lady of Belmont and the Jew – the one an emasculating seductress, the other a castratingly evil creditor. Shakespeare, however, inserts into the time between Antonio's signing of Shylock's bond, and Bassanio's winning the 'golden fleece' an incident which alters the focus of the resolution: the clandestine marriage of the usurer's daughter, Jessica. This incident, dovetailing first with Bassanio's departure for Belmont, and then with Shylock's discovery of the wreck of Antonio's ships, enables the displacement of any reservations we might have about the thrifty motivation of Bassanio's love for Portia onto Shylock's thrift, which crucially fails, unlike Bassanio's, to employ itself in making itself credible, or beloved.

Criticism of the trial scene has traditionally interpreted Shylock's rigid refusal to listen to, or make, any emotional appeal concerning his case as a sign of his representing the legalistic 'Old Testament' reasoning of the Jews, as opposed to the equity of Christians, informed by the Gospel. It might also be explained as a kind of allegory of the rigidity of the English common law with respect to evidence under seal; for, as I have outlined, the development of an equity at common law was an effect of reluctance to change the positive law on the irreversibility of bonds by mere verbal evidence of their discharge.[18] Yet for those who have been moved by the eloquence of Shylock's response to the scorn of Antonio in the first act, his representation in the trial scene may seem frustrating, and dramatically inexplicable. For though he is urged by the Duke to explain his desire to pursue a useless suit against Antonio, he refuses:

You'll ask me why I rather chose to have
A weight of carrion flesh, than to receive
Three thousand ducats: I'll not answer that!
But say it is my humour, – is it answer'd?
... Some men there are love not a gaping pig!
Some men are mad when they behold a cat!
And others, when the bagpipe sings i' th' nose,
Cannot contain their urine – ... now for your answer
As there is no firm reason to be rend'red
Why he cannot abide a gaping pig,
Why he a harmless necessary cat,
Why he a woollen bagpipe, but of force
Must yield to such inevitable shame
As to offend himself being offended:
So I can give no reason, nor I will not ...

(IV.i.40–59)

This refusal of Shylock's frustrates an invitation to be dramatic, to plead the case of a father betrayed and a householder robbed by the Christians to whom he gave credit. As such, it may also be read as signalling Shylock's exclusion from participation in a certain kind of economy – the economy of *uncertainty* or probable reason. For Shylock's insistence on the invalidity of any but a 'firm reason' resembles the scholastic refusal to recognize humanism's affirmation of the practical value of arguments based in uncertainty; it is the latter, the humanistic model that defines 'reason' elsewhere in Shakespeare; in *Twelfth Night* and *As You Like It*, for example, 'reason' means probable persuasion, a clever or emotive argument, valid only as part of the timeliness and particularity of its application to the circumstances of the occasion.[19] Othello offers a an illuminating contrast to Shylock here; where the latter fails to recognize the practical value of probable reason, the former moves the Senate to pass judgement in his favour by narrating and making dramatically probable the mitigating circumstances of his case. In *The Merchant of Venice*, however, Shakespeare's suggestion of an alignment between Hebraic thought, scholastic logic and the irreversibility of the positive law on evidence under seal enables a facile identification of skill in rhetorical probability (Portia's finding of an equitable 'loophole for error' in her interpretation of the sentence of the bond) with a Christian monopoly of the injunction to be merciful in the exaction of debts.[20]

233

When the Duke objects, 'This is no answer, thou unfeeling man', Shylock replies: 'I am not bound to please thee with my answers' (IV.i.63–5). Rhetorically speaking, it is as if Shylock has misunderstood what 'binds' men and assures them of thrift and fortune; while his sealed bond comes undone in the rhetorical uncertainty of its own expression, he is denied recognition of the extent to which everyone in a verisimilar style of drama is 'bound to please', obliged to become credible, persuasive. In Shylock's case it is because the stealing away of Jessica is not articulated in this scene as an emotionally powerful 'reason' for his anger that the incident becomes something else: a proof of the comic ineffectuality of his notion of 'thrift', and what it 'betrays' about his psychic condition. Thus critics associate Shylock's concern with bodily continence – the image of the man unable to control his bladder at the sound of the bagpipe – with a miserly, self-defeating attempt to close off the apertures of his house and keep Jessica and the ducats safe inside: 'when you hear the drum / And the vile squeaking of the wry-necked fife' he says to Jessica, 'stop my house's ears, I mean my casements . . . do as I bid you, shut doors after you, / Fast bind, fast find, – / A proverb never stale in thrifty mind' (II.v.29–54). Much is made of the bagpipe image as Shylock's unconscious 'justification of his own moral incontinency'.[21] But the image of the bagpipe as dangerously eliciting involuntary disclosure is first applied, by the inquistive Solanio, to the discreet 'sadness' of Antonio:

> Nature hath fram'd strange fellows in her time:
> Some that will evermore peep through their eyes,
> And laugh like parrots at a bagpiper;
> And other of such vinegar aspect,
> That they'll not show their teeth in way of smile
> Though Nestor swear the jest be laughable.
>
> (I.i.51–6)

Antonio's sadness is superficially opposed to the impatience of Gratiano to embrace risk, to laugh and be indiscreet, yet both are equally crucial contributions to the dramatic economy of Bassanio's plot. For as Gratiano's 'commends and courteous breath' (II.ix.90) render dramatically effective the uncertainty of Bassanio's means, so Antonio's sad discretion when confronted by Salanio and Salerio, the gossips of the Rialto, keeps his credit good for Bassanio's sake, in spite of the supposition or uncertainty of his means at sea. As Gratiano and Bassanio exploit the pleasurable, flirtatious quality of uncertainty, Antonio sustains its anxiety; in *Il Pecorone*, Ansaldo observes phlegmatically 'e usanza che delle navi rompano in mare' – 'it is normal that ships get wrecked at sea'.[22] Thus sadness, or discretion, is also a practical manifestation of Antonio's love for Bassanio. Shakespeare transforms Ansaldo's simple investment in Gianetto's courteous plausibility ('I will love you better, the more you make yourself beloved') into Antonio's and Bassanio's relation of humanist *amicitia*, a bond forged through the secret consultation and execution of plots and economic projects. Antonio's love and credit is thus interpreted by Bassanio as a guarantee of confidence in his consultative discretion: 'to you, Antonio / I owe the most in money and in love, / And from your love I have a warranty / To unburthen all my plots and purposes / How to get clear of all the debts I owe' (I.i.130–4). Prudential consultation over the probability of good fortune parallels the credit (expressed as a love so unbounded as to require no assurance of return) with which Antonio furthers Bassanio's project.

If Antonio, Bassanio and Gratiano all express a consciousness of the contribution of uncertainty to the rhetorical probability of Bassanio's chance of good fortune, then theirs is, like Petruchio's in *The Taming of the Shrew*, a notion of thrift which takes decorum, or dramatic effect, into the calculation of costs and returns. By Shylock's crucial failure to exploit the emotional probability of his case, we see that it is his function in the play to locate and make explicit the principles of calculation and anxious mistrust that are both necessary, and necessarily disavowed, by the Xenophonic or Ciceronian prudence that contributes to the happiness of the Christians. Shylock's frankness and loquacity on the subject of the need for assurances and locks represents a miscalculation of the value of discretion; or, to put it another way, Shylock fulfils the tropical function of the housewife in the humanist discourse of good husbandry, who is defined by the stigma of thrifty anxiety even as Christian 'husbandry' becomes, by her definition, an activity at once more fortunate and more magnanimous. As Walter Lynne's Xenophonic housewife admits the superiority of the decorous and timely speech of her husband to all her household contrivance ('I knowe, that he dyd more wyth one worde, than I can do in a hole day'[23]) so Shylock's 'fast bind, fast find / A proverb never stale in thrifty mind' (II.v.52–3) compares pathetically with

Bassanio's prudential calculation of the returns he is like to gain by his courtesy:

> O my Antonio, had I but the means
> To hold a rival place with one of them,
> I have a mind presages me such thrift
> That I should questionless be fortunate.
>
> (I.i.173–6)

It is surely for this reason that Shylock distinguishes himself by the example of Jacob who, in the Protestant literature of thrift and husbandry fulfils (along with Paul's words on the imperative of household provision, 1 Timothy 4:8) the legitimating function of the housewife in Xenophon's *Oeconomicus*. We find, for example, in Coverdale's much imitated and reprinted *Christen State of Matrimonye*:

> If thy wife be vertuouse and trustye, let her be also carefull in kepyng and providing for thy house. For sich studye ... is not foreboden for the godly patriarch Jacob thought it necessary for him and his wyfe to be studiouse for their houshold [marginalia: Gen. xxx], Paul affirming it, if a man provide not for his owne household, he denieth the faith and is an infidel.[24]

The episode to which Bullinger and all his imitators in the literature of good husbandry refer is Genesis 30, which Shylock narrates in justification of his practice of 'thrift' in taking interest on loans (I.iii.72–85). Jacob was cheated by Laban, who promised him hire for his service, but after seven years gave him for a wife not Rachel for whom he had served, but Leah, her elder sister. After another seven years, Jacob earned Rachel, but as the two wives and their handmaids competed industriously in bearing him children, he soon had a large number of dependents, for whom he was still forced to provide out of the paltry wages given him by Laban. His protest to Laban forms the crux of Protestant arguments on the compatibility of prudent calculation and Christian ethics, but it also sets in motion the story which Shylock tells to Antonio and Bassanio:

> And Laban said unto him, I pray thee, if I have found favour in thine eye, tarry, for I have learned by experience that the LORD hath blessed me for thy sake.

... And he said unto him, Thou knowest how I have served
thee, ... the LORD hath blessed thee since my coming: and
now *when shall I provide for mine own house also*?

(Genesis, 30:27–30)[25]

Laban offers him hire on his own terms, and Jacob proposes to
take all Laban's speckled and spotted goats and sheep; he then
performs the famous trick with the wands narrated by Shylock,
and gains enough in the way of herds and flocks to establish
himself as a patriarch, and the master of a great household.
Commentators have been puzzled by Shylock's choice of the Jacob-
Laban story as a justification for the taking of interest; the editor of
the Arden edition remarks, in a note to I.iii.72–85, that 'The Laban
story has not been found in any 16th-c book on usury'. Within the
Protestant discourse of good husbandry, however, it crops up
again and again, as a justification of 'Just keping of the house like
Christian folke':

The man in his gayning and occupying must be just & fayth-
full ... for faythfulnes ever abydeth when unfaythfulnes &
craftynes destroy themselves: as ye see in the faithful dealing
of Jacob and the covetouse desayt of Laban.[26]

In his use of the Jacob-Laban story as a justification of usury,
Shylock parodies and lays bare its legitimating function in the
Protestant discourse of good husbandry. At the same time, however, this parody works to dissociate and insulate the economic
prudence of the Christian husbands in the play from the calculation, deception and theft that ensures the success of their rhetorically mediated projects. Belying the dominant concerns of the prose
fiction, poetry and drama of the 1560s–1580s, *The Merchant of
Venice* displaces humanism's rhetorical problematization of the
signs of love and friendship between men, and locates the displaced anxiety within an imaginatively compelling fiction of
paranoid thrift and racial hatred – a fiction of Jewish otherness.

This partial and inconclusive reading of *The Merchant of Venice*
may seem an inappropriate conclusion to a book which has been
about the centrality of fictions of women to the rhetoric of
humanism. In another way, however, it is perfectly appropriate,
for it returns us to where this book began, with Xenophon's
Oeconomicus, the text which offered a model for representations
of the practical and economic value of humanism through the

celebration of a humanist *habitus* of flexible self-mediation, of decorous facility in translating exemplary reading into daily practice. This book has been trying to unravel such humanist discourses of the rhetorical economies and textualized friendships of men in order to cast new light on Renaissance representations of women, and on women's access to literary production. However, if it can conclude with the unexpected finding that the fiction of 'Shylock the Jew' is also marked by implication in such discourses, then this suggests that the subject has still more to reveal for our understanding of humanist texts and their functions in sixteenth-century English culture. The wealth of the usurer's daughter is not yet exhausted.

NOTES

INTRODUCTION

1 Shakespeare, *King Lear*, ed. Kenneth Muir (London: Methuen, 1972), I.i.98–9, p. 9. Further references to this edition will appear in the text.

2 Shakespeare, *Hamlet*, ed. Harold Jenkins (London: Methuen, 1982), III.iv.45–8, p. 321.

3 See sonnet 29 in Stephen Booth (ed.), *Shakespeare's Sonnets* (New Haven: Yale University Press, 1977), pp. 27–9; Aemilia Lanyer, 'The description of Cooke-ham' in Germaine Greer *et al.* (eds), *Kissing the Rod* (London: Virago, 1988), line 105, p. 48. An exception to this critical tendency is John Barrell's essay, 'Editing out: the discourse of patronage and Shakespeare's twenty-ninth sonnet' in *Poetry, Language and Politics* (Manchester: Manchester University Press, 1988), pp. 18–43.

4 Mervyn E. James, 'A Tudor magnate and the Tudor State' in *Society, Politics and Culture* (Cambridge: Cambridge University Press, 1986), pp. 54–5.

5 Marcel Mauss, *The Gift: The Form and Reason for Exchange in Archaic Societies*, tr. W.D. Halls (London: Routledge, 1990), p. 36.

6 Desiderius Erasmus, *Parabolae sive Similia*, tr. R.A.B. Mynors in *The Collected Works of Erasmus*, vol. 23, ed. Craig R. Thompson (Toronto: University of Toronto Press, 1978), pp. 123–277, p. 131. For the Latin, see Erasmus, *Parabolae sive Similia*, ed. J.C. Margolin, part 1, *Opera Omnia Desiderii Erasmi Roterodami* (Amsterdam: North Holland Publishing Co., 1975), V: 1–332. I was first alerted to this fascinating letter by Natalie Zemon Davis's essay, 'Beyond the market: books as gifts in sixteenth-century France', *Transactions of the Royal Historical Society* 33 (1983), 69–88.

7 Mauss, *The Gift*, p. 61.

8 Anon., *Amis and Amiloun* in Henry Weber (ed.), *Metrical Romances of the Thirteenth, Fourteenth and Fifteenth Centuries*, 2 vols (Edinburgh, 1810), II:375, 382.

9 Davis, 'Beyond the market', 77; on the *topos* of the literary token as able to make present the absent friend, see Lisa Jardine, *Erasmus, Man of Letters: The Construction of Charisma in Print* (Princeton, NJ: Princeton University Press, 1993), p. 31.

10 Erasmus, *Parabolae*, pp. 131–2.
11 *Ibid.*
12 A version of this argument is given by Juliet Dusinberre, *Shakespeare and the Nature of Women* (London: Macmillan, 1975).
13 See, for example, Joan Kelly, 'Did women have a Renaissance?' in *Women, History and Theory* (Chicago: University of Chicago Press, 1984), pp. 19–50; Lisa Jardine, *Still Harping on Daughters* (Hassocks, Sussex: Harvester, 1983); Anthony Grafton and Lisa Jardine, 'Women humanists: education for what?' in *From Humanism to the Humanities* (London: Duckworth, 1986), pp. 29–57; Ann Rosalind Jones, *The Currency of Eros: Women's Love Lyric in England 1540–1620* (Bloomington: Indiana University Press, 1990), pp. 11–35. Of course, there has been a wealth of excellent feminist scholarship devoted to the recovery of sixteenth-century women's writing – an example is the collection of essays edited by Margaret Hannay, *Silent but for the Word: Tudor Women as Patrons, Translators and Writers of Religious Works* (Ohio: Kent State University Press, 1985) – but the constraints upon women's entry into the new literary culture of humanism are nevertheless abundantly clear.
14 Gayle Rubin, 'The traffic in women: notes on the "political economy" of sex' in Rayna Reiter (ed.), *Towards an Anthropology of Women* (New York: Monthly Review Press, 1975), p. 173.
15 Christiane Klapisch-Zuber, 'The cruel mother' in *Women, Family and Ritual in Renaissance Italy,* tr. Lydia Cochrane (Chicago, University of Chicago Press, 1985), pp. 117–19.
16 Patricia Parker, *Literary Fat Ladies: Rhetoric, Gender and Property* (London: Methuen, 1987), pp. 3, 98.
17 Michel de Certeau, *The Practice of Everyday Life*, tr. Steven Rendall (Berkeley: University of California Press, 1984), pp. 79, 81–2.
18 See Matteo Bandello, 'Mirabile beffa fatta da una gentildonna a dui baroni del regno d'Ongaria' in *Tutte le Opere*, 2 vols, ed. Francesco Flora (Milan: Mondadori, 1952), I:242–63; William Painter, *The Second Tome of the Palace of Pleasure* (London: Henry Bynneman, 1567), fols. 292[r]–309[r]; George Whetstone, *The Rocke of Regarde* (London: Robert Waley, 1576), sigs G5[r]–H4[v].
19 Whetstone, *Rocke of Regarde*, sig. G6[r].
20 Painter, *Palace of Pleasure*, fol. 297[r].
21 *Ibid.*, fol. 309[r].

1 THE HOUSEWIFE AND THE HUMANISTS

1 Larry Silver's *The Paintings of Quinten Massy* (Oxford: Phaidon, 1984) devotes a chapter to Metsys' link with Erasmus. The painting is also known as *Le Banquier et sa femme*; however, as Raymond de Roover makes clear, there was no clear distinction between these functions in Northern Europe during the fourteenth and fifteenth centuries; indeed, in Antwerp every burgher had a right to open a public moneychanging practice, and by the second half of the fourteenth century, such practices were regularly used by individuals as places

in which to deposit spare cash. See Raymond de Roover, *Money, Banking and Credit in Medieval Bruges* (Cambridge, Mass.: Harvard University Press, 1948), pp. 175, 247. On the Erasmus–Gilles diptych, see Lorne Campbell, Margaret Mann Phillips, Hubertus Schulte and J.B. Trapp, 'Quentin Matsys, Desiderius Erasmus, Pieter Gillis and Thomas More', *The Burlington Magazine* 120 (1978), 716–24; Lisa Jardine, *Erasmus, Man of Letters: the Construction of Charisma in Print* (Princeton NJ: Princeton University Press, 1993), pp. 27–39.

2 Erwin Panofsky, *Early Netherlandish Painting* (Cambridge, Mass.: Harvard University Press, 1953), 2 vols, I:189, 354; H. Clifford Smith, 'The Legend of S. Eloy and S. Godoberta by Petrus Christus', *The Burlington Magazine* 25 (1914), 326–35; E.P. Richardson, '"The Detroit St. Jerome" by Jan Van Eyck', *Art Quarterly* 19 (1956), 227–34 and Erwin Panofsky, 'Jan Van Eyck's *Arnolfini* Portrait', *The Burlington Magazine* 64 (1934), 117–27.

3 See, for example, Marinus Van Reymerswaele, *Two Tax Gatherers* in the Sainsbury Wing of the National Gallery, London. In *Money, Banking and Credit*, de Roover reproduces from the Museo Nazionale, Florence, a version of *The Moneylender and his Wife* by Van Reymerswaele. Others hang in Munich (Alta Pinacotheca), Madrid (Prado), Antwerp (Musée Royal des Beaux Arts) and Windsor Castle.

4 Svetlana Alpers, *The Art of Describing: Dutch Art in the Seventeenth Century* (Harmondsworth: Penguin, 1989), introduction, p. xxi.

5 *Ibid.*, p. 179.

6 Jardine, *Erasmus, Man of Letters*, pp. 27–39.

7 De Roover, *Money, Banking and Credit*, pp. 172–247.

8 Miles Coverdale, *The Christen State of Matrimonye* (London, 1541); Heinrich Bullinger, *Der Christlich Eestand* (Zurich: Christoffel Froschower, 1579); see John K. Yost, 'The value of married life for the social order in the early English Renaissance', *Societas* 6 (1976), 25–39.

9 See Kathleen M. Davies, 'The sacred condition of equality – how original were Puritan doctrines of marriage?', *Social History* 5 (1977), 579–80, 564n.; see also Derrick S. Bailey, *Thomas Becon and the Reformation of the Church in England* (London: Oliver and Boyd, 1952), p. 22.

10 Coverdale, *Christen State*, sig. J2^v.

11 John Winkler, *The Constraints of Desire: the Anthropology of Sex and Gender in Ancient Greece* (London: Routledge, 1990), p. 23.

12 John Dod and Robert Cleaver, *A Godlie Forme of Household Government: for the ordering of private families* (London: Thomas Marshe, 1612), sig. L4^r.

13 Davies, 'Sacred condition of equality', p. 570.

14 Nancy Armstrong, *Desire and Domestic Fiction: a Political History of the Novel* (Oxford: Oxford University Press, 1987), pp. 18–19; see also p. 110.

15 Catherine Belsey, *The Subject of Tragedy: Identity and Difference in Renaissance Drama* (London: Methuen, 1985), pp. 159–60.

16 Xenophon, *Oeconomicus*, tr. E.C. Marchant (London: Heinemann, 1929) vii.23–35, pp. 420–5. For the derivation of the pseudo-Aristotelian

Oeconomia from Xenophon, see Aristotle, *Economics*, tr. E.S. Forster in vol. X of *The Works of Aristotle*, ed. J.A. Smith and W.D. Ross (Oxford: Clarendon Press, 1921), p. x.

17 Richard Hyrde, tr. of Juan Luis Vives, *A very frutefull and pleasant boke, called the instruction of a Christien woman* (London: T. Berthelet, 1541), sig. M1^{r}.

18 M.I. Finley, 'Aristotle and economic analysis', *Past and Present* 47 (1970), 3–25, 22.

19 Davies, 'Sacred condition of equality', p. 577.

20 *Ibid*., pp. 576–7.

21 Richard Whitford, *A Werke for Householders* (London: R. Redman, 1537), sig. F5^{v}; see Aristotle, *Economics*, 1345^{a}, and Josef Soudek, 'Leonardo Bruni and his public: a statistical and interpretative study of his annotated Latin version of the (Pseudo-) Aristotelian *Economics*', *Studies in Medieval and Renaissance History* 5 (1968), 51–136.

22 Erasmus, *Apopthegmatum Opus* (Paris: Johannes Roigny, 1533), sig. A2^{r}; Lawrence Humphrey, *The Nobles, or of Nobilitye* (London: Thomas Marshe, 1563), sig. Y5^{v}; Bruni is cited by Soudek, 'Leonardo Bruni and his public', 66; for Johannes Herrold, see J. Margolin, introduction to Erasmus' *Encomium Matrimonii* in *Opera Omnia Desiderii Erasmi Roterdami* (Amsterdam: North Holland Publishing Co., 1975), V: 364.

23 Whitford, *A Werke for Householders*, sigs F5^{r} and F6^{v}; see also below, p. 63.

24 De Roover, *Money, Banking and Credit*, p. 11; for a provocative interpretation of the anxieties faced by early modern capitalists on this account, see Lyndal Roper, 'Stealing manhood: capitalism and magic in early modern Germany', *Gender and History* 3 (1991), 4–22, 14.

25 Abbot Paynton Usher, *The Early History of Deposit Banking in Mediterranean Europe* (Cambridge, Mass.: Harvard University Press, 1943), pp. 12–34; on foreign exchange as a credit system, see Raymond de Roover, *Gresham on Foreign Exchange* (Cambridge, Mass.: Harvard University Press, 1949), pp. 94–106.

26 Jan Ympyn Christoffels, *A notable and very excellent woorke, expressing and declaryng the maner and forme how to kepe a boke of accomptes or reconynges, verie expedient and necessary to all Marchantes* (London, 1547), sig. C2^{r}.

27 Christoffels, *A notable woorke*, sig. C2^{r}; see also Thomas Wilson, *A Discourse uppon Usurye by waye of Dialogue and oracions* (London: Richard Tottel, 1572), sigs P6^{r}-7^{v}; de Roover, *Foreign Exchange*, p. 177.

28 J.S. Brewer, J. Gairdner and R.S. Brodie (eds), *Letters and Papers, Foreign and Domestic, of the Reign of Henry VIII* (London: Eyre & Spottiswoode, 1862–1932), 21 vols, vol. 13, pt 1, p. 536; see J.L. Bolton, *The Medieval English Economy* (London: J.M. Dent and Sons, 1980), pp. 342–3.

29 R.H. Tawney, introduction to Thomas Wilson, *A Discourse Upon Usury* (London: Frank Cass, 1925), pp. 160–1 explains that while the Act repealed the 1552 Act under which persons taking any interest whatsoever were to forfeit interest and principle, reviving the Act of 1545 under which persons taking more than 10 per cent were to forfeit

the treble value of their wares and profits, any transaction involving less than 10 per cent would give no legal security to the creditor. For the credit crisis, see G.D. Ramsay, *The City of London in International Politics at the Accession of Elizabeth Tudor* (Manchester: Manchester University Press, 1975), pp. 58–61; the effect of the 1571 Act, see Norman Jones, *God and the Moneylenders: Usury and Law in Early Modern England* (Oxford: Basil Blackwell, 1989), ch. 2.

30 Roper, 'Stealing manhood', pp. 10–11.

31 Heiko Oberman, *Masters of the Reformation: The Emergence of a New Intellectual Climate in Europe*, tr. Dennis Martin (Cambridge: Cambridge University Press, 1981), p. 130.

32 Oberman, *Masters of the Reformation*, p. 146; on Deuteronomy see Benjamin Nelson, *The Idea of Usury: From Tribal Brotherhood to Universal Otherhood* (Chicago: Chicago University Press, 1969).

33 Jones, *God and the Moneylenders*, pp. 1–5.

34 Richard Hitchcocke, *A Pollitique Platt* (London: John Kingston, 1580), sig. **1^r; for Hitchcocke's proposal to use interest on loans, see sig. A4^v and table. Cicero is cited by John Dee in his *Brytannicae Reipublicae Synopsis* for which see William Sherman, 'A reader's guide to the Elizabethan Commonwealth', *Journal of Medieval and Renaissance Studies* 20 (1990), 300n. For the 'commonweal' ideology of Elizabethan economic projects, see Joan Thirsk, *Economic Policy and Projects* (Oxford: Clarendon Press, 1978), pp. 33–50.

35 See Walter Nicgorski, 'Cicero's Paradoxes and his idea of utility', *Political Theory* 12 (1984), 557–78, 565–7.

36 Robert Whittinton, *The thre bookes of Tullyes offyces both in latyn tonge in englysshe* (London: Wynkyn de Worde, 1534), sig. Q3^v, 'formula, qua officium cognoscitur', sigs Q5^r-Q6^v.

37 Nicholas Grimald, *Marcus Tullius Ciceroes thre bookes of duties* (London: Richard Tottel, 1558), sigs O7^v-O8^r.

38 Kurt Singer, 'Oikonomia: an inquiry into the beginnings of economic thought and language', *Kyklos* 11 (1958), 29–57, 40.

39 Victoria Kahn, 'Humanism and the Resistance to Theory' in Patricia Parker and David Quint (eds), *Literary Theory/Renaissance Texts* (Baltimore: Johns Hopkins University Press, 1986), p. 377; see also Terence Cave, *The Cornucopian Text* (Oxford: Clarendon Press, 1978).

40 Cave, *Cornucopian Text*, p. 35.

41 Cicero, *De Officiis*, tr. Walter Miller (London: Heinemann, 1913), I.xxvii–xxviii, pp. 95–103; see Whittinton, *Tullyes offyces*, sig. I1^r, 'So it is that this temperaunce that we interpretate so as I have sayd is a scyence of oportunitie of tyme to do any thynge, but this same selfe defynycion may be the defynicion of prudence'. See Victoria Kahn, *Rhetoric, Prudence and Skepticism in the Renaissance* (Ithaca and London: Cornell University Press, 1985), p. 35.

42 Gentian Hervet, *Xenophons Treatise of Householde* (London: T. Berthelet, 1534), sig. A1^r. There were further editions in 1544, 1557 and 1573. For comparing the Greek, I have used E.C. Marchant's parallel text; I have also benefited from Leo Strauss, *Xenophon's Socratic Discourse* (Ithaca and London: Cornell University Press, 1970).

43 See John Archer Gee, *The Life and Works of Thomas Lupset* (New Haven: Yale University Press, 1928), pp. 1–121.

44 For the associations of humanists such as Lupset, Starkey and Hervet both with the Poles and with Erasmus, see James McConica, *English Humanism and Reformation Politics* (Oxford: Clarendon Press, 1966); Gordon Zeeveld, *Foundations of Tudor Policy* (Cambridge, Mass.: Harvard University Press, 1948); Thomas F. Mayer, *Thomas Starkey and the Commonweal* (Cambridge: Cambridge University Press, 1989).

45 Compare, 'This boke of householde, full of high wisdome, written by the noble philosopher Xenophon, the scholer of Socrates, the which for his swete eloquence, and incredible facilitie, was surnamed Musa Attica, that is to sai, the songe of Athenes', Hervet, *Treatise of Householde*, sig. A1^r, with M.T. Ciceronis, *Cato Maior Seu de Senectute*, D. Erasmi annotationibus illustratus (Paris: Michael Vascosan, 1536) sig. I8^r: 'Xenophon Socratis discipulus ob elegantiem dulcedinem & incredibilem dicendi facilitatem, musa attica appellatus est.'

46 Hervet, *Treatise of Householde*, sig. A2^r. Henceforward all references to this edition will appear in the text.

47 Davies, 'Sacred condition of equality', p. 572.

48 Michel Foucault, *The Use of Pleasure*, vol. 2 of *The History of Sexuality*, tr. Robert Hurley (Harmondsworth: Penguin, 1984), p. 152.

49 James Tatum, *Xenophon's Imperial Fiction: On the Education of Cyrus* (Princeton, NJ: Princeton University Press, 1989), p. 192.

50 *Ibid.*, pp. 189–92; in the *Oeconomicus*, the 'Cyrus' figured is Cyrus the Younger, who never in fact became king, but as Tatum affirms, p. 41, 'the association between the older and the younger Cyrus later turned into a literary project in its own right'.

51 Humphrey, *The Nobles*, sig. I8^{r-v}.

52 *Ibid.*, sig. X2^r.

53 Tatum, *Xenophon's Imperial Fiction*, p. 197, pp. 98–106.

54 Cicero, *De Senectute*, tr. William A. Falconer (London: Heinemann, 1923), XVII: 59–60, pp. 70–3.

55 O.B. Hardison, *The Enduring Monument: A Study of the Idea of Praise in Renaissance Literary Theory and Practice* (Chapel Hill: University of North Carolina Press, 1962), pp. 72–9.

56 Sir Thomas Elyot, *The Boke named the Governour* [1531] (London: J.M. Dent, 1907), p. 45.

57 See Dudley Fenner, *The Artes of Logike and Rhetorike* (London, 1584).

58 See J. Wayne Baker, 'Heinrich Bullinger and the idea of usury', *Sixteenth Century Journal* 5 (1974), 49–70, 51–8; and Nelson, *Idea of Usury*, ch. 2.

59 Heinrich Bullinger, *Von dem unverschampten fräfel* (Zurich: Christoffel Froschower, 1531), fols 156^r and 157^{r-v}; I am very grateful to my father, John Hutson, for translating Bullinger's difficult German. We note that Wayne Baker translates 'den der ander mit siner arbeyt ... gewunnen hat' as 'which he has earned for the other with his work' ('Bullinger and the idea of usury', 62), but the grammar would seem to construe as 'which the other has earned with his work'. This does not affect the general sense of approving a profit share between loan-

capitalist and venturer.

60 Bullinger, *Fräfel*, fols 70ᵛ-72ʳ.

61 An English translation of the *Fräfel* was published; see John Veron Sennoys, *A most necessary and frutefull Dialogue between the seditious libertin or rebel Anabaptist and the true obedient Christian* (London: John Oswen, 1551), but it omits Bullinger's pro-usury arguments.

62 Bullinger, *Fräfel*, fol. 71ᵛ.

63 Shakespeare, *The Merchant of Venice*, ed. John Russell Brown (London: Methuen, 1955), I.iii.64–90, 26n.

64 Bullinger, *Christlich Eestand*, fol. 76ʳ; Coverdale, *Christen State*, sig. J2ᵛ.

65 Bullinger, *Christlich Eestand*, fol. 75ʳ; Coverdale, *Christen State*, sig. J2ʳ.

66 *Ibid.*

67 Bullinger, *Christlich Eestand*, fol. 77ᵛ; Coverdale, *Christen State*, sig. J3ʳ.

68 Bullinger, *Christlich Eestand*, fol. 76ᵛ.

69 Thomas Lupset, *An Exhortacion* in Gee, *Works*, pp. 250–1; for Paul Withypoll's friendship with Cromwell, see G.R. Elton, *Reform and Renewal: Thomas Cromwell and the Commonweal* (Cambridge: Cambridge University Press, 1973), p. 65; on Paul and Edmund Withypoll's careers, see G.C. Moore-Smith, 'Edmund Withypoll' in *Archiv für das studium der neuern sprachen und Literaturen* n.s. 43 (1922), 183–9.

70 Lupset, *An Exhortacion*, in Gee, *Works*, p. 247 (sig. C3ᵛ). Gee notes that in the 1560 editon of *Tho. Lupsets Workes*, the phrase 'Matens, masse or a sermon' becomes, 'thee sevice'. Nevertheless, it is striking to note that a reader of the 1560 edition has marked with marginal annotations passages which relate to the soul's danger through bargaining; i.e., sigs F6ʳ⁻ᵛ; sig. F7ʳ; sig. G4ʳ, sig. G5ʳ, sigs I2ᵛ-3ᵛ, sig. I6ʳ, sigs J8ᵛ–K3ʳ, sigs K5ʳ–6ʳ. For a description of the business community as one in which being 'in charity' with one's neighbours was considered vital, see Susan Brigden, 'Religion and social obligation in early sixteenth–century London', *Past and Present* 103 (1984), 67–112.

71 Lupset, *An Exhortacion* in Gee, *Works*, pp. 250–1 (sigs C8ᵛ–D1ʳ); this passage is marked with a pointing hand in the 1560 edition.

72 *The Correspondence of Erasmus*, tr. R.A.B. Mynors (Toronto: University of Toronto Press, 1987), VII: 16–25; for the identification of More as 'ideal husband' here with the exemplary husband in Erasmus' *Coniugium*, see n. 27, p. 355; for the Latin, see *Opus Epistolarum Des, Erasmis Roterdami*, ed. P.S. Allen, vol. 4 (Oxford: Clarendon Press, 1922), pp. 12–23. For Erasmus' recognition of analogies between the effects of verisimilitude in portraiture and in the printed familiar epistle, see Jardine, *Erasmus, Man of Letters*, pp. 30–1.

73 *Correspondence*, VII: 19–20; *Opus Epistolarum* IV: 17–18.

74 *Correspondence*, VII: 24; *Opus Epistolarum*, IV: 21, lines 262–5.

75 *De Copia Verborum ac Rerum*, ed. Betty I. Knott, vol. 3, *Opera Omnia Desiderii Erasmi Roterdami* (Amsterdam: North Holland Publishing, 1972), pp. 258–79.

76 *Correspondence*, VII: 21; *Opus Epistolarum* IV: 18.

77 Bullinger, *Christlich Eestand*, fol. 75ʳ; *The Works of Thomas Nashe*, 5 vols, ed. R.B. McKerrow (Oxford: Basil Blackwell, 1966), II:107.

78 See Silver, *Quinten Massys*, p. 137, citing Alexander van Fornenebergh,

Den Antwerpischen Protheus (1658), pp. 26–7. I have not yet been able to obtain this book.

79 Lupset, *An Exhortacion* in Gee, *Works*, pp. 247, 256; for reading as continuous with participation in the Mass, see Margaret Aston, 'Devotional Literacy' in *Lollards and Reformers: Images and Literacy in Late Medieval Religion* (London: Hambledon Press, 1984), p. 124 and Susan Brigden, *London and the Reformation* (Oxford: Clarendon Press, 1989), pp. 14–16.

2 ECONOMIES OF FRIENDSHIP

1 Giovanni Boccaccio, *Decameron*, 2 vols, ed. Antonio Enzo Quaglio (Milan: Garzanti, 1974), II:901.

2 *Il Decamerone dim. Giovanni Boccaccio*, ed. Girolamo Ruscellai (Venice: Vicenzo Valgusio, 1552), p. 461. For 'capital' Ruscellai gives 'istima'.

3 Pierre Bourdieu, *Outline of a Theory of Practice*, tr. Richard Nice (Cambridge: Cambridge University Press, 1977), p. 177.

4 Edward Hake, *Of Golds Kingdom in this Unhelping Age* (London: John Windet, 1604), sigs E2^v-E3^v, sig. A4^r.

5 Paul Millet, *Lending and Borrowing in Ancient Athens* (Cambridge: Cambridge University Press, 1991), pp. 9–36, 32–3 ; see also Marcel Mauss, *The Gift: The Form and Reason for Exchange in Archaic Societies* (London: Routledge, 1990) and Marshall Sahlins, 'On the sociology of primitive exchange' in *Stone Age Economics* (London: Routledge, 1988), pp. 185–275. For a sixteenth-century citation of Hesiod's rule of reciprocity, see George Turberville, *A plaine Path to perfect Virtue* (London: Henry Bynneman, 1568), sig. C2^r.

6 Sir Hugh Platt, *The Floures of Philosophie* (London: Henry Bynneman, 1581; first published in 1572), sig. M1^{r-v}.

7 Isabella Whitney, *A Sweet Nosgay or pleasant Posye: contayning a hundred and ten Phylosophicall Flowers* (London: Richard Jones, 1573), sig. B4^v.

8 *Ibid.*, sig. B5^r.

9 William Harrys, *The Market or fayre of Usurers* (London: Steven Mierdman, 1550), sig. D4^v.

10 Whitney, *Sweet Nosgay*, sig. E2^v.

11 Hake, *Golds Kingdom*, sigs F1^{r-v}.

12 Boccaccio, *Decameron*, II:904–5.

13 'Titus and Gisippus' is one of the three most favoured, by sixteenth-century writers, of Boccaccio's hundred *novelle*; for its influence, see Louis Sorieri, *Boccaccio's Story of Tito e Gisippo in European Literature* (New York: Comparative Literature Series, 1937), pp. 99, 152 and *passim*; Charles Tyson Goode, 'Sir Thomas Elyot's "Titus and Gysippus"', *MLN* 37 (1922), 1–11; Samuel Lee Wolf, 'A source of *Euphues, the Anatomy of Wit*', *MP* 7 (1910), 577–85; Herbert T. Wright, *Boccaccio in England from Chaucer to Tennyson* (London: Athlone, 1957) and Laurens J. Mills, *One Soul in Bodies Twain* (Bloomington, Indiana: The Principia Press, 1937), pp. 97–108 and p. 410, n. 121.

14 Sir Thomas Elyot, *The Boke named the Governour* [1531] (London: J.M. Dent, 1907), pp. 154–5.

15 See Bourdieu, *Theory of Practice*, pp. 5–19.

16 Boccaccio, *Decameron* II:888; Elyot, *Governour*, p. 167.

17 Elyot, *Governour*, pp. 173–4.

18 *Ibid.*, p. 177.

19 *Ibid.*, p. 179.

20 *Ibid.*, p. 181.

21 Bourdieu, *Theory of Practice*, p. 186.

22 John Lyly, *Euphues: the Anatomy of Wit* (1578) in Paul Salzman (ed.), *An Anthology of Elizabethan Prose Fiction* (Oxford: Oxford University Press, 1987), pp. 103, 114; see Wolf, 'A source of *Euphues*' 581n.; Thomas Watson, *The HEKATOMPATHIA, or Passionate Centurie of Love* (London: John Wolf, 1582), sig. I4^r. George Pettie, *A Petite Pallace of Pettie his Pleasure*, ed. Herbert Hartman (London: Oxford University Press, 1938), p. 47.

23 See John J. Major, *Sir Thomas Elyot and Renaissance Humanism* (Lincoln, Nebraska: University of Nebraska Press, 1964), pp. 256–9; Mills, *One Soul in Bodies Twain*, pp. 28–39, 103; Sorieri, *Boccaccio's Story of Tito e Gisippo*, p. 4.

24 Elyot, *Govenour*, p. 177; Boccaccio, *Decameron*, II:901.

25 Naomi Tadmor, '"Family" and "Friend" in *Pamela*: a case study in the history of the Family in eighteenth-century England', *Social History* 14 (1989), 289–306, 300; Lawrence Stone, *The Family, Sex and Marriage 1500–1800* (London: Weidenfeld and Nicolson, 1977), pp. 79–80.

26 John Harington, *The booke of freendeship of Marcus Tullie Cicero* (London: Thomas Berthelet, 1550), sig. B2^v.

27 For the translation of Cicero's *utilitas* as 'profit', see Robert Whittinton, *The thre bookes of Tullyes offyces both in latyn tonge and in englysshe* (London: Wynkyn de Worde, 1534), sig. L3^r. Book II, concerning *utilitas* begins:

> I suppose I have sufficiently shewed in this first booke howe offyces be deduced out of honesty and out of all kindes of vertue. It foloweth that I must procede to those maner of offices which pertayne to the cleane kepynge of this lyfe and to the substance of richesse and habundance of suche thynges as men occupye / Wherein I sayde bothe it is to be asked what is profytable and what is not profytable.
>
> (sig. K2^r)

For the notion that the humanist model of friendship coincides exactly with the interests of the commonweal, see Major, *Sir Thomas Elyot*, p. 259; Cicero and Thomas Wilson think otherwise; see Cicero, *De Officiis*, tr. Walter Miller (London: Heinemann, 1925), III.x, p. 310 and Thomas Wilson, *Three orations of Demosthenes* (London: Henrie Denham, 1570), sig. A1^r.

28 Thomas Lupset, *An Exhortacion to yonge men* (London: Thomas Berthelet, 1535) sig. C4^r.

29 Harington, *Booke of freendeship*, sig. A4^v.

30 *Ibid.*, sigs A3^r-A4^r.
31 Boccaccio, *Decameron*, II:904.
32 See above, pp. 47–9.
33 Claude Lévi-Strauss, *The Elementary Structures of Kinship* revised edition, tr. James Harle Bell, John Richard von Sturmer and Rodney Needham (Boston: Becon Press, 1969), p. 481; see also Gayle Rubin's brilliant critique, 'The traffic in women: notes on a political economy of sex' in R. Reiter (ed.), *Towards an Anthropology of Women* (New York: Monthly Review Press, 1975), pp. 157–210.
34 Georges Duby, *Medieval Marriage: Two Models from Twelfth-Century France*, tr. Elborg Foster (Baltimore: Johns Hopkins University Press, 1978), p. 13; see also David Herlihy, *Medieval Households* (Cambridge, Mass.: Harvard University Press, 1985), pp. 79–88.
35 Thomas Starkey, *A Dialogue between Reginald Pole and Thomas Lupset* (*c.* 1533), ed. Kathleen Burton (London: Chatto and Windus, 1948), pp. 140–1. On Cromwell's part in commissioning the *Dialogue*, see G.R. Elton, 'Reform by statute: Thomas Starkey's *Dialogue* and Thomas Cromwell's policy', *Proceedings of the British Academy* 16 (1968), 165–88, 169–70. On the 'bachelor' households of the English nobility at the beginning of the sixteenth century, see Kate Mertes, *The English Noble Household 1200–1600* (Oxford: Basil Blackwell, 1988), pp. 57–8.
36 Starkey, *Dialogue*, p. 141. See also Starkey's treatise in the form of a letter to Henry VIII written about 1536, in which poverty/underpopulation and matrimony/tillage are continually elided in phrases such as: 'the *penury* of pepul & inhabitantys in your cyties and townys' or '*plant* therein *men lyvyng in lawful matrimony* wherby the nomber of your pepul shalbe hereafter much increasyd' (my italics) in Sidney J. Herrtage (ed.), *England in the Reign of Henry Eighth* part 1: *Starkey's Life and Letters* (London, 1878), pp. xlviii–lxii.
37 Eric Carlson, 'Marriage reform and the Elizabethan High Commission', *Sixteenth Century Journal* 21 (1990), 437–51. See also David Logan, 'The Henrican Canons', *Bulletin of the Institute of Historical Research* 48 (1974), 99–103, and G.R. Elton, *Reform and Renewal: Thomas Cromwell and the Commonweal* (Cambridge: Cambridge University Press, 1973).
38 Richard Taverner, *A ryght frutefull Epystle devysed by the moste excellent clerke Erasmus in laude and prayse of matrymony* (London: R. Redman, 1532), sig. B1^r. On Taverner, see James McConica, *English Humanism and Reformation Politics* (Oxford: Clarendon Press, 1966), p. 117, and John K. Yost, 'Taverner's use of Erasmus and the Protestantisation of English Humanism', *Renaissance Quarterly* 23 (1970), 266–76.
39 Taverner, *Epystle*, sig. A2^r.
40 David Clapam, *The Commendation of Matrimony made by Cornelius Agrippa* (London: Thomas Berthelet, 1545), sig. A2^r.
41 Starkey, *Dialogue*, p. 79.
42 Mervyn E. James, 'The concept of order and the Northern Rising, 1569' in *Society, Politics and Culture: Studies in Early Modern England* (Cambridge: Cambridge University Press, 1986), pp. 271–2; 'The Lyfe

of Ipomydon' in Henry Weber (ed.), *Metrical Romances of the Thirteenth, Fourteenth and Fifteenth Centuries*, 2 vols (Edinburgh, 1810), II:54.

43 Mertes, *Noble Household*, pp. 170–9; on p. 174 Mertes notes that a copy of Elyot's *Governour* was bought for the charges of Sir H. Willoughby of Wollaton in 1549.

44 Elyot, 'the ancient huntyng of Greekes, Romanes and Persianes', *Governour*, p. 83. In Xenophon, hunting is justified by Cyrus' father as a means of learning how to take strategic advantage of the enemy in battle; see Xenophon, *Cyropaedia*, 2 vols, tr. Walter Miller (London: Heinemann, 1914), I.vi.35–40, pp. 118–25.

45 Edward Hake, *A Touchstone for this time present* (London: Thomas Hacket, 1574), sig. F1^r.

46 Lawrence Humphrey, *The Nobles or of Nobilitye*, sig. H8^v.

47 *Ibid.*, sig. E6^r.

48 For the impact of Starkey's proposals on subsequent economic policy, see Elton, 'Reform by Statute', 174–88 and, in R.H. Tawney and E. Power (eds), *Tudor Economic Documents*, 3 vols (London: Longman Greene and Co., 1924), 'Policies to reduce this realme unto a prosperous welth and estate' (1549), III:311–45; 'Considerations delivered to the Parliament, 1559', I:325–30. The eventual results of these policies were to create a 'consumer society' of England, which was far from what Starkey or other 'commonwealthsmen' ever envisaged: see Joan Thirsk, *Economic Policy and Projects: The Development of a Consumer Society in Early Modern England* (Oxford: Clarendon Press, 1978) and A.L. Beier, 'Engine of manufacture: the trades of London', in A.L. Beier and Roger Finlay (eds), *London: The Making of the Metropolis 1500–1700* (London: Longman, 1986), pp. 141–67.

49 Starkey, *Dialogue*, p. 85. Starkey's distrust of artificers making luxury goods may be understood in terms of the preference, in an economy where cash is scarce, to reserve it for exchanging for 'substantial' goods of raw material, rather than 'wasting' it on the labour of artificers working that material; see Thirsk, *Economic Policy and Projects*, pp. 14–16 and my own *Thomas Nashe in Context* (Oxford: Clarendon Press, 1989), pp. 15–37.

50 Starkey, *Dialogue*, p. 124.

51 Taverner, *Epystle*, sigs B6^{r-v}, C5^v, D1^r.

52 Lévi-Strauss, *Elementary Structures of Kinship*, p. 485; see also Rubin, 'Traffic in women', p. 174.

53 Starkey, *Dialogue*, pp. 22–4.

54 See Lisa Jardine, 'Humanistic logic' in Charles B. Schmitt, Quentin Skinner, Ekhart Kessler and Jill Kray (eds), *The Cambridge History of Renaissance Philosophy* (Cambridge: Cambridge University Press, 1988), pp. 173–98, p. 175; 'practical certainty' is Victoria Kahn's phrase; see *Rhetoric, Prudence and Skepticism in the Renaissance* (Ithaca and London: Cornell University Press, 1985), p. 20.

55 Warren Boutcher, 'Florio's Montaigne: translation and pragmatic humanism in the sixteenth century', unpublished Ph.D. thesis, Cambridge University, 1990, p. 10; see also Jardine 'Humanistic logic', pp. 187–92.

56 S.F. Bonner, *Roman Declamation in the Late Republic and Early Empire* (Liverpool: Liverpool University Press, 1949), p. 11 and *passim*. See the same author's *Education in Ancient Rome from the Elder Cato to the Younger Pliny* (London: Methuen, 1977). On the association between declamation and humanistic logic, or 'reasoning abundantly', see Lisa Jardine, *Erasmus, Man of Letters* (Princeton, NJ: Princeton University Press, 1993), p. 136 and Joel B. Altman, *The Tudor Play of Mind* (Berkeley: University of California Press, 1978), pp. 28–63.

57 Quintilian, *The Institutio Oratoria of Quintilian*, 4 vols, tr. H.E. Butler, (London: Heinemann, 1935), II:190–311.

58 Quintilian, *Institutio Oratoria*, V.viii; II:190–1.

59 See Anthony Grafton and Lisa Jardine, *From Humanism to the Humanities: Education and the Liberal Arts in Fifteenth and Sixteenth-Century Europe* (London: Duckworth, 1986), pp. 79, 68–82; also Nancy Streuver, 'Lorenzo Valla: Humanist Rhetoric and the critique of the classical languages of morality' in James J. Murphy (ed.), *Renaissance Eloquence* (Los Angeles: University of California Press, 1983), pp. 191–206, 202.

60 Erasmus, *Opera Omnia* vol. 3: *De Copia Verborum ac rerum*, ed. Betty I. Knott (Amsterdam: North Holland Publishing, 1972), pp. 230–3 and notes.

61 Taverner, *Epystle*, sigs A7ʳ, B4ʳ and B6ʳ⁻ᵛ.

62 Terence Cave, *The Cornucopian Text* (Oxford: Clarendon Press, 1978), p. 22.

63 David Starkey, 'Intimacy and innovation: the rise of the Privy Chamber 1485–1547' in *The English Court from the Wars of the Roses to the Civil War* (London: Longman, 1987), p. 85.

64 See Thomas Chaloner, *Of the office of servauntes* (London: Thomas Berthelet, 1534), sigs B8ʳ⁻ᵛ, C4ʳ⁻ᵛ. For Cousin's service in Erasmus' household, see Franz Bielaire, *La Familia d'Erasme* (Paris: Librairie Philosophique, 1968) and Lucien Febvre, 'Un Secretaire d'Erasme: Gilbert Cousin et la Reform en Franche-Comte', *Société de l'Histoire du Protestantisme Français* (1907), 97–148.

65 'Sir Thomas Chaloner the Elder (1525–65)', *DNB* 9:457 and Richard Hakluyt, *The Principal Navigations, Traffiques and Discoveries of the English Nation*, 12 vols (Glasgow: James McLehose and Sons, 1903–5), V: 70–1.

66 Elyot, *Governour*, 'Howe the studentes in the lawes of this realme may take excellent commoditie by the lessons of sondry doctrines', pp. 64–6; R.M. Fisher, 'Thomas Cromwell, humanism and educational reform', *Bulletin of the Institute of Historical Research* 50 (1977), 151–63; see also J.H. Baker, 'English law and the Renaissance' in *The Legal Profession and the Common Law* (London: Hambledon, 1986), pp. 461–76 and Alessandro Guiliani, 'The influence of Rhetoric on the law of evidence and pleading', *Juridical Review* 7 (1962), 216–51.

67 Herrtage, *Starkey's Life and Letters*, p. lxxii.

68 Hannah H. Gray, 'Renaissance humanism: the pursuit of eloquence', *Journal of the History of Ideas* 24 (1963), 497–514, 511; for William Marshall's authorship of the English translation of Valla, *A Treatyse of*

the Donation gyven unto Sylvester Pope of Rome by Constantine (London, 1534) see McConica, *English Humanism and Reformation Politics*, p. 136; for Marshall's authorship of the a poor law based on Starkey's *Dialogue* and his own translation of the ordinance at Ypres, see G.R. Elton, 'An early Tudor Poor Law', *Economic History Review* 6 (1953), 55–67.

69 The 'witty argumentes, quycke reasons' of Agricola are given as Clapam's motive for translation, *Commendation of Matrimony*, sig. A3^r. Compare William Harrington's refusal to use 'proofs wholly the work of art' when opening the causes whereby matrimony is to be commended in *In thys boke are conteyned the commendacions of matrymony* (London: John Skot, 1528), sig. A2^v.

70 Elton, *Reform and Renewal*, pp. 16–25.

71 Anthony Grafton and Lisa Jardine, 'Studied for action: how Gabriel Harvey read his Livy', *Past and Present* 129 (1990), 32–73; Jardine, 'Gabriel Harvey, scholar-reader: knowledge transactions and private services in the 1590s', unpublished research paper; William Sherman, '"Official Scholars" and "Action Officers": research intelligence and the making of Tudor policy in early modern England', unpublished research paper delivered at the London Renaissance Seminar, 1990; also Sherman, 'Dee's *Britannicae Republicae Synopsis*: a reader's guide to the Elizabethan commonwealth', *Journal of Medieval and Renaissance Studies* 20 (1990), 293–315.

72 Starkey, *Dialogue*, p. 21; see also Lupset, *An Exhortacion*, sigs A2^r-A3^v, where the communicative action of the text has *amicitia* as its pretext.

73 Taverner, *Epystle*, sigs A3^r-4^v.

74 Stephen Booth (ed.), *Shakespeare's Sonnets* (New Haven: Yale University Press, 1977), pp. 6–7, 18–19, 48–9, and 15. See also Katherine Wilson, *Shakespeare's Sugared Sonnets* (London, 1974), pp. 46–67 and my 'Why the lady's eyes are nothing like the sun' in Clare Brant and Diane Purkiss (eds), *Women, Texts and Histories 1500–1760* (London: Routledge, 1992) pp. 14–20. Thomas Wilson, *The Rule of Reason, conteynyng the Arte of Logique* (London: Richard Grafton, 1551) derives his example of an argument drawn from 'similitude' from the section of Erasmus' *Encomium Matrimonii* in which a bachelor is like the bad husband who tends only the 'redy grown': sig. P.1^r.

75 The main source seems to be the story of the merchants of Egypt and Baghdad as told in Petrus Alphonsus, *Disciplina Clericalis*; see Arthur Lee Collingwood, *The Decameron: its Sources and Analogues* (London: David Nutt, 1909), pp. 330–43.

76 Cornelia C. Coulter, 'Boccaccio's knowledge of Quintilian' *Speculum* (1958), 490–6, 493.

77 In Book XIV of the *Genealogia Deorum*, Boccaccio recalls Quintilian's denunciation of those declaimers who neglect 'artificial proof' and concentrate on ornament (V.xii.17), to support his own refutation of critics who claim that the works of poets are superficial and empty. See Charles C. Osgood (ed.), *Boccaccio on Poetry* (Princeton: Princeton University Press, 1930), pp. 52–4. For *Translatio studii* see Ernst Robert Curtius, *European Literature in the Latin Middle Ages*, tr.

Willard R. Trask (London: Routledge and Kegan Paul, 1953), p. 29; 'Sophronia' sounds like an ideal harmony between the Greek virtues of *sophia* (wisdom) and *phronesis* (prudence).

78 Elyot, *Governour*, p. 164.

79 John Hazel Smith (ed.), *Two Latin Comedies by John Foxe the Martyrologist* (Ithaca: Cornell University Press, 1973), pp. 54–197. *Locii communes* or 'places' of argument are explained by Wilson, *Rule of Reason*, as 'the restyng corner of an argument, or els a marke whiche giveth warning to our memorie that we may speake probablie, either on the one parte, or the other, of all causes that fall in question', sig. J5^r. Treatment of the *locii* entered humanist logic from Quintilian; see Grafton and Jardine, *Humanism to the Humanities*, p. 78.

80 Antony Cope, *The Historie of two the Most Noble Capitaines of the worlde, Anniball and Scipio* (London: T. Berthelet, 1544), sig. X2^r. See also Livy, *The War Against Hannibal*, tr. Aubrey de Selincourt (Harmondsworth: Penguin, 1965), p. 412. The failures of previous generals may be ascribed to Hannibal's exploitation of the unhappy relations between them and those second-in-command; i.e., Scipio the Elder and Sempronius, Fabius Maximus and first Minucius and then Marcellus, pp. 78–9, 115, 253–4.

81 Elyot, *Governour*, p. 292.

82 Duby, *Medieval Marriage*, p. 13.

83 R. Howard Bloch, *Etymologies and Genealogies: a Literary Anthropology of the French Middle Ages* (Chicago: Chicago University Press, 1983), p. 75; this and the following paragraph paraphrase Bloch's argument, pp. 80–107.

84 *Ibid.*, pp. 182–4.

85 *Ibid.*, p. 108.

86 Citations are from Anon., *Sir Eglamour of Artoys* (London: John Walley, *c*. 1546); I also consulted Frances A. Richardson (ed.), *Sir Eglamour of Artois* (London: Early English Text Society, no. 256, 1965). For the dating and popularity of sixteenth-century editions of the romance, see R.S. Crane, *The Vogue for Medieval Chivalric Romance during the English Renaissance* (Menasha, Wisconsin, 1919), p. 37 and C.R. Baskerville, 'An Elizabethan Eglamour play', *MP* 19 (1917), 759–60. *Sir Degore*, published in the early sixteenth century by William Copland, may be read similarly.

87 R. Howard Bloch, *Medieval French Literature and Laws* (Berkeley: University of California Press, 1977), p. 9.

88 *Ibid.*, p. 224.

89 Robert Bartlett, *Trial by Fire and Water: the Medieval Judicial Ordeal* (Oxford: Clarendon Press, 1986), p. 126; see also J.H. Baker, *Introduction to English Legal History* (London: Butterworth, 1979), p. 63.

90 See Duby, *Medieval Marriage*, pp. 4–6; also Beatrice Gottlieb, 'The meaning of clandestine marriage' in Robert Wheaton and Tamara Hareven (eds), *Family and Sexuality in French History* (Philadelphia: Pennsylvania University Press, 1980); James Brundage, *Law, Sex and Christian Society in Medieval Europe* (Chicago: Chicago University Press, 1987), pp. 551–75.

91 William Harrington, *Commendacions of matrymony*, sig. A4^{r-v}.
92 Gottlieb, 'Clandestine marriage' and Diana O'Hara, '"Ruled by my friends": aspects of marriage in the diocese of Canterbury c.1540–1570', *Continuity and Change* 6 (1991), 9–41; Erwin Panofsky, 'Jan Van Eyck's *Arnolfini* Portrait', *The Burlington Magazine* 64 (1934), 117–27.
93 Compare Bloch, *Etymologies and Genealogies*, p. 193 and Crane, *Vogue for Medieval Chivalric Romance*, p. 11.
94 See McEdward Leach (ed.), *Amis and Amiloun* (London: Early English Text Society o.s., no. 203, 1937) and 'The Lyfe of Ipomydon' in vol. 2 of Weber (ed.), *Metrical Romances*.
95 See Herbert T.Wright, *Early English Versions of the Tales of 'Guiscardo and Ghismonda' and 'Titus and Gisippus' from the Decameron* (London: Early English Text Society o.s., no. 205, 1937), pp. 153–61; introduction, p. lxxxi.
96 Elyot, *Governour*, p. 172.
97 Tina Krontiris, *Oppositional Voices: Women as Writers and Translators of Literature in the English Renaissance* (London: Routledge, 1992). The phrase cited comes from Krontiris' reading of the episode in which Trebatio impersonates the husband negotiated for Princess Briana by her father in Margaret Tyler's translation of Diego Ortunez, *Mirrour of Princely Deedes and Knighthood* (London: Thomas East, 1578), sigs B3^{v}-C5^{r}. Krontiris understands the clandestine marriage as a union of pure love, unmotivated by dynastic concern, but since the romance as a whole retrospectively establishes Trebatio's dynasty through his clandestine marriage, this is more than a little misleading.
98 Elyot, *Governour*, p. 181.

PART II ANXIETIES OF TEXTUAL ACCESS

1 Sir Thomas Elyot, *A Preservative Agaynste deth* (London, 1534), sigs A2^{v}-3^{r}.
2 Edward Hake, *A Touchstone for this time present* (London: Thomas Hacket, 1574), sig. F1^{r}.
3 Thus, for example, Shakespeare derived the plot of *All's Well that Ends Well* from the *novella* of Giletta of Narbona in William Painter's *Palace of Pleasure* (London: Henry Denham, 1566), fols 95^{r}-100^{v}, while the plot of *Romeo and Juliet* comes (perhaps via Painter) from Pierre Boaistuau, *Histoires Tragiques Extraictes des Oeuvres Italiennes de Bandel* (Paris: Vincent Sertenas, 1559) and that of *Much Ado about Nothing* comes from François de Belleforest, *Le Troisiesme Tome des Histoires Tragiques* (Lyons: Pierre Rollet, 1574), fols 475^{r}-514^{v}. 'Hamlet' is found in Belleforest, *Le Cinquiesme Livre des Histoires Tragiques* (Lyons: Benoist Rigaud, 1576), pp. 197–302. The story of 'The Dutchess of Savoie' (Painter, *Palace of Pleasure*, tome I, novel xiv, fols 226^{r}-258^{v}) is alluded to in the 'lamentation of a woman being wrongfully defamed' in the 1584 edition of *A Handful of Pleasant Delights*, ed. Hyder E. Rollins (Cambridge Mass.: Harvard University Press, 1924), pp. 56–7 and by George Pettie, *A Petite Pallace of Pettie his Pleasure* (1576), ed. Herbert Hartman (London: Oxford University Press, 1938), p. 6; the

story of 'Dom Diego' figures also in George Whetstone, *The Rocke of Regard* (London: Robert Waley, 1576) and Richard Lynche, *Diellia: Certaine Sonnets, adioned to the amorous Don Diego and Genivera* (London: Henry Olney, 1596); 'wofull *Monsieur Dom Dieg*' is mentioned in Hyder E. Rollins (ed.), *A Gorgeous Gallery of Gallant Inventions* (1578) (Cambridge Mass.: Harvard University Press, 1926), p. 41. For a general account of the indebtedness of George Pettie and Barnabe Riche to Painter and Fenton, see René Pruvost, *Matteo Bandello and Elizabethan Fiction* (Paris, 1937), pp. 75–99. See also Donald Stone Jr. 'Belleforest's Bandello: a bibliographical study', *Bibliotheque d'Humanisme et Renaissance* 36 (1972), 489–99 and René Sturel, *Bandello en France aux XVIᵉ Siècle* (Paris: E. de Boccard, 1918).

4 This is not the place to begin a discussion of the innumerable ways in which Shakespeare's plays rehearse the 'anxieties of textual access' that are the subject of this chapter, but the reader may be referred to a forthcoming article by Lisa Jardine and myself on 'Pedagogy and the technology of textual affect: Erasmus' familiar letters and Shakespeare's *King Lear*'.

5 Caroline Lucas, *Writing for Women: The Example of Woman as Reader in Elizabethan Romance* (Milton Keynes: Open University Press, 1989).

6 This part of the argument of this chapter derives from my article, 'Fortunate travelers: reading for the plot in sixteenth-century England' in *Representations* 41 (1993), 83–103.

3 FROM ERRANT KNIGHT TO PRUDENT CAPTAIN

1 Margaret Tyler, *The Mirrour of Princely deedes and Knighthood* (London: Thomas East, 1578), sig. Y7ʳ.

2 *Ibid.*, sig. D3ᵛ.

3 *Ibid.*, sig. Z1ᵛ.

4 Tina Krontiris, *Oppositional Voices: Women as Writers and Translators of Literature in the English Renaissance* (London: Routledge, 1992), p. 54.

5 George Duby, *Medieval Marriage: Two Models from Twelfth-Century France*, tr. Elborg Foster (Baltimore: Johns Hopkins University Press, 1978), pp. 4–5.

6 Tyler, *Mirrour of Knighthood*, sig. E1ᵛ; compare Diego Ortunez de Calahorra, *Espejo de Principes y Cavalleros* (Medina del Campo, 1583), fol. 14ʳ.

7 Tyler, *Mirrour of Knighthood*, sigs A2ʳ⁻ᵛ, A3ʳ.

8 *Ibid.*

9 See Alan Stewart, 'The bounds of sodomy: textual relations in early modern England', unpublished Ph.D. thesis, London University, 1993, p. 98.

10 Helen Hackett, '"Yet tell me some such fiction": Mary Wroth's *Urania* and the "Femininity" of Romance' in Clare Brant and Diane Purkiss (eds), *Women, Texts and Histories 1575–1760* (London: Routledge, 1992), pp. 39–68.

11 Lucas, *Writing for Women*, p. 18.

12 *DNB*, 'William Painter'.

13 Painter, *The Second Tome of the Palace of Pleasure* (London: Henry Denham, 1567), sigs *3^{r-v}.

14 *Ibid.*, sig. *4^r.

15 *Ibid.*, sig. *2^v.

16 On the futility of this project, see Edith Kern, 'The Romance of novel/ novella' in Peter Demetz *et al.* (eds), *The Disciplines of Criticism* (New Haven: Yale University Press, 1968).

17 Sir Philip Sidney, *The Countess of Pembroke's Arcadia*, ed. Maurice Evans (Harmondsworth: Penguin, 1977), p. 95.

18 Lucas, *Writing for Women*, pp. 40–1.

19 Geoffrey Fenton, *Certaine Tragicall Discourses* (London: Thomas Marshe, 1567), fol. 1^r.

20 See Pruvost, *Bandello and Elizabethan Fiction*, p. 109; Painter writes that Boccaccio is worth translating for the 'order of writing', but Bandello is best followed in 'the French Translators, then the barren soile of his owne vaine . . . being a Lombard'; *Palace of Pleasure*, tome I 'To the Reader', sig. *3^{r-v}. Francois Belleforest calls Bandello 'rude & grossier en son Lombard', *Continuation des Histoires Tragiques* (Paris: Vincent Sertenas, 1559), sig. A3^r.

21 Belleforest, *Continuation des Histoires Tragiques*, sig. A3^r.

22 See Jean Robertson, 'Sidney and Bandello', *The Library*, 5th series, 21, (4) (1966), 326–8.

23 Matteo Bandello, *Tutte le Opere*, 2 vols, ed. Francesco Flora (Milan: Mondadori, 1952), II:336–46; see Belleforest, 'simplesse du seigneur de Virle', *Continuation des Histoires Tragiques*, fols 145^r–180^r, Painter, *Second Tome*, fols. 268^r–292^r.

24 R. Howard Bloch, *Medieval French Literature and Laws* (Berkeley: University of California Press, 1977), p. 199.

25 Anon., *Sir Eglamour of Artoys* (London: John Waley, n.d.), sig. B3^v.

26 *Ibid.*, sigs B4^r, C4^r.

27 Nicolas de Hereberay, *Le Premier Livre de Amadis de Gaule* (Paris: Denis Janot, 1540), ch. 6, 'Comme Vrgande la mescogneue apporta une lance au Damoysel de la mer'.

28 'The Lyfe of Ipomydon' in Henry Weber (ed.), *Metrical Romances of the Thirteenth, Fourteenth and Fifteenth Centuries*, 2 vols (Edinburgh, 1810), II:294.

29 Painter, *Second Tome*, fol. 286^v.

30 George Gascoigne, *The Complete Works*, 2 vols, ed. J.W. Cunliffe (Cambridge: Cambridge University Press, 1907), I:351.

31 *Ibid.*, I:5.

32 *Ibid.*, I:6.

33 Fenton, *Tragicall Discourses*, fol. 245^v.

34 *Ibid.*, fol. 245^r.

35 William Sherman, '"Official Scholars" and "Action Officers": research intelligence and the making of policy in early modern England' (paper delivered to the London Renaissance Seminar, 1990).

36 Charles Hughes (ed.), 'Nicholas Faunt's Discourse touching the Office

of Principal Secretary of Estate &c (1592)', *English Historical Review* 20 (1905), 507–8.

37 *DNB*, 'Sir Hugh Platt 1552–1611'.

38 Hutson, 'Fortunate travelers', pp. 86–7.

39 Conyers Read, *Mr Secretary Walsingham*, 2 vols (Oxford: Clarendon Press, 1925), I:18.

40 Aristotle, *Nich. Eth.*, VI.vi–viii.9; Sir Thomas Elyot, *The Boke named the Governour* [1531] (London: J.M. Dent, 1907), p. 96.

41 Victoria Kahn, *Rhetoric, Prudence and Skepticism* (Ithaca and London: Cornell University Press, 1985), p. 35.

42 Elyot, *Governour*, p. 97.

43 Terence Cave, *The Cornucopian Text* (Oxford: Clarendon Press, 1979), p. 131.

44 Richard Morison, *The Stratagemes, Sleyghtes and Policies of warre . . . by S. Julius Frontinus* (London: Berthelet, 1539); Antony Cope, *The Historie of two the Moste Noble Capitaines of the worlde, Anniball and Scipio* (London: Berthelet, 1544); Peter Whitehorne, *The Arte of Warre . . . by Nicholas Machiavel* (London, 1566); Arthur Golding, *The eyght bookes of C.J. Caesar* (London, 1565); William Barker, *The bookes of Xenophon contayning the discipline, schole and education of CYRUS* (London: Reynold Wolf, 1552).

45 Elyot, *Governour*, p. 102.

46 *Ibid.*, pp. 45–6.

47 Philip Sidney, *A Defence of Poetry*, ed. Jan Van Dorsten (Oxford: Oxford University Press, 1966), p. 24.

48 Read, *Secretary Walsingham*, I:18.

49 Barker, *Xenophon . . . education of CYRUS*, sigs E3r–6r.

50 Whitehorne, *Arte of Warre* (1573 edition), sig. R1^r; sigs P.1^r–P.4^v.

51 Morison, *Frontinus*, Book I, cap. xii, Book II, cap. vii, sig. G5^r.

52 Sidney, *Defence*, pp. 24, 40.

53 *Ibid.*, p. 53.

54 R. Edwards, *The Paradyse of daynty devises* (London: Henry Disle, 1578), sig. C4^r.

55 H.C. Hamilton (ed.), *Calendar of State Papers, Ireland 1586–8* (London, 1877), p. 193.

56 *Ibid.*, p. 194.

57 Fenton, *Tragicall Discourses*, fols 226^v–227^r.

58 *Ibid.*, fol. 231^r.

59 *Ibid.*, fols 244^v, 250^r.

60 *Ibid.*, fols 286^r, 296^v.

61 Lucas, *Writing for Women*, p. 54.

62 For example, Pettie, *Pallace of Pleasure*, pp. 60–1, 164–5, 175.

63 George Pettie, *The Civile Conversation of M. Steeven Guazzo* (London: Richard Watkins, 1581), sig. J1^r.

64 Juliet Fleming, 'The ladies' man and the age of Elizabeth' in James Grantham Turner (ed.), *Sexuality and Gender in Early Modern Europe* (Cambridge: Cambridge University Press, 1993), pp. 158–81.

65 As, for example, 'The letter of G.P. to R.B. Concerninge this Woorke' in Pettie, *Pallace of Pleasure*, p. 6,

follow this advise: if you bee free, that you come not into bondes; if you bee bounde, *ut te redimas captum quam queas minimo*; for trust me, the broade blasphemy of Pigmalion, and the sodaine *Apostacie*, or rather right conversion of *Alexius*, have setled me in this fayth, that I think him *Ter[que] quater[que] beatum, qui a consortio mulierum se conhibere potest*.

The first Latin phrase, meaning 'ransom yourself as cheaply as you can' was a favourite quotation from Terence's *Eunuch* (see below, Chapter 6) suggesting something like 'make love but don't promise her anything'. The second phrase, '[he is] thrice and four times blessed who can manage without a wife' ensures that the rhetorical husbandry of the *Pallace* remains just that: a fictional fashioning of women as proof that instrumental friendships between men now operate through texts.

4 USURERS' DAUGHTERS AND PRODIGAL SONS

1 Mattea Bandello, *Tutte le Opere*, 2 vols, ed. Francesco Flora (Milan: Mondadori, 1952), I:571.
2 Virginia Woolf, *A Room of One's Own* (London: Panther, 1977), p. 47.
3 Lisa Jardine, 'Humanistic logic' in Charles Schmitt *et al.*, *The Cambridge History of Renaissance Philosophy* (Cambridge: Cambridge University Press, 1988), p. 175.
4 Richard Helgerson, *The Elizabethan Prodigals* (Berkeley: University of California Press, 1976).
5 Roger Ascham, *The Schoolmaster* (1570), ed. Lawrence V. Ryan (Charlottesville: Virginia University Press, 1974), p. 69.
6 Stephen Gosson, *Playes confuted in five Actions* (London: Thomas Gosson, n.d.), sig. D5^v.
7 Paul Millet, *Lending and Borrowing in Ancient Athens* (Cambridge: Cambridge University Press, 1991), p. 32.
8 Marcel Mauss, *The Gift*, tr. W.D. Halls (London: Routledge, 1990), p. 37.
9 William Painter, *The Second Tome of the Palace of Pleasure* (London: Henry Bynneman, 1567), sigs *3^{r-v}.
10 The quotation here is from George Pettie, *A Petite Pallace of Pettie his Pleasure*, ed. Herbert Hartman (London: Oxford University Press, 1938), p. 23; for this formulation of prodigality, see Terence Cave's critique of Panurge's praise of debts in '"Or donné par don": échanges metaphoriques et materiels chez Rabelais', forthcoming in the published proceedings of a conference on 'Or, monnaie, échange dans la culture de la Renaissance', Lyons, 1991.
11 Warren Boutcher, 'Florio's Montaigne: translation and pragmatic humanism in the sixteenth century', unpublished Ph.D. thesis, Cambridge University, 1990, p. 46.
12 George Gascoigne *The Complete Works*, 2 vols, ed. J.W. Cunliffe (Cambridge: Cambridge University Press, 1907), I:5–6.
13 See the modern edition of the 1573 *Adventures of Master F.J.* in Paul Salzman (ed.), *An Anthology of Elizabethan Prose Fiction* (Oxford: Oxford University Press, 1987), p. 21.

14 See, for example, the secretary's reply to F.J.'s first conditional promises written in a letter to Dame Elinor. The secretary writes:

> although I found no just cause to credit your coloured words, yet have I thought good hereby to requite you with like courtesy . . . If I could persuade myself that there were in me any coals to kindle such sparks of fire, I might yet peradventure be drawn to believe that your mind was frozen with like fear.

This is a concession to F.J.'s protestation of love, but it avoids accountability by a hypothetical construction ('if I could persuade') so that everything depends on the probability of F.J.'s persuasion. When, by contrast, Dame Elinor is forced by the departure of her secretary to write her own letters, she demonstrates no rhetorical skill at guarding herself from accountability for what she promises: 'I have found in my chamber diverse songs which I think to be of your making', she writes, 'and I promise you they are excellently made, and I assure you that I will be ready to do for you any pleasure that I can during my life.' (*Adventures of Master F.J.* in Salzman, *An Anthology of Elizabethan Prose Fiction*, pp. 8–9, 15).

15 Gascoigne, *Works*, I:5–6.

16 Thomas Lodge, *An Alarum Against Usurers* (London: Thomas East, 1584) reprinted in *The Complete Works of Thomas Lodge*, 4 vols, ed. E. Gosse (London: Hunterian Club, 1883), I:5.

17 See John Dover Wilson, 'Euphues and the prodigal son', *The Library* n.s. 10 (1909), 337–61.

18 George Whetstone, *The Rocke of Regarde* (London: Robert Waley, 1576), sigs *2^v-*3^r, sig. O4^r.

19 Isabella Whitney, *A Sweet Nosgay, or pleasant Posye: contayning a hundred and ten Phylosophicall Flowers* (London: Richard Jones, 1573), sigs. E3^r and E6^r. Further references to this edition will appear in the text. On Whitney, see Ann Rosalind Jones, *The Currency of Eros: Women's Love Lyric in Europe 1540–1620* (Bloomington: Indiana University Press, 1990), pp. 36–52; R.J. Fehrenbach, 'Isabella Whitney, Sir Hugh Plat, Geoffrey Whitney and "Sister Eldershae"', *ELN* 21 (1983), 7–11 and Betty Travitsky, '"The Wyll and Testament" of Isabella Whitney' *ELR* 10 (1980), 80–95.

20 Margaret Tyler, *Mirrour of Princely Deedes* (London: Thomas East, 1578), sig. A2^r; Barnabe Googe, *Eglogs, Epitaphes and Sonnettes* (London: Thomas Colwell, 1563).

21 Marshall Sahlins, 'On the sociology of primitive exchange' in *Stone Age Economics* (London: Routledge, 1988), pp. 191–204.

22 On Erasmus' use of the printed familiar epistle in this way, see Lisa Jardine, *Erasmus, Man of Letters* (Princeton, NJ: Princeton University Press, 1993), pp. 14–26.

23 Natalie Zemon Davis, 'Beyond the market: books as gifts in sixteenth-century France', *Transactions of the Royal Historical Society* 33 (1983), 69–88.

24 David Clapam, *The Commendation of Matrimony* (London: Thomas Berthelet, 1545), sig. C4^r.

25 See my *Thomas Nashe in Context* (Oxford: Clarendon Press, 1989), pp. 127–31.

26 For the sexualization of women's relation to rhetoric, see Nancy Vickers, 'The blazon of sweet beauty's best': Shakespeare's *Lucrece*' in Patricia Parker and Geoffrey Hartman (eds), *Shakespeare and the Question of Theory* (London: Methuen, 1985), pp. 95–115 and Patricia Parker, *Literary Fat Ladies* (London: Methuen, 1987).

27 See William Painter's version of the Artexerxes story in *The Palace of Pleasure* (London: Henry Denham, 1566), tome I, novel ix, fol. 25ʳ.

28 Richard Stanihurst, *The First Fowre Bookes of Virgil his Aeneis translated into English* (Leiden: John Pates, 1582), sig. A4ᵛ. For other uses of Artaxerxes, see Pierre de la Primaudaye, *Academie Française* (Paris: Guillaume Chaudière, 1580), sig. *4ʳ; Thomas Lupton, *Sivqila: Too good, to be true* (London: Henry Bynneman, 1580), sig. A4ʳ.

29 Thomas Nashe, *The Works*, 5 vols, ed. R.B. McKerrow (Oxford: Basil Blackwell, 1966), III:124.

30 Lawrence Humphrey, *The Nobles or of Nobilitye* (London: Thomas Marshe, 1563), sig. B7ʳ.

31 Fenton, 'A Wonderful Vertue in a gentlman of Syenna on the behalfe of his enemye . . . and the other to retorne his courtesye with equall frendship' in *Certaine Tragicall Discourses* (London: Thomas Marshe, 1567), fols 4ʳ–36ʳ; see also Painter, *Second Tome*, fols 350ᵛ-375ᵛ; subsequent references to Fenton's version will appear in the text.

32 Bandello, *Opere*, I:582–3.

33 Gascoigne, *Works*, I:5.

34 Thomas Heywood, *A Woman Killed with Kindness* in Keith Sturgess (ed.), *Three Elizabethan Domestic Tragedies* (Harmondsworth: Penguin, 1985), II.i.1–11, p. 203.

35 *Ibid.*, V.i.95–6,153, pp. 256–8.

36 *Ibid.*, II.i.57–63, p. 205.

37 *Ibid.*, II.iii.33–53, p. 211.

38 *Ibid.*, V.iii.7–9, p. 260.

39 See, for example, Max Weber, *The Protestant Ethic and the Spirit of Capitalism*, tr. Talcott Parsons (London: Allen and Unwin, 1930); Thomas Wilson, *A Discourse Upon Usury*, ed. R.H. Tawney (London: Frank Cass, 1962, 1925); Lawrence Stone, *The Crisis of the Aristocracy* (Oxford: Clarendon Press, 1965), pp. 505–46; R. de Roover, *Money, Banking and Credit in Mediaeval Bruges* (Cambridge, Mass.: Harvard University Press, 1948); R. de Roover, *Gresham on Foreign Exchange* (Cambridge, Mass.: Harvard University Press, 1949); J.T. Noonan, *The Scholastic Analysis of Usury* (Cambridge, Mass.: Harvard University Press, 1957); Abbot Paynton Usher, *The Early History of Deposit Banking* (Cambridge, Mass.: Harvard University Press, 1943); Benjamin Nelson, *The Idea of Usury* (Chicago: Chicago University Press, 1969); Norman Jones, *God and the Moneylenders: Usury and Law in Early Modern England* (Oxford: Basil Blackwell, 1989); Eric Kerridge, *Trade and Banking in Early Modern England* (Manchester: Manchester University Press, 1988); Jacques le Goff, *Your Money or Your Life: Economy and Religion in the Middle Ages*, tr. Patricia Ranum (New York: Zone Books,

1988); Heiko Oberman, *Masters of the Reformation*, tr. Dennis Martin (Cambridge: Cambridge University Press, 1981); R.M. Helmholz, 'Usury and the medieval English church courts', *Speculum* 61 (1986), 364–80.

40 Whetstone, *Rocke of Regarde*, sig. A1ʳ.

41 Paul Salzman, *English Prose Fiction 1558–1700: a Critical History* (Oxford: Clarendon Press, 1985), p. 11.

42 Bandello, *Opere*, I:68.

43 The historical Bianca Maria was the heiress of a wealthy merchant family in Casale whose nobility had been established in 1464. See Adelin Charles Fiorato, *Bandello: Entre l'histoire e l'ecriture* (Firenze: Leo S. Olschki, 1979), p. 544.

44 Painter, *Second Tome*, fol. 211ʳ. References to Painter's and Fenton's versions will appear in the text, distinguished as 'F' and 'P'.

45 See François de Belleforest, *Le second Tome des histoires Tragiques* (Paris: Vincent Norment, 1565), fol. 48ᵛ, and the definition of 'la lie' and 'lier' in Randle Cotgrave, *A Dictionarie of the French and English Tongues*, reproduced from the edition of 1611 (Columbia: University of South Carolina Press, 1950).

46 See, for example, Lodge, *Complete Works*, I:5; Whetstone, *Rocke of Regarde*, sig. *3ʳ; Edward Hake, *Newes Out of Powles Churchyarde* (London: Richard Jones, 1579), sig. A4ʳ.

47 Bandello, *Opere*, I:59.

48 See below, and Diana O'Hara, '"Ruled by my friends": aspects of marriage in the diocese of Canterbury c.1540–1570', *Continuity and Change* 6 (1991), 9–41.

49 Belleforest, *Le second Tome*, sig. E4ᵛ.

50 Elyot, 'Of faythe or fidelitie', *The Boke named the Governour* [1531] (London: J.M. Dent, 1907), p. 211.

51 *Ibid.*, 'Of promise and covenant', p. 224; see also Thomas Lupton, *Sivqila*, sig. T2ʳ.

52 R.E. Helmholz, 'Assumpsit and Fidei Laesio', *Law Quarterly Review* 91 (1975), 406–32.

53 J.H. Baker, *An Introduction to English Legal History* (London: Butterworth, 1979), pp. 267–87; J.H. Baker, 'English law and the Renaissance' in *The Legal Profession and the Common Law* (London: Hambledon, 1986), p. 463; J.H. Baker, *The Reports of Sir John Spelman*, 2 vols (London: Selden Society, 1978), II:37–43.

54 Baker, *John Spelman*, II:64, 258.

55 *Supposes . . . by George Gascoigne of Grayes Inne*, in Gascoigne, *Works*, I:207; John Hazel Smith (ed.), *Two Latin Comedies by John Foxe the Martyrologist* (Ithaca and London: Cornell University Press, 1973), I.iii, p. 70.

56 T.E. Hartley, *Proceedings in the Parliaments of Elizabeth I* vol. I (Leicester: Leicester University Press, 1981), p. 233. Where Gascoigne has 'the fulkers', Ariosto has 'l'ebreo', the jew. See Ludovico Ariosto, *Tutte le Opere*, 5 vols, vol. 4, *Commedie*, ed. Angela Casella *et al.* (Milan: Mondadori, 1974), p. 218.

57 On the crisis of credit in the 1570s, see G.D. Ramsay, *The City of London*

In International Politics at the Accession of Elizabeth Tudor (Manchester: Manchester University Press, 1975), p. 58.

58 R. Edwards, *The Paradyse of Dainty Devises* (London: Henry Disle, 1578), sigs B4^r, C1^{r-v}, C3^{r-v}, R3^r; see especially the poem of Jasper Heywood, which begins, 'My friend, if thou wilt credit me in ought, / To whom the truth in tryall well appears', sig. B4^r, and the poem by R.D. which begins, 'Is this the truste that faithfull freendes can finde?', sig. C1^v.

59 Thomas Lupton, *Sivqila*, sig. U1^v; for bonds, see Baker, *English Legal History*, pp. 266–73; Edith G. Henderson, 'Relief from bonds in the English Chancery in the mid-sixteenth century', *American Journal of Legal History* 8 (1974), pp. 299–306.

60 Whetstone, *Rocke of Regarde*, sig. N4^r.

61 Anon., *A Newe Interlude of Impacyente Poverte*, ed. R.B. McKerrow (1911) in W. Bang (ed.), *Materialen zur Kunde des alteren Englischen Dramas*, 44 vols (Louvain, 1911), XXXIII: 6, 10.

62 Gascoigne, *Works*, I:349; Whetstone, *Rocke of Regarde*, sig. O4^r. For the perception that the problem of credit was one which was affecting 'young gentlemen' rather than tradesmen, see the speech made against Thomas Wilson in the Parliament of 1571, Hartley, *Parliaments of Elizabeth I*, p. 231.

63 Heywood, *Woman Killed with Kindness*, II.iii.55–6, p. 209; IV.i.17, p. 234; Whetstone, *Rocke of Regarde*, sigs L3^r and N1^r. Thomas Lodge's *Alarum Against Usurers* explicitly characterizes the usurer as an accomplished hypocrite. For a study of the association between the hypocrites of theatre and marketplace, see Jean-Christophe Agnew, *Worlds Apart: The Market and the Theater in Anglo-American Thought 1550–1750* (Cambridge: Cambridge University Press, 1986).

64 See Thomas Wilson, *A Discourse uppon Vsurye, by waye of Dialogue and oracions* (London: R. Tottel, 1572), sigs C2^r, F4^r; William Harrys, *The market or fayre of Vsurers* (London: Steven Meirdman, 1550), sigs C2^r, D5^v.

65 Lupton, *Sivqila*, sig. T1^v.

66 John Guy, 'Law, equity and conscience in Henrician jurist thought' in John Guy and Alistair Fox, *Reassessing the Henrician Age: Humanism, Politics and Reform 1500–1530* (Oxford: Basil Blackwell, 1986), pp. 179–98; see also Baker, *John Spelman*, II:37–43.

67 Christopher St German, *Hereafter followeth a Dyalogue in Englgysshe betwyxt a Doctour of Dyvynte and a Student in the Lawes of Englande: Of the groundes of the sayde Lawes and of Conscyence* (London: Peter Treverys, 1530), sig. I1^r.

68 Baker, *John Spelman*, II:38.

69 Guy, 'Law, equity and conscience', p. 184.

70 See Guy, 'Law, equity and conscience', p. 183; Aristotle, *Ethics*, V.x; Boutcher, 'Florio's Montaigne', pp. 16–17.

71 Baker, *John Spelman*, II:40–3; Edward Hake, *Epieikeia: A Dialogue on Equity in Three Parts*, ed. D.C. Yale (New Haven: Yale Law Library Publications, 1953), pp. 123–6.

72 Baker, *John Spelman*, II:255–8.

73 David Ibbetson, 'Assumpsit and debt in the early sixteenth century: the origins of the Indebitatus count', *Cambridge Law Journal* 41 (1982), 42–61, 146.

74 Baker, *John Spelman*, II:262–72; Baker, 'The origins of the "doctrine" of consideration 1535–1585' in *Legal Profession and Common Law*, pp. 369–92.

75 Marie Axton, *The Queen's Two Bodies: Drama and the Elizabethan Succession* (London: Royal Historical Society, 1977), pp. 19–37.

76 Sharrington v. Strotton in Edmund Plowden, *The Commentaries or Reports* (London, 1761), pp. 305–6.

77 Belleforest, *Le seconde Tome*, sig. E3^r; Philip Sidney, *The Old Arcadia*, ed. Katherine Duncan-Jones (Oxford: World's Classics, 1985), p. 348.

78 In the preface to Book II of the *De Officiis*, Cicero makes Fortune's ability to argue *in utramque partem* one of the predicates of the need to reconcile honesty and expediency: 'Magnam vim esse in fortuna in utramque partem, vel secundas ad res vel adversas, quis ignorat?' ('Who fails to comprehend the enormous, two-fold power of fortune for weal and for woe?'); see Victoria Kahn, *Rhetoric, Prudence and Skepticism* (Ithaca and London: Cornell University Press, 1985), p. 69.

PART III THE THEATRE OF CLANDESTINE MARRIAGE

1 Andrew Gurr, *Playgoing in Shakespeare's London* (Cambridge: Cambridge University Press, 1987), p. 149.

2 Diana O'Hara, '"Ruled by my friends": aspects of marriage in the diocese of Canterbury c.1540–1570', *Continuity and Change* 6 (1991), 11–13.

3 Laura Gowing, citing 'Anne Foote c. Lancelot Grimshawe' 8/6/1610, in 'Women, sex and honour: the London Church courts, 1572–1640', unpublished Ph.D thesis, London University, 1993, p. 108.

4 *Ibid.*, p. 117.

5 Shakespeare, *Othello*, ed. M.R. Ridley (London: Methuen, 1958), I.ii.11–17, p. 15.

6 *Ibid.*, I.iii.67–9, p. 25; I.iii.61–3, 108, pp. 25–7; III.iii.370–2, p. 115.

7 See, for example, the comments of Ridley in the notes to the Arden edition, on Desdemona's behaviour, II.i.109–66, 'It is unnatural. Desdemona's natural instinct must surely be to go to the harbour' and at IV.iii.35, 'What did Shakespeare intend by this sudden transition to Lodovico? . . . One is tempted to wonder whether there has not been a misattribution of speeches.'

8 Geoffrey Fenton, *Certaine Tragicall Discourses* (London: Thomas Marshe, 1567), fol. 297^r.

9 Shakespeare, *Othello*, I.i.104, p. 10. I do not mean, of course, to suggest that the traditional means of expressing friendship by hospitality ceased with the advent of humanism; see Lawrence Stone, *The Crisis of the Aristocracy* (Oxford: Clarendon Press, 1965), pp. 42–9, 555–66, 581–4.

10 Stephen Orgel, 'Nobody's perfect: or, why did the English Renaissance stage take boys for women?', *South Atlantic Quarterly* 88 (1989), 7–29, 17.

11 Orgel, 'Nobody's Perfect', p. 13.

12 *Ibid.*, p. 8.

13 *Ibid.*, p. 12.

14 *Ibid.*, p. 10.

15 Admittedly, T.W. Baldwin, *Shakespeare's Five Act Structure* (Urbana: University of Illinois Press, 1947) presses the case for Terentian structure too pedantically, as Wolfgang Riehle, *Shakespeare, Plautus and the Humanist Tradition* (Cambridge: D.S. Brewer, 1990) points out, p. 99. However, Riehle has a Plautine axe to grind; the issue is that a quasi-Aristotelian theory of plot based on artificial proofs was undeniably made known to the dramatists of the English Renaissance through humanist editions of Terence and Plautus, which analysed them according to the theories of Donatus and Evanthius. See Marvin T. Herrick, *Comic Theory in the Renaissance* (Urbana: University of Illinois Press, 1950) and Georgia S. Nugent, 'Ancient theories of comedy: the treatises of Evanthius and Donatus', in Maurice Charney (ed.), *Shakespearean Comedy* (New York: New York Literary Forum, 1980).

16 Shakespeare, *The Taming of the Shrew*, ed. Brian Morris (London: Methuen, 1981), Induction, line 140, p. 170.

17 See Leo Salingar, *Shakespeare and the Traditions of Comedy* (Cambridge: Cambridge University Press, 1974), p. 69; and Patricia Russell, 'Romantic narrative plays 1570–1590' in John Russell Brown and Bernard Harris (eds), *Elizabethan Theatre*, Stratford on Avon Studies, 9 (London: Edward Arnold, 1966).

18 Andrew Gurr, 'The bear, the statue and hysteria in *The Winters Tale*', *Shakespeare Quarterly* 34 (1983), 420–5, 421.

19 Gurr, *Playgoing in Shakespeare's London*, pp. 80–97, p. 81.

20 *Ibid.*, p. 107. For an interesting interpretation of Maningham's structural perception of *Twelfth Night*, see Leo Salingar, 'The design of *Twelfth Night*', *Shakespeare Quarterly* 9 (1958), 117–39.

21 Charles Estienne, *Les Abusez: Comedie faite à la mode des Anciens* (Paris: Estienne Groulleau, 1549), sig. A2^r.

22 *Ibid.*, sig. A3^r.

23 Shakespeare, *As You Like It*, ed. Agnes Latham (London: Methuen, 1975), IV.i.151–60, p. 100.

24 *Ibid.*, V.iv.118, p. 127.

5 HOUSEHOLD STUFF

1 See *The Self Tormenter* in John Sergeaunt (tr.), *Terence*, 2 vols (London: Heinemann, 1912), I:138–9, 142–3.

2 John Foxe, *Titus et Gesippus* in *Two Latin Comedies by John Foxe the Martyrologist*, ed. John Hazel Smith (Ithaca: Cornell University Press, 1973), p. 105.

3 Interestingly, Stephen Greenblatt has recently written of Christopher Columbus as a 'reader of signs' rather than an 'observer' in *Marvellous Possessions* (Oxford: Clarendon Press, 1991), p. 86.

4 Ben Jonson, *The Works*, 11 vols, ed. C.H. Herford and Percy Simpson (Oxford: Clarendon Press, 1925–52), III:218; see also Joel Altman, *The Tudor Play of Mind* (Berkeley: University of California Press, 1978), p. 185.

5 Jonson, *Works*, III:233, 218.

6 Katherine Eisaman Maus, 'Horns of dilemma: jealousy, gender and spectatorship in English Renaissance drama', *ELH* 54 (1987), 561–83, 563.

7 Foxe, *Two Latin Comedies*, pp. 72–3, 104–5.

8 Maus, 'Horns of dilemma', pp. 576, 578.

9 Terence Cave, *Recognitions: A Study in Poetics* (Oxford: Clarendon Press, 1988), pp. 282–5.

10 *Pub. Terentii Comoediae Sex, iam denno scholijs illustratae* (six comedies by Terence, now newly illustrated with scholarly commentaries, including those of Melanchthon and Erasmus) (Vratislaviae: Scharffenburg, 1574), sig. 4^v.

11 Sergeaunt (tr.), *Terence*, I:144–5.

12 *Ibid.*

13 *Pub. Terentii Comoediae Sex*, sig. O5^r.

14 Altman, *Tudor Play of Mind*, p. 133.

15 *Ibid.*, p. 136.

16 See Donatus, 'De Tragoedia et Comoedia' in *Pub. Terentii Comoediae Sex*, sig. D3^r; Altman, *Tudor Play of Mind*, p. 133.

17 Altman, *Tudor Play of Mind*, p. 133n.

18 See Peter Brooks, *Reading for the Plot* (New York: Vintage Books, 1985), p. 18, and Roland Barthes, *S/Z*, tr. Richard Miller (New York: Farrar, Straus and Giroux, 1974), pp. 84–6. For 'error' as a dilatory space, see Patricia Parker, *Literary Fat Ladies: Rhetoric, Gender and Property* (London: Methuen, 1987), p. 17.

19 Sergeaunt (tr.), *Terence*, I:24–5.

20 Aelius Donatus, *Aeli Donati quod fertur Commentum Terenti*, 3 vols, ed. Paul Wessner (Teubner: Lipsae, 1902), I:97; see also Altman, *Tudor Play of Mind*, p. 133.

21 T.W. Baldwin, *Shakespeare's Five Act Structure* (Urbana: University of Illinois Press, 1947), p. 179.

22 *Pub. Terentii Comoediae Sex*, sig. D&^{v}.

23 John Rastell, *Terens in englysh* (London, 1520), sig. A2^r.

24 See the introduction by Edmond H. Beame and Leonardo G. Sbrocchi to *The Comedies of Ariosto* (Chicago: University of Chicago Press, 1975), p. xii.

25 Lyndal Roper, *The Holy Household: Women and Morals in Reformation Augsburg* (Oxford: Clarendon Press, 1989), p. 4.

26 See Marvin T. Herrick, *Tragicomedy: Its Origins and Development in Italy and France* (Urbana: University of Illinois Press, 1962), pp. 17–46; John Palsgrave, *The Comedye of Acolastus translated in oure englysshe tongue after such maner as chyldern are taughte in the grammar schoole*, ed. P.L.

Carver (London: EETS, 1937).

27 M. Christopherus Stummelius, *Studentes, comoedia de vita studiosorum*, with a preface by Jodicus Willichus (Frankfurt: Johannes Eichorn, 1550), sigs C6^v-D2^v; sigs A4^v-5^r. For the notoriety of the *Eunuchus* rape speech, see Carlo Ginzburg, 'Titian, Ovid, and sixteenth-century codes for erotic illustration' in *Myths, Emblems, Clues*, tr. John and Anne Tedeschi (London: Hutchinson, 1986), pp. 77–8.

28 Palsgrave, *Acolastus*, pp. 145, 172.

29 Geoffrey Fenton, *A forme of Christian pollicie* (London: Rafe Newberry, 1574), pp. 146–7.

30 Altman, *Tudor Play of Mind*, pp. 107–29.

31 Whitney, *Sweet Nosgay*, sig. E7^v; on the continuum between deliberative drama at court and at the inns of court, see Marie Axton, *The Queens Two Bodies* (London: Royal Historical Society 1977), *passim*.

32 Compare the text of the *Supposes* in George Gascoigne, *An Hundreth Sundrie Flowres* (London: Richard Smith, 1573), sigs B2^r-K3^v, with that of *The Posies of George Gascoigne* (London: Richard Smith, 1575), sigs A2^r-F4^v.

33 George Gascoigne *The Complete Works*, 2 vols, ed. J. W. Cunliffe (Cambridge: Cambridge University Press, 1910), II:6; the discovery of the place for error is at V.vii, when the tutor, Gnomaticus, reveals to the Markgrave Severus, a deception that enables Severus to execute punishment with equity, pp. 81–2.

34 George Whetstone, *The Right Excellent and Famous History of Promos and Cassandra: Devided into Two Commical Discourses* (London, 1578) in Geoffrey Bullough (ed.), *Narrative and Dramatic Sources of Shakespeare*, 8 vols (London: Routledge, 1968), II:443.

35 Stephen Gosson, *Playes confuted, in five Actions* (London: T. Gosson, n.d.), sigs C6^r-7^r.

36 Xenophon, *Cyropaedia*, I.6.26–39; Niccolo Machiavelli, *Discorsi sopra la prima deca di Tito Livio* in *Il Principe e altre opere politiche*, ed. D. Cantimori (Milan: Garzanti, 1976), III.39, pp. 445–6: 'E Senefonte nelle vita di Ciro mostra che andando Ciro ad assaltare il re d'Armenia, nel divisare quella fazione ricordo a quegli suoi che questa non era altro che una di quelle cacce' and II: 13, p. 278. For an analysis of the 'fraud' or sophistry to which Machiavelli refers, see James Tatum, *Xenophon's Imperial Fiction* (Princeton, NJ: Princeton University Press, 1989), pp. 134–45.

37 See Leah L. Otis, *Prostitution in Medieval Society* (Chicago: University of Chicago Press, 1985), p. 13.

38 Sergeaunt (tr.), *Terence*, I:334–5.

39 Otis, *Prostitution*, p. 28.

40 Roper, *Holy Household*, p. 93.

41 Ruth Mazo Karras, 'The regulation of brothels in later medieval England', *Signs* 14 (1989), 399–433.

42 Otis, *Prostitution*, p. 10.

43 Roper, *Holy Household*, p. 112.

44 An example of the 'continuity' argument is Martin Ingram's 'The reform of popular culture? Sex and marriage in early modern

England', in Barry Reay (ed.), *Popular Culture in Seventeenth-Century England* (London: Routledge and Kegan Paul, 1988), pp. 129–65. For a critique of Ingram's position, see Ian W. Archer, *The Pursuit of Stability: Social relations in Elizabethan London* (Cambridge: Cambridge University Press, 1991), pp. 248–9.

45 See Eric Joseph Carlson, 'Marriage reform and the Elizabethan High Commission', *Sixteenth Century Journal* 21 (1990), 436–51, 440n.; see also Donald Logan, 'The Henrician Canons', *Bulletin of the Institute of Historical Research* 48 (1974), 88–103; Edward Cardwell, *The Reformation of Ecclesiastical Laws* (Oxford, 1850); Edward Cardwell, *Synodalia: a Collection of Articles of Religious Canons ... 1547–1719*, 2 vols (Oxford, 1842); R.H. Helmholz, *Roman Canon Law in Reformation England* (Cambridge: Cambridge University Press, 1990) and Norman L. Jones, 'An Elizabethan bill for the reformation of ecclesiastical law', *Parliamentary History* 4 (1985), 184–6.

46 Carlson, 'Marriage reform', p. 442; G.R. Elton, 'Reform by Statute: Thomas Starkey's *Dialogue* and Thomas Cromwell's policy', *Proceedings of the British Academy* LIV (1968), 165–88; and see above, Chapter 2, pp. 82–3.

47 For the correspondence between Burghley and Fleetwood, see Thomas Wright (ed.), *Queen Elizabeth and her Times: A Series of Orginal Letters*, 2 vols (London: Henry Colburn, 1838). Thomas Norton (co-author of the tragedy *Gorboduc*) was responsible for presenting a new edition of the bill for the Reformation of Ecclesiastical Laws to Parliament in 1571; his 'Instructions to the Lord Mayor of London, 1574–5' are published in J.P. Collier (ed.), *Illustrations of Old English Literature*, 3 vols (London, 1866), III:12–13. Both Fleetwood and Norton were key figures in the 1570s movement to suppress theatres, see E.K. Chambers, *The Elizabethan Stage*, 4 vols (Oxford: Clarendon Press, 1923), I:265.

48 Ian W. Archer, *The Pursuit of Stability* (Cambridge: Cambridge University Press, 1991), p. 250.

49 *Ibid.*

50 *Ibid.*, p. 251.

51 See Beatrice Gottlieb, 'The meaning of "clandestine marriage"', in Robert Wheaton and Tamara K. Hareven (eds), *Family and Sexuality in French History* (Philadelphia: Pennsylvania University Press, 1980); Steven Ozment, *When Fathers Ruled: Family Life in Reformation Europe* (Cambridge, Mass.: Harvard University Press, 1983), pp. 25–49; James A. Brundage, *Law, Sex and Christian Society in Medieval Europe* (Chicago: Chicago University Press, 1987), pp. 551–75; Martin Ingram, *Church Courts, Sex and Marriage in England 1570–1640* (Cambridge: Cambridge University Press, 1987), pp. 125–67; R. Houlbrooke, 'The making of marriage in mid-Tudor England', *Journal of Family History* 10 (1985), 339–52.

52 Nicholas Lesse, *The Censure and judgement of ... Erasmus: whyther dyvorsemente betwene man and wyfe stondeth with the lawe of god* (London: widow of John Herforde, 1550), sigs. F6^v-7^r; sig. I4^r.

53 *Ibid.*, sigs F6; G1^r; G3^r; G8^v; I^r; I7^r; see Roper, *Holy Household*, p. 157.

54 See Brundage, *Law, Sex and Christian Society*, pp. 553, 562; Roper, *Holy Household*, pp. 132–64; Richard M. Smith, 'Marriage processes in the English past: some continuities' in Lloyd Bonfield, Richard Smith and Keith Wrightson (eds), *The World We Have Gained* (Oxford: Basil Blackwell, 1986) pp. 77–8; for the *Edit Contre les mariages Clandestins* see F. Isambert, *Recueil general des anciennes lois françaises*, vol. 13 (1546–59) (Paris, 1822), pp. 469–70.

55 Helmholz, *Roman Canon Law in Reformation England*, p. 69.

56 James Gairdner and R.H. Brodie (eds), *Letters and Papers Foreign and Domestic of the Reign of Henry VII* (London: Eyre and Spottiswoode, 1894), XIV: 401, 441; XVIII: 99.

57 Lesse, *The Censure of Erasmus*, sig. E5^r; sig. K4^v.

58 Chambers, *Elizabethan Stage*, I:277 ; Carlson, 'Marriage reform and the Elizabethan High Commission', p. 443; Archer, *Pursuit of Stability*, p. 243.

59 Chambers, *Elizabethan Stage*, IV:273.

60 Richard Whitford, *A Werke for housholders* (London: R. Redman, 1537), sig. D7^r.

61 Edward Hake, *A Touchstone for this time present* (London: Thomas Hacket, 1574), sig. C1^r.

62 *Ibid.*, sigs C3^r-G4^v.

63 See R.J. Fehrenbach, 'A letter sent by the maids of London (1567)', *ELR* 14 (1984), 299.

64 Francis Kinwelmarsh in R. Edwards, *The Paradyse of daynty devises* (London: Henry Disle, 1578), sig. F4^r.

65 Fleetwood to Burghley, 5 August 1575 in T. Wright, *Queen Elizabeth and her Times*, p. 20.

66 Belleforest, *Le Seconde Tome des Histoires Tragiques* (Paris: Vincent Norment, 1565), sig. E4^r.

67 Fleetwood to Burghley, 5 August 1575 and 18 July 1583 in Wright, *Queen Elizabeth and her Times*, II:21, 204–6.

68 Whetstone, *Promos and Cassandra* in Bullough (ed.), *Narrative and Dramatic Sources*, II:491, 468.

69 *Ibid.*

6 WHY DO SHAKESPEARE'S WOMEN HAVE 'CHARACTERS'?

1 M. Accius Plautus, *Opera*, ed. Dionys. Lambinus (Paris: Joannes Macaeus, 1576), Act IV, p. 71. The phrase occurs at two other points in the play; in the prologue Mercury explains how Jupiter, 'unknown to her husband, borrows Alcmena upon interest and makes her pregnant' ('occoepit Alcmenam clam virum / Vsuramque eius corporis coepit sibi / Et gravidam fecit is eam compressu suo'), pp. 4–5; and in Act I, scene ii, announcing the arrival of Jupiter with Alcmena, 'a wife he has taken up at interest' (*uxore usuraria*), p. 38.

2 John Foxe, *Titus et Gesippus* in *Two Latin Comedies*, ed. John Hazel Smith (Ithaca: Cornell University Press, 1973), p. 102.

3 Nicholas Udall was the author of *Floures for Latine Speakynge selected and gathered oute of Terence* (London: T. Berthelet, 1533); on Udall, see William Tydeman's edition of *Ralph Roister Doister* in *Four Latin Comedies* (Harmondsworth: Penguin, 1984).

4 Joel Altman, *The Tudor Play of Mind* (Berkeley: University of California Press, 1978), p. 150.

5 Thomas Wilson, *The Rule of Reason, conteinynge the Arte of Logike* (London: John Kingston, 1563), sigs S2^v-3^v.

6 Udall, *Ralph Roister Doister* in Tydeman, *Four Tudor Comedies*, p. 197.

7 Natalie Zemon Davis, *The Return of Martin Guerre* (Cambridge, Mass.: Harvard University Press, 1983), p. 107.

8 Jean de Coras, *Arrest Memorable du Parlement de Tholose contenant une Histoire prodigeuse d'un suppose mary* (Paris: Gaillot du Pré, 1572), sig. *2^r: 'plaisante & recreative', 'incertaine & doubteuse', 'triste, piteuse & miserable pour le regard de l'hipocrisie & simulation descouverte'.

9 Davis, *Martin Guerre*, p. 112.

10 Michel de Montaigne,

> je vis en mon enfance un proces, que Corras, conseiler de Toulouse, fit imprimer, d'un accident étrange, de deux hommes qui se presentaient l'un pour l'autre. Il me souvient (et ne me souvient d'autre chose) qu'il me semble avoir rendu l'imposture de celui qu'il jugea coupable si merveilleuse et excedant de si loin notre connaissance ... que je trouvai beaucoup d'hardiesse en l'arrêt qu'il l'avait condemmné a être pendu.

'Des Boiteux', *Oeuvres Complètes*, ed. Robert Barral (Paris: du Seuil, 1967), p. 415.

11 Coras, *Arrest Memorable*, annotation 38, sigs D6^v-7^v.

12 *Ibid.*, sig. D8^v: 'Cyrus, Roy des Perses sçavoit bien dire tous les noms de ses soldats.' Scipio Africanus would, of course, be an examplar for one whose identity is projected in uncertainty: 'Scipio never said a word to diminish belief in these marvels: on the contrary, he tended to strengthen it by deliberately refusing either to deny openly or openly to affirm the truth.' Livy, *The War with Hannibal*, tr. Aubrey de Selincourt (Harmondsworth: Penguin, 1965), p. 380.

13 Davis, *Martin Guerre*, p. 115. For Boiastuau, see Michel Simonin, 'Notes sur Pierre Boiastuau', *Bibliothèque d'Humanisme et Renaissance* 38 (1976), 328–30. The edition I have used of the *Arrest Memorable* is bound up with Coras' *Paraphrase sur l'Edict des Marriages clandestinement contractez* in a collection of marital disputes entitled *Histoire Tragique et Arrests de la Cour de Parlement de Tholose* (BL 15384, 1–3), which suggests a perceived association between the project of the Boaistuau-Belleforest *Histoires Tragiques* and that of the publication of these trials of clandestine marriage.

14 Jean de Coras, *Paraphrase sur l'Edict des marriages clandestinement contractez par des enfans de famille contre le gré et vouloir de leur peres et meres* (Paris: Gaillot du Pré, 1572), fol. 8^r:

Ce sont nos arguments et raisons, lesquels bien entendues sont ...

assez fortes, pour rendre nos adversaires harrassez et hors d'aleine: toutesfois, leur donnerons nous encore . . . des authoritez, & des Exemples, pour les rafreschir, & . . . gaigner, s'ils ne sont du tout impersuasibles, & inexorables.

15 *Ibid.*, fols 5ᵛ, 10ʳ, 14ʳ; 'avoir plus d'egard à la conservation du publiq & tranquilité des subjets, qu'à conserver l'autorité des peres sur les enfans'.

16 Coras, *Arrest Memorable*, sigs D6ʳ, B5ʳ.

17 Davis, *Martin Guerre*, p. 110.

18 Terence Cave, *Recognitions: A Study in Poetics* (Oxford: Clarendon Press, 1988), p. 13.

19 Coras, *Arrest Memorable*, annotation 3, sig. A4ʳ.

20 See Plautus, *Opera*, pp. 69–75; Coras, *Arrest Memorable*,

Enfin Blepharo est esleu arbtire, pour juger lequel des deux est le vray Amphytrio, qui pour l'entiere similitude, qui estoit entre eux, ne sceut onqcues discerner l'un de l'autre . . . Quoy, voyant Iuppiter, pour monstrer l'innocence d'Alcmena, descouvre au long tout la faict à Amphitrio, & le remet en paix & amitié avec sa femme.

(sig. A4ᵛ)

21 Plautus, *Opera*, IV.3, p. 75.

22 W.W. Greg (ed.), *Gesta Grayorum 1688* (London: Malone Society Reprints, 1914), pp. 22–3.

23 Shakespeare, *The Comedy of Errors*, ed. R.A. Foakes, (London: Methuen, 1962), I.i.2–4. Further references to scene and line number in this edition will appear in the text.

24 Gascoigne, *The Complete Works*, 2 vols, ed. J.W. Cunliffe (Cambridge: Cambridge University Press, 1907), II:82.

25 *Ibid.*, II:86.

26 Philip Melanchthon, preface to Terence's *Andria, Pub. Terentii Comeodiae Sex* (Vratislaviae, 1574), sig. D7ᵛ.

27 Philip Sidney, *The Old Arcadia*, ed. Katherine Duncan-Jones (Oxford: World's Classics, 1985), pp. 181, 189; Ariosto, 'La Cassaria', IV.viii in *Tutte le Opere*, 5 vols, ed. Cesare Segre (Milan: Mondadori, 1974), IV:48–9; Terence, *Phormio*, 2 vols, tr. John Sergeaunt (London: Heinemann, 1912), II:68–81.

28 Plautus, *Pseudolus* in *Works*, 5 vols, tr. Paul Nixon (London: Heinemann, 1932), IV:192–3.

29 P.L. Hughes and J.F. Larkin (eds), *Tudor Royal Proclamations*, 3 vols (New Haven: Yale University Press, 1969), II:381.

30 George Whetstone, *A Mirour for Magestrates of Cyties* (London: Richard Jones, 1584), sigs A4ʳ, H1ʳ, J3ʳ.

31 Gascoigne, *Works*, I:352; Robert Whittinton, *The thre bookes of Tullyes offyces* (London: Wynkyn de Worde, 1534), sig. I1ʳ; see also Victoria Kahn, *Rhetoric, Prudence, Skepticism* (Ithaca and London: Cornell University Press, 1985), p. 35.

32 Rudolf K. Wittkower, 'Chance, time and virtue', *Journal of the Warburg and Courtauld Institutes* (1937–8), 313–21.

33 Walter Lynne, *The vertuous scholehous of ungracious women* (n.d.), sig. A8ᵛ.

34 Michel de Certeau, *The Practice of Everyday Life*, tr. Stephen Rendall (Berkeley: University of California Press, 1984), pp. 79, 81–2.

35 See Wells' remarks on II.i.7–8 in Stanley Wells (ed.), *The Comedy of Errors* (Harmondsworth: Penguin, 1972), p. 132 and his emendation of the line in Stanley Wells and Gary Taylor (eds), William Shakespeare, *The Complete Works: Original Spelling Edition* (Oxford: Clarendon Press, 1986), p. 295.

36 Plautus, *Amphitryon*, tr. Paul Nixon (London: Heinemann, 1928), pp. 90–1.

37 Patricia Parker, *Literary Fat Ladies* (London: Methuen, 1987) p. 17.

38 James L. Sanderson, 'Buff jerkin: a note to 1 Henry IV', *English Language Notes* 4 (1966–7), 92–5.

39 *Ibid.*

40 Leah Marcus, 'The Shakespeare editor as shrew tamer' *ELR* 22 (1992), 177–200, 178.

41 *Ibid.*, 200.

42 *Ibid.*, 178.

43 Andrew Gurr, *Playgoing in Shakespeare's London* (Cambridge: Cambridge University Press, 1987), p. 149.

44 Shakespeare, *The Taming of the Shrew*, ed. Brian Morris (London: Methuen, 1981), Ind.i.129–30, p. 161. Further references to act, scene, and line in this edition will appear in the text.

45 E.K. Chambers, *The Elizabethan Stage*, 4 vols (Oxford: Clarendon Press, 1923), IV:318–19.

46 Terence, *The Eunuch* in John Sergeant (tr.), *Terence*, 2 vols (London: Heinemann, 1912), I:292–5. See Carlo Ginzburg, 'Titian, Ovid and sixteenth-century codes for erotic illustration' in *Myths, Emblems, Clues*, tr. John and Anne Tedeschi (London: Hutchinson, 1986), pp. 77–95.

47 M. Christopherus Stummelius, *Studentes, comoedia de vita studiosorum* (Frankfurt: Johannes Eichorn, 1550), sigs C6ᵛ-D2ᵛ.

48 Ariosto explicitly derives the plot of *I Suppositi* from Terence's *Eunuch*; see *Opere*, IV:197.

49 Gascoigne, *Works*, I.240. The fiction derives from Plautus' *Captivi*.

50 Shakespeare, *The Taming of the Shrew*, introduction, pp. 136, 82.

51 Geoffrey Fenton, *A forme of Christian pollicie* (London: Rafe Newberry, 1574), p. 144. On theatre's association with marketplace mockery in the sixteenth century, see C.R. Baskervill, *The Elizabethan Jig* (Chicago: Illinois University Press, 1929), *passim* and Adam Fox, 'Popular literature and its readership in early modern England', unpublished research paper, presented at the conference on reading, Magdalene College, Cambridge, 1992.

52 Ariosto, *Opere*, IV:199: 'Credo che in casa sino le lettiere e le casse e li usci abbino li orrechi.'

53 *Ibid.*, IV:227–8, 252.

54 On household solidarity, see Juliet du Boualy, 'Lies, mockery and family integrity', in J.G. Peristinay (ed.) *Mediterranean Family Structures* (Cambridge: Cambridge University Press, 1976), pp. 389–406.

55 Katherine Eisaman Maus, 'Horns of dilemma: jealousy, gender and

spectatorship in English Renaissance drama', *ELH* 54 (1987), 561–83.

56 Stephen Gosson, *Playes confuted in five Actions* (London: Thomas Gosson, 1582), sigs C6ʳ-7ʳ.

57 Diana O'Hara, '"Ruled by my friends": aspects of marriage in the diocese of Canterbury c.1540–1570', *Continuity and Change* 6 (1991), 21.

58 *Ibid.*, 28.

59 Erasmus, *Coniugium*, in *The Colloquies of Erasmus*, ed. and tr. C.R. Thompson (Chicago: University of Chicago Press, 1965), p. 121.

60 See Erasmus, *Coniugium*, p. 116 and Juan Luis Vives, *De Officio Mariti* (Bruges, 1529), sigs L1ʳ-2ᵛ. For the question of female chastity as a signifier for the increased anxiety over privacy consequent upon humanist and mercantile writing practice, see Stephanie Jed, *Chaste Thinking: the Rape of Lucretia and the Birth of Humanism* (Bloomington: Indiana University Press, 1989), pp. 74–120.

61 Ruth Nevo, *Comic Transformations in Shakespeare* (London: Methuen, 1980), p. 49.

CONCLUSION

1 Shakespeare, *The Merchant of Venice*, ed. John Russell Brown (London: Methuen, 1955), V.i.15–6, p. 125; subsequent references to this edition will appear in the text.

2 For an analysis of usury according to this definition, see Benjamin Nelson, *The Idea of Usury: From Tribal Brotherhood to Universal Otherhood* (Chicago: University of Chicago Press, 1969). 'Negative reciprocity' is Marshall Sahlins' phrase, see *Stone Age Economics* (London: Routledge, 1988), pp. 185–276.

3 Bryan Chyette, *Constructions of 'the Jew' in English Literature and Society: Racial Representations 1875–1945* (Cambridge: Cambridge University Press, 1993), pp. 2–3.

4 Joseph Shatzmiller, *Shylock Reconsidered: Jews, Moneylending and Medieval Society* (Berkeley: University of California Press, 1990), pp. 71–103.

5 J.M. Rigg, Hilary Jenkinson and H.G. Richardson (eds), *Calendar of the Plea Rolls of the Exchequer of the Jews*, 4 vols (London: Jewish Historical Society, 1905–72); see also Cecil Roth, *A History of the Jews in England* (Oxford: Clarendon Press, 1941), pp. 38–90.

6 See Shatzmiller, *Shylock Reconsidered*, p. 101 and Wolfgang von Stromer and Michael Tosh, 'Zur Buchführung der Juden in Spatmittelalter', in Jürgen Schneider (ed.), *Wirtschaftskrafte und Wirtschaftswege*, 5 vols (Nurnberg, 1978), I:387–40, 399.

7 Sholomo Eidelberg, 'Marufia in Rabbenu Gershon's Responsa', *Historia Judaica* 15 (1953), 59–66.

8 For these causes of the crisis in credit relations see above, pp. 139–47 and notes. On the absence of a Jewish moneylending presence in England during this period, see Roth, *History of the Jews in England*, p. 89; though Tawney cites the case of a Jew being penalized for usury in the introduction to his edition of Thomas Wilson's *A Discourse Upon Usury*, ed. R.H. Tawney (London: Frank Cass, 1962), p. 21n., his

reference is actually to the Plea Rolls of the Jews' Exchequer, which makes it pre-expulsion. All Wilson's own references to Jewish moneylenders in the *Discourse* are explicitly pre-1290, see pp. 232, 269, 283. See also J.L. Bolton, *The Medieval English Economy* (London: J.M. Dent, 1980), pp. 338–41. Recent research has broadened our knowledge of Jewish presence in sixteenth-century London; see, for example, Roger Prior's work on Aemilia Lanyer's family, the Bassanos, 'Jewish musicians at the Tudor court', *The Musical Quarterly* 69 (1983), 253–65. James Shapiro, 'Shakespeare and the Jews', *The Parkes Lecture* (University of Southampton, 1992), argues for a more pervasive Jewish presence in sixteenth-century England than most historians have allowed; the examples he gives, interestingly enough, are mostly of men serving in the capacity of scholar-readers and translators. On the mercantilist arguments for the official 'readmission' of the Jews to England see Jonathan Israel, *European Jewry in the Age of Mercantilism 1550–1750* (Oxford: Clarendon Press, 1985), pp. 158–60.

9 R. Po-Chia Hsia, *The Myth of Ritual Murder: Jews and Magic in Reformation Germany* (New Haven: Yale University Press, 1988), esp. pp. 42–65.

10 Shapiro, 'Shakespeare and the Jews', p. 19.

11 Thomas Nashe, *Works*, 5 vols, ed. R.B. McKerrow (Oxford: Basil Blackwell, 1966), II:305, 314.

12 For *Othello*, see above, p. 155; for Orlando, Shakespeare, *As You Like It* ed. Agnes Latham (London: Methuen, 1975), II.vii.100–1, III.ii.125.

13 Giovanni Fiorentino, *Il Pecorone* (Milan: Giovanni Antonio, 1558), fol. 32^v.

14 *Ibid.*

15 See Rudolf K. Wittkower, 'Time, chance and virtue', *Journal of the Warburg and Courtauld Institutes* 1 (1937–8), 313–21; another play in which the negotiation of good fortune in civil life is throughout referred to in metaphors of tempests and skilful navigation is *Twelfth Night*.

16 See Erasmus, *On Copia of Words and Ideas*, ed. and tr. D.B. King and H.D. Rix (Milwaukee: Marquette University Press, 1963), p. 11:

Just as there is nothing more admirable or splendid than a speech with a rich copia of words overflowing in a golden stream, so it is, assuredly, such a thing as may be striven for at no slight risk, because, according to the proverb: 'Not every man has the luck to go to Corinth.'

See also William Painter, *The Palace of Pleasure* (London: Henry Denham, 1566), tome I, fol. 38^r, which attributes the story behind this proverb, of Demosthenes and Lais of Corinth, to a classical book called *Cornucopia*.

17 Fiorentino, *Il Pecorone*, fol. 36^r.

18 See, for example, John Russell Brown's introduction to the Arden edition, pp. l–liii. For equity at common law, see above, pp. 144–6.

19 For example, *Twelfth Night*, ed. J.M. Lothian and T.W. Craik (London: Methuen, 1975), III.i.25, III.ii.2–4.

20 Interestingly, Heiko Oberman notes a similar negative association in Erasmus' writing between Judaic and scholastic thought; see Heiko Oberman, 'Three sixteenth-century attitudes to Judaism: Reuchlin, Erasmus and Luther' in Bernard Cooperman (ed.), *Jewish Thought in the Sixteenth Century* (Cambridge, Mass.: Harvard University Press, 1983), p. 341.

21 John Gross, quoting Norman Holland in *Shylock: a Hundred Years in the Life of a Legend* (London: Chatto and Windus, 1992), p. 71.

22 Fiorentino, *Il Pecorone*, fol. 35^r.

23 Walter Lynne, *The vertuouse scholehous of ungracious women* (n.d.), sig. A8^v.

24 Miles Coverdale, *The Christen State of Matrimonye* (London: 1541), sig. J2^r, and see above, pp. 41–5.

25 See, for example, Heinrich Bullinger, *Von dem unverschampten fräfel* (Zurich: Christoffel Froschower, 1531), fol. 70^r.

26 Coverdale, *Christen State of Matrimonye*, sig. J2^v.

PRIMARY SOURCES

Anon., *Amis and Amiloun* ed. McEdward Leach, London, Early English Text Society o.s., no. 203, 1937.

—— *A Gorgeous Gallery of Gallant Inventions* [1578], ed. Hyder E. Rollins, Cambridge, Massachusetts, Harvard University Press, 1926.

—— *A Handful of Pleasant Delights* [1584], ed. Hyder E. Rollins, Cambridge, Massachusetts, Harvard University Press, 1924.

—— *A Newe Interlude of Impacyente Poverte* [1560], ed. R.B. McKerrow in W. Bang (ed.), *Materialen zur Kunde des alteren Englischen Dramas*, Louvain, 1911.

—— *Sir Eglamour of Artoys*, London, John Walley, n.d.

—— *Sir Eglamour of Artois*, ed. Francis A. Richardson, London, EETS, 1965.

Ariosto, Ludovico, *Tutte le Opere*, 5 vols, ed. Cesare Segre, Milan, Mondadori, 1974.

—— *The Comedies of Ariosto*, tr. Edmond H. Beame and Leonardo G. Sbrocchi, Chicago, University of Chicago Press, 1975.

Ascham, Roger, *The Schoolmaster* (1570), ed. Lawrence V. Ryan, Charlottesville, Virginia University Press, 1974.

Bandello, Matteo, *Tutte le Opere*, 2 vols, ed. Francesco Flora, Milan, Mondadori, 1952.

Barker, William, *The viii bookes of Xenophon contayning the discipline, schole and education of CYRUS*, London, Reynold Wolf, 1552.

Belleforest, François de, *Continuation des Histoires Tragiques*, Paris, Vincent Sertenas, 1559.

—— *Le Seconde Tome des Histoires Tragiques*, Paris, Vincent Norment, 1565.

—— *Le Troisiesme Tome des Histoires Tragiques*, Lyons, Pierre Rollet, 1574.

—— *Le Cinquiesme Livre des Histoires Tragiques*, Lyons, Benoist Rigaud, 1576.

Blundeville, Thomas, *The True Order and Methode of Wryting and reading Hystories*, London, William Seres, 1574.

Boaistuau, Pierre, *Histoires Tragiques Extraictes des Oeuvres Italiennes de Bandel*, Paris, Vincent Sertenas, 1559.

Boccaccio, Giovanni, *Il Decamerone dim. Giovanni Boccaccio*, ed. Girolamo Ruscellai, Venice, Vincenzo Valgusio, 1552.

—— *Boccaccio on Poetry*, ed. Charles C. Osgood, Princeton, NJ, Princeton University Press, 1930.

—— *Decameron*, 2 vols, ed. Antonio Enzo Quaglio, Milan, Garzanti, 1974.

Bullinger, Heinrich, *Von dem unverschamptem fräfel*, Zurich, Christoffel Froschower, 1531.

—— *Der Christlich Eestand*, Zurich, Christoffel Froschower, 1579.

Calendar of the plea rolls of the Exchequer of the Jews, 4 vols, ed. J.M. Rigg, Hilary Jenkinson and H.G. Richardson, London, Jewish Historicial Society, 1905–72.

Chaloner, Thomas, *Of the office of servauntes, a boke made in Latin by one Gylbertus Cognatus and newly Englyshed*, London, Thomas Berthelet, 1534.

Ciceronis, M.T., *Cato Maior Seu de Senectute*, Paris, Michael Vascosan, 1536.

Clapam, David, *The Commendation of Matrimony, made by Cornelius Agrippa*, London, Thomas Berthelet, 1545.

Cope, Antony, *The Historie of two the Most Noble Capitaines of the worlde, Anniball and Scipio*, London, Thomas Berthelet, 1544.

Coras, Jean de, *Paraphrase sur l'Edict des Marriages clandestinement contractez par les enfans de famille, contre le gré & consentement de leurs peres & meres*, Paris, Gaillot du Pré, 1572.

Cotgrave, Randle, *A Dictionarie of the French and English Tongues* (1611), Columbia, University of South Carolina Press, 1950.

Coverdale, Miles, *The Christen State of Matrimonye*, London, 1541. Translation of Heinrich Bullinger, *Der Christlich Eestand*, Zurich, Christoffel Froschower, 1579.

Dod, John, and Cleaver, Robert *A Godlie Forme of Householde Government; for the ordering of private families*, London, Thomas Marshe, 1612.

Donatus, *Aeli Donati quod fertur Commentum Terenti*, 3 vols, ed. Paul Wessner, Teubner, Lipsae, 1902.

Edwards, Richard, *The Paradyse of daynty devises*, London, Henry Disle, 1578.

Elyot, Sir Thomas, *The Boke named the Governour* [1531], London, J.M. Dent, 1907.

Erasmus, Desiderius, *Apopthegmatum Opus*, Paris, Johannes Roigny, 1533.

—— *Opus Epistolarum Des, Erasmis Roterdami*, 12 vols, ed. P.S. Allen, Oxford, Clarendon Press, 1906–58.

—— *On Copia of Words and Ideas*, ed. and tr. D.B. King and H.D. Rix, Milwaukee, Marquette University Press, 1963.

—— *The Colloquies of Erasmus*, tr. C.R. Thompson, Chicago, University of Chicago Press, 1965.

—— *Opera Omnia Desiderii Erasmi Roterdami recognita et adnotatione critica instructa notisque illustrata*, Amsterdam, North Holland Publishing Co., 1969– .

—— *Collected Works of Erasmus*, 66 vols, Toronto, University of Toronto Press, 1974–88.

Estienne, Charles, *Les Abusez: Comedie fait à la mode des Anciens*, Paris: Estienne Groulleau, 1549.

Fenton, Geoffrey, *Certaine Tragicall Discourses written out of French and Latine*, London, Thomas Marshe, 1567.

—— *A forme of Christian pollicie*, London, Rafe Newberry, 1574.

Foxe, John, *Two Latin Comedies*, ed. John Hazel Smith, Ithaca, Cornell University Press, 1973.

Gascoigne, George, *A Hundreth Sundrie Flowres*, London, Richard Smith, 1573.

—— *The Complete Works*, 2 vols, ed. J.W. Cunliffe, Cambridge, Cambridge University Press, 1907.

—— 'The Adventures of Master F.J.' in Paul Salzman (ed.), *An Anthology of Elizabethan Prose Fiction*, Oxford, Oxford University Press, 1987.

Giovanni, Il Fiorentino, *Il Pecorone*, Milan, Giovanni Antonio, 1558.

Golding, Arthur, *The eyght bookes of C.J. Caesar*, London, 1565.

Googe, Barnabe, *Eglogs, Epitaphes and Sonnettes*, London, Thomas Colwell, 1563.

Gosson, Stephen, *Playes confuted in five Actions*, London, T. Gosson, n.d.

Grimald, Nicholas, *Marcus Tullius Ciceroes thre bookes of duties*, London, Richard Tottel, 1558.

Hake, Edward, *A Touchstone for this time present*, London, Thomas Hacket, 1574.

—— *Newes out of Powles Churchyarde*, London, Richard Jones, 1579.

—— *Of Golds Kingdome in this unhelping Age*, London, John Windet, 1604.

—— *Epiekeia: A Dialogue on Equity in Three Parts*, ed. D.C. Yale, New Haven, Yale Law Library Publications, 1953.

Harington, John, *The booke of freendeship of Marcus Tullie Cicero*, London, Thomas Berthelet, 1550.

Harrington, William, *In this boke are conteyned the commendacions of matrymony imprynted at the instaunce of Mayster Polydore Vergyl*, London, John Skot, 1528.

Harrys, William, *The market or fayre of Vsurers*, London, Steven Mierdman, 1550.

Herberay, Nicholas de, *Le Premier Livre de Amadis de Gaule . . . traduict nouvellement d'espagnol en Francoys*, Paris, Denis Janot, 1540.

—— *Le Second Livre de Amadis de Gaule, traduict nouvellement d'espagnol en Francoys*, Paris, Denis Janot, 1541.

Hervet, Gentian, *Xenophons Treatise of Householde*, London, T. Berthelet, 1534.

Heywood, Thomas, *A Woman Killed with Kindness* in Keith Sturgess (ed.), *Three Elizabethan Domestic Tragedies*, Harmondsworth, Penguin, 1985.

Hughes, Paul L. and Larkin, James F. (eds), *Tudor Royal Proclamations*, 3 vols, New Haven, Yale University Press, 1969.

Humphrey, Lawrence, *The Nobles or of Nobilitye*, London, Thomas Marshe, 1563.

Hyrde, Richard, *A very frutefull and pleasant boke, called the instruccion of a Christen woman*, London, T. Berthelet, 1529. Translation of Joannes L. Vives, *De Institutionae foeminae Christianae*, Antwerp, F. Byrckman, 1524.

Isambert, François, *Receuil général des anciennes lois françaises*, Paris, 1822, vol. 13.

Jonson, Ben, *The Works*, ed. C.H. Herford and Percy Simpson, Oxford, Clarendon Press, 1925–52.

Lesse, Nicholas, *The Censure and judgement of . . . Erasmus: whyther dyvorsement betwene man and wyfe stondeth with the lawe of god*, London, Widow of John Herforde, 1550.

Livy, *The War with Hannibal*, tr. Aubrey de Selincourt, Harmondsworth, Penguin, 1965.

Lodge, Thomas, *The Complete Works*, ed. E. Gosse, London, Hunterian Club, 1883.

Lupset, Thomas, *An Exhortacion to yonge men, perswading them to walke the patheway that leadeth to honeste and goodnes: writen to a frend*, London, T. Berthelet, 1535.

—— *Tho. Lupsets workes*, London, 1560.

—— *The Life and Works of Thomas Lupset*, ed. John Arthur Gee, New Haven, Yale University Press, 1928.

Lupton, Thomas, *Sivqila: Too good, to be true*, London, Henry Bynneman, 1580.

Lyly, John, *The Plays of John Lyly*, ed. Carter A. Daniel, London, Associated University Presses, 1988.

Lynche, Richard, *Diella, Certaine Sonnets, adjoyned to the amorous Poeme of Dom Diego and Ginevra*, London, Henry Olney, 1596.

Lynne, Walter, *The vertuous scholehous of ungracious women: a godly dialogue . . . of two Systers . . . out of the land of Meissen*, n.d.

Machiavelli, Niccoló, *Il Principe e altre opere politiche*, ed. D. Cantimori, Milan, Garzanti, 1976.

Marshall, William, *The forme and maner of subvention or helping for pore people practysed in Hypres*, London, T. Berthelet, 1535.

Montaigne, Michel de, *Oeuvres Completes*, ed. Robert Barral, Paris, du Seuil, 1967.

Morison, Richard, *The Strategemes, Sleyghtes, and policies of warre, gathered together by S. Julius Frontinus*, London, T. Berthelet, 1539.

Ortunez, Diego de Calahorra, *Espejo de Principes y Cavalleros*, Medina del Campo, 1583.

Painter, William, *The Palace of Pleasure*, London, Henry Denham, 1566.

—— *The Second Tome of the Palace of Pleasure*, London, Henry Bynneman, 1567.

Palsgrave, John, *The Comedy of Acolastus translated in oure englysshe tongue*, ed. P.L. Carver, London, EETS, 1937.

Paynell, Thomas, *The most excellent . . . Treasurie of Amadis of Fraunce*, London, Henry Bynneman, 1567.

Pettie, George, *The Civile Conversation of M. Steeven Guazzo*, London, Richard Watkins, 1581.

—— *A Petite Pallace of Pettie his Pleasure* (1576), ed. Herbert Hartman, London, Oxford University Press, 1938.

Platt, Hugh, *The floures of philosophie with the pleasures of poetrie*, London, Henry Bynneman, 1581.

Plautus, M. Accius, *Opera*, ed. Dionys. Lambinus, Paris, Johannes Macaeus, 1576.

—— *Works*, tr. Paul Nixon, 5 vols, London, Heinemann, 1932.

Plowden, Edmund, *The Commentaries or Reports*, London, Catherine Lintot and Samuel Richardson, 1761.

Primaudaye, Pierre de la, *Academie Française*, Paris, Guillaume Chaudière, 1580.

Proceedings in the Parliaments of Elizabeth I, vol. 1, ed. T.E. Hartley, Leicester, Leicester University Press, 1981.

Rastell, John, *Terens in englysh*, London, 1520.

Riche, Baranabe, *Alarme to England...conteyning the decay of warlike discipline, to be perused by Gentlemen, such as are desirous by service to seek their own deserved prayse and the preservation of their Country*, London, Christopher Barker, 1578.

Saint German, Christopher, *Hereafter followeth a Dyologue in Englysshe betwyxt a Doctour of Dyvynyte and a Student in the Lawes of Englande: Of the groundes of the sayd Lawes and of Consyence*, London, Peter Treverys, 1530.

Sidney, Philip, *The Old Arcadia*, ed. Katherine Duncan-Jones, Oxford, World's Classics, 1985.

Stanihurst, Richard, *The First Fowre Bookes of Virgil his Aeneis translated into English*, Leiden, John Pates, 1582.

Starkey, Thomas, *A Dialogue between Reginald Pole and Thomas Lupset*, ed. Kathleen Burton, London, Chatto and Windus, 1948.

—— *Starkey's Life and Letters*, vol. 1 of *England in the reign of Henry VIII*, ed. Sidney J. Herrtage, London, 1878.

Stummelius, Christopherus, *Studentes, comoedia de vita studiosum*, with a preface by Jodicus Willichus, Frankfurt, Johannes Eichorn, 1550.

Taverner, Richard, *A ryght frutefull Epystle devysed by the moste excellent clerke Erasmus in laude and prayse of matrymony*, London, R. Redman, 1532.

R.H. Tawney and E. Power (eds), *Tudor economic documents*, London, Longman Green and Co., 1924.

Terence, *Pub. Terentii Comoediae Sex editae, sudio et labore Phillippi Melanchthonis ac Erasmi Roterdami*, Vratislaviae, 1574.

Turberville, George, *A plaine Path to perfect Vertue*, London, Henry Bynneman, 1568.

Tyler, Margaret, *The Mirrour of Princely deedes and Knighthood*, London, Thomas East, 1578. Translation of Diego de Calahorra Ortunez, *Espejo de Principes y Cavalleros*, Medina del Campo, 1583.

Udall, Nicholas, *Apophthegmes, that is to saie, prompte, quicke, wittie and sententious saiynges, of certain Emperours, Kynges, Capitaines, Philosophers, and Oratours ... profitable to rede, partely for all maner of persones, & especially for Gentlemen, first gathered of ... Erasmus*, London, Richard Grafton, 1542.

—— *Ralph Roister Doister* in William Tydeman (ed.), *Four Tudor Comedies*, Harmondsworth, Penguin, 1984.

Walter, William, *Here begynneth the hystory of Tytus and Gesyppus* [1523] in Herbert T. Wright (ed.), *Early English Versions of ... Titus and Gisippus*, London, EETS, o.s., no. 205, 1937.

Watson, Thomas, *The HEKATOMPATHIA or Passionate Centurie of Love*, London, John Wolf, 1582.

Weber, Henry (ed.), *Metrical Romances of the Thirteenth, Fourteenth and Fifteenth Centuries*, 2 vols, Edinburgh, 1810.

Whetstone, George, *The Rocke of Regarde*, London, Robert Waley, 1576.

—— *the Right Excellent and Famous History of Promos and Cassandra: Devided into Two Commical Discourses*, London, 1578.

—— *A Mirour for Magestrates of Cyties*, London, Richard Jones, 1584.

Whitehorne, Peter, *The Arte of Warre . . . by Nicholas Machiavel*, London, John Wright, 1573.

Whitford, Richard, *A Werke for housholders*, London, R. Redman, 1537.

Whitney, Isabella, *A Sweet Nosgay, or pleasant Posye contayning a hundred and ten Phylosophicall flowers*, London, Richard Jones, 1573.

Whittinton, Robert, *The thre bookes of Tullyes offyces both in latyn tonge & in englysshe*, London, Wynkyn de Worde, 1534.

Wilson, Thomas, *The Rule of Reason, conteynynge the Arte of Logique*, London, Richard Grafton, 1551.

—— *The Arte of Rhetorique*, London, Richard Grafton, 1553.

—— *The Rule of Reason, conteinynge the Arte of Logike . . . newlie corrected*, London, John Kingston, 1563.

—— *A Discourse uppon Vsurye, by waye of Dialogue and oracions*, London, Richard Tottel, 1572.

—— *A Discourse upon Usury*, ed. R.H. Tawney, London, Frank Cass, 1962.

Wright, Thomas (ed.), *Queen Elizabeth and her Times: A Series of Original Letters*, 2 vols, London, Henry Colburn, 1838.

Xenophon, *Cyropaedia*, 2 vols., tr. Walter Miller, London, Heinemann, 1914.

—— *Oeconomicus*, tr. E.C. Marchant, London, Heinemann, 1929.

SECONDARY SOURCES

Adams, Robert P., '"Bold bawdry and open manslaughter": the English New Humanist attack on medieval romance', *Huntington Library Quarterly* 23 (1959–60), 33–44.

Alpers, Svetlana, *The Art of Describing: Dutch Art in the Seventeenth Century*, Harmondsworth, Penguin, 1989.

Altman, Joel, *The Tudor Play of Mind*, Berkeley, University of California Press, 1978.

Archer, Ian W., *The Pursuit of Stability: Social Relations in Elizabethan London*, Cambridge, Cambridge University Press, 1991.

Armstrong, Nancy, *Desire and Domestic Fiction: A Political History of the Novel*, Oxford, Oxford University Press, 1987.

Aston, Margaret, *Lollards and Reformers: Images and Literacy in Late Medieval Religion*, London, Hambledon Press, 1984.

Axton, Marie, *The Queen's Two Bodies: Drama and the Elizabethan Succession*, London, Royal Historical Society, 1977.

Bailey, Derrick S., *Thomas Becon and the Reformation of the Church in England*, London, Oliver and Boyd, 1952.

Baker, J.H., *The Reports of Sir John Spelman*, 2 vols, London, Selden Society, 1978.

—— *An Introduction to English Legal History*, London, Butterworth, 1979.

—— *The Legal Profession and the Common Law*, London, Hambledon, 1986.

Bakhtin, Mikhail, *Rabelais and his World*, tr. Helene Iswolsky, Cambridge, Massachusetts, MIT Press, 1968.

Baldwin, T.W., *Shakespeare's Five Act Structure*, Urbana, University Of Illinois Press, 1947.

Barthes, Roland, *S/Z*, tr. Richard Miller, New York, Farrar, Straus and Giroux, 1974.

Bartlett, Robert, *Trial by Fire and Water: The Medieval Judicial Ordeal*, Oxford, Clarendon Press, 1986.

Baskervill, C.R., 'An Elizabethan Eglamour play', *Modern Philology* 19 (1917), 759–60.

—— *The Elizabethan Jig*, Chicago, Illinois University Press, 1929.

Belsey, Catherine, 'Disrupting sexual difference: meaning and gender in the comedies' in John Drakakis (ed.), *Alternative Shakespeares*, London, Routledge, 1985.

—— *The Subject of Tragedy: Identity and Difference in Renaissance Drama*, London, Methuen, 1985.

Bielaire, Franz, *La Familia d'Erasme*, Paris, Librairie Philosophique, 1968.

Bloch, R. Howard, *Medieval French Literature and Laws*, Berkeley, University of California Press, 1977.

—— *Etymologies and Genealogies: A Literary Anthropology of the French Middle Ages*, Chicago, Chicago University Press, 1983.

Bolton, J.L., *The Medieval English Economy*, London, J.M. Dent and Sons, 1980.

Bonner, S.F., *Roman Declamation in the Late Republic and Early Empire*, Liverpool, Liverpool University Press, 1949.

—— *Education in Ancient Rome from the Elder Cato to the Younger Pliny*, London, Methuen, 1977.

Boulay, Juliet du, 'Lies, mockery and family integrity' in J.G. Peristiany (ed.), *Mediterranean Family Structures*, Cambridge, Cambridge University Press, 1976.

Bourdieu, Pierre, *Outline of a Theory of Practice* tr. Richard Nice, Cambridge, Cambridge University Press, 1977.

Boutcher, Warren, 'Florio's Montaigne: translation and pragmatic humanism in the sixteenth century', unpublished Ph.D. thesis, Cambridge University, 1990.

Brigden, Susan, 'Religion and social obligation in early sixteenth-century London', *Past and Present* 103 (1984), 67–112.

—— *London and the Reformation*, Oxford, Clarendon Press, 1989.

Brooks, Peter, *Reading for the Plot: Design and Intention in Narrative*, New York, Vintage Books, 1985.

Brundage, James A., *Law, Sex and Christian Society in Medieval Europe*, Chicago, Chicago University Press, 1987.

Bush, Douglas, 'The Petite Pallace of Pettie his Pleasure', *Journal of English and Germanic Philology* 27 (128), 162–9.

Campbell, Lorne *et al.*, 'Quentin Matsys, Desiderius Erasmus, Pieter Gillis and Thomas More', *The Burlington Magazine* 120 (1978), 716–24.

Cardwell, Edward, *Synodalia: A Collection of Articles of Religious Canons. . .* 1547–1719, 2 vols, Oxford, 1842.

—— *The Reformation of Ecclesiastical Laws*, Oxford, 1850.

Carlson, Eric, 'Marriage reform and the Elizabethan High Commission', *Sixteenth Century Journal* 21 (1990), 436–51.

Cave, Terence, *The Cornucopian Text*, Oxford, Clarendon Press, 1979.

—— *Recognitions: a Study in Poetics*, Oxford, Clarendon Press, 1988.

—— "'Or donne par don": échanges métaphoriques et materiels chez Rabelais', forthcoming in the proceedings of 'Or, monnaie, échange dans la culture de la Renaissance', conference, Lyons, 1991.

Certeau, Michel de, *The Practice of Everyday Life*, tr. Steven Rendall, Berkeley, University of California Press, 1984.

Chambers, E.K., *The Elizabethan Stage*, 4 vols, Oxford, Clarendon Press, 1923.

Chyette, Bryan, *Constructions of 'the Jew' in English Literature and Society: Racial Representations 1875–1945*, Cambridge, Cambridge University Press, 1993.

Collingwood, Arthur Lee, *The Decameron: Its Sources and Analogues*, London, David Nutt, 1909.

Coulter, Cornelia C., 'Boccaccio's knowledge of Quintilian', *Speculum* (1958), 490–6.

Crane, R.S., *The Vogue for Medieval Chivalric Romance during the English Renaissance*, Menasha, Wisconsin, 1919.

Curtius, Ernst Robert, *European Literature in the Latin Middle Ages*, tr. Willard R. Trask, London, Routledge and Kegan Paul, 1953.

Davies, Kathleen M., 'The sacred condition of equality – how original were Puritan doctrines of marriage?', *Social History* 5 (1977), 563–80.

Davis, Natalie Zemon, *Society and Culture in Early Modern France* (1965) Oxford, Polity Press, 1987.

—— 'Beyond the market: books as gifts in sixteenth-century France', *Transactions of the Royal Historical Society* 33 (1983), 69–88.

—— *The Return of Martin Guerre*, Cambridge, Massachusetts, Harvard University Press, 1983.

—— *Fiction in the Archives*, Stanford, California, Stanford University Press, 1987.

Duby, George, *Medieval Marriage: Two Models from Twelfth-Century France*, tr. Elborg Foster, Baltimore, Johns Hopkins University Press, 1978.

Eidelberg, Sholomo, 'Marufia in Rabbenu Gershon's Responsa', *Historia Judaica* 15 (1953), 59–66.

Elton, G.R., 'An early Tudor Poor Law', *Economic History Review* 6 (1953), 55–67.

—— 'Reform by statute: Thomas Starkey's *Dialogue* and Thomas Cromwell's policy', *Proceedings of the British Academy* LIV (1968), 165–88.

—— *Reform and Renewal: Thomas Cromwell and the Commonweal*, Cambridge, Cambridge University Press, 1973.

Febvre, Lucien, 'Un Secretaire d'Erasme: Gilbert Cousin et la reforme en Franche-Comte', *Société de l'Histoire du Protestantisme Français* (1907), 97–148.

Fehrenbach, R.J., 'Isabella Whitney, Sir Hugh Plat, Geoffrey Whitney and "Sister Eldershae"', *English Language Notes* 21 (1983), 7–11.

—— 'A letter sent by the maids of London (1567)', *English Literary Renaissance* 14 (1984), 285–305.

Finley, M.I., 'Aristotle and economic analysis', *Past and Present* 47 (1970), 3–25.

Fiorato, Adelin, Charles, *Bandello: Entre l'histoire e l'écriture*, Firenze, Leo S. Olschki, 1979.

Fisher, R.M., 'Thomas Cromwell, humanism and educational reform', *Bulletin of the Institute of Historical Research* 50 (1977), 151–63.

Foucault, Michel, *The Use of Pleasure*, tr. Robert Hurley, Harmondsworth, Penguin, 1984.

Fox, Adam, 'Popular literature and its readership in early modern England', unpublished research paper presented at the conference on reading, Magdalene College, Cambridge, 1992.

Friedman, Alice T., *House and Household in Elizabethan England*, London, University of Chicago Press, 1989.

Ginzburg, Carlo, *Myths, Emblems, Clues*, tr. John and Anne Tedeschi, London, Hutchinson, 1986.

Goode, Charles Tyson, 'Sir Thomas Elyot's "Titus and Gysippus"' *Modern Language Notes* 37 (1922), 1–11.

Gottlieb, Beatrice, 'The meaning of clandestine marriage' in Robert Wheaton and Tamara K. Hareven (eds), *Family and Sexuality in French History*, Pennsylvania, Philadelphia University Press, 1980.

Gowing, Laura, 'Women sex and honour: the London church courts, 1572–1640', unpublished Ph.D. thesis, London University, 1993.

Grafton, Anthony and Jardine, Lisa, *From Humanism to the Humanities: Education and the Liberal Arts in Fifteenth and Sixteenth-Century Europe*, London, Duckworth, 1986.

—— 'Studied for action: how Gabriel Harvey read his Livy', *Past and Present* 129 (1990), 32–73.

Greenblatt, Stephen, *Shakespearean Negotiations*, Oxford, Clarendon Press, 1988.

—— *Marvellous Possessions*, Oxford, Clarendon Press, 1991.

Gray, Hannah H., 'Renaissance humanism: the pursuit of eloquence', *Journal of the History of Ideas* 24 (1963), 497–514.

Gross, John, *Shylock: a Hundred Years in the Life of a Legend*, London, Chatto and Windus, 1992.

Guiliani, Alessandro, 'The influence of rhetoric on the law of evidence and pleading', *Juridical Review* 7 (1962), 216–51.

Gurr, Andrew, 'The bear, the statue and hysteria in *The Winter's Tale*', *Shakespeare Quarterly* 34 (1983), 420–5.

—— *Playgoing in Shakespeare's London*, Cambridge, Cambridge University Press, 1987.

Guy, John, 'Law, equity and conscience in Henrician jurist thought' in John Guy and Alistair Fox, *Reassessing the Henrician Age: Humanism, Politics and Reform 1500–1530*, Oxford, Basil Blackwell, 1986.

Hackett, Helen, '"Yet tell me some such fiction": Mary Wroth's *Urania* and the "Femininity of Romance"' in Clare Brant and Diane Purkiss (eds), *Women, Texts and Histories*, London, Routledge, 1992.

Hardison, O.B., *The Enduring Monument: A Study of the Idea of Praise in Renaissance Literary Theory and Practice*, Chapel Hill, University of North Carolina Press, 1962.

Hedley, Jane, 'Allegoria: Gascoigne's master trope', *English Literary Renaissance* 11 (1981), 148–63.

Helmholz, R.E., 'Assumpsit and Fidei Laesio', *Law Quarterly Review* 91 (1975), 406–32.

—— 'Usury and the medieval English church courts', *Speculum* 61 (1987), 364–80.

—— *Roman Canon Law in Reformation England*, Cambridge, Cambridge University Press, 1990.

Henderson, Edith, 'Relief from bonds in the English Chancery in the mid-sixteenth century', *American Journal of Legal History* 8 (1974), 299–306.

Herlihy, David, *Medieval Households*, Cambridge, Massachusetts, Harvard University Press, 1985.

Herrick, Marvin T., *Comic Theory in the Renaissance*, Urbana, University of Illinois Press, 1950.

—— *Tragicomedy: its Origins and Development in Italy and France*, Urbana,

University of Illinois Press, 1962.

Houlbrooke, Ralph, 'The making of marriage in mid-Tudor England', *Journal of Family History* 10 (1985), 339–52.

Hutson, Lorna, *Thomas Nashe in Context*, Oxford, Clarendon Press, 1989.

—— 'Why the lady's eyes are nothing like the sun' in Clare Brant and Diane Purkiss (eds), *Women, Texts and Histories 1500–1760*, London, Routledge, 1992.

—— 'Fortunate travelers: reading for the plot in sixteenth century England', *Representations* 41 (1993), 83–103.

Ibbetson, David, 'Assumpsit and debt in the early sixteenth century: the origins of the Indebitatus count', *Cambridge Law Journal* 41 (1982), 142–61.

Ingram, Martin, *Church Courts, Sex and Marriage in England 1570–1640*, Cambridge, Cambridge University Press, 1987.

—— 'The reform of popular culture? Sex and marriage in early modern England' in Barry Reay (ed.), *Popular Culture in Seventeenth-Century England*, London, Routledge and Kegan Paul, 1988.

Israel, Jonathan, *European Jewry in the Age of Mercantilism 1550–1750*, Oxford, Clarendon Press, 1985.

James, Mervyn E., *Society, Politics and Culture: Studies in Early Modern England*, Cambridge, Cambridge University Press, 1986.

Jardine, Lisa, *Still Harping on Daughters: Women and Drama in the Age of Shakespeare*, Hassocks, Sussex, Harvester, 1983.

—— 'Humanistic logic' in Charles B. Schmitt, Quentin Skinner, Eckhard Krasler and Jill Kraye (eds), *The Cambridge History of Renaissance Philosophy*, Cambridge, Cambridge University Press, 1988.

—— *Erasmus, Man of Letters: the Construction of Charisma in Print*, Princeton, NJ, Princeton University Press, 1993.

Jones, Ann Rosalind, *The Currency of Eros: Women's Love Lyric in Europe, 1540–1620*, Bloomington, Indiana University Press, 1990.

Jones, Norman L., 'An Elizabethan bill for the reformation of ecclesiatical law', *Parliamentary History* 4 (1985), 184–6.

—— *God and the Moneylenders: Usury and Law in Early Modern England*, Oxford, Basil Blackwell, 1989.

Kahn, Victoria, *Rhetoric, Prudence and Skepticism in the Renaissance*, Ithaca and London, Cornell University Press, 1985.

—— 'Humanism and the resistance to theory' in Patricia Parker and David Quint (eds), *Literary Theory and Renaissance Texts*, Baltimore, Johns Hopkins University Press, 1986.

Karras, Ruth Mazo, 'The regulation of brothels in later Medieval England', *Signs* 14 (1989), 399–433.

Krontiris, T., *Oppositional Voices: Women as Writers and Translators of Literature in the English Renaissance*, London, Routledge, 1992.

Lévi-Strauss, Claude, *The Elementary Structures of Kinship* revised edition, tr. James Harle Bell, John Richard von Sturmer and Rodney Needham, Boston, Beacon Press, 1969.

Lievsay, J.L., *Stefano Guazzo and the English Renaissance 1575–1675*, Chapel Hill, University of Carolina Press.

Logan, Donald, 'The Henrician Canons', *Bulletin of the Institute of Historical Research* 48 (1974), 99–103.

Lucas, Caroline, *Writing for Women: The Example of Woman as Reader in Elizabethan Romance*, Milton Keynes, Open University Press, 1989.

Marcus, Leah, 'The Shakespeare editor as shrew tamer', *English Literary Renaissance* 22 (1992), 177–200.

Maus, Katherine Eisaman, 'Horns of dilemma: jealousy, gender and spectatorship in English Renaissance drama', *ELH* 54 (1987), 561–83.

Mauss, Marcel, *The Gift: the Form and Reason for Exchange in Archaic Societies*, tr. W.D. Halls, London, Routledge, 1990.

McConica, James, *English Humanism and Reformation Politics*, Oxford, Clarendon Press, 1966.

Mertes, Kate, *The English Noble Household 1200–1600*, Oxford, Basil Blackwell, 1988.

Millet, Paul, *Lending and Borrowing in Ancient Athens*, Cambridge, Cambridge University Press, 1991.

Mills, Laurens J., *One Soul in Bodies Twain*, Bloomington, Indiana, Principia Press, 1937.

Moore-Smith, G.C., 'Edmund Withypoll', *Archiv für das studium der neuern sprachen und Literaturen*, n.s., 43 (1922), 183–9.

Nelson, Benjamin, *The Idea of Usury: From Tribal Brotherhood to Universal Otherhood*, Chicago, University of Chicago Press, 1969.

Nevo, Ruth, *Comic Transformations in Shakespeare*, London, Methuen, 1980.

Nicgorski, Walter, 'Cicero's Paradoxes and his idea of utility', *Political Theory* 12 (1984), 557–78.

Nugent, Georgia S., 'Ancient theories of comedy: the treatises of Evanthius and Donatus' in Maurice Charney (ed.), *Shakespearean Comedy*, New York, New York Literary Forum, 1980.

Oberman, Heiko, *Masters of the Reformation: The Emergence of a New Intellectual Climate in Europe*, tr. Dennis Martin, Cambridge, Massachusetts, Harvard University Press, 1981.

—— 'Three sixteenth-century attitudes to Judaism: Reuchlin, Erasmus, Luther' in Bernard Cooperman (ed.), *Jewish Thought in the Sixteenth Century*, Cambridge, Cambridge University Press, 1983.

O'Hara, Diana, '"Ruled by my friends": aspects of marriage in the diocese of Canterbury c.1540–1570', *Continuity and Change* 6 (1991), 9–41.

Orgel, Stephen, 'Nobody's perfect: or, why did the English Renaissance stage take boys for women?', *South Atlantic Quarterly* 88 (1989), 7–29.

Otis, Leah, L., *Prostitution in Medieval Society*, Chicago, University of Chicago Press, 1985.

Panofsky, Erwin, 'Jan Van Eyck's *Arnolfini* portrait', *The Burlington Magazine* 64 (1934), 117–27.

—— *Early Netherlandish Painting*, 2 vols, Cambridge, Massachusetts, Harvard University Press, 1953.

Parker, Patricia, *Literary Fat Ladies: Rhetoric, Gender and Property*, London, Methuen, 1987.

Perry, Ben Edwin, *The Ancient Romances*, Berkeley and Los Angeles, University of California Press, 1967.

Po-Chia Hsia, R., *The Myth of Ritual Murder: Jews and Magic in Reformation Germany*, New Haven, Yale University Press, 1988.

Pocock, J.G.A., *The Machiavellian Moment*, Princeton, NJ, Princeton University Press, 1978.

Prior, Roger, 'Jewish musicians at the Tudor court', *The Musical Quarterly* 69 (1983), 253–65.

Pruvost, René, *Matteo Bandello and Elizabethan Fiction*, Paris, 1937.

Ramsay, G.D., *The City of London in International Politics at the Accession of Elizabeth Tudor*, Manchester, Manchester University Press, 1975.

Read, Conyers, *Mr Secretary Walsingham*, 2 vols, Oxford, Clarendon Press, 1925.

Richardson, E.P., '"The Detroit St. Jerome" by Jan Van Eyck', *Art Quarterly* 19 (1956), 227–34.

Robertson, Jean, 'Sidney and Bandello', *The Library*, 5th series, 21(4) (1966), 326–8.

Roover, Raymond de, *Money, Banking and Credit in Mediaeval Bruges*, Cambridge, Massachusetts, Harvard University Press, 1948.

—— *Gresham on Foreign Exchange*, Cambridge, Massachusetts, Harvard University Press, 1949.

Roper, Lyndal, *The Holy Household: Women and Morals in Reformation Augsburg*, Oxford, Clarendon Press, 1989.

—— 'Stealing manhood: capitalism and magic in early modern Germany', *Gender and History* 3 (1991), 4–22.

Rubin, Gayle, 'The traffic in women: notes on a "political economy" of sex' in R. Reiter (ed.), *Towards an Anthropology of Women*, New York, Monthly Review Press, 1975.

Rueger, Zofia, 'Gerson's concept of equity and Christopher St. German', *History of Political Thought* 3 (1982), 1–30.

Russell, Patricia, 'Romantic Narrative Plays 1570–1590' in John Russell Brown and Bernard Harris (eds), *Elizabethan Theatre*, Stratford on Avon Studies, 9, London, Edward Arnold, 1966.

Sahlins, Marshall, *Stone Age Economics*, London, Routledge, 1988.

Salingar, Leo, *Shakespeare and the Traditions of Comedy*, Cambridge, Cambridge University Press, 1974.

Salzman, Paul, *English Prose Fiction 1558–1700: a Critical History*, Oxford, Clarendon Press, 1985.

Sanderson, James L., 'Buff jerkin: a note to 1 Henry IV', *English Language Notes* 4 (1966–7), 92–5.

Schaeffer, John D., 'The use and misuse of Giambattista Vico: rhetoric, orality and theories of discourse' in H. Aaram Veeser (ed.), *The New Historicism*, London, Routledge, 1989.

Shapiro, James, 'Shakespeare and the Jews', *The Parkes Lecture*, University of Southampton, 1992.

Shatzmiller, Joseph, *Shylock Resonsidered: Jews, Moneylending and Medieval Society*, Berkeley, University of California Press, 1990.

Sherman, William, '"Official Scholars" and "Action Officers" : research intelligence and the making of Tudor policy in early modern England', unpublished research paper delivered at the London Renaissance Seminar, 1990.

—— 'Dee's *Britannica Republicae Synopsis*: a reader's guide to the Elizabethan commonwealth', *Journal of Medieval and Renaissance Studies* 20 (1990), 293–315.

Silver, Larry, *The Paintings of Quinten Massys*, Oxford, Phaidon, 1984.

Simonin, Michel, 'Notes sur Pierre Boiastuau', *Bibliothèque d'Humanisme et Renaissance* 38 (1976), 328–30.

Simpson, A.W.B., 'The place of Slade's case in the history of contract', *Law Quarterly Review* 74 (1958), 381–96.

Singer, Kurt, 'Oikonomia: an inquiry into the beginnings of economic thought and language', *Kyklos* 11 (1958), 29–57.

Skinner, Quentin, 'The State' in Terence Ball, James Farr and Russell L. Hanson (eds), *Political Innovation and Conceptual Change*, Oxford, Clarendon Press, 1989.

Smith, H. Clifford, 'The Legend of S. Eloy and S. Godoberta by Petrus Christus', *The Burlington Magazine* 25 (1914), 326–35.

Smith, R.S., 'A woad growing project at Wollaton in the 1580s', *Transactions of the Thoroton Society* 65 (1961), 27–46.

Smith, Richard M., 'Marriage processes in the English past' in Lloyd Bonfield *et al.* (eds), *The World We Have Gained*, Oxford, Basil Blackwell, 1986.

Sorieri, Louis, *Boccaccio's Story of Titus and Gisippus in European Literature*, New York, Comparative Literature Series, 1937.

Soudek, Josef, 'Leonardo Bruni and his public: a statistical and interpretative study of his annotated Latin version of the (Pseudo-) Aristotelian *Economics*', *Studies in Medieval and Renaissance History* 5 (1968), 51–136.

Starkey, David, *The English Court from the Wars of the Roses to the Civil War*, London, Longman, 1987.

Stone, Donald Jr, 'Belleforest's Bandello: a bibliographical study', *Bibliothèque d'Humanisme et Renaissance* 36 (1972), 489–99.

Stone, Lawrence, *The Family, Sex and Marriage*, London, Weidenfeld and Nicolson, 1977.

Strauss, Leo, *Xenophon's Socratic Discourse*, Ithaca and London, Cornell University Press, 1970.

Stromer, Wolfgang von and Tosh, Michael, 'Zur Buchfürung der Juden in Spatmittelater' in Jürgen Sneider (ed.), *Wirtshaftskrafte und Wirthschaftswege*, 5 vols, Nurnberg, 1978, I:387–40.

Sturel, René, *Bandello en France aux XVIᵉ Siècle*, Paris, E. de Boccard, 1918.

Tadmor, Naomi, '"Family" and "Friend" in *Pamela*: a case study in the history of the family in eighteenth-century England', *Social History* 14 (1989), 289–306.

Tatum, James, *Xenophon's Imperial Fiction: On the Education of Cyrus*, Princeton, NJ, Princeton University Press, 1989.

Thirsk, Joan, *Economic Policy and Projects: The Development of a Consumer Society in Early Modern England*, Oxford, Clarendon Press, 1978.

Travitsky, Betty, '"The Wyll and Testament" of Isabella Whitney', *English Literary Renaissance* 10 (1980), 80–95.

Usher, Abbot Paynton, *The Early History of Deposit Banking*, Cambridge, Massachusetts, Harvard University Press, 1943.

Vickers, Nancy, '"The blazon of sweet beauty's best": Shakespeare's

Lucrece' in Patricia Parker and Geoffrey Hartman (eds), *Shakespeare and the Question of Theory*, London, Methuen, 1985.

Wall, Wendy, 'Isabella Whitney and the Female Legacy', *ELH* 58 (1991), 35–62.

Wayne Baker, J., 'Heinrich Bullinger and the idea of usury', *Sixteenth Century Journal* 5 (1974), 49–70.

White, Hayden, *Metahistory: The Historical Imagination in Nineteenth Century Europe*, Baltimore, Johns Hopkins University Press, 1975.

Wilson, Katherine, *Shakespeare's Sugared Sonnets*, London, Allen and Unwin, 1974.

Winkler, John J., *The Constraints of Desire: The Anthropology of Sex and Gender in Ancient Greece*, London, Routledge, 1990.

Winchester, Barbara, *Tudor Family Portrait*, London, Jonathan Cape, 1955.

Wittkower, Rudolph K., 'Chance, time and virtue', *Journal of the Warburg and Courtauld Institutes* 1 (1937–8), 313–21.

Wolf, Samuel Lee, 'A Source of *Euphues, The Anatomy of Wit*', *Modern Philology* 7 (1910), 577–85.

Wright, Herbert T., *Boccaccio in England from Chaucer to Tennyson*, London, Athlone, 1957.

Zeeveld, Gordon, *Foundations of Tudor Policy*, Cambridge, Massachusetts, Harvard University Press, 1948.

INDEX